Kafka

By the same author

Biography

BRUCE CHATWIN

A LIFE OF MATTHEW ARNOLD

WORLD ENOUGH AND TIME:
THE LIFE OF ANDREW MARVELL

ALDOUS HUXLEY: AN ENGLISH INTELLECTUAL

Poetry

PLAUSIBLE FICTIONS

Fiction

A SHORT BOOK ABOUT LOVE

REMEMBERING CARMEN

Criticism

AFTER ARNOLD: CULTURE AND ACCESSIBILITY

Kafka

NICHOLAS MURRAY

Yale University Press
NEW HAVEN & LONDON

First published in 2004 in Great Britain by Little, Brown
and in the United States by Yale University Press

Quotations from the following are reprinted by permission of The Random House Group Ltd: *The Trial*, Idris Parry (trans.), Martin Secker & Warburg, 1994; *The Man Who Disappeared*, Michael Hoffman (trans.), Martin Secker & Warburg, 1996; *The Castle*, J. A. Underwood (trans.), Martin Secker & Warburg, 1997; *The Great Wall of China*, Malcolm Pasley (trans.), Martin Secker & Warburg, 1991; *Metamorphosis and Other Stories*, Malcolm Pasley (trans.), Martin Secker & Warburg, 1992; *The Diaries of Franz Kafka 1910–1913*, Joseph Kresh (trans.), Martin Secker & Warburg, Greenberg (trans.), Martin Secker & Warburg, 1949; *Letters to Felice*, Erich Heller and Jurgen Born (eds.), James Stern and Elisabeth Duckworth (trans.), Martin Secker & Warburg, 1974; *Letters to Milena*, Tania and James Stern (trans.), Willy Haas (ed.), Martin Secker & Warburg, 1953. *From Letters to Ottla and the Family*, Nahum Glatzer (ed.), Richard and Clara Winston (trans.), copyright © 1974, 1982 by Shocken Books; used by permission of Schocken Books, a division of Random House, Inc.

Printed in the United States of America.

Library of Congress Control Number: 2004107048

ISBN 0-300-10631-9 (cloth : alk. paper)

A catalogue record for this book is available from the British Library.

The paper in this book meets the guidelines for permanence and durability of the Committee on Production Guidelines for Book Longevity of the Council on Library Resources.

10 9 8 7 6 5 4 3 2 1

Contents

Since I am nothing but literature
Da ich nichts anderes bin als Literatur

Franz Kafka

It is through writing that I keep a hold on life
Durch mein Schreiben halte ich mich ja am Leben

Franz Kafka

Altogether he is a man who wants nothing but the absolute, the ultimate in all things
Überhaupt ist er ein Mensch, der nur das Unbedingte will, das Äußerste in Allem

Max Brod

PART I

Prague

I

At the gates of the New Jewish Cemetery in the Prague suburb of Strašnice, a lean and ancient custodian emerges to greet the visitor. He gestures towards a cardboard box, set on a small chair, from which one is invited to select a paper yarmulke, or skull-cap. With a dry smile, he accepts, on this bitterly cold February morning, the substitute of a woolly hat. Over his shoulder, it is impossible to miss a spotted white enamel sign, which reads, above a slender black arrow, DR FRANZ KAFKA.

It was another such dull day – in spite of the date – in the late afternoon of 11 June 1924, when the doctor of law was buried here, among the dark, ornate gravestones of the Prague Jewish bourgeoisie. Coming upon the grave at the end of a gravel path, one is immediately struck by its difference: a grey, tapering, Cubist lozenge on which are printed the names of Kafka and the parents he preceded to the grave. In its formal simplicity, its shapely lightness, its unobtrusive but wholly original presence, it could not be more fitting as a memorial to a writer whose unique genius continues to fascinate the world and to baffle its attempts at interpretation.

One cannot spend long in Prague, where Kafka was born and where almost all of his short life was lived, without becoming aware both of how much he belongs to this place and of how much it belongs to him. 'Kafka was Prague and Prague was Kafka,' declared his friend Johannes Urzidil.[1] Yet Prague is now the capital of the Czech Republic, an independent state of the new Europe, which does not any longer speak the language in which Kafka wrote. He was born, in 1883, into one of the major cities of the Austro-Hungarian Empire, whose official language, that of the Habsburg Dual Monarchy, was German. And Kafka was a Jew in a city where the Jews were almost wholly Germanized. This would have been a complex enough starting point for any writer, but for Kafka there were myriad additional tensions that contributed both to the complexity of his art and to the anguish of his personal life. He wanted only to write. 'I am nothing but literature,' he asserted.[2] But the world set up for him a series of obstacles: an unsympathetic family, a demanding professional career, poor health, and the constantly receding prospect of a marriage he craved. The peculiar flavour of his books – the now universalized 'Kafkaesque' – derives from this sense of being unhoused, unable to find accommodation in a mysteriously antagonistic world. From guilt, but like Joseph K in *Der Prozess/The Trial* he felt himself to be an accused without a formal accusation, a criminal without a crime. From exclusion, like the land surveyor who cannot breach the baffling protocols of *Das Schloss/The Castle* in order to establish himself in its orbit. From hope for a new life and a personal remaking, like the hero of *Der Verschollene/The Man Who Disappeared.* From self-lacerating pain: the dream of oneself being metamorphosed into a repellent and monstrous creature. And eventually from a terminal illness that put paid to all hope.

But to see Kafka as a quivering neurasthenic, someone who knew only how to suffer, would be a travesty. His quiet, reflective, solitary personality also diffused warmth, wit, a sense of pleasure in life, just as much as a consciousness of its pains. He had friends, he was part of a lively and stimulating circle of remarkable Prague writers and intellectuals; he was successful in his career and popular with his colleagues; he relished his escapes into the countryside and outdoor pursuits; he enjoyed a modest but enviable reputation as a writer even if his major novels were unpublished in his lifetime; and he was attractive to women and enjoyed their company. However much he was tormented by private fears and lonely anxieties, he was loved by all who came into contact with him.

In the years following his death, when his position in world literature was being established, a habit arose of seeing Kafka as a quasi-religious writer, an allegorist of religious themes, a modern Everyman. At the same time, a somewhat abstracted Kafka emerged, one much suited to the temper of mid-twentieth-century European and American intellectuals. Absurdists and existentialists took him up with great relish. Slowly, however, in the second half of the twentieth century, a more nuanced picture of Kafka began to develop. Ignorance about his Prague background, his Jewishness, the details of his personal life, was countered by a flow of informed studies and especially by the appearance of letters and diaries that filled out the picture of the historical Kafka: a particular man in a particular place at a particular time.

This is the Kafka presented in this biography. Inescapably, the story must begin in Prague.

One day in the autumn of 1920,[3] Kafka approached the window of his parents' apartment in the luxurious Oppelthaus building in the heart of Prague. He turned to his companion in the room, the Jewish scholar Friedrich Thieberger, who was his Hebrew teacher, executed a few circular movements with his hand, and declared: 'Within this little circle my whole life is contained.'[4] From the window he could see the Altstädter Ring (Old Town Square) and Niklasstrasse (or Mikulášská),[5] as well as his school, his university and his office.

Standing in the square today, it is possible to recapture that Kafka conspectus. Facing east from the Oppelthaus (on the north side of the square) one can see the ornate baroque façade of the Palais Kinský. At the right-hand corner, the ground-floor premises, which today house the Kafka Bookshop, were from 1912 onwards the location of his father's fancy-goods shop. In the rear of the building was the German Gymnasium, which Kafka attended as a schoolboy. One's eye now travels southwards to the corner of the square where Celetná Street (Kafka would have known it as Zeltnergasse) leads off in the direction of two of the family houses and the shop's former premises. Facing the south side of the square next, we see the house called 'At the Unicorn', where Kafka, as an undergraduate, attended Berta Fanta's famous salon. This side of the square eventually meets the start of a smaller square, Malé náměstí, where, pushing past the crowds of tourists watching the figures come and go on the famous Apostle Clock on the Old Town Hall, one sees the Minuta House with its elaborate external *sgraffito* – another temporary home for the restlessly moving Kafka family. Stepping back into the main square, a short walk along the western side brings one to the north-west corner, where one may see what is left (merely the original portal) of the house in which Kafka was born and which now houses the Kafka Exhibition. With a little more time to spare, one may see on foot most of the buildings associated with Kafka in the surrounding streets of the Old Town.[6] It is a striking physical reminder of the rootedness in one place of a writer who, in his imagination, transcended all boundaries.

Yet Kafka's roots were not securely planted. He may have lived most of his life in Prague, but he was never wholly at ease there – though it is not easy to conceive of any place in which Kafka would have been totally comfortable. Given his provenance as a Prague German Jew, in the last days of the Habsburg Empire, he experienced unavoidable frictions resulting from his membership of what has been called a ghetto with invisible walls.[7]

The Kafkas did not originally come from the historic Prague

Ghetto that was finally swept away in the writer's lifetime in a ruthless act of slum clearance. They were village Jews – *Dorfjuden* – from the rural hinterland of southern Bohemia. Kafka's grandfather, Jakob (1814–89), was the kosher butcher in the Czech-speaking village of Wossek – today's Osek – near Strakonice. Osek at that time had a sizeable Jewish community and the Kafkas lived in a lane known as 'In the Jews' Quarter'; eight of them in a tiny hovel. The Jewish cemetery remains in the village. The family, described by their historian as 'a very typical Bohemian Jewish family',[8] probably spoke some version of Yiddish, or 'Jewish-German', but also Czech. That they also spoke German is clear from Jakob's gravestone, which, in addition to Hebrew inscriptions, has the injunction '*Friede seiner Asche!*' ('May his ashes rest in peace').[9]

Jakob, who was said to be ' a big, powerful man',[10] had a hard life in Osek, struggling to bring up six children in rural poverty. He married late in life, at the age of thirty-five, in 1849, the year after the relaxation of laws that prohibited all Jews save for the eldest child in a family from marrying. His wife, Franziska Platowksi, was described by her daughter-in-law as 'a delicate, hard-working woman, who, despite all trouble and difficulties, brought up her children well and they were the only happiness in her life'.[11] She also had a reputation in the village as a healer and her grandson would later develop an interest in natural medicine.

The couple's fourth child, Hermann (1852–1931), in the traditional manner of the self-made man, would never let his children forget the hardships he had suffered, and which were undoubtedly genuine. 'It is unpleasant to listen to Father talk with incessant insinuations about the good fortune of people today and especially of his children, about the sufferings he had to endure in his youth,' Kafka wrote in his diary at the age of twenty-eight.

> No one denies that for years, as a result of insufficient winter clothing, he had open sores on his legs, that he often went hungry, that when he was only ten he had to push a cart through the villages [delivering kosher meat] even in winter and very early in the morning – but, and this is something he will not understand, these facts, taken together with the further fact that I have not gone through all this, by no means lead to the conclusion that I have been happier than he, that he may pride himself on these sores on his legs, which is something he assumes and asserts from the very beginning, that I cannot appreciate his past sufferings, and that, finally, just because I have not gone through the same sufferings I must be endlessly grateful to him. How gladly I would listen if he would talk on about his youth and parents, but to hear all this in a boastful and quarrelsome tone is torment.[12]

Hermann, the big burly man who so frightened his sensitive young son, would clap his hands together and exclaim in exasperation, 'Who can understand that today! What do the children know?' His relatives were sometimes brought in to act as reinforcements: Aunt Julie, for instance, Hermann's younger sister, who had 'the huge face of all Father's relatives. There is something wrong and somewhat disturbing about the set or colour of her eyes.' At the age of ten she had been hired out as a cook. 'In a skimpy wet skirt, in the severe cold, she had to run out for something, the skin on her legs cracked, the skimpy skirt froze and it was only that evening, in bed, that it dried.' Small wonder that Hermann Kafka was so driven, when he later arrived in Prague, by the need to make good and to be seen to do so, to achieve social distinction, to live at smart addresses (the explanation for all those removals from one part of the Old Town to the other), and to side with the German-speaking elite. His son would always be torn between admiration for his father's practical wisdom and strength and distaste for his macho boasting. Nor could Franz ever forgive his father's utter lack of interest in his writing.

At the age of fourteen Hermann was sent out of the family home to earn his living pushing a cart as an itinerant pedlar. At twenty he joined the army, rising in his three years to the rank of platoon commander, or *Zugführer*. In later years his singing of old military songs would be one of the ways in which he liked to emphasise his pro-Austrian patriotism.[13] Equally, when it suited his business interests, he would stress later in Prague his fondness for all things Czech, even to the point of misleadingly telling the Census that Czech was the language spoken in the family home. Franz, for his part, refused to collude in this deception. The family in fact spoke German – though Hermann was said to swear in Yiddish.

From his Bohemian roots, Hermann Kafka brought to his business life in Prague the symbol of the Kafka name. His business stationery boasted a jackdaw – '*kavka*' in Czech – which is a reminder of the oppression of the Jews in the Habsburg Empire. In October 1781 Emperor Joseph II had issued an Edict of Toleration, or *Toleranzpatent*. By modern standards, 'toleration' might not seem *le mot juste*, for, as well as affirming the principle of religious toleration and opening up all forms of trade and commerce to Jews (though they were still barred from owning land in the countryside), it aimed to make Austrian Jews more useful to the state. Like Marcuse's 'repressive tolerance', it gave with one hand and controlled with the other. Jews were encouraged to establish their own government-supervised elementary schools. Universities and institutes of higher education opened up to Jews. But meanwhile the use of Hebrew and Yiddish in business records was banned, and in 1782 legislation forced Jews to abandon their Jewish patronymics and adopt German personal and family names.[14] Many plumped for names of animals and birds, and it is probable that a late eighteenth-century Kafka ancestor chose the family name, or had it forced upon him by imperial officials.[15] 'Don't be surprised at the Jews' lack of attachment to their names,' wrote Joseph Roth. 'For Jews their names have no value because they are not their names . . . They have compulsory aliases. Their true name is the one by which they are summoned to the Torah on the Sabbath and on holy days: their first Jewish name, and the Jewish first name of their father.'[16] It was not until late in the century that followed the *Toleranzpatent* that the Jews in Bohemia became properly emancipated and began the move to the city. Hermann Kafka was a typical example of this social movement.

On Kafka's mother's side there was a different inheritance. Julie Kafka came from a more bourgeois family who had been successful in the textile and brewery trades in Poděbrady (Podiebrad) on the River Elbe. Her father, a cloth-maker from Humpolec in eastern Bohemia, had married well. A house in Podiebrad and a shop came as a dowry with his bride. As Kafka's friend, literary executor and first biographer Max Brod put it: 'Here we find scholars, dreamers, inclined to eccentricity, and others driven by this inclination to the adventurous, the exotic, or the freakish and reclusive.'[17] It is easy to see why Kafka was drawn to this strand of his ancestry. In some handwritten notes made for her family in the 1930s, Julie sketched a picture of her family background. Her grandfather on her mother's side, Adam Porias, was 'a devout Jew and a well-known Talmud scholar' with a successful drapery shop in Podiebrad which he neglected in favour of his Talmudic studies. When he and his wife moved to Prague late in life they had a fine house on Old Town Square with a scholarly library on the first floor above the shop. He bathed every day, winter and summer, in the Elbe, even if this necessitated breaking the ice with a pick-axe. One of Adam's brothers was even more religious and was mocked by his schoolfriends for wearing the tassels of his prayer shawl over his coat. Another brother was a doctor who converted to Christianity, one of several apostates on Julie's side of the family, in spite of frequent claims that they were more devout than the Kafkas.[18] Among these were Julie's rich brothers, Rudolf, Alfred and Josef Löwy.

In a diary entry Kafka discussed his relatives, but only on his mother's side. 'In Hebrew my name is Amschel,' he wrote, 'like my mother's maternal grandfather [Adam Porias], whom my mother, who was six years old when he died, can remember as a very pious and learned man with a long, white beard. She remembers how she had to take hold of the toes of the corpse and ask forgiveness for any offence she may have committed against her grandfather.'[19] Julie's mother, Esther Löwy, died of typhus at the age of twenty-eight, leaving the three-year-old Julie and three brothers. Esther's mother, in Kafka's words, 'became melancholy, refused to eat, spoke with no one' and then, a year after the death of her daughter, went for a walk and did not return. Her body was found in the Elbe. Two more brothers were born after Julie's father, Jakob, remarried a year later. It may well have been this rapid remarriage after her daughter's death that contributed to Esther's mother's suicide.

Kafka's Löwy uncles captured his imagination, and, as will be seen later, influenced his writing of *The Man Who Disappeared.* Uncle Alfred became a director of the Spanish railways (which might have accounted for his forced conversion); Uncle Siegfried (another of Julie's brothers), Kafka's favourite, became a country doctor in Triesch, Moravia; and Uncle Rudolf (a bachelor, like his stepbrother Alfred), who was a book-keeper in a brewery, converted to Catholicism and became steadily more eccentric, though not to the extent of his own uncle, Nathan, whom Julie described as 'crazy Uncle Nathan'. Rudolf was used by Hermann as another stick with which to beat his son. 'Rudolf all over!' he would exclaim when Kafka 'committed some apparent stupidity'. Hermann considered Rudolf 'extremely ridiculous, an indecipherable, too friendly, too modest, solitary, and yet almost loquacious man'. The constant drumming in of this comparison made Kafka feel as though his *faux pas* were 'a consequence of a fundamental flaw of my nature' and, in spite of his perceiving no real affinity with Rudolf, his father's curse 'resulted in my at least starting to resemble this uncle of mine'.[20]

The distinction between the Kafkas and the Löwys was endorsed by Franz. It begins to sound like a pretty little Lawrentian fable in the making – the rough, animal father and the sensitive, artistic mother with whom the artistic child formed an exclusive bond. But it was not like that at all. Though Hermann Kafka was certainly not a bookish man, playing cards after supper being the limit of his cultural sophistication, his roughness and boorishness were never knowingly underestimated by his resentful son. And Julie, though well meaning, never really grasped the significance for her son of writing as a sacred vocation. She thought of it as his more or less harmless 'pastime' (*Zeitvertrieb*). As Max Brod wrote: 'Franz's mother loves him very much, but she has not the faintest idea who her son is and *what his needs are*. Literature is a "pastime"! Mein Gott! As though it did not eat our hearts out, willing victims though we are. Frau Kafka and I have often had words over this. All the love in the world is useless when there is total lack of understanding.'[21]

There were two very powerful reasons for this lack of mutual understanding (though in fairness to Kafka's parents he must have been a difficult child). The first was the business, which demanded all of Hermann and Julie's attention and left very little time either for intellectual pursuits or for taking an interest in their son's literary aspirations. The second was the kind of childhood each had experienced. It is truer to say that their childhoods were virtually non-existent. Hermann had been put to work as a boy and Julie, aged five when her father had remarried, had been forced to look after three brothers and two stepbrothers. The model of family life was hard and unremitting; it left very little leisure for honing what are now called 'parenting skills'. In his mid-thirties Kafka wrote the famous *Brief an den Vater/Letter to the Father*, a furious, pamphlet-length indictment of his father's indifference and of his responsibility for his son's failure to reach an accommodation with life. It will be considered in more detail later, but even if it had ever been sent (it was not), it is unlikely that its reproachful barbs would have penetrated the hide of Hermann Kafka. Parents and son simply spoke a different language. 'I have always looked on my parents as persecutors,'[22] Franz once wrote. He had a horror of family life:

> I cannot live with people; I absolutely hate all my relatives, not because they are wicked, not because I don't think well of them . . . but simply because they are the people with whom I live in close proximity. It is just that I cannot abide communal life . . . Seen in a detached way, I enjoy all people, but my enjoyment is not so great that, given the necessary physical requirements, I would not be incomparably happier living in a desert, in a forest, on an island, rather than here in my room between my parents' bedroom and living room.'[23]

This is the domestic matrix out of which came the terrifying claustrophobia and self-disgust of Gregor Samsa in *Die Verwandlung/Metamorphosis*.

2

Franz Kafka was born in the centre of Prague on 3 July 1883, a year after the marriage of his father to Julie Löwy. Hermann Kafka had arrived in the city on the Vltava, after quitting the army in the 1870s, to establish himself in the retail drapery trade. He specialized in *Galanteriewaren*, or fancy goods, which included haberdashery, fashion accessories, walking-sticks and parasols. He was thirty when he married Julie Löwy and their first child was born in the 'House of the Tower', at the edge of the old Jewish Ghetto, just off the Old Town Square, on the corner of Karpfengasse and Maiselgasse (today, respectively, Kaprova and Maislova). The house was later demolished, but the doorway still remains as part of the newer building.

In later life, Kafka considered that being the first-born – 'of which I am the sad but perfect example'[1] – bestowed considerable disadvantages when compared with the experience of subsequent siblings:

> These late-born ones are at once surrounded by a variety of partly undergone, partly striven-for realizations, experiences, discoveries, conquests, by their brothers and sisters, and the advantages, advice and encouragement gained by this close and wholly interdependent family life are enormous. By then the family is far better equipped to deal with them . . . the parents . . . have learned from their

> mistakes . . . and automatically these late-born ones are settled more warmly in the nest; *less attention is paid to them* [my italics].

This is typical of Kafka's deep ambivalence towards his family. He wanted to be left alone, for his solitary and particular individuality, his *Eigentümlichkeit*, to be reverenced. But at the same time he was demanding and quick to indict failures of parenting.

Julie Kafka described her new baby as 'a delicate but healthy child'.[2] Two years later, she gave birth to Georg, 'a pretty, vigorous child',[3] who died fifteen months later from measles; and in 1887 Heinrich was born, but he survived for only six months. In Kafka's view, both boys died 'through the fault of the doctors',[4] with the result that: 'I was the only child until 4–5 years later my three sisters arrived, separated by one and two years respectively. Thus I lived alone for a very long time, battling with nurses, old nannies, spiteful cooks, unhappy governesses, since my parents were always at the shop.' This loneliness in early childhood can hardly have failed to leave its mark on the psyche of a shy, delicate child. One of Kafka's biographers, Ernst Pawel, has speculated that Franz may have resented the appearance of the two rivals for his parents' attention ('pretty, vigorous' certainly seems a little fonder than 'delicate but healthy'), and, after fantasizing about their deaths, may have been consumed with guilt when they did shortly thereafter die.[5] It is an interesting idea, but Kafka himself never indicated that he might have felt that way. Of the three sisters, Gabriele ('Elli'), Valerie ('Valli') and Ottilie ('Ottla'), it was the youngest, Ottla, who was his favourite.

On 16 September 1889, at the age of six, Franz left this solitary enclosure for the world of education. Since the family lived always in the centre of the Old Town, it was a short walk from the striking Minuta House – the fifth residence since Kafka's birth – in the Kleiner Ring (Small Town Square or Malé náměstí) to the Deutsche Knabenschule (German School for Boys) on the Fleischmarkt (Meatmarket). Thirty years later, Kafka recalled these first walks to school: 'Our cook, a small, dry thin person with a pointed nose and hollow cheeks, yellowish but firm, energetic and superior, led me every morning to school. We lived in the house which separates the Kleiner Ring from the Grosser Ring. Thus we walked first across the Ring, then into Teingasse, then through a kind of archway in the Fleischmarktgasse down to the Fleischmarkt.'[6] On these walks with the cook, every morning for about a year, she would threaten to tell the teacher how naughty he had been at home:

> As a matter of fact I probably wasn't very naughty, but rather stubborn, useless, sad, bad-tempered, and out of all this probably something quite nice could have been fabricated for the teacher. I knew this so didn't take the cook's threat too lightly. All the same, since the road to school was enormously long I believed at first that anything might happen on the way (it's from such apparent childish light-heartedness that there gradually develops, just because the roads are not so enormously long, this anxiousness and dead-eyed seriousness.)[7]

The small boy doubted that the cook would dare to talk to 'the world-respect-commanding teacher' and told her so. She replied, between 'thin, merciless lips', that she most certainly would, whether he believed it or not, and the threat intensified.

> School in itself was already enough of a nightmare, and now the cook was trying to make it even worse. I began to plead, she shook her head, the more I pleaded the more precious appeared to me that for which I was pleading, the greater the danger; I stood still and begged for

> forgiveness, she dragged me along, I threatened her with retaliation from my parents, she laughed, *here* she was all-powerful, I held on to the shop doors, to the cornerstones, I refused to go any further until she had forgiven me, I pulled her back by the skirt (she didn't have it easy either), but she kept dragging me along with the assurance that she would tell the teacher this, too; it grew late, the clock on the Jakobskirche struck 8, the school bells could be heard, other children began to run, I always had the greatest terror of being late, now we too had to run and all the time the thought: She'll tell, she won't tell – well, she didn't tell, ever, but she always had the opportunity and even an apparently increasing opportunity (I didn't tell yesterday but I'll certainly tell today) and of this she never let go. And sometimes . . . she stamped her foot in the street in anger about me and the coal merchant woman would sometimes be standing there, watching.

There are several ways to read this anecdote. At one level it is a frightening childhood experience of the type usually associated with an authority figure and carried by many adults throughout a lifetime. From another point of view it is a sign that Kafka could well have been a spoiled, difficult child who needed a firm hand. He was, it seems, considered something of a mummy's boy because he was always taken to school in spite of its proximity to his home.[8] At another level, too, it could be the playing out of complex class and nationalistic tensions. The cook would almost certainly have been Czech in a reasonably well-to-do German-Jewish household of which little Franz was the darling scion. The silent stare of the coal merchant woman would have seen and understood this. Would a knowing look have passed between the two women, unknown to Franz?

When Hermann Kafka had come to Prague to establish

himself in business he had made a number of decisions about how he would place himself. Newly arrived from the provinces, from a Czech village, he would have seen himself initially as a Czech. But for some years Bohemia in general and Prague in particular had been taut with political and ethnic tensions. Allegiances mattered. Fairly lukewarm in his practice of the Jewish religion (for which he would later be reproached by his son), Hermann nevertheless took the view that his future lay with the prosperous Prague German-Jewish elite which dominated business and social life in Prague. The German names given to all six children and the choice of the German elementary school – pointedly ignoring the alternative Czech primary school which only 10 per cent of Jewish children attended – were confirmation of the group with which he and his son were to be aligned.

At the end of the nineteenth century, the Austrian provinces of Bohemia and Moravia, including the city of Prague, were undergoing rapid social and political change. The tensions caused by this swiftly evolving environment sometimes found expression in physical violence. Bohemia had become the industrial powerhouse of the region, and the industrialized workers began to form trade unions and to constitute a sizeable industrial proletariat. There was a resurgence of pan-German nationalism, as well as its rival, Czech nationalism. Clashes between opposing factions were frequent, and Austrian troops were regularly called in to restore order. For periods of Kafka's youth, Prague was under direct rule from Vienna. In such movements as the Young Czech Party an unpleasant anti-Semitism flourished as part of the nationalist programme, exacerbated by the fact that the workers were invariably Czech while their bosses were invariably Jewish.

Gradual removal of the laws constraining Jewish citizens of the Empire had resulted in a drift of Jews such as Hermann Kafka from the country to the city. There was a Czech Jewish movement and Hermann seems to have joined briefly the synagogue in Heinrichgasse (Jindřišská), which was the first in Prague to preach in Czech. But he soon threw in his lot with the German-Jewish section of society. Nevertheless, during the anti-Semitic riots of December 1897 in the city, his shop escaped attack from the mobs because he was considered sufficiently Czech not to be a target. An apocryphal story relates that the mob paused outside his shop in the Old Town and shouted: 'Leave Kafka alone; he's Czech.'[9]

At the turn of the century, nationalist sentiment and racial hatred intensified in what were now the dying years of the Austro-Hungarian Empire. Habsburg rule would expire with the First World War, at the end of which the new Czechoslovakian Republic headed by Tomáš Masaryk was established. Masaryk, in 1899, had been the brave defender of Leopold Hilsner, a Jewish shoemaker wrongfully accused of the murder on Easter Eve of a young woman, Agnes Hruza. The claim was that the girl had been raped and ritually slaughtered and her blood used in the preparation of matzos for Passover. It was a familiar return of the old blood-libel against Jews, and the case has been described as 'Eastern Europe's equivalent of the Dreyfus affair'.[10] Masaryk, whose example showed that Czech self-determination had no necessary connection with racial hatred, later recalled the bitter opposition he had encountered when he published a pamphlet in Hilsner's defence, and the sight of 'the timid faces of so many of my acquaintance who suddenly gave me a wide berth'.[11] Kafka's awakened interest in his Jewish roots in his late twenties, his disapproval of his father's neglect of his Jewish heritage, and his later interest in the nascent Zionist movement, however qualified that was, all have deep historical roots in the situation of Jews in late nineteenth-century and early twentieth-century Prague.

Austrian Jews had finally achieved full emancipation only in the 1860s, whereas Jews had been settled in Prague since the tenth century. It is a strange experience today to sit quietly in the

Staronová ('Old–New' or Altneu) Synagogue in Prague – the oldest functioning synagogue in Europe – and look up at what seems a rather odd architectural style of Gothic ribbed vaulting. Begun in the thirteenth century, when Jews were forbidden from becoming architects, the job is thought to have been done by Franciscan builders working on a nearby convent. It is set in the heart of what was once the notorious Prague Ghetto, a walled enclave, insanitary, crowded and squalid.[12] The famous Rabbi Löw, legendary creator of the golem, was a presence here in the golden age of Prague Jewry. When Emperor Joseph II removed the gates of the ghetto in his reforming period in the 1780s, the area was named Josefov in his honour. After the revolutions of 1848 Jews were allowed to settle outside the ghetto walls and were granted equal status as citizens. The more prosperous Jews moved out to residential suburbs, and their place was taken by every kind of lowlife character, vice rubbing shoulders with extreme Orthodoxy and piety. As a result, only 20 per cent of the ghetto district was Jewish by 1890. Three years later, during Kafka's boyhood, the process of sweeping away the narrow, twisting streets was begun and the area sanitized. Today it is a neat district of the inner city much visited by international tourists.

In 1900 Jews formed less than 7 per cent of the population of Prague and the inner suburbs,[13] but their power, wealth and influence were considerable. Many Jews chose assimilation or acculturation in order to escape the poverty and restrictions of ghetto life. The path of bourgeois entrepreneurial and professional life was the obvious one to take, and more than half of all Bohemian Jews in the second half of the nineteenth century were engaged in commerce and finance, with a further 15 to 25 per cent in the professions. What is striking about the Prague Jewish community was that it possessed no industrial working class of any significance. According to Gary Cohen, 'The great majority of the Prague Jews adopted the culture of Austria's German middle class. The large-scale linguistic and cultural

Germanization of the Bohemian Jews had begun in the reign of Emperor Joseph II, when the government established schools for the Jews with German as the language of instruction.' By around 1860 German had virtually replaced the regional Jewish dialect known by its detractors as *Mauscheldeutsch* as the main language spoken in the larger Jewish communities. German was the language of commerce, public administration and education. It was natural that the Prague Jews should choose this language, although they would still need to have some knowledge of Czech. This did not mean that they were embraced by that other minority – the German Christians – but they increasingly began to move in the German cultural sphere in Prague. This trend was accelerated by the rise of Czech nationalism in the second half of the nineteenth century. Social and economic resentment from the small Czech shopkeepers, craftsmen and skilled workers fuelled street protests sporadically from the 1840s right up to the outbreak of the First World War.

Class as much as religion determined the Prague Jewish Germanization and the relatively small number of poor Jews did start to align themselves with the Czechs after the mid-1880s. In the old Jewish quarter, in this period leading up to the clearance of the ghetto, the Czech-Jewish movement won some electoral support, but the overwhelming majority of middle-class Jewry continued the process of Germanization, notwithstanding their tendency – again exemplified by Hermann Kafka – to tell the Census that they spoke Czech in the home, as their *Umgangssprache*. Only 45 per cent of Prague Jews claimed to speak German in the 1900 Census, which was plainly not accurate.

The Germans overall began to develop their own forms of cultural life in Prague, and the German Casino (in spite of its name it was a social club) was founded in 1862 as the nerve centre of the German community. Jews formed nearly half of the membership of this socially select institution and did not feel the need to play down their Jewishness. Kafka's cousin, Bruno, was an influential member of the German Club, the Casino's political arm, and the shared values of political liberalism, civil liberties and anti-clericalism created a bond between Jewish and Gentile Germans. Together they were still a minority and they therefore needed each other. There was, however, less fraternization in the private sphere. As Cohen puts it: 'However much Jews desired and achieved acceptance in the public life of Prague's German society, only a tiny number joined in family relationships with non-Jews.'

The Czechs, however, had quite a different view of all this. To them, the Prague Germans – Jew and Gentile alike – formed a powerful elite, occupying positions of power and influence out of all proportion to their numbers (in 1900, 34,000 out of a total city population of around 450,000). They spoke the language of the imperial power and seemed to the Czech minority to be prone to a certain haughtiness. Their separate theatres, clubs, newspapers and institutions of community life constituted a kind of cultural apartheid. Some slight residue of this spirit continues to the present day. Controversy broke out in Prague in 2000 when the city council proposed to rename the tiny square in front of Kafka's birthplace Franze Kafky Náměstí (Franz Kafka Square). There were objections from the local mayor, and Marta Zelezná of the Franz Kafka Society told the BBC that the city has 'an ambivalent relationship' with its most famous writer. 'He's not viewed as "our" writer because he was Jewish and because he wrote in German,'[14] she said. Banned in the communist era as decadent, Kafka's work is only now being brought out in a complete Czech translation. In the Czech edition of *Who's Who in History* his name does not appear. The square was renamed, but the ambivalence lingers.

At the end of the nineteenth century the Czechs saw the Germans as a class of rulers. According to the Czech writer Pavel Eisner:

> They consisted of the Germanized or foreign nobility, the holders of high or intermediate positions in the government, the officers of the Prague garrison, the industrialists and wholesalers, the other rich high bourgeois, the professors at the University and Institute of Technology, and the German actors, and also the fluctuating element of German students who were only temporarily in Prague and never became part of the city on the Vltava. There had never been a German hinterland in the immediate environs of Prague.[15]

Eisner saw this as a social and linguistic ghetto. 'To this Ghetto with invisible walls the German Jew in Prague attached himself.' When one considers the facts – that the Prague German Jew was an industrialist, prosperous businessman, leading bank official, a doctor or lawyer with a large practice, a university professor; that almost all wholesale merchandising and almost all import and export trade was carried on by Jews; and that the whole business of expensive fashion goods was a Jewish monopoly – it is not hard to see why there was resentment and why traditional anti-Semitic stereotyping flourished. 'As a businessman the German Jew in Prague had only Czech workers – there were no others – and Czech foremen,' wrote Eisner. 'Businessman or not, the domestic servants were always Czech. So also were the janitor, the coachman and chauffeur, the greengrocer, the milkmaid, the marketwoman, the charwoman, and the washerwoman.'

The Kafka household embodied this caste system. The servants and nursemaids were Czech, as were all the menial staff: Hermann Kafka famously branded his Czech shop staff as 'paid enemies'.[16] It was probably only from these social inferiors that any living Czech was learned. And it was invariably from lower-class Czech women that the young scions of the German bourgeoisie such as Kafka received their sexual initiation.

The Prague German attended German schools, a German university and probably read one of the two Prague German daily newspapers, *Bohemia* (which was far from being pro-Czech) and the *Prager Tagblatt*, or the weekly *Montagsblatt*, all three of which were run by Germans.

The rural Sudeten Germans from the Sudetengau, or border district, were probably just as much alienated from the Prague Germans and their cosmopolitan, avant-garde tastes as were the Czechs. When, however, Eisner compares Prague German society to the European colony in Shanghai, one begins to suspect that he overestimates the extent of the mutual incomprehension.[17]

Certainly Kafka was an exception, speaking Czech, as will be seen later, with some fluency, and taking an interest in the Czech language and culture. What should really concern us here is the extent to which this experience of growing up in a rather rarefied, separate world added still further to his natural disposition to feel alienated from his surroundings, his sense of not belonging. In particular, language was a central issue. Kafka, though in no sense an ideological or programmatic writer, always had a keen political awareness, a sympathy for the underdog and a mistrust of the powerful. Living at a time of Czech struggle for self-determination from a sclerotic, conservative empire run from Vienna, he would have been acutely aware of what was at stake. His epoch in Prague was characterized, in the words of Emmanuel Frynta, as 'a time of transition and revolt, when the ground was unsteady beneath one's feet, a time without present, without attachment, without anchorage'.[18]

As he arrived at primary school on the Fleischmarkt, the tensions inherent in the six-year-old Kafka's situation would be seen and felt – once he had shaken himself free from the restraining hand of the malevolent cook – in the taunts and missiles of the boys going into the Czech primary school next door. So violent were the clashes between Czech and German schoolboys that one of Kafka's later friends, Oskar Baum, lost his eyesight permanently in one of these tussles. 'At a very early age a sense of guilt and of not being welcome was forced upon him,' argues Emmanuel Frynta. Above the Czech primary school was inscribed the injunction: 'A Czech child belongs in a Czech school.' Kafka's teacher on that first day was Hans Markert, but, according to Hugo Hecht, one of Kafka's schoolfellows, the only teacher who made any impression on the boys was Moritz Beck, 'an outstanding teacher who took an interest in pupils out of school life'. Kafka, though shy and nervous, was 'always a model pupil, often the star pupil; the teacher liked this modest, quiet, good pupil very much'.[19] Hecht can remember only one incident when the perfect schoolboy attracted censure. One beautiful spring morning Kafka was so absorbed by a sparrow that had come to rest on the sill of the open window that he failed repeatedly to answer when his name was called by the teacher.

Franz would remain at the Deutsche Knabenschule, playing in the corridors and classrooms during breaks because it had no proper exercise yard, and absorbing such framed maxims from the walls as 'Speech is silver; silence is golden', for four years. Then Hermann was faced with deciding on the next step of his eldest child's education. He resolved to send the ten-year-old to the German Gymnasium, where he would begin in earnest the process of intellectual self-discovery.

3

On 20 September 1893, ten-year-old Franz Kafka entered the Altstädter Deutsches Gymnasium, the strict and austere German grammar school housed in the rear of the Palais Kinský. Its official title – 'The Imperial and Royal [*Kaiserlich und Königliche*] State Gymnasium with Instruction in the German Language' – in its monarchical pomposity recalls the satirical world of Kakania (those two royal initials combined with an obvious scatological intent in the invention of Kafka's contemporary, the Viennese novelist Robert Musil, whose *Der Mann ohne Eigenschaften/The Man without Qualities* (1930) laid bare the last days of Habsburg society). As Franz Baumer put it: 'A musty atmosphere and a conservative, philistine spirit permeated this institution, which was built wholly on the principle of a dry pragmatism coupled with a pronounced authoritarian relationship between teacher and student. It was in the nature of things that the former monopolized the grand stairway while the latter had to use the service staircase.'[1]

In spite of Kafka's insistence that he was a 'slowly developing' and 'timid' child,[2] he once again impressed his contemporaries by being diligent and successful – mathematics aside – within the constraints of the traditional syllabus, which concentrated on the classics taught with little imagination or flair. His father had chosen the humanistic Gymnasium rather than the more modern Realschule. The latter would have prepared his son for a business career. Hermann may have been motivated by a growing realism about the likely capacity of Franz as a practical businessman; or by social ambition, for the Gymnasium traditionally supplied the imperial administration with its top civil servants and lawyers. The syllabus gave no instruction in modern languages or literature, and music, physical education and art were optional subjects only. From the start of the third year about half of the school time was devoted to Latin and Greek, yet in his copious later reading Kafka hardly ever mentioned a classical author. His favourite teacher seems to have been the Darwinian natural history master, Adolf Gottwald. His form-master was a Catholic priest of the Piarist Order, Emil Gschwind, most of whose pupils were Jewish. 'Our Gymnasium was not a frightful trench, it was on the other hand a symptom of the insular apartness in which most Prague Jews lived at the start of the 1900s,'[3] said his school contemporary Emil Utitz. The sole Czech pupil in the eighth and final year of the class above Kafka's at the Gymnasium, Zdenko Vanek, remembers having to leave the lesson when the rabbi arrived to instruct his classmates, who were almost all the sons of Jewish manufacturers and shopkeepers. Vanek remembers Kafka as 'a quiet, brooding and reflective type'.[4]

Kafka made only a few friends at school, including: Hugo Bergmann, the Zionist philosopher; Rudolf Illowý, the socialist thinker; Ewald Příbram, whose father was helpfully president of the insurance firm where Kafka would later work; and Oskar Pollak, the art historian. Bergmann, who had also been with Kafka at primary school, recalled his friend as something of a rebel, more of a socialist than a Zionist: 'We both experienced the thrill of nonconformity,'[5] he claimed. The pair pointedly remained seated during the playing of the patriotic 'Watch on the Rhine' during an outing of the Altstädter Kollegentag, a senior boys' club to which all were expected to belong.[6] Kafka, like any intelligent student, passed through various intellectual phases – atheistic, pantheistic and socialist. He was very enthusiastic about the freedom of the Boers around 1900 and was said to wear in his buttonhole (in spite of his desire to be invisible) the red carnation – *rote Nelke* – of the socialist tendency. Vanek recalls that Kafka was already, at the Gymnasium, a keen reader of sociological periodicals and intellectual monthlies, a habit that he maintained throughout his life. It was around this time that he began to read *Der Kunstwart*, a cultural monthly founded and edited by the husband of Richard Wagner's niece, Ferdinand Avenarius. The magazine was influenced by Nietzsche, as was Kafka at this time, and it had a lofty aesthetic and a slightly overwrought style, together with a *völkisch* sentimentality, against which Kafka eventually reacted.

Kafka was a good arguer, according to Bergmann, the latter having to defend his Zionism against the intellectual assault of his friend. Kafka remembered this a good many years later, when he recalled arguing 'the existence of God with Bergmann in a talmudic style either my own or imitated from him. At the time I liked to begin with a theme I had found in a Christian magazine (I believe it was *Die christliche Welt*) in which a watch and the world and the watchmaker and God were compared to one another, and the existence of the watchmaker was supposed to prove that of God.'[7] Kafka also revealed to Bergmann his desire to become a writer, but any attempts from this time were probably destroyed. He was certainly seen by his friend as an eager bookworm. When they both passed a bookseller's window in the Old Town Square, Kafka asked Hugo to sing out the title of any book in the shop window, promising that he would name the author. His success in this feat duly impressed his friend.

Hugo Hecht, Kafka's primary-school friend who followed him to the Gymnasium, remembered Kafka as a very well-behaved pupil – 'always very pure'[8] – who declined to take part in the normal ribald sexual talk of adolescent schoolboys. He was 'very nicely dressed' but also 'somewhat remote and distant from us'.[9] He seemed to his contemporaries to live, as it were, behind 'a glass wall',[10] not unfriendly or haughty, but reserved. He always responded to conversational approaches and wasn't a spoilsport, but he would never make the first move. He was, said Emil Utitz, 'quiet, shy and a little mysterious'.[11]

Academically, Kafka was well above average and was often in receipt of star reports, but this was not how he chose to represent his situation to himself. He later complained to his father that the latter's attitude was constantly undermining his self-esteem. He never thought he would pass out of the first class at primary school, but not merely did he succeed in doing so, he won a prize. It was a similar story with the entrance examination to the Gymnasium. At the end of his first year there, he thought he would fail again, but,

> I went on and on succeeding. What this produced, however, was not confidence, on the contrary, I was always convinced – and I positively had the proof of it in your forbidding expression – that the more things I was successful in, the worse the final outcome would inevitably be. Often in my mind's eye I saw the terrible assembly of the masters . . . meeting in order to examine this unique, outrageous case, to discover how I, the most incapable and in any case the most ignorant of all, had succeeded in creeping up as far as this class, which now, when everybody's attention had at last been focused on me, would of course instantly spew me out, to the high delight of all the righteous, now liberated from this nightmare. Living with such fantasies is not easy for a child. In these circumstances, what could I care about my lessons?[12]

In spite of Kafka's ardent self-flagellation here, though, he evidently *did* care about his lessons and matriculated easily after eight years at the Gymnasium (even if he pretended that his triumph had been the result of 'cheating'). At least one schoolfriend, Hugo Bergmann, couldn't quite see what Kafka had to complain about. When visiting his friend's home on Celetná he was deeply impressed by the fact that Franz possessed not only a large desk (*Schreibtisch*), at which the two could sit and do their homework, but his own room, which enjoyed a fine view of the busy street.

Lukewarm as the Kafkas were in the observance of their Jewish religion, Kafka did go through the ceremony of his bar-mitzvah on 13 June 1896. Many years later he recalled: 'The 13th birthday is a special occasion. Up near the altar in the temple I had to recite a piece learned by heart with great difficulty, then at home I had to make a brief speech (also learned by heart). I also received many presents.'[13] The measure of Hermann Kafka's assimilation may be gauged from the fact that the printed invitations sent out for this event referred to it as a 'confirmation'. Franz was bored by religion at this time, and the bar-mitzvah meant no more to him than 'some ridiculous learning by heart . . . something like the ridiculous passing of an examination'.[14]

During his last summer holiday from school, in 1900, Kafka spent a brief period with his favourite uncle, Siegfried, a country doctor in Triesch (Třešt), and then joined his parents at the Bohemian town of Roztoky (Rostok), on the Vltava, seven miles north of Prague, which the Baedeker of that year describes succinctly as 'amidst fruit-trees'. The Kafkas were staying in the house of the Roztoky postmaster, and Franz lost no time in cultivating the acquaintance of the postmaster's daughter, Selma Robitschek. They spent much time together in the forest, with Kafka reading aloud from – naturally – the works of Nietzsche. On 4 September he wrote a note in her album: 'as though words could carry memories'.[15]

Back in Prague later that month, Kafka settled down for his final year at the Gymnasium. Once again, in 1901, he passed the necessary examinations. The summer was spent with Uncle Siegfried at the North Sea island resorts of Helgoland and Norderney, preparing himself for university in the autumn.

In a later notebook entry – one of those that are partly autobiographical, partly a draft story, and which therefore should be interpreted with care – Kafka wrote: 'When I think about it, I must say that my education has done me great harm in some respects. This reproach applies to a multitude of people – that is to say, my parents, several relatives, individual visitors to our house, various writers, a certain particular cook who took me to school for a year, a crowd of teachers . . . a school inspector, slowly walking passers-by; in short this reproach twists through society like a dagger.'[16] This is probably what Kafka felt, and it is common for highly original and creative minds to find fault with their schooling. On the other hand, he was never inclined to pass over an opportunity to paint the blackest picture he could. Mathematics, however, could legitimately be entered as a grievance against himself. Years later he recalled the agony of a particular school day:

> I saw the professor up there leafing through his notebook probably in search of my name, and I compared my inconceivable lack of knowledge with that spectacle of strength, terror and reality. I wished, half-dreaming with fear, that I could get up like a ghost, dash ghostlike between the benches, fly past the professor as light as my knowledge of mathematics, somehow penetrate the door, pull myself together outside and be free in the lovely air which, in all the world known to me, did not contain tensions such as those in the schoolroom . . . But it didn't happen like this.[17]

In fact, the teacher called him out, gave him a task involving the use of logarithmic tables, and, when he couldn't find the tables in his desk, said to him, 'You crocodile!' and gave him a mark of 'poor'. This at least prevented the public demonstration of his ignorance that would inevitably have followed. The strange moral drawn by Kafka from this routine classroom event was that one could 'disappear' from such a painful reality 'and the possibilities were infinite and one could even "die" while living'. This faculty of self-absenting, self-negating was one which Kafka learned to hone in these early years.

Kafka was far more influenced by his private experience, and by his home life, than he was by his school – though one shouldn't underestimate the importance of the rote-learning of German classics such as Goethe (whom he nevertheless admired unreservedly), nor his encounter with such modern Czech literary classics as Božena Němcová's *The Grandmother* (1855). In *Letter to the Father*, Kafka made clear what he thought about the upbringing he had received. He conceded that he was probably

> obstinate, as children are. I am sure that Mother spoilt me too, but I cannot believe I was particularly difficult to manage, I cannot believe that a kindly word, a quiet taking of me by the hand, a friendly look, could not have got me to do anything that was wanted of me . . . not every child has the endurance and fearlessness to go on searching until it comes to the kindliness that lies beneath the surface. You can only treat a child in the way in which you are constituted, with vigour, noise, and hot temper, and in this case this seemed to you, into the bargain, extremely suitable, because you wanted to bring me up to be a strong brave boy.[18]

It's easy to see the problem here. Hermann's rough, vigorous handling of the ultra-sensitive boy, in order to fashion him in his own likeness as a tough survivor in the battle of life, was not flexible enough – even if the harried businessman could have found the time to devote to the task – to accommodate the special demands made by his son.

Kafka claimed that his father was 'completely tied to the business, scarcely able to be with me even once a day' and therefore, when he did manifest himself, the effect was all the more frightening. He recalled in particular an incident from his childhood when, after persistently 'whimpering' for water – 'probably partly to be annoying, partly to amuse myself' – Hermann swept his son out of bed and carried him out on to the *pavlatche* (a characteristic balcony running around the inner courtyard of a Prague apartment building) and left him there alone in his nightshirt facing the closed door. As far as Kafka was concerned, this was 'typical of your methods of bringing up a child and their effect on me. I dare say I was quite obedient afterwards for a period, but it did me inner harm.' The boy could not reconcile the trivial offence with the terror of parental Law (Kafka gave the word an upper-case initial at key points in the fiction). 'Even years afterwards I suffered from the tormenting fancy that the huge man, my father, the ultimate authority, would come almost for no reason at all and take me out of bed in the night and carry me out on to the *pavlatche*, and that therefore I was such a mere nothing for him.' In reality, Hermann probably stomped back to his game of cards reflecting that worse was dealt out to him when he was a naughty child in Osek.

Kafka, however, was relentless. This incident he saw as merely 'a small beginning' whose fruit was 'this sense of nothingness that often dominates me' and which 'comes largely from your influence'. He claimed that what he needed was 'a little encouragement, a little friendliness, a little keeping open of my road, instead of which you blocked it for me'. He touchingly recalled his father's delight when young Franz saluted and marched smartly, as Hermann had done in his days in the Austrian forces, 'but I was no future soldier'. Hermann urged his son to eat heartily, drink beer with his meals and repeat drinking songs –

'but nothing of this had anything to do with my future'. Even his father's physical presence depressed him. Kafka had a lifelong love of swimming but when the two of them undressed in the same bathing-hut: 'There was I, skinny weakly, slight, you strong, tall, broad.' The boy felt himself physically inferior not only in his father's eyes, 'but in the eyes of the whole world, for you were for me the measure of all things'. This sense of disparity in physical strength between himself and his father remained with Kafka for the rest of his life and is powerfully present in his major fiction, such as *Das Urteil/The Judgement*, which had already been published when the indictment of *Letter to the Father* was written.

When Hermann played the tyrannical patriarch in a small room ('From your armchair you ruled the world') his son winced as his father gaily rubbished, one after the other, the Czechs, the Germans and the Jews. 'Your opinion was correct, every other was mad, wild, *meschugge*, not normal . . . For me you took on the enigmatic quality that all tyrants have whose rights are based on their person and not on reason.' This had a disabling effect on the boy. He was unable to articulate his frail, immature thoughts and ideas in this noisy and dogmatic court: 'All these thoughts, seemingly independent of you, were from the beginning loaded with the burden of your harsh and dogmatic judgements; it was almost impossible to endure this and yet to work out one's thoughts with any measure of completeness and permanence.' The fact that his father was the all-powerful arbiter, the Law, meant that nothing his son could say, think or do could be weighed in the balance against the sheer physicality of his opposition and contempt: 'Courage, resolution, confidence, delight in this or that, did not endure to the end when you were against whatever it was or even if your opposition was merely to be assumed; and it was to be assumed in almost everything I did.'

In the more routine aspects of child-rearing, such as conduct at table – one of the few places where Hermann regularly spent time with his son – the father's hearty appetite resulted in a series of bullying injunctions to his son (who later developed a very fastidious approach to food and became a vegetarian) to eat up and eat fast and to observe rules that the father himself did not. The result was that the world seemed to the young Kafka to be divided into three zones: 'One in which I, the slave, lived under laws that had been invented only for me and which I could, I did not know why, never completely comply with; then a second world, which was infinitely remote from mine, in which you lived, concerned with government, with the issuing of orders and with annoyance about their not being obeyed; and finally a third world where everybody else lived happily and free from orders and from having to obey. I was continually in disgrace.'

The consequence of this family situation – described with such unremitting insistence by Kafka that it can weary the reader – was that: 'I lost the capacity to talk.' The quietness, the keeping of his own counsel, the tendency to reply only when spoken to, which his fellow pupils observed, was the result of being shouted down by the all-powerful father: 'What I got from you . . . was a hesitant, stammering mode of speech, and even that was too much for you, and finally I kept silence, at first perhaps from defiance, and then because I couldn't either think or speak in your presence. And because you were the person who really brought me up, this has had its repercussions throughout my life.' As with many bullies, obedience could sometimes earn as much condemnation as outright defiance would have done. Accordingly, when Kafka was 'too docile . . . completely dumb, cringed away from you, hid from you, and only dared to stir when I was so far away from you that your power could no longer reach me', this was interpreted as a further offence to his father. 'Your extremely effective rhetorical methods in bringing me up, which never failed to work with me anyway, were: abuse, threats, irony, spiteful laughter and – oddly enough – self-pity.'

One of Hermann's threats to the young boy – it sounds like a piece of colourful Yiddish – was: 'I'll tear you apart like a fish.' The result of this constant undermining of the boy's self-esteem was that: 'I lost confidence in my own actions. I was wavering, doubtful.' Franz was aware, however, that at least something of what he had become by the time he was an adult was the result of his own nature and not wholly the fault of this rambunctious system of nurture. He admitted therefore that: 'you only intensified what was already there, but you did greatly intensify it, simply because where I was concerned you were very powerful and you employed all your power to that end'. And when Kafka goes on to indict his father's use of irony and sarcasm one wonders if a small dose of the former in the son might have saved him some suffering. To some extent he did become dulled to the constant tirade: 'One became a glum, inattentive, disobedient child, always trying to escape from something and in the main to escape within oneself. So you suffered, and so we suffered.' There were, of course, moments of tenderness, all the more poignant for being so obviously rare, as when Hermann came into Kafka's sickroom 'and out of consideration for me only waved your hand to me. At such times one would lie back and weep for happiness, and one weeps again now, writing it down.'

Reading this indictment one can easily forget that Kafka had two parents. He allowed that 'Mother was illimitably good to me', but in a sense she was almost too good. As a result of her attempts to restrain what might have been a useful adolescent defiance, she drove Franz back into his father's orbit, in the interests of keeping the peace: 'Mother unconsciously played the part of a beater during a hunt.' Hermann never beat his son – though he was fond of theatrical threats, such as laying his braces over the back of the chair as if to prepare for a thrashing. This then became further grounds for reproach because 'a huge sense of guilt' built up when the boy was let off – it having been made so abundantly clear that he deserved to be beaten. Julie

Kafka was 'too devoted and loyal' to Hermann 'to have been able to constitute an independent spiritual force, in the long run, in the child's struggle'. It was hard for her to be thus in the middle of this theatre of war: 'it was Mother on whom we relieved our wild feelings'.

The cumulative effect of this domestic conflict for the growing Gymnasium boy was to undermine his self-confidence. Hermann's edgy paranoia towards the outside world, so characteristic of the self-made man, was deeply damaging: 'this mistrust, which for me as a little boy was nowhere confirmed in my own eyes, since I everywhere saw only people excellent beyond all hope of emulation, in me turned into mistrust of myself and into perpetual anxiety in relation to everything else'.

Kafka never lost his conviction that the whole course of his life was determined in these stuffy Prague family interiors. For that reason alone, the connection between the world of his childhood and the world of his mature fiction should not be underestimated: there is a striking congruence of themes in Kafka's life and art. *Letter to the Father* is a cleverly constructed document. Kafka later admitted to its deployment of artful rhetorical strategies, its 'lawyer's tricks' ('*advokatorischen Kniffe*').[19] It is one side of the story. It bears, in fact, many similarities to the letters written today by those who use 'recovered memories' to bring accusations of previously unrecalled incidents of childhood abuse.[20] One would very much like to hear from the other side. [21]

But even if we allow for a degree of exaggeration or paranoia, Kafka's fictions are often governed by a system of thought and perception analogous to the nightmare world of fear, uncertainty and guilt he describes in this letter to his father. It is a world which frightened, hypersensitive children know and feel as true, however much sensible adults will tell them to snap out of it. Even in the *Letter* Kafka knew that he had to distinguish between what he, as a person, would have been like in *any* family, in any system of child-rearing, and what he became as a result of the particular family environment in which he developed. In the end *how things are perceived* may be the fact that matters, the fact that is incontrovertible. Irrespective of whether Kafka was *right* to blame his father for the man his son was, for the life he lived, the conflict determined the shape of his world – the world adumbrated in his fiction, his letters, his diaries. It is a world always fiercely consistent, and one in which he never ceased to judge himself as harshly as he judged others.

4

In November 1901 Kafka began his studies at the German Ferdinand Karl University in Prague. This intensely literary eighteen-year-old – who had barely scraped through the mathematical part of the Gymnasium syllabus, and only with Hugo Bergmann's help (the latter, unlike Kafka, graduated from the Gymnasium with honours) – joined Hugo in lectures in chemistry. The reasoning behind the choice of chemistry was that only two traditional professions were open to Jews – law and medicine – and since neither appealed to Franz or Hugo, they were persuaded to try chemistry by the rumour that employment opportunities existed in the chemical industry. Bohemia at this time was the industrial centre of the Dual Monarchy, and the factory chimneys smoked.

Bergmann and Kafka attended the lectures at the Chemical Institute of the university given by Professor Goldschmied, a baptized Jew, but soon discovered that they had no aptitude whatsoever for laboratory work. Bergmann stuck it out for a year before switching to mathematics, physics and philosophy. Kafka lasted a mere two weeks before transferring to the subject which he had initially rejected, law, although he also attended August Sauer's lectures on German literature, as well as those on art history. Sauer was an enthusiast for the nineteenth-century masters of German narrative prose such as Franz Grillparzer, Adalbert Stifter, Heinrich von Kleist and Johann Peter Hebel, whose clarity of language and thought and whose narrative vigour were such potent influences on the formation of Kafka's own style.

Kafka, however, soon grew irritated with Sauer's sentimental *völkisch* nationalism. Although the University of Prague, founded in 1348, was one of the oldest in Europe, it had split in 1882, the year before Kafka's birth, into two faculties – Czech and German – and nationalist feelings ran high in both. There were even separate entrances and exits for Czech and German students. Like most German-Jewish students, Kafka soon joined the Lese- und Redehalle der Deutschen Studenten (Reading and Lecture Hall for German Students), a club of mostly Jewish students which had an excellent library and organized literary readings, exhibitions, concerts and discussion groups. Kafka was particularly interested in its Section for Literature and Art. It was after delivering a paper on Schopenhauer and Nietzsche to the Section on 23 October 1902, at the start of Kafka's second year, that the aspiring writer Max Brod, who was to play such a defining role in Kafka's life and in the forging of his posthumous literary reputation, first met Kafka. At that time, Kafka had completed a dry and unstimulating year of Roman and German law, philosophy and German art history, and was gasping for intellectual air in the Hall. Brod – seen as a dazzlingly clever law student, musician, poet and future novelist – provoked an argument when he described Nietzsche as 'a fraud'. This was certainly not Kafka's view, and a vigorous discussion ensued as the two walked home.

Max Brod, who, in spite of his early gifts, is not now very highly regarded as a novelist, dedicated himself to the nurturing of Kafka's reputation. He has been criticized, sometimes unmercifully,[1] both for his insistence on Kafka's religious, if not saintly, personality and for the quality of his editorial practice in preparing Kafka's work for posthumous publication. On the other hand, he helped, in Kafka's lifetime, a writer who needed a little gentle promotion, and he saved his work from destruction in two senses: he took the unpublished manuscripts with him to Israel in 1939 in flight from the Nazis and took steps to protect them further during a period of political unrest in the Middle East in the late 1950s. They eventually reached Oxford in 1961, where they are now in the Bodleian Library.[2] Most importantly of all, Brod's refusal to carry out Kafka's dying request that all his unpublished work be destroyed gave the world the three major novels, much of the shorter fiction, the letters and the diaries.

Brod remembered the undergraduate Kafka in his outward appearance as 'deeply unobtrusive – even his elegant suits, which were mostly dark blue, were as unobtrusive and reserved as himself'.[3] The adult Kafka was now emerging. His contemporaries agree that he was tall, slim, dark-haired, well built, neatly but unshowily dressed, reserved and shy, with a delicate, courteous manner. Everyone noticed his eyes, which were dark (the most common adjective is *dunkel*), gleaming and suggestive of unexpressed depth.[4] So beguiling and haunting was the intensity of his large and luminous eyes that many forgot to notice the colour. A bewildering variety of colours is registered by those who published their recollections of meetings with him – steel blue, steel grey, black, brown.[5] Although the consensus appears to be for grey with a hint of blue, it is certainly difficult to brush aside the evidence of the *braun* recorded by his last, intense love, Dora Diamant. She recalled:

> The essential characteristics of his face were the very open, sometimes even wide-open eyes, whether he was talking or listening. They were not staring in horror, as it has been said of him; it was rather more an expression of astonishment. His eyes were brown and shy. When he spoke they lit up . . . not so much irony as mischievousness – as if he knew of something that other people didn't

> know. But he was entirely without solemnity . . . His wrists were very slender, and he had long, ethereal fingers which took on shape while he was telling a story . . . Kafka was always cheerful.[6]

Fred Bérence, the Swiss writer who met Kafka in 1921, was of the opinion that 'No photo of him can convey the modest charm of this man. He was tall, well built, very dark-haired, extremely well dressed; he produced a very natty impression. I remember two dark eyes, which smiled out from a pale countenance, and in which I thought I saw golden spangles dance. His dying voice became in the course of a conversation ever more lively, warm, full toned and colourful.'[7]

One of Kafka's colleagues at his workplace recalled his 'lustrous, raven-black hair, dark eyes and a rapid walk'.[8] Another, speaking when illness had begun to make its mark, also remembered the raven-black hair 'and contrasting grey eyes. Through his build and his thoughtful abstraction he made a very timid and reticent impression . . . His face was often very serious and severe, his eyes shining and glowing.'[9] Kafka's acquaintance Gustav Janouch, who is regarded today as an unreliable witness in his *Conversations with Kafka* (1953), nevertheless concurs with the dark brows and the lively brown face, his 'small bony hand' and 'large grey glittering eyes'. Janouch thought Kafka 'spoke through his face', and loved gestures, though using them sparely.[10] Kafka would have agreed about 'my long bony hand with fingers like those of a child and an ape'.[11]

This was the Kafka who was beginning, as an undergraduate, to define himself and, in the eyes of those who knew him later, he never quite lost his boyish appearance. In his thirties he looked like an eighteen-year-old. Although happy to be flirtatious, he was still sexually immature. At school – where his classmates knew him as someone who did not take part in sexual banter – he had felt at a disadvantage. One evening, possibly when he was about sixteen and coming to the end of his time at the Gymnasium,[12] he went for a walk with his parents on the Josefplatz and began to reproach them, 'in a stupidly boastful, superior, proud, cool (that was spurious), cold (that was genuine), and stammering manner, as indeed I usually talked to you' for having left him in ignorance of sexual matters. He told them that he had to find these things out from his friends, exaggerating the 'great dangers' such ignorance had put him in (while admitting that he was not such a total innocent about 'the usual sexual misdemeanours of city children'). His father listened patiently to this outburst before adding matter-of-factly that he could give young Franz 'some advice about how [you] could go in for these things without danger' – presumably suggesting that Franz could visit a prostitute. Franz had half expected such an offer and may have been trying to extract it 'in keeping with the pruriency of a child over-fed with meat and all good things, physically inactive, everlastingly occupied with himself'. But when the offer came, he recoiled, seeing it as concrete evidence of how little mutual trust there was between father and son – 'actually the first direct instruction bearing on real life that I ever received from you' – and also that what it really meant was 'the filthiest thing possible' – another contemptuous gesture from a sexually normal married man towards a son whom he was ready to push, together with his uncontrolled sexual nature, 'down into this filth'. Kafka's interpretation is revealing, as is the tone of fastidious repulsion and the repeated use of the word 'filth' to describe normal adolescent sexuality. Ultimately, he would not receive his sexual initiation until after his twentieth birthday.

Intellectually, too, Kafka was uncertain and confused as a teenager. After a year of chopping and changing in his university courses he began to explore the idea of leaving Prague in order to complete his studies at the University of Munich. On 17 October 1902 he went there,[13] but the project came to nothing – perhaps because his father was not prepared to fund it. This was perhaps unfortunate, because at this stage of Kafka's development such a move away from home might have been extremely beneficial. It could have made him more responsible for himself and forced him to break out of the negative bind with his parents.

During the summer the Kafkas had received a visit from Uncle Alfred Löwy, who was by now director-general of the Spanish railways, and whose breath of abroad blew into the constrained interior of the Kafka's first-floor apartment at No. 3 Celetná, in the house known as 'At the Three Kings'. This was where Kafka lived with his family from 1896 to 1907, by which time he was twenty-four. Kafka made a special trip back to Prague from Libechov (Liboch), a village on the Elbe 25 miles north of Prague where he had been staying for the summer, in order to see Uncle Alfred. He told his best university friend, Oskar Pollak, that shortly before his uncle's arrival, 'I had the weird, unfortunately very weird notion of begging him, no, not begging, asking, whether he mightn't know some way to help me out of this mess, whether he couldn't guide me to some place where at last I could start afresh and do something.'[14] Uncle Alfred, perhaps fearing to sow discord in the family, reacted by humouring Franz but making no promises. The vague terms – 'some way . . . some place . . . something' – used by a normally very precise writer eloquently express Kafka's confusion and sense of being lost during the summer of 1902 as the second university year beckoned. It was, he told Pollak, 'a strange time',[15] in which he gave himself over to bucolic rhapsodizing: 'I sit in the garden and tell the children . . . fairy tales.'

By the end of 1902, Kafka was ensconced again in Prague, his dreams of flight grounded. 'Prague doesn't let go. Either of us,'[16] he confided in Pollak. 'This old crone has claws [*Dieses Mütterchen hat Krallen*]. One has to yield, or else. We would have to set fire to it on two sides, at the Vyšehrad and at the

Hradčany [the two hills overlooking Prague]; then it would be possible for us to get away.' This comment on Prague is often quoted out of context as if it were Kafka's final judgement on the city rather than a young man's spasm of temporary exasperation. Kafka's Prague, like the Dublin of his contemporary James Joyce, who was just about to take flight at this time to Paris for a lifetime in exile, would indeed not let go. But it is not clear that Kafka, in spite of occasional half-hearted attempts, was ever seriously determined to escape its claws until the very end of his life, and there was much about the city he loved, especially on his walks through its green spaces.

Of much more significance in these first undergraduate years was the fact that Kafka was beginning to exhibit, in letters to friends, hints of the writer to come. He had begun writing in his early teens but he later destroyed all those attempts. In the same letter to Pollak just quoted he put on display for the first time that imaginative, fabulating mode that was to become so natural to him. He invented a tale of 'Shamefaced Lanky [*schamhaften Langen*] and Impure in Heart', the former a self-portrait, the latter Emil Utitz, his Gymnasium friend. Shamefaced Lanky's head sticks out through the roof, his feet protrude through the windows and he has 'clumsy, skinny, spidery fingers'. He is visited by his ebullient and loquacious friend from the city, Impure in Heart, and when the latter leaves, Lanky weeps: 'His heart ached and he could not tell anyone.' The awkwardness, bizarre physical transformations, and quiet, helpless despair are proleptic hints of *Metamorphosis*.

In spite of his new friendship with Max Brod and his encounters with like-minded young thinkers in student societies, such as Paul Kisch (brother of the writer Egon Erwin Kisch (1885–1948), who later threw himself into a variety of left-wing causes), Kafka entered his second undergraduate year still a solitary figure. For the whole of that year he concentrated on his legal studies and took his examinations in historical law in the summer of 1903.

Then his long career as a valetudinarian began in August with a visit to the 'Weisser Hirsch' Sanatorium of Dr Lahmann near Dresden. He scribbled cheerfully to Paul Kisch, over a picture postcard of gentlemen in swimming trunks, hosing each other down, while enjoying their *Luftbad*: 'Here you drink air instead of beer and bathe in air instead of water.'[17] Back in Prague in early September to prepare for his third academic year, he reflected in a letter to Oskar Pollak, from whom he hadn't heard all summer, on the 'high hopes' with which he had originally entered on the summer that was now evaporating: 'perhaps you were even dimly aware of what I wanted out of this summer. I'll say it: to bring out at one stroke what I believe I have in me (I don't always believe it) . . . I've become healthier . . . stronger, been with people a good deal, can talk with women . . . but the summer has brought me none of the miracles.'[18]

Still writing in the mannered *Kunstwart* idiom that he was soon to abandon for his carefully precise mature style, Kafka admitted that his instinctive solitariness was 'repulsive'. He tried to assure himself that he believed in the injunction: 'honestly lay your eggs out in the open and the sun will hatch them; better to bite into life than bite your tongue; honour the mole and its ilk but don't make it into one of your saints'. He promised to put together a bundle of everything he had written to date, 'original or derivative', excluding his childhood things (which might have included the plays he wrote for family entertainments: 'as you see, this misery's been on my back from early on'). He excluded what he had destroyed, his projected pieces ('whole countries to him who has them and sand to everyone else') and the sort of writing which was too embarrassing to share with anyone ('for we shudder to stand naked and be fingered by others, even if we have begged on our knees for that very thing'). He told Pollak, 'this whole past year I have written almost nothing'. He wanted a candid assessment from his friend of all that he had done so far. 'Because – this is why I want it – what is dearest and hardest of mine is merely cool, in spite of the sun, and I know that another pair of eyes will make everything warmer and livelier.'

Kafka had arrived at the point eventually reached by all tyro writers, where the shyness, self-consciousness and doubt that seem to urge keeping it all under wraps – or tossing it on the fire – conflict with the realization that writing stands or falls by its ability to engage 'another pair of eyes', and that it must be put to the test of another judgement. What is most noticeable about the twenty-year-old Kafka is the centrality of *writing* in his life at this time. Law studies, politics, all other kinds of student activity are nothing compared with the obsession of his life. When he told Pollak that he was taking 'a piece of my heart, packing it neatly in a few sheets of inscribed paper, and sending it to you', this was more than a piece of empty rhetoric. Kafka's loneliness even in the presence of friends is candidly stated:

> We are as forlorn as children lost in the woods. When you stand in front of me and look at me, what do you know of the griefs that are in me and what do I know of yours . . . we human beings ought to stand before one another as reverently, as reflectively, as lovingly, as we would before the entrance to hell . . . For me, you were, along with much else, also something like a window through which I could see the streets. I could not do that by myself, for tall though I am I do not yet reach to the windowsill.[19]

Kafka would always need – and would find – such human windows on the world, helping to connect his interior life to the world out there, the world of the Sunday clerks in Wenceslas Square (Wenzelsplatz or Václávské náměstí) in Prague with 'their red carnations and their stupid and Jewish faces [*ihre dummen und jüdischen Gesichter*] and their clamour'.[20] In the meantime he was determined to keep writing – whatever the omens for success: 'So many powers within me are tied to a stake, which might possibly grow into a green tree.'

Kafka's reading was also proceeding apace. He had spent the summer of 1903 reading the work of the German philosopher Gustav Fechner (1801–87) and the medieval German mystic Meister Eckhart. As the third year started he concentrated more exclusively on law, having put behind him the courses on German literature and language, the history of art, music, psychology and classical philology. He was taught canon law by Professor Singer, state law by Professor Ulbrich, civil law by Professor Krasnapolski and civics by Professor Rinteln. Anna Pouzarová, the governess of his three sisters, who had joined the household when Kafka was nineteen, in October 1902, remembered his room, where two volumes of Roman law sat on the desk. 'The young man was very diligent, always sitting at his desk.'[21] He was always kind and courteous to the Czech servants, but nevertheless struck them as rather reserved and shy, uninterested in gossip and banter: 'The young man was tall, thin, of an earnest nature, and said little. He spoke in a quiet, soft voice. He wore mostly dark suits and sometimes a round, black hat. I never saw him excited, nor did he ever laugh out loud.' Anna also suspected him of occasionally sleeping on the floor as a form of therapeutic discipline. She once caught sight of all the sisters lying on the carpet doing breathing exercises according to their brother's instructions.

It would be wrong, however, to conclude that Kafka led a wholly monastic existence. In July 1903 his first sexual encounter – typically for a young man of his class – was with a working-class Czech girl. Opposite the house in Celetná was a dress-shop, in the door of which a shop assistant used to stand. Pacing up and down his room in order to memorize the 'senseless facts'[22] of 'the disgusting Roman law' for his first state examination in the autumn, Kafka kept coming back to the window to look at the girl. Incredibly, this shy young man began to communicate with the girl in sign language. He indicated that he would fetch her at 8 p.m. When he came down in the evening he found that she was with another man, but since Kafka was 'afraid of the whole world' one more person to fear was of no account. The other man took the girl's arm but she signalled that Kafka should follow. The man and the girl went as far as Schützen Island (Střelecký ostrov), where they drank beer, with Kafka at the next table. Next they walked back to the girl's apartment somewhere near the Fleischmarkt, where the man bade farewell and the girl ran into the house. But then she re-emerged and with Kafka went to a hotel in Malá Strana (the Little Quarter or Kleinseite). 'Even before we got to the hotel all this was charming, exciting, and horrible, in the hotel it wasn't different. And when, towards morning (it was still hot and beautiful) we walked home over the Karlsbrücke [Karluv most] I was actually happy, but this happiness came from the fact that at last I had some peace from the ever-yearning body, and above all it came from relief that the whole experience hadn't been *more* horrible, *more* obscene.' He was with 'the girl' (who never acquired an identity) again two nights later, but shortly afterwards went with his parents to Aussig for his summer holidays, where he 'played around a bit' with another girl, thus turning the first into 'a bitter enemy, and yet she was a good-natured friendly girl . . . followed me all the time with her uncomprehending eyes'.

That 'enmity' was also caused by sexual guilt on the part of the young bourgeois who had allowed himself to be sullied by a shop-girl. He also turned on her because at the hotel she

> in all innocence had made a tiny repulsive gesture (not worthwhile mentioning), had uttered a trifling obscenity (not worthwhile mentioning), but the memory remained – I knew at that instant that I would never forget it and simultaneously I knew, or thought I knew, that this

> repulsiveness and smut, though outwardly not necessary, was inwardly however very necessarily connected with the whole thing, and that just this repulsiveness and obscenity (whose little symptom had only been her tiny gesture, her trifling word) had drawn me with such terrible power into this hotel, which otherwise I would have avoided with all my remaining strength.

The sexual politics implicit in this narrative could be analysed at length. This autobiographical confession was made in a letter written nearly two decades later to Kafka's lover Milena Jesenská. He recalled this experience for her in order to explain why he had remained sexually reticent. Some biographers hint at impotence, but it seems more likely that some form of physical reserve or slowness of sexual response constrained, but did not necessarily prevent, Kafka's engagement in sexual activity.[23] Dora Diamant, his last love, was frequently asked about this aspect of Kafka, and in a recently discovered journal she writes of a passage in his diary where he mentions a relationship with an anonymous 'B' in which 'there are effusions which are not released but must spend themselves in being repulsed',[24] an obscure enough passage which could mean just about anything, including an ordinary friendship where there was insufficient reciprocation. She then observed that Kafka was 'sensuous like an animal – or like a child. Wherever does the assumption of Franz as an ascetic come from?'[25] Kafka's physical immaturity, his boyishness, created, in Max Brod's view, 'a certain temporary mistrust of his sexual capacity',[26] and he *was* perennially anxious, but there is no evidence of impotence. On the contrary, there is a good deal of evidence of sexual relationships with both prostitutes and other women.

In the years following his sexual initiation with the shop-girl, that experience in the hotel in the Malá Strana came back to haunt Kafka. 'My body, sometimes quiet for years, would then be shaken to the point of not being able to bear it by this desire for a small, a very specific abomination [*einer ganz bestimmten Abscheulichkeit*], for something slightly disgusting, embarrassing, obscene, even in the best that existed for me there was something of it, some small nasty smell, some sulphur, some hell.'[27] Not content with linking this fleeting encounter to his general sense of social dysfunction, Kafka went on to draw another startling conclusion: 'This urge had in it something of the eternal Jew, being senselessly drawn, wandering senselessly through a senselessly obscene world.' He became grateful for the moments when he was not thus tormented, even if it meant an apparent physical coolness towards his current partner, and even though, 'During those periods, as long as they lasted, I was always alone.'

In a letter to Oskar Pollak in November 1903, in which Kafka listed his reading, he concluded: 'Some books seem like a key to unfamiliar rooms in one's own castle.'[28] Just as writing was to Kafka an essential means of realizing himself as a human being, so his reading was undertaken in a similar spirit of extreme seriousness. Early in the new year of 1904 he told Pollak that he had been reading the diaries of the German dramatist Friedrich Hebbel (1813–63) and had been at one and the same time intimidated by the record of a life 'which towers higher and higher without a gap'[29] and exhilarated by the experience. In a wonderful passage about the grandeur of reading he writes: 'I think we ought to read only the kind of books that wound and stab us. If the book we are reading doesn't wake us up with a blow on the head, what are we reading it for? . . . we need the books that affect us like a disaster, that grieve us deeply, like the death of someone we loved more than ourselves, like being banished into forests far from everyone, like a suicide. A book must be the axe for the frozen sea inside us [*Ein Buch muß die Axt sein für das gefrorene Meer in uns*].'[30]

It is characteristic of Kafka that a volume of diaries should wield the axe as much as a fictional work. He remained a passionate reader of letters and biographies of writers, sometimes preferring them to the creative works themselves, and there is a strong case for treating his own volumes of letters and diaries as works written with the creative energy and imaginative wholeness of works of art. Alongside those tomes of Roman law, he was continuing to consume Amiel, Byron, Franz Grillparzer, Eckermann's *Conversations with Goethe*, Goethe's letters as well as those of Grabbe and du Barry, and, of current work, he would have read Thomas Mann's short story about the tensions of the artistic life, 'Tonio Kröger', in the journal *Die Neue Rundschau*. He may also have started to read Flaubert – one of the principal writers in his personal pantheon – at around this time.

And some time during 1904 he began to write the first of the fictions that have survived, *Beschreibung eines Kampfes/Description of a Struggle*.

5

Description of a Struggle, which was begun some time after 1902 and possibly as late as 1904, is Kafka's first significant work of prose fiction. It was never published in his lifetime – though some parts of it were recycled and published in 1909 in the periodical *Hyperion.* The story exhibits both the arresting originality of Kafka's fictional imagination and the remarkable individuality of his style. It was the first work that Max Brod remembered Kafka reading aloud to him: 'I went about with Kafka for several years without knowing that he wrote,'[1] claimed Brod, whose relationship with Kafka was now beginning to develop in the measure that the friendship with Oskar Pollak waned.

Kafka's language was quite different from that of his fellow Prague Germans. It has already been noted how isolated politically and sociologically the Prague Germans were from their Czech neighbours. Kafka was exceptional in taking a genuine interest in Czech culture and language – he even subscribed to a Czech philological journal – as most of his fellow German speakers (roughly 34,000 out of central Prague's population of 450,000) were indifferent to the cultural life of the Czechs. According to Klaus Wagenbach, the Kafka scholar whose analysis of this phenomenon has been most influential (though it is now starting to be challenged),[2] most of the Prague German writers exhibited a 'romantic obliviousness to the real world'[3] because they were cut off from the sources of ordinary life, ordinary language and the living idiom around them. If one accepts this argument, the Prague German writers lived in linguistic as well as social isolation, writing in a literary dialect that had no connection with ordinary speech. It was, claimed Wagenbach, a paper German (*papierenes Deutsch*). There was something decadent, unhealthy, and overwrought about the work of these writers, he implied. 'The imagination grew luxuriantly like splendidly poisonous blossoms from a swamp, unbridled sexuality flourished in baroque confusion. [The Prague writers] wanted to discover a new world, but all they did was put powder and make-up on this one or set it on fire and celebrate the conflagration,' wrote one critic.[4] In the writing of Kafka's contemporaries such as Paul Leppin, language, Wagenbach argues, 'is used to trick the reader; everything is artificial, sweet-smelling, inflated . . . This lack of taste . . . [is] typical of the whole Prague School.' By contrast, Kafka's 'concise, neutral, sparse, logically constructed language' was a repudiation of the mannered excess of such writers as Gustav Meyrink and Rilke in his early years.

Heinrich Teweles, editor of the German-language journal *Bohemia*, complained that 'the stream of our language threatens to dry up . . . In Prague, we have no German people from whom the language can be reproduced; we are nothing but cultural Germans.'[5] These writers used a Viennese or High German dialect, which had a particular Prague German inflection. 'Even Kafka's speech had a distinct Prague colouring,' Wagenbach maintains. Years later, in a letter to Max Brod and Felix Weltsch written in 1920 from a sanatorium in Merano, Kafka told of how a fellow guest, an Austrian general, 'with his sharp ears schooled in the Austrian army',[6] enjoyed pinning him down as a Prague German. Czech influenced the pronunciation of Prague German (sometimes called 'Little Quarter German'), as well as its syntax and vocabulary. Wagenbach concludes that 'In his early letters and stories, a lingering uncertainty in High German usage and vocabulary is undeniable.' One might add that this is hardly surprising. There are variations in the English spoken in Wales, Scotland and Ireland (to look no further) that are perfectly normal. Moreover, they enrich British English rather than impoverish it. Nevertheless, it is clear that Kafka, notwithstanding his respect for Czech language and culture, elected to see himself as a German writer and his models were the classical German writers such as Goethe, Kleist and Stifter. Kafka's language became 'a personalized Prague German, purified of almost all local influence'. According to the writer Franz Werfel, Kafka found an alternative to the shortcomings of an etiolated Prague German literary language 'by imposing an extreme rigour on the verbal material offered to him by his environment. He scrutinized it suspiciously, almost pedantically, because he lacked a native fluency and confidence.'[7] Kafka, however, would have been unique even if he had been brought up in the bustle of the Viennese coffee houses. His originality cannot be confined to one source.

Description of a Struggle refers directly to the specific topography of Prague in a way that was rarely matched in Kafka's subsequent fiction. From the very outset his writing was characterized both by extreme precision and extreme opacity. Kafka was, as Erich Heller put it, 'the creator of the most obscure lucidity in the history of literature, a phenomenon that, like a word one has on the tip of one's tongue, perpetually attracts and at the same time repels the search for what it is and means'.[8] André Gide thought that 'The realism of his images continually surpasses one's power of imagination, and I could not say which I admire more: the "naturalist" representation of a fantastic world, made credible by the meticulous accuracy of its images, or the assured boldness of turning towards the mysterious.'[9] The special paradox of this distinctive mode of writing – pure, exact, vivid, and yet so often difficult if not impossible to explain or decipher – has inevitably led critics to look for allegorical significance, as if there were some concrete dimension to which these stories 'refer', if one could only find the key. But there are no such keys. It is more helpful to see these pieces as symbols rather than allegories, their strangeness and suggestiveness to be relished, like an Imagist poem, rather than laboriously (and probably inadequately) decoded. *Description of a Struggle* feels like the projection of the fears and fantasies of the author. It opens with a closed domestic interior, an atmosphere of strange sexuality, an imagined 'friend', who may be no more than an alter ego. In the section titled 'A Walk', the imagination is seen as a countervailing force to the world of daily necessity, an escape for the dysfunctional individual ('Thus I toyed with my future life and tried stubbornly to forget'). In another passage, 'Conversations with a Supplicant', the narrator declares, 'of all these people who behave so irresolutely, so absurdly as a result of their confusion, I alone seem worthy of hearing the truth about myself'. He later asks: 'What is it that makes you all behave as though you were real? Are you trying to make me believe I am unreal . . . ?' In the 'Continued Conversation between the Fat Man and the Supplicant', he notes: 'contact with a human body is always repugnant to me'. All these strangely juxtaposed elements clearly come from Kafka's own feelings, anxieties and obsessions at this time about where he fits into the surrounding world.

A comment made around the time this piece was being written sheds some light on that uncertainty. Kafka explains why he has decided not to join Max Brod and his group at a fancy-dress ball: 'A mob of friends is useful only in revolutions when all act together and simply.'[10] He tells Brod that something of oneself is lost in company where the reactions of a crowd 'distort' the perceptions of the individual: 'They put you in a false position.' And again, he told Oskar Pollak: 'When someone extends a cool hand to me, it makes me feel good, but when he takes my arm I find it embarrassing and incomprehensible.'[11] Kafka's normal desire for sympathetic company was in conflict with his desire for solitude – for more than solitude, for invisibility. 'Do you know what is special about some people?' he asks his friend. 'They are nothing, but they cannot show it, cannot show it to their own eyes, that is what is special about them.' In these letters Kafka often conveys what he means to say in short, invented parables, and in them he is preoccupied with inventing the self through language: 'It's fine if we can use words to cover ourselves up from ourselves, but even better if we can adorn and drape ourselves with words until we have become the kind of person that in our hearts we wish to be.'[12]

Yet, in spite of these delicate movements of withdrawal, these evasions of intimacy, Kafka was also pursuing a lively social life. He was interested in political and social issues and liked to attend political meetings – as a quiet listener rather than as an activist. (Some have argued that Kafka was an active participant in radical political activity – but this view is based largely on the testimony of the anarchist Michael Mares, whose recollection that Kafka was arrested, and let off with a token fine, after a demonstration now seems to have been the result of a mistaken identification.[13]) His Gymnasium socialism was probably still with him, though, and there were many anarchist meetings taking place in Prague which he attended. In particular, an organization called the Young People's Club, a centre for anarchist youth founded in 1900, staged political lectures in Prague between 1903 and 1910 which attracted the attention of the police. The latter banned club members in 1906 from making a collection for wives and families of unemployed miners in north Bohemia (a stronghold of the anarchists) and as its anti-militarist tone became more pronounced it was watched even more closely by the police until it was eventually closed down in 1910 and members of its committee put on trial. Since Kafka received an official police clearance in 1906 when he started to do some court work after graduating in law, and since the documents were signed by the arch-anarchist-hunter Inspector Karel Slavicek, who testified to Kafka's being 'unmarried, of Jewish faith and good behaviour',[14] it is unlikely that he was anything more than a fellow-traveller at most. Classical anarchism, with its libertarian emphasis on the freedom of the individual in opposition to the hierarchical power of the state, of society, of the family, would have appealed to Kafka, with his belief in the precious freedom of the self, its inviolable particularity, its *Eigentümlichkeit*.

Another claim on Kafka's social self was the elite café society of Prague, where philosophy, politics, literature and just about everything else were discussed. At the Café Louvre followers of the philosopher Franz Brentano gathered, and several of his disciples, Anton Martý, Oskar Kraus and Alfred Kastil, were teachers at the university. Kafka heard Martý lecture there and was a regular attendee at the Louvre symposia. Brentano's philosophy, with its emphasis on ethics based on rigorous self-analysis, would have held a clear appeal for Kafka, who later discovered the work of Kierkegaard, cherishing especially his *Fear and Trembling* (1843), that rigorous examination of faith and the ethical. Emphasis on self-analysis would, in addition, push Kafka further into his intense interior world.

Brentano's ideas were also discussed at the famous Prague salon of Berta Fanta. She was the wife of a leading Prague pharmacist whose daughter married Kafka's schoolfriend Hugo Bergmann in 1908. Her imposing house 'At the Unicorn' can still be seen today dominating the Old Town Square. It became a meeting-place of the German elite who discussed Brentano and other philosophers such as Fichte, Kant and Hegel. They also ventured into more fashionable esoteric areas such as spiritualism, Indian wisdom, the doctrines of Madame Blavatsky and Rudolf Steiner's theosophy. Writers such as Meyrink, Franz Werfel, Willy Haas, Max Brod and Kafka attended, as did the scientist Albert Einstein and the physicist Gerhard Kowaleski. The young conductor Otto Klemperer and the poet Rainer Maria Rilke also graced the salon from time to time.

Kafka was in two minds about the Fanta Salon. Quite apart from his natural reluctance to take part in group activities, he had intellectual doubts about some of this fashionable mish-mash. According to Leopold Kreitner, who knew him at that time, Kafka 'was mostly a silent listener, only occasionally interposing a relevant question or a pungent remark, thus bringing the "elevated" discussion down to earth. Eventually he stayed away, disgusted with the snobbery into which these nights had degenerated.'[15] One evening the distinguished German poet Else Lasker-Schüler, author of the *Hebrew Ballads* (1913), who was known in Berlin for her outrageous Bohemianism, was at the Fanta Salon. Spilling out at midnight on to the square, she announced with typical affectation that she was the 'Prinz von Theben' for the night and sank to her knees, improvising an ode on the cobbles in the moonlight. This attracted the attention of a policeman who asked who she was. Drawing herself up to her full height, she declared, 'I am the Prinz von Theben!' This was too much for Kafka, who announced, 'She is no Prinz von Theben but *eine Kuh vom Kurfürstendamm* [a cow from Kurfürstendamm in Berlin].'

Later, Kafka and his friends congregated in the Café Arco (whose patrons were satirized as the Arconauts) and the Cafés Français and Continental. At the Arco, according to Kreitner, they would on occasion slip from philosophy into perusal of the head waiter's 'well-stocked pornographic library' or adjourn to Madame Goldschmidt's establishment, where, in this pre-war period, there was dancing, the best coffee in the city and various scantily clad 'hostesses' whose professional services were available for a set fee of ten imperial crowns.

In Kafka's letters at this time there are fleeting references to 'prostitutes',[16] an 'Indian dancing girl',[17] and 'the twenty-three-year-old girl . . . who provided me with a miracle of a Sunday'.[18]

It is likely that Kafka's sexual experiences were much more frequent throughout his life with girls of this kind than with women of his own class. Affairs with the latter were invariably carried out by correspondence. The women in his novels are nearly always closer to the stereotype of the whore than that of the madonna.

In the autumn of 1904 Kafka made a new friend in the future writer Oskar Baum, whose blindness was a horribly real reminder of the violence that frequently erupted between Czechs and Germans in Prague. It was in such a boyhood scrap that Baum had been blinded. At their first meeting (Brod had gone to read a new story to Baum and had brought Kafka along with him) the blind young man was deeply impressed by Kafka:

> He knew he was in the presence of a blind man. And yet, as Brod was introducing him, he bowed silently to me. It was, you might think, a senseless formality in my case, since I couldn't see it. His hair, which was smoothed down, touched my forehead for a moment as he bowed, probably because the bow that I made at the same time was a little too violent. I was moved in a way that for the moment I could see no clear reason for. Here was one of the first people in the world who made it clear that my deficiency [*sic*, '*Mangel*'] was something that concerned nobody but myself – not by making allowances or being considerate, not by the faintest change in his bearing. That was what he was like. He stood so far from the accepted utility formulas that he affected one in this way. His severe, cool reserve was so superior in depth of humanity to the ordinary run of kindness – which I otherwise recognize when I am first introduced to people in a pointless increase in warmth of words, or tone of voice, or shake of the hand.[19]

After this, Kafka plunged into his final academic year of legal studies through the autumn and winter of 1904 to 1905. In the summer of 1905 he rewarded himself with a trip to a small town in Moravian Silesia called Zuckmantel. He arrived at the end of July at the sanatorium run by Dr Ludwig Schweinburg. Kafka always enjoyed such places (until he became seriously ill) and he wrote brightly to Brod a month later: 'I am frivolous; this is my fourth week in a sanatorium in Silesia, where I mingle a great deal with people and womenfolk, and have become rather lively.'[20] Although Kafka was represented by his friends as an intense young man, private and apart, shy and silent, there was nevertheless something about a sanatorium that always perked him up. Perhaps it was the Teutonic order of such places, the way everything was arranged, and the consequent fact that one could enjoy the simple luxury of being a patient in a gently collegiate atmosphere of health-seeking. He liked Zuckmantel so much that he returned the following year.

Dr Schweinburg's was a relatively young establishment and it practised various modish new therapies.[21] There was more air-bathing (*Luftbäder*), as in Dresden in 1903, hydrotherapy and 'electric light baths' – not to mention a 'vaginal-cooling machine' – all aimed at tackling the malady of neurasthenia. Many years later, during a difficult relationship, Kafka referred to 'that sweetness one experiences in a relationship with a woman one loves, such as I had in Zuckmantel'[22] and, a little later, he confessed again that 'I have never yet been intimate with a woman apart from that time in Zuckmantel.'[23] Although this was a reference to the following year when he returned to the sanatorium (and, since we know that he had been sexually intimate with a woman by now, he was clearly referring not to a sexual initiation alone but to authentic emotional intimacy), it is more than likely that there was also female company on the first visit. 'At all periods of his life women felt themselves drawn to Franz,' Brod recalled, 'he himself doubted he had this effect, but the fact cannot be disputed.'[24] The sanatorium offered many opportunities for the exercise of Kafka's charm. Refreshed by this period of stay, Kafka moved on to Strakonice with his mother and three sisters to visit his aunts Anna and Julie in the family village in southern Bohemia.

Kafka's return to Prague in the autumn of 1905 was grim, for he now had to face the rigours of dreary law exams. Moreover, the cramming put more pressure on his fragile constitution. The series of three exams went by the chilling Latin title of *Rigorosum*. The first took place on 7 November and was on Austrian civil and criminal law. The second, on 16 March 1906, was on constitutional and international law; and the third, Roman, German and canon law, was taken on 13 June 1906. A mere five days later, Kafka scraped through with a pass ('three out of five votes judging his performance adequate'[25]) and was awarded his doctor of law degree by Professor Alfred Weber (brother of the renowned sociologist). He had come through in part by using Brod's notes on finance law, which 'saved me three months of my life'.[26] His claim that he and the examiner 'arrived at the loveliest rapport' and that the other exams were 'fun, too, although I did not know very much' can be interpreted only as some species of mad irony.

What Kafka would do next was not clear. He had no ideas about a profession and he wanted simply to write. There was no question of avoiding work, but he was indifferent to what it would be. Economic necessity (and in Hermann Kafka's household nobody would be carried) meant that without delay he went to work in a law firm in the Old Town. It was run by Dr Richard Löwy, who, because of his name, is often assumed to have been Franz's uncle, but was no relation at all.

After August in Zuckmantel, Kafka returned to Prague to do one year's mandatory work experience as a lawyer in the courts, first in the district court in Prague, then in the criminal court. Very little is recorded of his opinion of this experience, other than a sardonic comment to Brod when it was over: 'I have accomplished nothing at all during my year of court clerking . . . a profession becomes harmless as soon as one is able to cope with it. I would make a constant fool of myself during working hours – even though there are only six of them.'[27] Indeed, the only remarkable thing that happened in the winter of 1906–7 was the appearance of a book review by Brod in the Berlin monthly *Die Gegenwart* in February 1907. In it, Brod praised Kafka – who had not yet published a word – for his style, alongside three established writers, Heinrich Mann, Frank Wedekind and Gustav Meyrink. Whether this was a prank or a genuine attempt by Brod to give his friend a leg-up is not clear. Kafka joked that 'it will now become an indecent act for me to publish something later, for that would blast the delicacy of this first public appearance'.[28]

Concluding wisely that 'my future is not rosy',[29] Kafka set off for Triesch, where he spent August 1907 'riding around on the motorbike a good deal, swimming a lot, lying nude in the grass by the pond for hours, hanging about the park until midnight with a bothersomely infatuated girl, have already tedded hay in the meadow, have set up a merry-go-round, helped trees after a storm, taken cows and goats to pasture and driven them home in the evening, played a lot of billiards, taken long walks, drunk a lot of beer, and I have even been in the temple too'. But he had spent most of his time with two 'very bright girls, extremely Social Democratic'. One was a nineteen-year-old language student, Hedwig Therese Weiler, from Vienna, who was visiting her grandmother: 'short, her cheeks are not constantly and boundlessly red; she is very nearsighted, and not only for the sake of the pretty gesture with which she places her pince-nez on her nose – whose tip is really beautifully composed of tiny planes. Last night I dreamed of her plump little legs. Such are the roundabout ways by which I recognize a girl's beauty and fall in love.'[30] Hedwig is not Kafka's first love, but she is the first to be identified, and he wrote to her frequently. His letters are tender, self-deprecating and admit to his anxieties about relationships: 'I do not even have that concern for people that you require . . . You see, I am a ridiculous person; if you are a little fond of me, it's out of pity; my part is fear.'[31] Through the late summer and autumn of 1907 Kafka's epistolary intimacy with Hedwig grew more intense, and he talked about persuading her to come to Prague. He might declare, 'How little use meetings in letters are; they're like splashings near the shore by two who are separated by an ocean,'[32] but he was establishing a pattern for future courtships. The correspondence with Hedwig would continue for two years.

Summer dalliance was all very well, but with the arrival of autumn came the need to find a permanent job. 'I need no occupation, the more so since I am not capable of it,'[33] he joked rather desperately to Brod, but a job was certainly necessary. He toyed with the idea of attending the Export Academy at Vienna and learning Spanish, in addition to his French and English. Perhaps Uncle Alfred would find an opening for them both in Spain 'or else we would go to South America or the Azores, to Madeira'. The second part of his experience at the criminal court (where he wrote love letters to Hedwig at his official desk) finished on 30 September 1907.

The very next day he started work in earnest.

6

On 1 October 1907 the twenty-four-year-old Kafka started work at the offices of the Italian insurance company Assicurazioni Generali, whose grandiose headquarters building can still be seen today on the waterfront at Trieste. He thus became another of those writer-clerks who have figured so largely in the history of literary modernism – one thinks of Borges, Eliot and Stevens – and whose work was done in the interstices of an office career.

For many of Kafka's friends, and for Kafka himself, this was not the consummation wished for him. Max Brod believed that Kafka's family could have afforded to send him abroad to study, to escape for a little, but that the young writer did not possess sufficient push to insist on this. His energies were inwardly directed and manifested themselves in what Brod called 'a passive tenacity' ['*passive Zähigkeit*'].[1] 'Herein perhaps lay the fatal weakness of his life. He suffered and kept silent.' Kafka, however, understood the special nature of the bargain struck by the literary clerks. The strain imposed by the need to fight for a clearing of creative space, a retention of vital energy, was compensated for by a purity of focus. There was no truck with the forces of opportunistic journalism and hack-work of a kind which have become even more menacing to young talent today than they were a century ago. 'Breadwinning and the art of writing must be kept absolutely apart,' Brod summed up. And so

Kafka went into a harness from which he would be released only by early retirement on grounds of ill-health, and an early death. Brod, who followed the same path, eventually concluded, after years of 'joyless hours' at a desk, that Kafka was wrong, but that it was 'a noble error' ['*einen edlen Irrtum*'].

Kafka was hoping eventually for one of the attractive public-sector jobs where a shift began early and ended by two or three in the afternoon, leaving time, after a period of recuperation, to write in the evening. The Assicurazioni offices, in Wenceslas Square, were a relatively short walk from the new family home at No. 36 Niklasstrasse, where the Kafkas had moved in June. It was a smart new apartment building in an area redeveloped from the ruins of the old Jewish ghetto. Called 'At the Ship', it had a lift and the top-floor flat had a view of the Vltava with a half-finished bridge, the Cech Bridge, which Kafka called 'Suicide Lane'.[2] In this apartment Kafka would write his 'breakthrough' story, *Das Urteil/The Judgement*, as well as *Die Verwandlung/Metamorphosis*, but for now it was the place from which he set out every morning, leaving the Vltava behind him and striding along Niklasstrasse, across the Old Town Square, towards, eventually, the Assicurazioni offices. The Assicurazioni, according to Franz Baumer, 'presented a classical image of dusty Austro-Hungarian bureaucracy'[3] and employees were required to sign a contract whose stipulations included: 'no employee has the right to keep any objects other than those belonging to the office under lock in the desk and files assigned for his use'. The hours were long – eight to six with unpaid overtime expected – and the office busy, but Kafka put a brave face on it. 'These weeks I shall have to study insurance incessantly,' he told Hedwig, 'but it is highly interesting.'[4] With Brod he was more frank: 'my afflictions, assuming that up to now they walked on foot, are now walking appropriately on their hands'.[5] He was in the habit of meeting Brod after work at the statue of the Virgin on the Old Town Square, where they would console each other and pick up their literary conversations.

A medical examination for the job revealed that Kafka was six feet tall and weighed just over sixty kilos (just under ten stone). The doctors found him 'healthy' but 'fragile', and recommended a second examination.[6] To cheer himself up, Kafka wrote an account to Hedwig: 'I come tearing out of the big portal at 6.15, regret the wasted quarter-hour, turn to the right and go down Wenzelsplatz, then meet an acquaintance [Brod] who walks along with me and tells me a few interesting things, come home, open the door of my room, your letter is there, I enter into your letter like someone who is tired of paths through fields and now walks into the woods. I lose myself, but that doesn't worry me. If only every day would end this way.'[7] Unfortunately it did not. His 'tiny salary of 80 crowns and an infinite eight to nine hours of work' meant that he was compelled to 'devour the hours outside the office like a wild beast'. Not previously accustomed to limiting his private life 'to six hours', and because he was also studying Italian 'and want to spend the evenings of these lovely days out of doors', he emerged from 'the crowdedness of my leisure hours scarcely rested'.[8] All that made it bearable (apart from the thought of Hedwig) was a dream that the foreign company might furnish the means of travel and escape, to Trieste, at least – 'I have some hopes of someday sitting in chairs in faraway countries, looking out of the office windows at fields of sugar cane or Mohammedan cemeteries' – but there was no escaping the fact that the work was 'dreary', and the promised geographical deliverance never came. It was not so much the work that vexed him as 'the sluggishness of swampy time . . . even in the last half-hour I feel the pressure of the eight hours just as much as in the first'.[9] He ached for the time to leave at six. And he was conscious of how little he was being stimulated: 'I have no stories, see no people; for my daily walk I scurry down four streets whose corners I have already rounded off, and across a square.'[10]

The writing was not going well, either, in these circumstances, and Kafka's anxiety was increasing: 'it's . . . fear, generalized fear of writing, of this horrible pursuit; yet all my unhappiness now is due to my being deprived of it.' The writing-desk was one workplace from which one could never clock-off. Such temporary distractions as the 'Army officers, Berliners, Frenchmen, painters, cabaret singers' with whom he suddenly found himself involved across a few evenings in November only added to the guilt at not writing.

However, one more substantial piece of writing does seem to have been worked on around this time. There is a fleeting reference in May 1907 in a letter to Brod to 'two chapters'[11] that he has shown his friend. He refers to it again two years later, in July 1909. This is the posthumously published (and unfinished) story *Hochzeitsvorbereitungen auf dem Lande/Wedding Preparations in the Country*. Brod thought the work was begun in 1907 because a first draft was written in the Gothic German script, which Kafka abandoned in 1908. Though fragmentary and incomplete, the piece is interesting, less abstract than *Description of a Struggle* and with much better (more particular) observation of people and the real world. It is less a vehicle for private fantasies and anxieties, and prefigures *Metamorphosis*. The Prague cityscape of buildings and streets ('the small nameplates of firms that were fixed to the door') and the urban scene are precisely rendered: 'The horses stretched their thin forelegs, daring as chamois in the mountains.' The narrative plays with ideas of identity and of separating the real from the outwardly appearing self through word play on the German grammatical terms '*man*' ('one') and '*ich*' ('I'). The central character is travelling by train into the countryside to get married (leaving behind his other self, which has been transformed into a beetle) and some of his fellow-passengers are salesmen in the haberdashery trade (Hermann Kafka's, of course). Into a superficially naturalistic narrative, Kafka manages to inject a sense of unease, at one point declaring of the countryside, with abrupt mystery, 'Nobody must dare to go there, but who could restrain himself?' Shortly afterwards the narrative breaks off because the rest of the manuscript is lost. Although this is frustrating, the work nevertheless shows Kafka's fictional skills being honed, and it points towards future developments in riddling, menaced narrative.

Meanwhile, something had to be done to create more time to write. Kafka began to see if he could pull a few strings to secure a job at the Post Office, where the working hours would be shorter, but that came to nothing, and the new year 1908 brought only further office gloom. He complained to Hedwig of an 'abominable week',[12] saw no end to it – 'I suppose one must earn one's grave' – and he felt that this time he really did belong on 'Suicide Lane'. He could, however, still make light of his fabulating habit: 'Permit me to pull such stories over me as a sick man draws sheets and blankets over himself.' And the beginning of 1908 brought a fine compensation, his first publication. The bimonthly magazine *Hyperion*, edited by Franz Blei, published in its January/February issue eight of the very short prose pieces that would later form part of Kafka's first book,[13] *Betrachtung* (*Meditation* or *Reflection*), published in 1913.

Brod's friendship was a source of great strength to Kafka. He joked with him about a plan to start their nightlife at five o'clock in the morning when they would be like all the swells at the Trocadero who had been up all night: in possession of empty pockets. On his birthday he told Max: 'my love for you is greater than myself and I dwell in it rather than it dwells in me . . . For a long time this love has saved me more often than you know.'[14] It was especially valuable to Kafka now, 'when I am more puzzled about myself than ever and when fully conscious feel half asleep, but so extremely light, barely existing – I go around as though my guts were black'. He redoubled his efforts to escape his job, applying 'uselessly, terribly uselessly' for a different position at the beginning of June. Eventually, though, his prayers were answered.

On 15 July he quit the Assicurazioni and on the 30th joined the Arbeiter-Unfall-Versicherungs-Anstalt für das Königreich Böhmen in Prag, a mouthful in any language, which translates as the Workers' Accident Insurance Institute for the Kingdom of Bohemia in Prague (henceforth 'the Institute'). In his two letters of application – one written in German and the other in Czech[15] – Kafka was keen to stress that he was fluent in spoken and written Czech, as well as competent in French and English. Ten years later, when the Czechoslovakian Republic was founded, Kafka's fluency in Czech would ensure that he kept his job in spite of being a 'German'. This was a different sort of organization from the commercial Assicurazioni Generali, being semi-public with (somewhat reluctant) funding from private-sector employers. The massive industrial expansion in Bohemia and a burgeoning trade union movement had led to the Institute's founding in 1891.

Kafka's job concerned the prevention of industrial accidents and appeals by employers against classification of trades under various categories of risk. He drafted responses to the frequently heated challenges by employers against their high-risk classifications, wrote policy and publicity documents, and represented the Institute in court. He also inspected factories in his district: the northern Bohemian industrial area around Reichenberg (Liberec). It was thus a very important and responsible job which drew fully on Kafka's legal and drafting skills. His first-hand knowledge of industrial injury and the sufferings of workers in factories where employers paid scant regard to safety procedures confirmed him in his natural sympathy for those at the bottom of the pile. 'How modest these men are,' he told Brod. 'They come to us and beg. Instead of storming the Institute and smashing it to little pieces, they come and beg.'[16]

Although Kafka always claimed that he was not very good at his job, this was not the opinion of his employers, who promoted him several times. Like many writers in such a position who know that their heart and soul are elsewhere, he may have been extra careful to discharge his duties diligently to avoid the charge of lack of commitment. An office colleague from this time, Alois Gütling, remembered him as tactful when handling people able to speak good office Czech, and much admired by colleagues for his legal acumen. Another colleague, who joined the Institute several years later, when Kafka was becoming ill, V. K. Krofta, recalled his habitual reserve: 'Through his build and his thoughtful abstractedness he made a very timid and a reticent impression; those around him considered him a kind of Don Quixote. He spoke an elegant literary Czech always with little pauses and the utmost concentration . . . He gesticulated vigorously when he wanted to emphasize his meagre sentences and words.'[17]

Kafka was popular in the office, though colleagues noted his boyish demeanour, as if Dr Kafka were not quite fully grown-up. They nicknamed him 'our office baby' ('*unser Amtskind*'), and Brod confirmed that there was 'a certain naivety in Kafka's make-up'.[18] This streak of infantilism in Kafka has often been passed over by his biographers, even though Kafka himself was aware of 'my childish appearance'[19] and knew that his immaturity contributed to his hypochondria. When he was twenty-eight he reflected 'how comforting Mother can be' when she ministered to him in sickness: 'I should wish that for myself once more, because then I should be weak, therefore convinced by everything my mother did, and could enjoy childish pleasure with age's keener capacity for gratification.'[20] Franz Baumer, too, talks of his 'sublime infantilism',[21] and an old schoolfriend, Friedrich Feigl, later asserted of Kafka at the end of his life: 'Fundamentally Kafka remained a boy, to whom it was not granted to grow old . . . he faced life with all the curiosity of the child, in spite of the fact that he was over forty.'[22] Taken together, these observations (all by people who knew Kafka personally) once again raise the question discussed earlier of whether Kafka's sexual anxieties ('I believe Kafka was afraid of bodily contact,' said Feigl) and his fear of social engagement and commitment to relationships, particularly with women, were the result of some kind of arrested maturity, of thwarted development.

On the other hand, in the rough and tumble of the workplace, Kafka learned precisely those lessons of ordinary life that he needed to learn. 'It is clear that Kafka derived a great amount of his knowledge of the world and life, as well as his skeptical pessimism, from his experiences in the office,' wrote Max Brod, 'and from having to deal with the long-drawn-out process of official work and from the stagnating life of files.'[23] Inevitably, his immersion in red tape and officialdom has been seen as the inspiration for the bureaucratic nightmares of *The Trial*. However, there is evidence from Brod that there was humour and playfulness in the office as well as dry, dusty hours of existential torment. Kafka once wrote Brod a Chaplinesque account of the world of health and safety in the workplace: 'In my four districts – apart from all my other jobs – people fall off the scaffolds as if they were drunk, or fall into the machines, all the beams topple, all embankments give way, all ladders slide, whatever people carry up falls down, whatever they hand down they stumble over. And I have a headache from all these girls in porcelain factories who incessantly throw themselves down the stairs with mounds of dishware.'[24]

Kafka's office writings have been collected into a volume[25] and tribute has been paid to the eloquent clarity of his contributions to annual reports on aspects of industrial injury (though his authorship of particular documents, which were written anyway in a rigid house style and format, cannot be ascertained exactly). The surprise is that anyone should have thought that

Dr Kafka would have written anything other than immaculate and precise prose (in much the same way, English Victorian scholars murmur admiration for the reports of school inspections drawn up by the poet Matthew Arnold). A true surprise would have been if he had *not* done so. The precise descriptions, for example, of 'Accident Prevention Regulations in the Use of Wood-Planing Machines', complete with illustrative engravings, find an echo in the hideous torture apparatus of *In Der Strafkolonie/In the Penal Colony.*

Kafka's work involved a certain amount of travel, and within a couple of months he was already sending postcards back to Brod from such places as Tetschen on the Elbe ('I'm at home in hotel rooms; I'm at home at once in hotel rooms, more than at home, really').[26] He was also soon given a short vacation and went to Spitzen on the Bavarian border, from where he told Brod: 'I am very happy and . . . it would be a great joy to me if you were here, for in the woods are things one could meditate on for years, lying in the moss.'[27] The trips and the holiday would have offered relief from the office grind, but this was scarcely arduous in any case. Kafka's hours were just 8 a.m. until 2 p.m., which included a fairly substantial mid-morning snack known as *Gabelfrühstückspausen.* Kafka was known to be a vegetarian and avoided sausages and pies, bringing instead a buttered roll, which he ate with yoghurt or milk.[28] The early clocking-off time meant that he could leave the offices in Na Poříčí (now a refurbished French hotel with a recent sculpted bronze of Kafka in the foyer and a 'Felice Brasserie') and walk home across Josefplatz (Náměstí Republiky), down Celetná, across the Old Town Square, and along Niklasstrasse, to the flat, where he could eat, sleep and then spend the evening and sometimes part of the night writing.

However, he was still lonely on occasions and remained alienated from his family. 'I am so urgently driven to find someone who will merely touch me in a friendly manner,' he told Brod shortly after his return to Prague from holiday, 'that yesterday I went to the hotel with a prostitute . . . I didn't comfort her since she didn't comfort me either.'[29] Just before Christmas he told Brod: 'I have been in despair for two years . . . each time I get up in the morning I cannot think of anything with power enough to provide consolation for me.'[30]

From 4 to 14 September 1909 Kafka, Brod and Brod's brother, Otto, took a holiday together at the Italian resort of Riva on Lake Garda. On the 11th, hearing that there was an air show not far away at Brescia, the three young men decided to pay a visit, none of them ever having seen an aeroplane. Kafka's account – 'The Aeroplanes at Brescia', published in the journal *Bohemia* on 29 September – was the result of a proposal that Brod and he should write rival accounts of the same event. Kafka, though it occasionally suited him to adopt a fogeyish pose towards new technology (we shall later encounter a comic account of his use of the office telephone) mostly exhibited an attitude of enthralled wonder, especially for recent innovations, such as cinema.[31] He was the keenest of the trio to go, while Brod had an ulterior motive. He was concerned that, after his first year of office work, Kafka was not writing enough (though he had managed to persuade him to allow two more pieces to be published in March in *Hyperion*: the two fragments of *Description of a Struggle*). 'Indeed, he sometimes lived for months in a kind of lethargy, in utter despair.'[32] The idea of a contest might provoke Kafka into action again, he thought. The three friends spent the night of the 10th in a room with a hole in the middle of the floor looking down to the taproom below. Next day, their pockets mercifully unpicked, they attended the show. Kafka's account is lively and amusing – he never wrote in this vein again – and he describes the fashionable crowds who had gathered to see such air heroes as Louis Blériot, who had flown over the Channel less than two months previously, and Glenn Curtiss. The three friends saw a plane bumping along the turf before take-off 'like an awkward performer on the dance floor', an elderly aristocratic woman 'whose face has the colour of dark yellow grapes' and celebrities such as the poet Gabriele d'Annunzio and the composer Giacomo Puccini strutting about the stands. And the great Blériot himself: 'He turns his eyes slowly in our direction, turns them away from us and then in another direction, but his look he always keeps to himself.'[33] Though not the first account of an air show (as is sometimes claimed), it is among the earliest and captures a moment of excitement at a new phenomenon of twentieth-century life.

Towards the end of 1909 Kafka began to keep a diary or notebook whose first entries date from the summer of that year but which began in earnest in 1910. This was a hybrid of conventional dated entries and attempts at fiction, fragments and aphorisms (the biographer needs to step carefully between the two). It marked a new phase in his introspection and self-analysis – or at any rate one that we may now begin to observe. Prior to this his reflections on his fate were often no more than one finds in the juvenilia of many young writers – vague aspiration, as yet unsatisfied ambition, impatience at the slowness of one's approach to success – but a new tone enters the notebook entries. Kafka is beginning to articulate a more comprehensive world view, of greater reach and depth, and most certainly of greater bleakness. His adolescent shyness and solitariness are slowly metamorphosing into the terrible existential loneliness – the self-lacerating agony – with which his mature writing (and his later correspondence) faced the world.

7

Early in 1910, Kafka's preoccupation with his health became more pronounced. At the end of January he had his stomach pumped, noting wryly: 'I have a feeling that disgusting things will come out.'[1] This seems to have had about as much effect as his regular practice of Müller exercises, and by the middle of March he was forced to report to Brod: 'Recently I had rheumatic pains in my shoulders, then they slid down to the small of my back, then into my legs, but instead of going into the ground as you might expect, they went up into the arms.'[2] The pains persisted into the spring: 'Everything I possess is directed against me . . . I am nothing but a mass of spikes going through me; if I try to defend myself and use force, the spikes only press in the deeper . . . I am tempted to say: God knows how I can possibly feel any more pain, since in my sheer urgency to inflict it upon myself I never get around to perceiving it.'[3] In his diary he confessed to 'despair over my body and over a future with this body'.[4]

For the rest of his short life Kafka would struggle with the inescapable reality of his body, its failings, its dysfunction, its eventual collapse into terminal illness. He was hypersensitive to changes in his physical condition. He was a hypochondriac. He fretted about his diet, his constitution, his need for physical exercise. His dissatisfaction was bound up with – and in a mutually causal relationship with – his difficulties in writing. For the first five months of 1910, he wrote, 'I could write nothing that would have satisfied me, and for which no power will compensate me, though all were under obligation to do so.'[5] There were distractions, though, such as the arrival in Prague of the Russian Ballet, who performed at the German Theatre. Kafka composed several descriptions in his diary of the dancer Eduardova. At the same time he recorded: 'I passed by the brothel as though past the house of a beloved.'[6] There were also visits to cafés and political meetings (though pressure of work sometimes forced Kafka to decline invitations to join his friends) and, if new work was slow to come, there was the gratification of further publication of short prose pieces in *Bohemia*. But most significant of all was the arrival of a group of actors from a Yiddish theatre group from Lemberg, the capital of Galicia, the most north-easterly province of the empire, bordering Russia, who performed at the Café Savoy in May. They made a great impression which would be cemented the following year when another troupe from the same town arrived in Prague.

In July 1910 Kafka woke one Sunday, after a night of interrupted sleep, to reflect on his 'miserable life'.[7] His self-analysis now developed a new theme, which would culminate in the famous *Letter to the Father* of 1919. He began to blame his parents for his problems. In his diary, as noted above, he listed those who had allegedly done him 'great harm' during his childhood, drafting the indictment several times and adding new details on each occasion, in a way that suggests it was as much a fictional projection as an autobiographical confession. Yet the burden of his complaint fits the facts as he saw them. He was convinced that his parents – and in particular his father – had 'spoiled a part of me . . . spoiled a good, beautiful part (in my dreams it appears to me the way a dead bride appears to others)'. Outwardly he might seem normal enough, 'a man like others', and 'like everyone . . . I have my centre of gravity inside me from birth, and this not even the most foolish education could displace. This good centre of gravity I still have, but to a certain extent I no longer have the corresponding body. And a centre of gravity that has no work to do becomes lead, and sticks in the body like a musket ball.'

In the course of drafting this long complaint, Kafka pauses to describe the view from a window – that from No. 36 Niklasstrasse – of the fishermen by the Vltava, the trolley buses on the Czech Bridge, seen as he puts down his pen to open the window on the hot July night. On this summer evening in Prague, he burnishes the indictment of 'my parents and relatives. That they have done me harm out of love makes their guilt all the greater, for how much good they could have done me out of love . . . my education has spoiled me more than all the people I know and more than I can conceive.'[8] This long-drawn-out reproach is followed by a story, 'Unhappiness', which centres on a 'bachelor' who has insufficient involvement with the world to be able to withstand its shocks: 'His nature is suicidal, therefore it has teeth only for his own flesh and flesh only for his own teeth. For without a centre, without a profession, a love, a family, an income; i.e. without holding one's own against the world in the big things . . . one cannot protect oneself from losses that momentarily destroy one.'[9] Like the bachelor in his story, Kafka felt that 'we and our acquaintances are indeed unknowable, for we are entirely concealed; I, for instance, am now concealed by my profession, by my imagined or actual sufferings, by literary inclinations etc., etc.'. In a startling image, Kafka writes of the bachelor that 'his conduct can make one think of the corpse of a drowned man which, borne to the surface by some current, bumps against a tired swimmer, lays its hands upon him and would like to hold on. The corpse does not come alive, indeed is not even saved, but it can pull the man down.'

Death by drowning, suicidal impulses, self-loathing and confusion about one's direction in life, a destructive relationship with parents: these themes are the raw material of Kafka's major literary breakthrough, *The Judgement*, still two years away. But how do they relate to the real Kafka, the twenty-seven-year-old accident insurance lawyer in the Prague summer of 1910? He had just been promoted to a permanent position with a higher salary. His literary work was beginning to appear in respected periodicals. He had a small circle of friends whose invitations were so pressing that he sometimes had to decline them. His work took him out into the world of contemporary industry where he saw life, the realities of the workplace. He attended political meetings. The hopelessly introverted, damaged, lonely bachelor of his private fictional fantasies seems hard to square with the external reality of his life at this time.

One persistent consolation throughout Kafka's life was the countryside. A thoroughly urban animal, he nevertheless loved the country and the open air. In spite of his tendency to deprecate his physical capacity, he liked to walk, kept a bicycle in his Prague flat, and enjoyed swimming at the Civilschwimmschule (Civilian Swimming School), a bathing and boating establishment moored on the opposite bank of the Vltava from the Old Town (it can be seen today), where he also kept a rowing boat. He took particular pleasure in rowing upstream and then allowing himself to drift back downstream, lying motionless in the bottom of the boat, which was known as a *Seelentränker* ('man-drowner'). 'Because of my extreme thinness this may have looked very funny from the bridge,'[10] he later recalled. That was certainly the reaction of one of the clerks from his office, who saw, from one of the Prague bridges, the skeletal figure drifting past, 'like the dead in their coffins just before the last judgement'. Kafka also liked horse-riding and took lessons in the sport.

In the country he was an addict of fresh air and sunbathing, nude, if he felt confident enough. In August he visited Saaz, sixty-five miles north of Prague, where a picture postcard to Brod observed: 'In spite of everything it isn't bad, you know, to lie against a pile of sheaves for a while and bury your face in them!'[11] His main holiday in 1910, however, was a trip to Paris with Brod. The two prepared for the trip by taking French lessons. Before he set off, Kafka had to carry out a difficult mission in the northern Bohemian town of Gablonz (Jablonec) as part of the Institute's long-running battle with employers over high-risk insurance premiums. His need to deliver a public lecture filled him with apprehension. 'I bring more anxiety to this than is needed to make it a success,'[12] he told Brod. Thanks to a report in the *Gablonzer Zeitung*, we know what Kafka eventually said in his public address at the Hotel Geling.[13] Entering the lions' den, he told the assembled employers that it was in their interests to fill in the Institute's forms correctly, and that if there had been errors in the rapid classification of enterprises – 37,000 in the course of a few months – they had not been intentional. Kafka went on to lament the poor levels of communication between employers and the Institute, which, since they were members of it, they should regard as their own body and not as an antagonist. In order to win over the disgruntled capitalists (in this instance mostly small firms) Kafka announced some concessions, such as an end to unannounced inspections, consultation with employers before introducing new classifications, and a determination on the part of the Institute to try harder to discuss and interpret new legislation in the professional journals. Under some angry questioning, Kafka conceded that some inspections might have been less than professionally conducted, and he had to listen to complaints about the slowness of the Institute in dealing with appeals (*Rekurse*) against classification. After this, Kafka no doubt felt he deserved his holiday.

On 8 October, Kafka, Max and Otto Brod set off for Paris, travelling via Nuremberg. Kafka took with him his usual consignment of ailments (and some new ones: a dislocated big toe and a painful leg), and, after a week, an outbreak of boils forced him back alone to Prague. He sent the other two a postcard on his return telling how the doctor was 'horrified by the appearance of my backside' and how he was 'sitting at home in the afternoon as in a tomb'.[14] This should have been an opportunity to resume his writing, but this was not going well. In a late-night diary entry the following month he resolved: 'I will not let myself become tired. I'll jump into my story even though it should cut my face to pieces.'[15]

The problem was work as well as ill-health, so a brief trip to Berlin in December, where he saw Schnitzler's first play, *Anatol*, and a performance of *Hamlet*, and – the high point – discovered a vegetarian restaurant, was very welcome and was followed by a further eight days off, probably using up his leave allowance. Kafka's vegetarianism was now firmly established, and it may have been on this trip to Berlin that he visited the Aquarium with a friend, Ludwig Hardt. His companion heard Kafka, who had recently resumed his pure vegetarian diet after eating meat and fish on medical advice, murmur to the glass wall of the fish-tank: 'Now I can look into your eyes with a clear conscience.'[16] In the Berlin restaurant Kafka consumed lettuce with cream, semolina pudding with raspberry syrup, gooseberry wine and finished with a cup of strawberry-leaf tea.

Return to Prague, however, meant a return to the physical distractions of the family apartment, which in turn were seen as a series of further obstacles to writing. The fuss attendant on the wedding of his eldest sister, Elli, to Karl Hermann had subsided, but the noise to which he was hypersensitive persisted in the apartment: 'Doors are now being opened everywhere as if walls were being smashed,'[17] he told Brod, shortly before Christmas. 'But above all, the centre of all the misery remains. I cannot write; I have not done a line I respect . . . My whole body warns me against every word; every word, before it lets me write it down, first looks around in all directions. The sentences literally crumble before me; I see their insides and then have to stop quickly.' In his private diaries, Kafka was even harsher on himself for this failure to write: 'It is as if I were made of stone, as if I were my own tombstone . . . Almost every word I write jars against the next . . . I ought to be able to invent words capable of blowing the odour of corpses in a direction other than straight into mine and the reader's face.'[18] His excessive scruple about what he had written (virtually everything he wrote in 1910 had been put aside and crossed out) hindered him in broaching new work. What he had rejected was 'a mountain, it is five times as much as I have in general ever written, and by its mass alone it draws everything that I write away from under my pen to itself'.

Kafka struggled to keep to his regular writing schedule of eight to eleven in the evening, but work and its pressures kept intruding, forcing him to reflect that 'I, so long as I am not freed of my office, am simply lost.'[19] Even his desk became an enemy, a reason for not being able to write: 'There is so much lying about, it forms a disorder without proportion.' Towards midnight on Christmas Eve 1910, Kafka was reduced to railing at the clutter of his desk's pigeonholes with its 'wads of old newspapers, catalogues, picture postcards', and his inability to make the most of the space he had won in which to write. Solitude at the desk was nevertheless vital to him if *anything* was to be done. 'Being alone has a power over me that never fails. My interior dissolves (for the time being only superficially) and is ready to release what lies deeper. A slight ordering of my interior begins to take place and I need nothing more, for disorder is the worst thing in small talents.'[20] A few days later, Kafka confesses: 'My strength no longer suffices for another sentence. Yes, if it were a question of words, if it were sufficient to set down one word and one could turn away in the calm consciousness of having entirely filled this word with oneself.'[21] What is fascinating about these reflections on his writing is the way in which Kafka seems to be moving into a direct, unmediated relationship with the sources of his creativity and his medium, language. Writing becomes a process of total surrender to the possibilities of expression – which are at once tantalizingly difficult to grasp and in their potential infinite – and is unconstrained by any considerations of social realism, genre expectations, ethical intent – indeed, any external desideratum at all except its being 'sufficient' to have 'entirely filled this word with oneself'. Kafka was raising the stakes of writing: it was no mere 'literary vocation'. He even feared to write down too much about himself at this juncture for fear of 'betraying my self-perception . . . for one should permit a self-perception to be established definitely in writing only when it can be done with the greatest completeness, with all the incidental consequences, as well as with entire truthfulness'.[22] By insisting on a goal of 'entire truthfulness', Kafka was giving another turn of the screw to the machine on which he was voluntarily stretching himself. Max Brod said of his friend: 'He had an unusual aura of power about him . . . the unintermittent compactness of his ideas could not endure a gap, he never spoke a meaningless word.'[23] By not allowing himself that 'gap', Kafka was ensuring that writing would come to seem to him – as it so patently seems to us who come in his wake reading his letters and private diaries and notebooks – virtually a matter of life and death.

Issues less vital than life and death raised by the restive small businessmen of Bohemia ensured that Kafka's diary for the first two months of 1911 was punctuated by business trips to inspect factories in Friedland (Frýdlant) (where there was an ivy-shrouded castle in the snow that could have stood in for the castle in his great novel) and Reichenberg. He left in late January and returned to Prague around 12 February. In Friedland he visited the Imperial Panorama – keeping Brod apprised of his movements by picture postcard – and in Reichenberg, where he put up at the Hotel Eiche, he found a vegetarian restaurant called Thalysia and went to the theatre three times in the intervals of his business at the Workers' Compensation Office.

He was reading, especially his literary idol Heinrich von Kleist ('he fills me as if I were an old pig's bladder'[24]), and writing when he could, noting at the beginning of the year that circumstances were now more friendly than they had been for a year, in spite of the unsympathetic family environment which always affected him deeply. He remembered an occasion when an uncle had picked up a piece of his writing and said to the other relatives in the room who watched him scan it: 'The usual stuff.'[25] Kafka's reaction was characteristically extreme: 'with one thrust I had in fact been banished from society . . . I got an insight into the cold space of our world.' His room became a place of retreat where such incidents could be avoided, but he could not avoid exhaustion or the nervous tension that his current lifestyle produced. He considered that he was 'completely overworked. Not by the office but my other work.' The six hours a day, from eight to two, which he was compelled to spend at work 'tormented' him because he was 'full of my own things'. He allowed that the office had 'a right to make the most definite and justified demands on me. But for me in particular it is a horrible double life from which there is probably no escape but insanity.' Yet at the centre of this frustration was a growing realization that he had something, though the expression of it was enigmatic and extraordinary. He told his diary that the 'special nature of my inspiration . . . is such that I can do everything, and not only what is directed to a definite piece of work. When I arbitrarily write a single sentence, for instance, "He looked out of the window," it already has perfection.'[26]

On 26 March 1911 Kafka attended the first of a series of theosophic lectures in Prague given by Dr Rudolf Steiner. He had already been introduced to theosophy at Berta Fanta's salon, but now he had a chance to see Steiner in the flesh. 'He is, perhaps, not the greatest contemporary psychic scholar,' thought Kafka, 'but he alone has been assigned the task of uniting theosophy and science.'[27]

Two days later, Kafka paid the great *savant* a visit at the Victoria Hotel on Jungmannstrasse (Jungmanova ulice) at three o'clock in the afternoon. Kafka fumbled with his hat until he found a place for it on a boot-stand, and Steiner asked: 'So you are Dr Kafka? Have you been interested in theosophy long?' Kafka had come prepared to lay out his dilemma: 'I feel that a great part of my being is striving towards theosophy, but at the same time I have the greatest fear of it. That is to say, I am afraid it will result in a new confusion which would be very bad for me, because even my present unhappiness consists only of confusion.'[28] Steiner listened to Kafka explaining this confusion, which was that everything that mattered to him had been in the literary field. 'And here I have, to be sure, experienced states (not many) which in my opinion correspond very closely to the clairvoyant states described by you, *Herr Doktor*, in which I completely dwelt in every idea, but also filled every idea, and in which I not only felt myself at my boundary, but at the boundary of the human in general.' Because Kafka considered he lacked 'the calm of enthusiasm, which is probably characteristic of the clairvoyant', he felt that in those clairvoyant states he did not write his best work. Steiner listened attentively, nodding sagely, while working his handkerchief into one nostril at a time to deal with the effects of a head cold. The young man explained that he had reached the realization that he could not live by literature alone, especially given 'the slow maturing of my work and its special character'. Health and Kafka's character militated against the uncertainties of a full-time literary career: 'I have therefore become an official [*Beamte*] in a social insurance agency.' Yet that was not the end of his dilemma, for he was torn apart by the work–writing opposition: a good night's writing spoiled his work at the office next day and vice versa. 'Outwardly, I fulfil my duties satisfactorily in the office [the records of the Institute show that he received regular commendations for his efficiency and skill], not my inner duties, however, and every unfulfilled inner duty becomes a misfortune that never leaves.' Kafka feared that a wholesale adoption of theosophy would simply open up a third front of anxiety and stress, but he wanted Steiner to tell him if this analysis was correct. Frustratingly, Kafka leaves his report there. We do not know what Steiner thought of this intense young man with his grave expression, neat attire and glowing eyes who had come to seek his guidance. It must have been one of the more remarkable encounters of his Prague trip.

Meanwhile, Kafka was taking care to address the physical as well as the spiritual man. On another factory inspection trip in May he paid a visit to Moriz Schnitzer, a natural therapist conveniently based in Kafka's patch at Warnsdorf (Varnsdorf) in northern Bohemia. Schnitzer diagnosed 'poison in the spinal cord'[29] and recommended a vegetarian diet, fresh air, sunbathing, and – music to Kafka's ears – staying away from doctors. Kafka had come to the view that doctors were not good for him, in part because, unlike the natural therapists, they did not take a holistic approach. He reported enthusiastically to Brod on the encounter with the 'magician'[30] Schnitzer, an industrialist who had become a practitioner of the 'nature cure' in the garden city of Warnsdorf and who had told Kafka he was 'living on the wrong lines'.

Kafka, although occasionally prone to mock the faddish aspects of the natural therapy industry, was seriously committed to its precepts. He slept with the window open all the year round, wore light clothing, avoided meat except when medical advice insisted on it at certain periods, and drank no alcohol. The next few summer months seem to have been good for him physically (though Brod noted in his diary that he still had to keep prodding his friend out of his depressions[31]). He wrote nothing during the period but had started to read about Dickens, an experience which prompted a reflection that a writer experiences a story within him, is 'pursued by it' and entirely given over to it, wherever it may lead. Once again Kafka was stressing how the writer is visited by something outside himself and allows himself to be taken over by the forces of inspiration. But as far as general well-being was concerned: 'I have stopped being ashamed of my body in the swimming schools in Prague, Königssaal and Czernoschitz. How late I make up for my education now, at the age of twenty-eight, a delayed start they would call it at the racetrack.'[32] Accordingly he set off on 26 August with Brod for a trip to Zürich, Lucerne, Lugano, Stresa and Paris, leaving behind his father, who was ill from work-related stress.

To pass the time, Kafka and Brod resolved to 'describe the trip and at the same time our feelings towards each other during the trip'.[33] Kafka's travel notes are not particularly striking and often focus on descriptions of women seen on the journey. In Italy, at Osteno, he experienced a 'shivery feeling at the sight of lizards wriggling on a wall'[34] and at Menaggio reflected on the fact that 'Every word of Italian spoken to one penetrates the great void of one's own ignorance.' At Milan, the cathedral was dismissed as 'a little tiresome'[35] compared with the attractions of the brothel 'Al Vero Eden', where Kafka, who was well used to such establishments, reflected: 'At home it was with the German bordello girls that one lost a sense of one's nationality for a moment, here it was with the French girls.'[36] Kafka was not a natural traveller – he hardly ever left Prague except to visit health spas and resorts and saw very little of Austria, never mind further afield – and, were it not for the keeping of a diary, he confessed he would not have been able to keep 'the deathly feeling of the monotonous passing of the days' at bay. From Milan, the two friends journeyed to Paris (where 'the two little Frenchwomen with their fat behinds'[37] were duly noted) to see the paintings of the Louvre and visit Versailles. They saw *Carmen* at the Opéra Comique and later Racine's *Phèdre*. Here there were 'sensibly conducted brothels' managed by strong women: 'In Prague already, I had often taken casual notice of the Amazonian character of brothels. Here it was even more pronounced.'[38] Kafka's reference to a 'lonely, long, absurd walk home' suggests that he may have declined the offered girl whose 'clenched fist held her dress together over her pudenda' and left Max to it. Kafka was particularly absorbed by the Paris Métro system, the tunnels and tracks. 'Because it is so easy to understand, the subway is a frail and hopeful stranger's best chance to think that he has quickly and correctly, at the first attempt, penetrated the essence of Paris.'[39]

On 13 September Kafka left Brod and travelled alone to the Swiss sanatorium at Erlenbach on Lake Zurich where he was meant to be writing his part of the joint novel *Richard and Samuel*, which they had started in the summer. But the 'activities' of the sanatorium – massage, gymnastics and gramophone concerts (with the sexes rigidly separated) – prevented any writing. The guests consisted largely of 'elderly Swiss women of the middle class'.[40] From here, Kafka returned to work on 20 September with one of his many illnesses having dissolved 'while the others look on in astonishment'.[41] The next month Lemberg's Yiddish theatre troupe returned to Prague, and Kafka was an eager member of the audience. The troupe's visit triggered something of a turning point in Kafka's self-awareness as a Jew. He embarked on an exploration of Jewish history and culture that would develop steadily throughout the remainder of his life.

8

On 30 September 1911 Kafka attended the Staronová (Altneu) Synagogue in Prague for Yom Kippur, the Day of Atonement. For the first time in his letters and diaries we encounter something more than a passing reference to his Jewish faith. In this ancient synagogue Kafka noted three pious Eastern Jews: 'Bowed over their prayer-books, their prayer shawls drawn over their heads, become as small as they possibly can.'[1] His unsparing writer's eye also, however, observed 'the family of a brothel owner'. In spite of the 'arabesque melodies' which spun out the words 'as fine as hairs', he came to the conclusion that 'I was stirred immeasurably more deeply by Judaism in the Pinkas Synagogue.' This reference is to the nearby synagogue which is now famous for its 1958 Holocaust Memorial.

Being stirred deeply by Judaism was apparently a new emotion for Kafka. The child of an assimilated Jew, lukewarm in his observance, Kafka had expressed only mild interest in Zionism as a student. The year 1911, however, marked a turning point. His encounter with the far from lukewarm Eastern Jews or Ostjuden – whose lives have been so unforgettably etched by Joseph Roth[2] – in the shape of the Yiddish theatre troupe which returned to Prague that year ignited a growing interest that would intensify in his final decade.

His Jewish inheritance became another bone of contention between Kafka and his father. In the famous, unsent *Letter to the*

Father of 1919 Kafka carefully distinguished three different attitudes towards Judaism that he believed his father had implanted in him. The first was guilt as a child at not going to the synagogue frequently enough or observing the ritual fasts: 'I thought that in this way I was doing a wrong not to myself but to you, and I was penetrated by a sense of guilt, which was of course always ready to hand.'[3] The next phase began when Kafka, as a growing boy, began to find it absurd that his father should use this 'insignificant scrap of Judaism' ('*Nichts von Judentum*') as a reproach to his son.

Hermann went to the synagogue only four times a year, and when there he was indifferent, observing the forms of the prayers merely (though he 'sometimes amazed me by being able to show me in the prayer-book the passage that was being said at the moment'), and being content if Franz merely put in an appearance. The latter 'yawned and dozed through the many hours (I don't think I was ever again so bored, except later at dancing lessons)' and did his best to 'enjoy the few little bits of variety there were', such as the opening of the Ark of the Covenant, 'which always reminded me of the shooting-stands where a cupboard door would open in the same way whenever one got a bull's eye, only with the difference that there something interesting always came out and here it was always just the same old dolls with no heads'. Kafka's deliberately flippant impiety here expresses his frustration at being dragged along to the synagogue for form's sake. He was also frightened as a child by his father's threat that he might be called to read the Torah: 'That was something I went in dread of for years.' But otherwise he was not 'fundamentally disturbed in my state of boredom', unless it was by the bar-mitzvah. Yet even that meant no more to him than 'the ridiculous passing of an examination'. When his father was called up to read the Torah, his son saw it merely as a social triumph for Hermann, and, when the latter sent him away when the prayers for the dead were read, it left him only with the impression that 'what was about to take place was something indecent'. At home the same pattern of superficiality was repeated with just the first evening of Passover being celebrated, and that in a way which 'more and more developed into farce, with fits of hysterical laughter'.

This was the practical inheritance of Judaism, coupled with a dose of social snobbery (pointing out millionaire Jews in the congregation) that Kafka believed he had received. The result was that 'precisely getting rid of it seemed to me the most effective act of "piety" one could perform'. Part of the problem was that Hermann himself, with his inherited Judaism 'from that ghetto-like little village community' in Osek, did have some genuine memory of a living Jewish tradition, however eroded by emigration to the town and during his military service. It gave him a sort of irreducible minimum so that 'at bottom the faith that ruled your life consisted in your believing in the unconditional rightness of the opinions prevailing in a particular class of Jewish society', but it was too little to be able to inspire a child: 'it all trickled away while you were passing it on'. Because the scraps that Hermann wanted to pass on – 'the few flimsy gestures you performed in the name of Judaism' – had no real force of persuasion, he had to resort to threats, angered by what he saw as his son's apparent obstinacy.

Kafka realized that what was happening in the case of his father was not an isolated phenomenon. 'It was much the same with a large section of this transitional generation of Jews, which had migrated from the still comparatively devout countryside to the towns.' When, however, Kafka began to embark seriously on a study of Judaism, his father's usual 'dislike in advance of every one of my activities' meant that, far from welcoming his son's rediscovery of a family tradition, it immediately became yet another *casus belli* between them. Hermann began to rail against the Jewish writings his son was starting to explore, claiming that they 'nauseated' him. Kafka interpreted this as an unacknowledged admission by his father of the weakness of his lip-service Judaism and of the Jewish upbringing he had given his son. Hermann 'did not wish to be reminded of it in any way, and reacted to all reminders with frank hatred'. In conclusion, Kafka felt that his 'new Judaism' suffered because it bore his father's curse within it, bitterly adding that 'in its development the fundamental relationship to one's fellow men was decisive, in my case that is to say fatal'. As always, in the negative and unhealthy relationship between father and son (in Kafka's version of it) there appeared to be no resolution in prospect and a 'fatal' outcome seemed predetermined. The legacy of permanent damage was also – one must add, monotonously – insisted upon.

The arrival of the Yiddish theatre troupe in October 1911 was a welcome diversion in Kafka's life. At the time he had been sleeping very badly ('I . . . feel myself rejected by sleep'[4]). This was to become a permanent problem for him and, according to some medical opinion could have been an early symptom, together with splitting headaches, of his tuberculosis. It was generally caused, however, by his anxieties about writing and by the struggle to write in the teeth of the demands of his professional life. In an extraordinary passage in his diary Kafka declares that his sleeplessness is caused by a powerful realization of what is at stake in his writing, of what, if he can only bring it off, he is capable of: 'I believe this sleeplessness comes only because I write. For no matter how little and how badly I write, I am still made sensitive by these minor shocks, feel, especially towards evening and even more in the morning, the approaching, the imminent possibility of great moments which would tear me open, which could make me capable of anything and in the general uproar that is within me and which I have no time to command, find no rest.'[5] The sleeplessness was aggravated by a nightmare, a 'horrible apparition', of a blind child, both of whose eyes were covered by a pair of spectacles, which were not fastened in the usual way, the support being drilled into the child's cheekbones. So traumatic was this dream that he recounted it the next day to his boss at the Institute, Eugen Pfohl. Kafka, having sensed the awesome challenge of releasing through writing those 'great moments', felt unequal to it as yet, and the nightmares were the working out of this unease: 'during the day the visible world helps me, during the night it cuts me to pieces unhindered'.[6] The next night he returned to the dilemma: 'In the evening and the morning my consciousness of the creative abilities in me is more than I can encompass. I feel shaken to the core of my being and can get out of myself whatever I desire.'[7] In reality, however, he was an official who must go to work in the office each day.

That very day, while dictating to his secretary, and searching for some phrase that would conclude the report, he states the problem in all its starkness: 'Finally I say it [the elusive phrase], but retain the great fear that everything within me is ready for a poetic work and such a work would be a heavenly enlightenment and a real coming-alive for me, while here, in the office, because of so wretched an official document, I must rob a body capable of such happiness of a piece of its flesh.'

The office was becoming unbearable, and even if he were to be told that he could leave at the end of the month he believed he couldn't hold out. He went through the motions of his work in a kind of numbness: 'And most of the time in the office I do what I am supposed to, am quite calm when I can be sure that my boss is satisfied, and do not feel that my condition is dreadful.'[8] At night the demons – 'the great agitation in me' ('*die große Bewegung*') – returned to torment him in his lonely room in a house where he felt no one understood him, and where he watched in the middle of the night the lights and shadows thrown on the walls and ceilings by the electric lights of Niklasstrasse and the Czech Bridge. Kafka's Prague was sometimes reduced to this: a tight domestic web wrapped around him as if he were a trapped insect. He was writing again now (and reading Dickens, who was always a great favourite of

Kafka's), but the small irritations of the family – for instance, his sister playing with a visiting card between her teeth – continued to plague his raw sensibility.

As if the battle between writing and work were not enough, a new source of anguish was about to torment Kafka. His brother-in-law, Elli's husband, Karl Hermann, a self-confident and worldly businessman, planned to set up a factory manufacturing asbestos, with Kafka as a joint partner.[9] Hermann Kafka was keen to see his son-in-law prosper in business and for his son to start making money for a change, instead of all that pointless scribbling in his room at night. Although Kafka almost immediately began to complain about this venture, to be known as the Prager Asbestwerke Hermann & Co., he seems to have begun by taking a surprisingly positive attitude to it, perhaps out of a desire to prove to his father that he was worthy of his respect. He told Karl Hermann's younger brother Paul that he had advised his father to invest in the firm, had persuaded Uncle Alfred Löwy to do likewise, and had even put some of his own money into it.

In October and November Kafka met Karl Hermann and the lawyer Dr Robert Kafka (son of Hermann Kafka's cousin, Heinrich) to draw up the contract of partnership. There is a profound irony in Kafka sponsoring an asbestos factory when today that product is known as one of the world's most horrifying industrial killers and its manufacture has been outlawed in most countries. This, of course, was not known at the time, asbestos being seen as an exciting new product. (By dying so young, Kafka, a man with a deep compassion for the hardships faced by industrial workers, was at least spared the anguish and guilt he would certainly have felt if he had lived to see the facts about asbestos come to the fore.) Kafka spent valuable time in autumn 1911 on the project. This involved consulting Dr Robert Kafka on the legal aspects of the factory, and while the latter was 'a very good storyteller . . . with the vivacious speech that one often finds in such fat, black Jews',[10] Kafka would rather have been elsewhere, specifically at the theatre.

The appearance of the troupe of Yiddish actors from Lemberg in Galicia was a gratifying distraction for the harried Kafka, and their performances thrilled him. After the first night at the Café Savoy on 4 October of the Yiddish play *Der Meschumed/The Apostate*, by Josef Lateiner, Kafka was immediately captivated, especially by Frau Flora Klug, the male impersonator. Kafka was under no illusions about the artistic quality of the Yiddish theatre, though he allowed himself to be moved by its cheap effects ('Some songs . . . made my cheeks tremble'[11]). He was, however, fascinated by what it represented, by its expression of a direct, passionate, earthy Jewish culture. The actors, it seemed to him, were 'very close to the centre of the community's life . . . people who are Jews in an especially pure form because they live only in the religion, but live in it without effort, understanding or distress'. As Ritchie Robertson puts it, 'In their company, Kafka could feel that he was no longer being labelled a Jew by the more or less hostile Gentile world; he was not compelled to accept other people's definitions of him; he was able to be a Jew and revel in it.'[12] The lonely, anxious, tormented, confused Kafka of those silent watches of the night suddenly found himself at the heart of a boisterous communal experience and one to which he felt himself entitled to claim allegiance. He was experiencing the unusual pleasure of discovering a place where he might belong. He wanted to know and see more of this theatrical tradition and to know more about Yiddish literature in general, 'which is obviously characterized by an uninterrupted tradition of national struggle that determines every work. A tradition, therefore, that pervades no other literature, not even that of the most oppressed people.'[13]

Noticing the protruding front teeth of one of the actresses, Fräulein Kaufman, Kafka reflected: 'If I reach my fortieth year, then I'll probably marry an old maid with protruding upper teeth left a little exposed by the upper lip.'[14] His hypochondria suggested to him that forty (the age when he would die) would not be reached because of a tension over the left half of his skull, which felt to him 'like an inner leprosy'.

On his 3 October visit to the Savoy, Kafka was more critical of the play – Abraham Goldfaden's *Sulamith*. He found it 'stubborn, hasty and passionate for the wrong reasons'[15] as an artistic endeavour – and the performance ended in farce. The actor Yitzhak Löwy – 'whom I would admire in the dust'[16] – should have appeared after the curtain call to invite everyone to the following night's performance. Instead a scuffle broke out between the actors which resulted in Löwy being ejected by the head waiter of the Savoy.

Löwy was the director and moving force behind the troupe, and he and Kafka became close friends – to the consternation of Hermann Kafka, who didn't want these wild, gypsy-like Jews in his house. 'Whoever lies down with dogs gets up with fleas'[17] was the proverb that Hermann tossed at his son as his comment on this undesirable liaison. The actor, at twenty-four years old, was four years younger than Kafka, and had been born in Warsaw into an ultra-Orthodox family of Hasidic Jews. He ran away at the age of seventeen to Paris, where he did odd jobs and dabbled in amateur Yiddish theatre, which would have been anathema to his Orthodox parents. After joining a professional troupe in 1907, he toured the Jewish communities of Europe. Later, after 1912, he settled in Berlin as a touring base. From Vienna in 1913 he wrote to Kafka in his imperfect grammar: 'You were after all the only one what was so good to me . . . the only one what spoke to my soul, the only one what half understood me.'[18] They last saw each other in Budapest in July 1917. Löwy – in a fate comparable to that of so many of the names that will be encountered in the following pages – died in the death camp of Treblinka in 1942. There is an amusing fictionalization of him in Isaac Bashevis Singer's story 'A Friend of

Kafka', where the narrator says of Kafka that he 'wanted to be a Jew, but he didn't know how. He wanted to live, but he didn't know this either . . . He was sunk to his neck in the bourgeois swamp.'[19]

The plays of the Yiddish theatre – or *Jargontheater*, as it was known – were mostly written between 1880 and 1910, and, according to one scholar, they were 'immune to the revolution in modern drama at that time'.[20] It is possible that some of the characteristics of Kafka's writing – such as his reliance on gesture and exaggerated action, as well as the dark humour and comic irony – may be traced back to the overemphatic acting styles of the Lemberg troupe. It was not long after his experience of the *Jargontheater* that he wrote *Das Urteil/The Judgement*, which was the first significant demonstration of his more dramatic style.

Unlike Hebrew, which is an ancient Semitic tongue, Yiddish is an Indo-European language that developed from medieval German and became the vernacular of the ghettoes of Eastern Europe. It was not really familiar – or welcome – to the Westernized Jews of Prague, which explains Hermann Kafka's negative reaction to it. This was precisely the sort of thing that, as an upwardly mobile businessman in the city, he was trying to leave behind. His son's passionate attachment to the *Jargontheater* was thus another form of rebellion against Hermann's world and person. It is also symptomatic of that power of sympathetic identification which he displayed with his interest in Czech culture. In a long entry in his diary on the phenomenon of a 'small literature',[21] Kafka argued, on the basis of what he knew about contemporary Jewish literature in Warsaw through Löwy, and of contemporary Czech literature through his own insight, that many of the 'benefits' of literature may be produced by a literature whose development 'is not in actual fact unusually broad in scope, but seems to be, because it lacks outstanding talents'. Those benefits included 'the stirring of minds, the coherence of national consciousness . . . the pride which a nation gains from a literature of its own and the support it is afforded in the face of the hostile surrounding world, this keeping of a diary by a nation [*dieses Tagebuchführen einer Nation*] which is something entirely different from historiography . . . the spiritualization of the broad area of public life . . . the constant integration of a people with respect to its whole that the incessant bustle of the magazines creates'. Kafka believed that in a small literature there was a more lively and direct involvement by the people in its promotion and defence: 'literature is less a concern of literary history than of the people'. In short, the social aspects of Yiddish literature appealed to this lonely, secluded talent.

Kafka attended about twenty Yiddish plays between the autumn of 1911 and the spring of the following year. He filled his notebooks with summaries of the plots and descriptions of the actors. He pumped Löwy for information about the customs and culture of the Eastern Jews, whom Kafka saw as somehow more authentic than the compromised, often assimilated Western Jews of his father's ilk. Even at a business meeting he found himself noticing 'the Eastern Jewish gestures' of his client and the 'temple melodies in the cadence of his speech'.[22] It is fair to say that Kafka had become obsessed.

Unfortunately, his theatre-going offered only temporary relief from the normal pressures on him: work, writing and the family business. One precious Sunday that should have been spent writing, instead saw him setting off to the working-class district of Žižkov to plead with his father's bookkeeper to return to work. As a protest at their boss's behaviour, the 'paid enemies'[23] (Hermann's term for his Czech staff) at the shop had given notice *en masse*. 'By soft words, cordiality, effective use of his illness, his size and former strength, his experience, his cleverness,'[24] the wily Hermann had persuaded all but the bookkeeper back to work. Kafka was sent to heal the breach, by deploying some 'Czech arguments', but his efforts seem to have been in vain. So another day was wasted, and the next he was lamenting: 'I finish nothing because I have no time and it presses so within me . . . Shall I be able to bear it long?'[25]

In contrast, after a reading by Löwy of Yiddish and Hebrew poems and sketches, he 'felt all my abilities concentrated'.[26] He was now in love with one of the actresses, Mania Tschissik, and filled his notebooks with descriptions of her acting and her person ('the sudden flutter of a shudder upon my cheekbone, which I always feel when I hear her voice'[27]). It was clearly a powerful sexual attraction, but it came to nothing.

These reflections on roots and belonging were causing Kafka to re-examine his relations with his family. 'Yesterday it occurred to me that I did not always love my mother as she deserved and as I could,' he noted, 'only because the German language prevented it. The Jewish mother is no "*Mutter*", to call her "*Mutter*" makes her a little comic . . . I believe that it is only the memories of the ghetto that still preserve the Jewish family, for the word "*Vater*" too is far from meaning the Jewish father.'[28] Kafka was increasingly open to those 'memories of the ghetto' because of the impact of the actors whose performances he was attending repeatedly. He started to read, as a supplement to Löwy's oral information, *The History of the Jews* by Heinrich Graetz, and consumed it with such passion that 'I had to stop here and there in order by resting to allow my Jewishness to collect itself.'[29]

Yet, in spite of this new arrival of energy and fresh perspective in his life, the irreducible struggle to write continued. Sitting at the family table where they were playing cards, 'with unusual uproar',[30] he could only reflect miserably on the fact that 'I lead a horrible, synthetic life . . . the possible happiness becomes ever more impossible.' There is a sense of life passing him by, of time running out. On 1 November he confessed: 'This afternoon the pain occasioned by my loneliness came upon me so piercingly and intensely that I became aware that the strength which I gain through this writing thus spends itself, a strength which I certainly have not intended for this purpose.'[31] His frustrations were taken out on himself, as a startling diary entry confirms: 'This morning, for the first time in a long time, the joy again of imagining a knife twisted in my heart.'[32] Might this have been an example of his own maxim that 'the impetuosity of language often leads one astray'[33]? The sheer noise and bustle of the Kafka apartment were enough to prevent any serious attempts at writing: 'I sit in my room in the very headquarters of the uproar of the entire house. I hear all the doors close . . . I hear even the slamming of the oven door in the kitchen. My father bursts through the doors of my room and passes through in his dragging dressing gown, the ashes are scraped out of the stove in the next room . . . a hushing that claims to be friendly to me raises the shout of an answering voice. The house door is unlatched and screeches as though from a catarrhal throat.'[34] When the canaries started to sing, Kafka was near to breaking point and thought 'that I might open the door a narrow crack, crawl into the next room like a snake and in that way, on the floor, beg my sisters and their governess for quiet'. Surely the transformation in *Metamorphosis* is gestating here. These interruptions meant that his writing was coming out in fits and starts: 'I have too little time and quiet to draw out of me all the possibilities of my talent . . . If I were ever able to write something large and whole, well shaped from beginning to end, then in the end the story would never be able to detach itself from me.'[35]

The persistence – and the hopelessness – of Kafka's love for Mrs Tschissik the actresss reminded him forcefully of the fact that not only had he failed to give birth to a satisfactory book, but he had failed in what was to become an increasingly important goal for him: marriage and raising a family. He never faltered in his belief that this was his proper destiny, but it was one that would forever elude him. At the lawyer's office, working on the contractual details of the asbestos factory, a clause was read out about shares in the company and the possible future wife and possible children of the partner, Dr Kafka. Franz found himself looking at a table with two large chairs and a smaller one around it: 'At the thought that I should never be in a position to seat in these or any other three chairs myself, my wife and child, there came over me a yearning for this happiness so despairing from the very start that in my excitement I asked the lawyer the only question I had left after the long reading, which at once revealed my complete misunderstanding of a rather long section of the agreement that had just been read.'[36] It was around this time that Kafka wrote the short piece which begins: 'It seems so dreadful to be a bachelor . . .' and which was published in his first collection of fiction, *Betrachtung*. He was beginning to wonder if he would become like his bachelor uncle Alfred Löwy in Madrid, and after a conversation with his mother about marriage and children towards the end of the year he was convinced 'how untrue and childish is the conception of me that my mother builds up for herself'.[37] She considered that if he were to get married and have children, all his hypochondria and anxiety would vanish, his interest in literature would decline to a professional man's sideline or hobby, and he would find himself concentrating on his career, like any normal person.

Needless to say, Kafka did not see it that way. Whatever the difficulties and obstacles he was currently experiencing, his intuition that he was capable of great things continued to possess him. One night he lay on his bed 'and again became aware of all my abilities as though I were holding them in my hand . . . capable of anything and restrained only by powers which are indispensable for my very life and are here being wasted'.[38]

Irrespective of whether his mother was right about his problems being to some degree psychosomatic, the fact is that Kafka's health – or, more broadly, his sense of his own body – clearly exerted a powerful influence over his writing and his sense of what he could achieve in that sphere. After a visit to the apartment by his former governess (about whom he was rather rude) Kafka threw himself on the bed and complained how 'my joints ache with fatigue, my dried-up body trembles towards its own destruction in turmoils of which I dare not become fully conscious, in my head are astonishing convulsions'.[39] Kafka was always able to find someone or something to blame for his distress, and this time it was his body: 'It is certain that a major obstacle to my progress is my physical condition,' he decided. 'Nothing can be accomplished with such a body [*Mit einem solchen Körper läßt sich nichts erreichen*]. I shall have to get used to its perpetual balking . . . My body is too long for its weakness, it hasn't the least bit of fat to engender a blessed warmth, to preserve an inner fire, no fat on which the spirit could occasionally nourish itself beyond its daily need without damage to the whole.'[40] He could see that his state of health was hampering his writing – 'On what circumstances my way of life makes me dependent!' – but it is not clear to what extent his health problems were real or imagined at this stage. There is no record of his being unable to go to work and no reports of visits to doctors. Perhaps his mother's robust scepticism wasn't entirely misplaced.

But the lamentations continued: 'Yesterday evening I felt especially miserable. My stomach was upset again . . . the dismal future immediately before me seemed not worth entering, abandoned . . . I once more thought about the more distant future. How would I live through it with this body picked up in a lumber room?'[41] A clue to one of the deeper causes of Kafka's malaise can be found in his reference to the Talmud, saying: 'A man without a woman is no person.' His rediscovered sense of his Jewish destiny told him that he should marry and have children. Perhaps an infatuation with a travelling player was not the best way to go about it.

Meanwhile, he continued to chase more of those random, fleeting intuitions about his destiny as a writer which fascinate in his diary entries. In December he finally finished his contribution to the joint novel with Brod, *Richard and Samuel*, judging it a success. 'Even more, I think that something is happening within me that is very close to Schiller's transformation of emotion into character. Despite all the resistance of my inner being I must write this down.'[42] He had 'a great yearning to write all my anxiety entirely out of me, write it into the depths of the paper just as it comes out of the depths of me, or write it down in such a way that I could draw what I had written into me completely. This is no artistic yearning.'[43] Reading Wilhelm Schäfer's life of the artist Karl Stauffer, he felt 'caught up and held fast by this powerful impression forcing its way into that inner part of me which I listen to and learn from only at rare intervals . . . I must write.'[44]

As 1911 drew to a close, and through the cloud of ill-health that seems to have hung over him in the middle of December, Kafka continued to reflect on his literary career and whether he could realistically devote himself to it full time. After an argument with his father about his indifference to the affairs of the asbestos factory, in which he said he could not take an active part while he remained at the Institute, he caught himself wondering if he really did want to write full time: 'I disputed my ability to devote all my time to literature.'[45] He thought that if ever he were 'set free' from the office he would 'yield at once to my desire to write an autobiography',[46] a project he never accomplished, though *Letter to the Father* showed what it might have been like. Nevertheless, he continued to work at the Institute and increasingly came to believe that literature was indeed the only vocation for him, the only way of living that gave meaning to his life, even if it made no sense to the rest of the world. His family, who saw his life 'going in a direction that is foreign and false'[47] to them, feared – and his father said so explicitly – that he would become 'a second Uncle Rudolf, the fool of the new generation of the family'. The factory was a running sore and caused him 'torment', and only his father's reproaches, Karl's silent disdain and his own guilt made him do the little that he did to take an interest. Precious hours were dedicated to it, and if he were to sacrifice any more it would lead to 'the complete destruction of my existence, which, even apart from this, becomes more and more hedged in'.[48]

The sense that Kafka was moving towards some sort of resolution – that he must realize these intuitions of literary potential or remain permanently frustrated and incomplete – had intensified throughout 1911. The new year would see him working through those frustrations finally to produce a major piece of literature.

9

Kafka was now moving steadily towards a total commitment to writing in order, in some sense, to define his whole existence. The obvious constraints on such an absolute dedication remained unchanged – work, family, the uncooperative physical body – but he now began to believe that his incapacity in other directions demanded a retrenchment to the one activity he knew he could do well. 'It is easy to recognize a concentration in me of all my forces on writing,'[1] he wrote in his journal at the beginning of January 1912.

> When it became clear in my organism that writing was the most productive direction for my being to take, everything rushed in that direction and left empty all those abilities which were directed towards the joys of sex, eating, drinking, philosophical reflection and above all music. I atrophied in all those directions. This was necessary because the totality of all my strengths was so slight that only collectively could they even halfway serve the purpose of my writing . . . My development is now complete and, so far as I can see, there is nothing left to sacrifice; I need only throw my work in the office out of this complex in order to begin my real life in which, with the progress of my work, my face will finally be able to age in a natural way.

The calm clarity with which Kafka sets out his programme for himself here, its serene logic, was not a harbinger of the reality to follow. He was about to enter into a period that would test his reserves of moral and intellectual strength to the utmost degree. His writing would triumph – he himself would see his performance during this year as a breakthrough – but his personal life would turn into a long and anguished trial, one in which he could not fathom why he was in the dock and on what charge.

Meanwhile, the Yiddish players were still in town, and Kafka was obsessively gathering information about them, about the life of Löwy, the habits and culture of the Ostjuden, and the history of Jewish literature. He read 'greedily'[2] a 500-page book by Pines, *L'Histoire de la Littérature Judéo-Allemande* – and continued to dote on the divine Mrs Tschissik. He found it increasingly hard, however, to ignore the inferior literary quality of the plays. Whereas the first discovery of them had made it possible for him to think that 'I had come upon a Judaism on which the beginnings of my own rested, a Judaism that was developing in my direction and so would enlighten and carry me farther along in my own clumsy Judaism,'[3] they were now moving him away from that goal. Nevertheless, 'The people remain, of course, and I hold fast to them.'

On 18 February Kafka organized an evening of recitations by Löwy in the Main Hall of the Jewish Town Hall in Prague. 'For two weeks I worried for fear that I could not produce the lecture. On the evening before the lecture I suddenly succeeded.'[4] Kafka felt, in the days running up to the event, that he had become 'more nervous, weaker, and have lost a large part of the calm on which I prided myself years ago . . . So little physical strength!'[5] In fact, he experienced a 'proud, unearthly consciousness during my lecture (coolness in the presence of the audience, only the lack of practice kept me from using enthusiastic gestures freely) . . . In all this are revealed powers to which I would gladly entrust myself if they would remain.'[6] Before the readings proper began, Kafka – who, in spite of his shyness, was an excellent reader and adored reciting from his own and others' work – stood up to deliver an address on the Yiddish language. He told his audience that he planned to say something 'about how much more Yiddish you understand than you think'.[7] He claimed that many of his Prague Jewish audience were so 'frightened' of the language 'that one can almost see it in your faces', conceding that 'dread of Yiddish, dread mingled with a certain fundamental distaste', was understandable. He then argued that Western European culture was well ordered, quiet and characterized by mutual understanding between people, making 'the tangle of Yiddish' inherently puzzling. It was the youngest European language, only four hundred years old. 'It has not yet developed any linguistic forms of a lucidity such as we need. Its idiom is brief and rapid.' No grammars of Yiddish existed, and it was essentially a spoken language in continuous flux: 'The people will not leave it to the grammarians.' Moreover, it consisted solely of foreign words that have passed through this shifting lexical landscape in a 'whirl of language', a 'linguistic medley of whim and law'. No doubt to a ripple of laughter in the Town Hall, Kafka declared: 'I think I have for the present convinced most of you, ladies and gentlemen, that you will not understand a word of Yiddish.'

Yet he went on to maintain that German speakers ought to be able to understand Yiddish, and that the familiar colloquial language of German Jews (he would be thinking of his own family, who pointedly stayed away from the lecture) seemed to be 'a remoter or a closer approximation to Yiddish'. For this reason, such people should be able to understand Yiddish 'intuitively' and once the language – 'and Yiddish is everything, the words, the Hasidic melody, and the essential character of this Eastern Jewish actor himself' – had taken hold of them they would shed their reserve. 'Then you will come to feel the true unity of Yiddish, and so strongly that it will frighten you, yet it will no longer be fear of Yiddish but of yourselves.' He hopes that this fear will fade, 'For we did not set out to punish you.'

This short address demonstrates the hold that Yiddish culture now had over Kafka. A certain excess of drama in the argument may be traceable to his infatuation with the swirling excess of its idiom. It is also worth noting that one of the poems he introduced was 'Die Grine' ('The Greenhorns') by Morris Rosenfeld, which concerns a group of new Jewish arrivals in America who are glimpsed by the poet walking along a street dragging their seedy luggage. By this time, Kafka may already have started to write his first novel, *Der Verschollene/The Man Who Disappeared* (formerly known by the title Brod gave it, *Amerika*), the theme of which is emigration to the New World.

Classical German literature – in the shape of Goethe – was not being neglected by Kafka in favour of the Yiddish writers. He had always been a devoted admirer of Goethe, and the previous month some books on him brought to Kafka by his friend Felix Weltsch had provoked 'a distracted excitement'[8] and a desire to write an essay on 'Goethe's Frightening Nature'. Several days later, immersed in books about Goethe, he was filled with a 'zeal, permeating every part of me'[9] which prevented him from writing. He had been reading both biographical works and the German writer's famous autobiography, *Dichtung und Wahrheit/Poetry and Truth*. Overwhelmed by the great poet, Kafka felt that 'an incessant excitement [exacerbated, of course, by preparing the Yiddish lecture] has been oppressing me for days . . . I read sentences of Goethe's as though my whole body were running down the stresses'. Kafka appears to have been working himself into a state of hyper-excitement such that even the 'beautiful silhouette' of Goethe in one of his books served as a reproach to Kafka's lowering sense of his own body: 'My impatience and grief because of my exhaustion are nourished especially on the prospect of the future that is thus prepared for me and which is never out of my sight.

What evenings, walks, despair in bed and on the sofa are still before me, worse than those I have already endured!'[10] He worried that his 'literary mission' was making him dangerously single-minded and 'heartless'.[11]

Many of Kafka's diary entries in the first months of 1912 are preoccupied with the need to concentrate his forces and produce the sustained work that he felt was in him. 'Complete knowledge of oneself. To be able to seize the whole of one's abilities like a little ball' [12] was one desideratum scribbled down in early April. In May the first chapter of his joint novel with Brod, *Richard and Samuel*, was published in the *Herderblätter*, edited by Willy Haas. He was now definitely at work on *The Man Who Disappeared* and was making it an anchor for his turbulent feelings: 'How I hold fast to my novel against all restlessness, like a figure on a monument that looks into the distance and holds fast to its pedestal.'[13] Later, he was struck by a similar observation made by another of his literary idols, Gustave Flaubert, who said in one of his letters: 'My novel is the cliff on which I am hanging, and I know nothing of what is happening in the world.'[14]

In June Kafka and Brod decided to take a holiday, in the course of which they would visit the Goethehaus at Weimar. They set off on the 28th for a month, but the vacation does not seem to have given Kafka any respite from his anxieties. He was in 'a prolonged, irresistible dissatisfaction'[15] at not being able to make progress on his novel and wondered bitterly if he were not being pursued by demons: 'Only a crowd of devils could account for our earthly misfortunes.' As usual, the two friends kept a travel diary, and their first stop after Dresden was Leipzig, where Brod took Kafka to meet the young publisher Karl Wolff, of the firm Ernst Rowohlt. Wolff later recalled the arrival of the pair on that afternoon of 29 June at the shabby editorial offices: Brod struck him as an impresario bringing in his shy star performer and Kafka seemed 'Silent, awkward, delicate, vulnerable, intimidated like a gymnast in front of the judges, convinced of the unlikelihood that through the impresario's praises his expectations would ever be fulfilled.'[16] Wolff was mesmerized by Kafka's 'beautiful eyes', touching expression and a complete absence of authorial self-regard. Kafka then said something to Wolff which the publisher had never heard from an author and would never hear again: 'I will always be as grateful to you for the return of my manuscript as for the publication.' Kafka was the most undemanding of authors from the publisher's point of view. Wolff, who was to publish Kafka's first book in 1913, said that he always felt fearful of penetrating into his world. He also felt that there was no development in Kafka: 'He would not become; he was. His first prose work knew his last, the last was his first.' Kafka observed laconically in his diary that night: 'Rowohlt was rather serious about wanting a book from me.'[17]

Next day Kafka arrived at Weimar late in the evening and walked at night to the Goethehaus. 'Recognized it at once . . . Felt the whole of our previous life share in the immediate impression.'[18] The following day they left their 'quiet, pretty hotel',[19] visited the Schillerhaus and then returned to the Goethehaus, where the study and bedroom struck Kafka as 'Sad, reminding one of dead grandfathers.' Kafka's attention was soon caught by a pretty young girl called Grete Kirchner, whose father was the custodian of the Goethehaus. Urged on by Max, Kafka eventually formed 'a definite contact',[20] but it was a rather unsatisfactory flirtation consisting of random sightings – at a strawberry festival, for instance, where he noted: 'The suppleness of her body in its loose dress.'[21] A photograph was taken with the couple on a bench, which survives.[22] 'She smiled at me meaninglessly, purposelessly, behind her father's back. Sad.' At another hasty meeting he presented Grete with a box of chocolates with a little heart and chain twined about it. Ultimately, though, he realized that this was going nowhere: 'Had nothing in common with her.'[23]

On 8 July Kafka and Brod parted. The former went on to the

Jungborn nature therapy (*Naturheilkunde*) establishment in the Harz Mountains. Founded in 1896 by Adolf Just, the private spa at Jungborn was dedicated to the natural way of life (*Naturleben*), which boiled down to nudism, hydrotherapy, mud packs and a vegetarian diet.[24] Kafka was particularly fond of the 'sun and air cabins' ('*Lichtlufthäuschen*') and relished the absence of orthodox doctors. Back in March he had railed against 'these revolting doctors! Businesslike, determined and so ignorant of healing . . . I wish I had the strength to found a nature-cure society.'[25] He soon settled in to his cabin in the woods, which was open on three sides, and attended a lecture on clothing by the nature-doctor, who told him to take 'atmospheric baths' (those '*Luftbäder*' again) at night but to avoid exposing himself to too much moonlight, which 'has an injurious effect'.[26]

Kafka slipped out of bed, presumably naked, and took his atmospheric baths in the meadow in front of his cabin. There were also group gymnastics (a photograph of Jungborn shows a field full of naked folk in rigid drill-patterns), hymn-singing, military bands, ball-playing in a big circle and hay-making. Kafka was a little shy about joining in the public nudist activities and was nicknamed 'the man in the swimming trunks' ('*der Mann mit den Schwimmhosen*'). He confided to his diary: 'When I see these stark-naked people moving slowly past among the trees . . . I now and then get light, superficial attacks of nausea . . . Old men who leap naked over hay-stacks are no particular delight to me, either.'[27] Another hilarious photograph (reproduced by Wagenbach) shows a senior military officer with an enormous handlebar moustache, a vast belly, a swordbelt, a towering Wilhelmine helmet, but nothing else, taking a salute from a junior officer with a mere spiked helmet and a strategically placed newspaper.[28]

Whatever the efficacy of the nature therapy, three weeks in the fresh air for the anxious, hard-worked Kafka, with no office, no family criticism, no worries about the asbestos factory to bother him, could only have been beneficial. He was reading voraciously in his cabin – the Bible, Schiller, Plato, Flaubert (*L'Éducation sentimentale*, one of his favourite books) – and keeping his usual eye out for pretty young women. He danced at an evening hop with a girl called Auguste who wore a white blouse with flowers embroidered over her arms and shoulders. The melancholy girl was about to enter a convent 'because of the bad experiences she had had'.[29] Then there was a teacher, Frau Gerloff, with an 'owl-like, vivacious young face . . . Her body is more indolent.'[30] But no serious attachment seems to have formed during this stay, even if Grete Kirchner did write. 'Do you suppose it is true that one can attach girls to oneself by writing?'[31] he asked Brod in a letter that, in view of future events, has a painfully unintended irony.

Although Kafka was trying to take the therapy seriously and 'stuffing himself like a sausage' to fatten himself up, his residual problems remained. One of these was the difficulty of relating to other people. 'I came here partly for people,' he told Brod. 'How do I live in Prague, after all? This craving for people, which I have and which is transformed into anxiety once it is fulfilled, finds an outlet only during vacations.' The other problem was writing. Each day Kafka went to the writing room at Jungborn, where he sat alone and unproductive for an hour, no advance being made on *The Man Who Disappeared*. He was stabbed by the familiar writer's pangs of self-doubt – 'today some insights into the inferiority of my writing dawned on me . . . But it does not matter, I cannot stop writing; it is therefore a pleasure that can be tested to the core without harm.' Nevertheless, he worried that there was something about his life and experience to date which left him undernourished as a writer, possibly a lack of excess: 'I have never been the sort of person who carried something out at all costs . . . What I have written was written in a lukewarm bath. I have not experienced the eternal hell of real writers [*die ewige Hölle der wirklichen Schriftsteller habe ich nicht erlebt*].'[32] In the years since Kafka's death some critics have felt the same. One of the most famous dissenters was the robust American critic Edmund Wilson, who wrote in 1950 that the reputation of Kafka was being 'wildly overdone'.[33] Wilson felt that Kafka was appealing to those precious intellectuals who found that he gave expression to 'their emotions of helplessness and self-contempt'. He admired Kafka as a short-story writer, but felt that the two most famous novels were 'rather ragged performances', not finished or properly worked out (the best part of Wilson's argument, which needs to be taken seriously). He also stressed Kafka's love of Flaubert and noted the failure of Kafka critics to give due weight to the Flaubertian irony of his writing in their rush to treat him as a tragic metaphysician. Wilson was unimpressed by the religious and metaphysical claims being made in mid-century for Kafka, and concluded devastatingly: 'What he has left us is the half-expressed gasp of a self-doubting soul trampled under. I do not see how one can possibly take him for either a great artist or a moral guide.'

There is little evidence that Kafka criticism took much notice of Wilson, but the challenge remains for those who wish to view Kafka objectively and to take his full measure (and one thinks also in this context of another potent dissenting opinion, that of Primo Levi, who wished that Kafka had moved more forcefully towards the light). Some of these critics, one feels, were not attending to Kafka's very real sense of wanting to be positive in the very way they outlined. In this context a comment by Jorge Luis Borges is more perceptive. He said of Kafka: 'One could define his work as a parable or a series of parables whose theme is the moral relation of the individual with God and with His incomprehensible universe. Despite this contemporary ambience, Kafka is closer to the Book of Job than to what has been called "modern literature". His work is based on a religious, and particularly Jewish, consciousness; its imitation in other contexts becomes meaningless.'[34] As Kafka's exploration of his Jewishness deepened, his sense of the need for some more solid foundation to a work of art grew. The argument that he wished his work destroyed after his death because he feared it would not yield that profounder hope is persuasive.

On 28 July Kafka returned to Prague and to more 'torment' over his writing. Rowohlt wanted to publish his first collection of fiction, *Betrachtung* (*Meditation* or *Reflection*), but he was anxious that some of the pieces were simply not good enough. Free of the usual authorial vanity, Kafka had gone to the other extreme of an excess of scrupulousness and challenged Brod to agree that it was wrong 'to have something bad published with my eyes open',[35] as he now believed was the case with his two fictional fragments 'Conversations with a Supplicant' and 'Conversations with a Drunk', published as *Description of a Struggle* in *Hyperion* back in the spring of 1909. There were worse things than being unpublished, and 'this damnable forcing oneself' was tearing him apart. In a premonition of that dying request to Brod to destroy all his unpublished work, Kafka declared to his friend: 'We can allow bad things to remain finally bad only on our deathbed.' To his journal, he complained: 'How much time the publishing of the little book takes from me and how much harmful, ridiculous pride comes from reading old things with an eye to publication.'[36] He resolved to avoid magazine and review publishing from now on 'if I do not wish to be content with just sticking the tips of fingers into the truth'. He wrote to Rowohlt an extraordinary letter that told of his enforced choice 'between satisfying my sense of responsibility and an eagerness to have a book among your beautiful books'.[37] He added: 'Isn't what is most universally individual in writers the fact that each conceals his bad qualities in an entirely different way?'

Kafka's touchstone of truth was found in one of his favourite writers, Franz Grillparzer (1791–1872), a dramatist whose novella *Der arme Spielmann*/*The Poor Musician* had just been given an 'inspired'[38] reading aloud by Kafka. Grillparzer, a playwright and short-story writer, is probably not now well known to English-speaking readers – no English translation even of the famous novella is currently in print – but he had an enormous influence on Kafka (who could not have ignored the father–son conflict at the heart of *Der arme Spielmann*). 'The way he can risk everything and risks nothing, because there is nothing but truth in him already,' marvelled Kafka. Grillparzer's diaries show that he too lived the frustrated life of a bureaucrat, in Vienna (where he was director of the court archive), and was engaged to a woman whom he could not make up his mind to marry.

On 14 August Kafka was at the home of Max Brod. That evening he made the acquaintance of a young businesswoman from Berlin, Felice Bauer. The encounter was sufficiently memorable for Kafka to write in his journal: 'Thought much of – what embarrassment before writing down names – F.B.'[39] He could not have known what a trial the relationship with this young woman would prove – for both of them – over the next five years. Kafka would tear himself apart over Felice, yet the experience came at just the moment when his writing was achieving a measure of success. The autumn of 1912 would thus be for Kafka an emotional and artistic upheaval quite without precedent in his life so far.

PART II

Felice

10

Felice Bauer (her family is said to have pronounced her first name in the French manner) was four years younger than Kafka. She was, he admitted at the end of his life, 'not beautiful', though he admired her 'slender, fine body'.[1] She was strong and capable, but her suitability for Kafka – and his for her – was never obvious.

Felice was born in Neustadt, Upper Silesia, on 18 November 1887. Her Viennese father had married the daughter of a Neustadt dyer, but in 1899 the family moved to Berlin, where her father worked for a foreign company as an insurance agent. Five years later he left to be with his mistress, and stayed away until 1910. After leaving school in 1908, Felice went out to work to help her mother support her four brothers and sisters. The other members of the family relied on her countervailing stability: her brother was a swindler who fled to America, and her unmarried elder sister was pregnant around the time Felice's relationship with Kafka began. Felice was the only member of the family to know this. She worked briefly as a shorthand-typist with the Odeon record company, then in 1909 joined the Berlin firm Carl Lindström, which manufactured a dictating machine known as the Parlograph. The machine – whose technology fascinated Kafka – looks today rather cumbersome: it was mounted on a wooden box about eighteen inches wide, six inches high and six inches deep. It consisted of a wax recording drum and a mouthpiece with the serpentine twist of a Middle Eastern hookah and an adjustable lever to control the speed of recording or playback on a scale from *langsam* to *schnell*. A perfectly preserved example can be seen today in the National Museum of Technology in Prague. Felice, one of the new breed of efficient businesswomen (*die Angestellte*[2]) at the start of the twentieth century, was soon promoted to executive secretary at the firm. In March 1913 the now reunited family moved from Berlin's East End to Wilmersdorfstrasse in the smart West End, where the suitor from Prague would be received and, somewhat balefully, assessed by the Bauers.

Felice was solidly middle class, and more interested in soft furnishings than in Franz Grillparzer. Kafka's final lover, Dora Diamant, who did not meet Felice and was presumably relying on Kafka's account, told an interviewer after the war: 'She was an excellent girl, but utterly bourgeois. Kafka felt that marrying her would mean marrying the whole lie that was Europe.'[3] This was an observation made with the benefit of hindsight, for Kafka initially pursued Felice with determination. She seems to have had no interest in his work, nor was she a source of great sexual attraction for him, as far as can be established. Because her letters to Kafka have not been preserved, in contrast to the hundreds of his that have survived, and because she never spoke about him in later years, it will never be known exactly how she saw the relationship. For Kafka, it was frequently a torment and one that added to the pressures on him as a writer. It is almost as if he chose to punish himself. 'For five years,' wrote Max Brod, 'Kafka's strivings to wrest a marriage with Felice from himself and the opposing circumstances were the prevailing motive in his life, the thorn in his creative work and in his harassed religious questionings.'[4] She remained 'an ideal figure [*eine Idealgestalt*] for Franz'. At the same time there is powerful evidence from his diaries and his long and frequent letters to her that he loved Felice during the five years of their involvement with each other. The bulky correspondence with her (the German edition is nearly 800 pages long and the English translation runs to nearly 600 closely printed, anguished pages, longer by far than any of Kafka's full-length fictional works) is sometimes gruelling to read, yet the biographer who wishes to understand Kafka cannot flinch from it. Invariably, letters were started late at night and completed in the early hours when Kafka should have been engaged on his literary work or catching up with his sleep. The first entry in Kafka's diary after he met Felice ('Wasted day. Spent sleeping and lying down'[5]) is ominous. As this correspondence lacks the voice of Felice herself, except in those rare instances when he quotes some phrase back to her in order to answer it, a picture of her can only be deduced. She possessed a strong personality ('you are not fickle'[6]). She increasingly found something slightly weird about her correspondent, whom she hardly ever met in person – this was an epistolary love affair. She too, one assumes, must have been as desperate to marry as Kafka was, and thus prepared to tolerate what should perhaps not have been tolerated. Eventually, after the final breach, she married a prosperous German businessman, moved to Switzerland in 1931, and the United States in 1936, where she died in 1960, five years after she had agreed to release the letters for publication. They were first published as a separate volume in 1967.

Kafka first wrote to Felice, on the letterhead of the Institute, on 20 September 1912. He reminded her of their meeting at the Brod family home and of her promise to allow him to accompany her to Palestine. They never made that trip together, though it was one that Kafka increasingly dreamed of making in his later years as his interest in Zionism grew. 'That night you looked so fresh, even pink-cheeked, and indestructible,' he later recalled of 13 August.[7] 'Did I fall in love with you at once, that night? . . . At first sight I was quite definitely and incomprehensibly indifferent to you.' As they passed into the music room,

Kafka made the 'silly remark' that 'she appeals to me no end' and held on to the table. After she left that night Kafka accompanied her, with Brod's father, to her hotel. 'I still know the precise place on the Graben [today Na Příkopě] where for no reason, yet deliberately owing to my uneasiness, desire and helplessness, I stumbled several times off the sidewalk onto the street. And then instead of ignoring Herr Brod and whispering in my ear: "Come with me to Berlin, drop everything and come!" you were borne aloft in the elevator.'[8] One can imagine what Kafka's reaction would have been had such a romantic solicitation actually been made – hesitation, deferral, inaction. In his diary, Kafka was more candid about that first meeting: 'She was sitting at the table. I was not at all curious about who she was, but rather took her for granted at once. Bony, empty face that wore its emptiness openly. Bare throat. A blouse thrown on. Looked very domestic in her dress although, as it later turned out, she by no means was . . . Almost broken nose. Blond, somewhat straight, unattractive hair, strong chin.'[9] In spite of these less than enraptured notes, Kafka looked at her closely for the first time as he took his seat for supper: 'By the time I was seated I already had an unshakeable opinion.' That tenacity, given the absence of the more obvious indicators of passion in this twenty-nine-year-old man for a twenty-five-year-old woman, is one of the more remarkable things about the five-year involvement with Felice.

This would anyway have been a stirring time for Kafka. Preparations were being made for the publication of *Betrachtung* in November. The contract was returned on 25 September. The tentative writer – who sounds as if he could not overcome his gratitude to the publisher for bringing the book out at all – asked only for the largest possible typeface and wondered (if it were not too much trouble) whether he could have 'a dark cardboard binding with tinted paper',[10] like the firm's edition of the *Anecdotes* of his revered Heinrich von Kleist.

Imminent publication was proving deeply unsettling for Kafka: 'I live as irrationally as is at all possible. And the publication of the thirty-one pages is to blame.'[11] He even found himself wishing that Rowohlt would send back the book 'and I could lock it up again as if it had all never happened, so that I should be only as unhappy as I was before'.[12]

These pre-publication jitters were contributing to his failure to make any progress with *The Man Who Disappeared*. A visit at this time by Uncle Alfred from Spain further unsettled Kafka, who asked his uncle how he managed to be at one and the same time dissatisfied and yet at home everywhere. His uncle replied that, after some pointless social engagement, 'I go home and regret that I didn't marry.'[13] Then his sister, Valli, announced her engagement. Marriage was in the air. But Kafka did not hear back from Felice until the end of September.

And then, out of this tangle of new emotion and old frustration, and excited literary expectation, on the night of 22 September 1912, Kafka sat down at his desk, in his room at No. 36 Niklasstrasse, at 10 p.m., and wrote without a break until the light of the new day. He had come through a Sunday 'so miserable I could have screamed (I had spent the entire afternoon silently circling around my brother-in-law's relatives, who were on their first visit to us)'.[14] He had completed at one sitting – '*in einem Zug*'[15] – the story *Das Urteil/The Judgement*. It was rightly perceived by Kafka as a breakthrough.

Interesting as the *Betrachtung* pieces were, the bold narrative confidence and dramatic clarity of *The Judgement* signalled a leap forward in Kafka's fictional technique. 'I was hardly able to pull my legs out from under the desk, they had got so stiff from sitting,' he wrote the next day. 'The fearful strain and joy, how the story developed before me, as if I were advancing over water. Several times during this night I heaved my own weight on my back. How everything can be said [*Wie alles gesagt werden kann*], how for everything, for the strangest fancies, there waits a great fire in which they perish and rise up again.' At two in the morning Kafka looked up at the clock for the last time. He wrote the last sentence – 'At that moment, the traffic was passing over the bridge in a positively unending stream' – as the maid walked through the anteroom at 6 a.m. She will have seen the undisturbed bed 'as though it had just been brought in'. He stretched and said to her: 'I've been writing until now.' He felt 'slight pains around my heart' and realized how his weariness had disappeared in the middle of the night. For Kafka the conclusion was clear: 'The conviction verified that with my novel-writing I am in the shameful lowlands of writing. Only *in this way* can writing be done, only with such coherence, with such a complete opening out of the body and the soul.'[16] He had let himself go, the story having emerged not as planned ('I meant to describe a war; from his window a young man was to see a vast crowd advancing across the bridge, but then the whole thing turned in my hands into something else'[17]).

That total surrender to the creative moment, the liberating experience of that coherence, or *Zusammenhang*, would, alas, visit Kafka rarely in the years that followed. It would remain his ideal, for which he would sacrifice everything – health, marriage, ordinary human contentment. But for now he could reflect, as he put it later, that 'the story came out of me like a real birth, covered with filth and slime'.[18]

When Kafka made his 'trembling entrance' into his sisters' room to read the story to them while it was still fresh, one of them (probably Ottla) said that the house in the story was 'like ours',[19] to which he replied flippantly: 'In that case, then, Father would have to be living in the toilet.' But the autobiographical element in the story was obvious. In his first reflections on it Kafka also referred to 'thoughts about Freud, of course'.[20] It is his first reference to the psychoanalyst, whose reputation was established firmly by this time, and the central importance of father–son conflict in Kafka's work generally (and in *The*

Judgement in particular) might seem to sanction a classic Freudian approach to its analysis. Kafka, however, appears to make no further explicit references to Freud, though it is possible that the latter influenced some of the images in such stories as *A Country Doctor*.[21] The looming presence in *The Judgement* of Georg Bendemann's father echoes the overwhelming presence in Kafka's life of his own father. It is, in many ways, the fictional counterpart to *Letter to the Father* and inhabits the same world and proceeds from the same fundamental analysis of father–son relationships. The judgement pronounced on Georg by his father at the end of the story – 'I sentence you to death by drowning' – and the son's eager compliance, declaring, as he throws himself into the river (which is hard not to think of as the Vltava), 'Dear parents, I have always loved you, all the same,' reflect Kafka's ambivalent, masochistic attitude to his own parents. The alternative to slaying the father is self-destruction. Georg's futile determination to keep on loving his father even if it brings no reciprocal gesture – the only love the father wants must be expressed through submission to his will – mirrors Kafka's desperate attempt to achieve a proper relationship with Hermann, above all to please him, to be worthy of him.

Also mirrored is the sheer *physicality* of Hermann Kafka's presence in his timid son's life: 'My father is still a giant of a man,' observes Georg even when his parent is ill. 'I am still much the stronger of us two,' the father boasts, and the showing of his scar is the display of ancient machismo, still with the power to mock his son's puny immaturity. Georg's fiancée, Frieda Brandenfeld (we are certainly meant to see Felice Bauer's initials here), is mocked by the father in a crude fashion when he mimics the lifting up of her skirts.

Kafka's self-doubt and self-loathing are projected into this story, including his sexual anxiety about his relationship with Felice (and the possible attitude of his father towards her), his failure to succeed in business in his father's eyes, and his failure to stand up to him, or to attain a proper adult balance with him ('How long you've delayed before coming to maturity!' Georg's father screams at him). There is something of Kafka in both Georg and in 'the friend from Russia' who fails as a businessman and is 'resigning himself to becoming a permanent bachelor'. The friend is in some degree an embodiment of the alternative Kafka, the path he might have taken (like that other man in the East, the actor Löwy?), even if escape led to lack of success. But Kafka later said that there was 'undoubtedly a great deal of my uncle [Alfred Löwy] in *The Judgement*'.[22] He also wrote later, 'The friend is the link between father and son, he is their strongest common bond . . . the father . . . uses the common bond of the friend to set himself up as Georg's antagonist. Georg is left with nothing . . . [O]nly because he himself has lost everything except his awareness of the father does the judgement, which closes off his father from him completely, have so strong an effect on him.'[23] Again, Georg's failure to tell the friend about the engagement could be seen as expressing Kafka's intuitive doubts about Felice. His father's final revelation that he has been writing secretly to the friend from Russia is a way of declaring that he has closed off that path of escape. The judgement follows.

After his first thrilled reaction to the story, Kafka later claimed that he could not understand the real meaning of *The Judgement*. 'I can't find any, nor can I explain anything in it,'[24] he rather surprisingly told Felice nine months later. 'But there are a number of strange things about it.' These included the echoes in the names – Georg has the same number of letters as Franz, Bende has the same number as Kafka, with 'Mann' being there 'probably to fortify him for his struggles'. There were many other parallels, 'all of which, needless to say, I only discovered afterwards'. Possibly Kafka was being deliberately disingenuous here in order to play down the autobiographical implications that the wary Felice may have been pondering.

More convincing was a later retrospective declaration, for the benefit of his lover Milena Jesenská, who was translating the story into Czech: 'Each sentence in this story, each word, each – if I may say so – music is connected with "fear". On this occasion the wound broke open for the first time during one long night.'[25] It is most likely that Kafka's fear – which at that later time of writing to Milena was a word (*Angst*) that was ever more frequently on the tip of his pen – was that the negative bind into which he had entered in relation to his father might never be broken.

The experience of excited fluency that Kafka discovered on the night of 22 September was one he hoped to repeat. In his diary around this time, Brod reports how his friend was in 'ecstasy' at the way his writing was going ('writes whole nights through'[26]). Kafka was still working on *The Man Who Disappeared*, but after one night of writing on 7 October ('I could have written all through the night and the day and the night and the day, and finally have flown away'[27]) he came down with a bump. Far from flying away, he was required, as a partner in the asbestos factory, to deal with certain unpleasant realities. His brother-in-law, Karl Hermann, was off on a fourteen-day business trip, and it was considered by the Kafka family that the factory could not be left in the hands of the foreman alone. This came on top of a recent family campaign to get Kafka to play more of a role. He complained to Brod: 'I was thinking only of how my mother whimpers to me almost every evening that I really should look in on the factory now and then to reassure Father, and of how my father has also said it to me much more strongly by looks and in other roundabout ways.'

The problem was that Kafka was totally unable to provide the necessary supervision. He felt guilty about it, especially because 'in everybody's opinion I bear the chief blame for the establishment of the factory – though I must have assumed this blame in a dream'. Kafka was trapped. It was the busiest time of the year at the shop, which ruled out either of his parents, so in addition to 'the old lament' of his mother 'blaming me for my father's bitterness and sickness', this new complaint was lodged. Even Ottla, his favourite sister and habitual companion in arms against Father, deserted to the enemy, with the result that 'I realized with perfect clarity that now only two possibilities remain open to me, either to jump out of the window once everyone has gone to sleep, or in the next two weeks to go daily to the factory and to my brother-in-law's office.' The former course would 'provide me with the opportunity of shedding all responsibility, both for the disturbance of my writing and for the orphaned factory' and the second would 'absolutely interrupt my writing – I cannot simply wipe from my eyes the sleep of fourteen nights'. It is clear that the consideration of suicide was not rhetorical. Kafka stood for a long time at the window, his head pressed against the pane, wondering whether to throw himself down into Niklasstrasse. Finally, he concluded sardonically that 'my staying alive interrupts my writing less than death', but towards his family his feelings were perfectly clear: 'I hate them all.'

The asbestos factory still stands today in the Žižkov district of Prague. It is now a grim, grey, concrete building, padlocked and derelict. At its height, the factory employed twenty-five people working fourteen gas-driven asbestos-making machines. It was finally liquidated in 1917.

When he read Kafka's near-suicidal letter, Brod was so alarmed ('I was gripped by cold horror'[28]) that he secretly wrote to Kafka's mother. Julie was equally shocked, and replied with shaking hands: 'I, who would give my heart's blood for any of my children, to make them all happy, am helpless in this case.' She proposed that, to spare her husband, who was ill at this time, she would pretend that Franz was making daily visits to the factory, but she would tell him not to do so and would look around instead for another partner to take over his role. The whole episode exposed the false confidence that Kafka expressed when he told Brod, 'nothing coming from outside could disturb my writing now'.

Kafka was further unsettled by the absence of letters from Felice. He heard nothing between 28 September and 23 October, for example. His own letters to her, though written with an inventive verve, were brutally candid about his nervous anxieties. He loved to conjure up the immediate physicality of the experience of writing to her, describing the desk at which he was sitting, or the arrangement of items in his room. 'There was a night when I wrote letters to you continuously while half-asleep, it felt like a continuous soft hammering.'[29] Sometimes he wrote from the Institute on headed paper ('I am just being questioned about insurance for convicts, my God!'[30]). He also started to ask insistent questions about her life in Berlin from which one derives the sense that she was not as forthcoming about herself as he would have wished, though Kafka's standard epistolary manner was to fire off a round of questions to his correspondent.

He told her that next spring Rowohlt would be publishing a *Yearbook of Poetry*, which would contain *The Judgement*. He was going to dedicate it 'To Fräulein Felice B', but wondered: 'Is this dealing too imperiously with your rights?'[31] Kafka repeatedly and somewhat obsessively recalled details of their first meeting on 13 August, such as when he stepped on her feet as they passed through a revolving door, and the fact that he mentioned too often the trip to Palestine. 'I still remember very clearly the way you put on your hat and stuck in the hatpins.'[32] He was delighted when she offered him scraps of information about herself, such as the fact that she had studied Hebrew. 'It also transpired that you were a Zionist and this suited me very well.'[33] He confessed to her that office work was 'completely foreign to me, and bears no relation to my real needs',[34] and told how he would caress her letters in his pocket while he was dictating to his secretary.

By the early part of November Kafka felt confident enough to address her as 'Fräulein Felice' rather than 'Fräulein Bauer' and to embark on the long project of setting before her the detailed inventory of his personal agonies. 'My life consists, and basically always has consisted, of attempts at writing, mostly unsuccessful [he has already forgotten the ecstasy of 22 September].'[35] But when he didn't write he was 'at once flat on the floor, fit for the dustbin. My energies have always been pitifully weak.' Whenever he tried to reach beyond his strength, 'I was automatically forced back, wounded, humbled, forever weakened.' Given that Felice was known for her tough competence as a young businesswoman, this is an interesting tack. 'Just as I am thin,' he went on, 'and I am the thinnest person I know (and that's saying something, for I am no stranger to sanatoria), there is also nothing to me which, in relation to writing, one could call superfluous, superfluous in the sense of overflowing.' He was now thinking all the time of her, but even that preoccupation was related to his writing, for 'my life is determined by nothing but the ups and downs of writing, and certainly during a barren period I should never have had the courage to turn to you'. He was amazed at how intimately she had become associated with his creative output, given that until recently he considered that the only time he did not think about her was when he was writing.

As she heard his complaints, Felice must have wondered what place was being constructed for her in this obsessional writer's existence: 'My mode of life is devised solely for writing, and if there are any changes, then only for the sake of perhaps fitting in better with my writing; for time is short, my strength is limited, the office is a horror, the apartment is noisy, and if a pleasant, straightforward life is not possible then one must try to wriggle through by subtle manoeuvres.' To ram the point home, he explained how in the previous six weeks his timetable had been to go to the Institute between 8 a.m. and 2.30 p.m., have lunch until three or three-thirty, retire to bed for a sleep (if his personal demons permitted it) until seven-thirty, get up, perform ten minutes of exercise naked at the open window, take an hour-long walk, then have dinner with the family. Then, at around 10.30 p.m. (but often it was as late as eleven-thirty), he would sit down to write, and go on, 'depending on my strength, inclination and luck, until 1, 2, or 3 o'clock, once even until 6 in the morning'. After the writing session ended there would be further exercises, a wash and finally, 'usually with a slight pain in my heart and twitching stomach muscles', to bed. Sleep, however, did not always come (gallantly he remembered to mention that wondering if there would be a letter from her was one factor in his sleeplessness), with the result that the next morning, when the inexorable cycle began again, he was bleary-eyed and exhausted, and 'I only just manage to start work with what little strength is left'.

In one of the long corridors at the Institute between him and his typist there was a 'coffinlike' trolley for the moving of files and documents, 'and each time I passed it I felt as though it had been made for me, and was waiting for me'. It is clear from a subsequent letter that Felice protested at this tone and was concerned about his health. He was forced to explain that his visits to sanatoria were only on account of 'my stomach and my general weakness, not forgetting my self-enamoured hypochondria [*selbst verliebten Hypochondrie*]'.[36] She had evidently advised moderation after reading his daily schedule, but he protested: 'Shouldn't I stake all I have on the one thing I can do? What a hopeless fool I should be if I didn't! My writing may be worthless; in which case, I am definitely and without doubt utterly worthless. If I spare myself in this respect, I am not really sparing myself, I am committing suicide.' It does not seem to have occured to him to suggest that a happy marriage to Felice might have been an alternative to this sense of worthlessness. The word 'love' had not yet been exchanged between them – 'on no account will I say it first'.

Kafka's insistence that his writing was the only thing that mattered to him is sometimes contradicted by friends and critics. Brod, for example, observed: 'His literary work was not the be-all and end-all for Kafka, however much many passages in his diary, if taken literally, might seem to say so.'[37] Franz Kuna claimed: 'Kafka's mistrust of literature as an institution was complete. His idea of paradise was a place where there were no books.'[38] The latter claim seems overstated. Although he was uninterested in the fatuities of the 'literary scene', and ploughed an often lonely furrow, Kafka was profoundly bookish, interested in, and subscribing to, literary reviews, publishers' catalogues and magazines with a bibliophile's passion for the shape, feel and look of books. As we have seen above, his whole life was arranged in a careful pattern to put writing at its centre. Brod said that, unlike Flaubert with his cult of art, Kafka had a religious concern with the truth, which was stronger than his aesthetic beliefs. But Brod's habit of making Kafka into a religious figure gets in the way here. Even if Kafka were actually more Flaubertian than Brod allows (there are good grounds for arguing that he was), there is a false dichotomy being set up between 'art' and 'truth' which is not helpful in understanding what writing meant to Kafka. It is certainly true that Kafka could envisage renunciation of art (evidenced by his deathbed wish that his work be destroyed – which it was given to Brod to countermand), but not in his lifetime, when it became the raft to which he clung.

At a more mundane social level, Kafka did not shun literary company, either. When Brod introduced him to the Austrian novelist Otto Stoessl (1875–1936), for example, at a Prague watering-hole called 'At the Sign of the Two Blackbirds' in October, Kafka was deeply impressed; so much so that he sent Stoessl a copy of his new book, *Betrachtung*, when it came out at the end of the year, stressing, 'Seeing and hearing you was a great encouragement to me at that time, and a remark you made then, "The novelist knows everything," still rings in my mind to this day.'[39]

Perhaps it is not surprising that Kafka's relationship with Felice faltered during the six months from their first meeting until their second in late March 1913. They had only letters to go on, and Kafka's seemed to lurch from artful gallantry to displays of raw self-loathing. It was as if he were determined that she should know the worst of him but also that he should know the worst about himself. Perhaps he was already convinced that his happiness was doomed. Elias Canetti, in his masterly analysis of the Felice correspondence, *Kafka's Other Trial* (1969), argues that in this first phase Kafka's deeper intent was 'establishing a connection, a channel of communication, between her efficiency and health and his own indecisiveness and weakness'.[40] This was, says Canetti, 'a magnificent period' in Kafka's writing and the letter-love for Felice furnished 'a source of strength sufficiently distant to leave his sensitivity lucid, not perturbed by too close a contact'. It was the first three months of the relationship that Kafka would later look back on as the perfect phase. After January 1913 it would never recapture that first flourish, in part because he began to see that Felice, from her response to *Betrachtung*, was not going to be able to provide the sustaining power he wanted from her – a power that would support his writing.

As the relationship developed, Kafka began to fear that he was tormenting Felice with his displays of pain, not to mention 'by my existence, my very existence'.[41] He was letting her know that his nature was such that nothing different could be expected. He had merely acquired 'one more unfulfilled longing to add to my other unfulfilled ones; and a new kind of self-confidence, perhaps the strongest I ever had, has been given to me within my general sense of lostness [*Verlorensein*]'. He was gaining a kind of strength, but was it at her expense? Whether from plain honesty or from that masochistic streak in his nature, Kafka let Felice know what an oddity he was. His mode of life she would find 'crazy and intolerable'. His vegetarianism, which he alleged caused his father (a butcher's son) to bury his head in the newspaper while his son ate, his dull aspect (wearing the same suit at home and at the office and in all seasons), and his faddish asceticism, neither smoking nor drinking alcohol, coffee or tea (a health stratagem negated by persistent sleeplessness), were set out in detail for her inspection. Nor did he omit the boyish demeanour: 'You take me for much younger than I am . . . depending on the perspicacity of the uninitiated onlooker I am taken for anything between 18 and 25.' He was twenty-nine.

A pattern began to emerge in the relationship of self-condemnation linked to compensating dependence on her, which must have seemed to Felice burdensome. After one session of misery he was 'seized with such longing for you that all I wanted to do was lay my head on the table for some kind of support'.[42] He did not keep from her his anxiety, following the birth of Elli's daughter, Gerti, in November, that 'I shall never have a child', and a more veiled hint that he doubted even the possibility of marriage. He told her that he could sustain his misery when he lived only for himself: 'But when I want to draw close to someone, and fully commit myself, then my misery is assured.' Things had become so bad by the start of the second week in November, barely three months after their first meeting, that he drafted a letter (unsent) that began 'you are not to write to me again. I would be bound to make you unhappy by writing to you, and as for me I am beyond help . . . Now quickly forget the ghost that I am.'[43] Felice was plainly reading letters similar to this one, with their 'utter and imperative self-torture',[44] in a state of some alarm. She described one of them to him as alien to her, which horrified him. Slowly, he began to make clear the nature of the problem, which was, in a sense, that there was a rival to her: his writing. He even proposed to shorten his long (and almost daily) letters to her in order to spend 'every ounce of myself on my novel', adding, 'which after all belongs to you'.[45] She might have doubted this, but he nevertheless gave a full account of the progress of *The Man Who Disappeared*, which 'takes place entirely in the United States of America' and was now at the sixth chapter. 'After 15 years of despairing effort (except for rare moments) this is the first major work in which, for the past 6 weeks, I have felt confidence.' Surely it was better to concentrate on this than to pump out these 'inaccurate, alarmingly incomplete, imprudent, dangerous letters to you'? And would she not 'abandon me to the terrible loneliness I feel in spite of all this'? But Felice was still unsure and wanted to know more about his extraordinary family situation, which interested her more than his writing. Sending her a short piece, '*Grosser Lärm*/Great Noise', which had just appeared in the Prague literary magazine *Herder-Blätter*,[46] and which ironically represented the Kafka apartment as 'the headquarters of noise', he pointed out that his youngest sister Ottla, now just twenty, 'is my best friend in Prague, and the other two [Elli and Valli] are both sympathetic and kind. It's only my father and I who hate each other gallantly.'

No doubt recognizing the toll these letters were taking, both on himself and his writing – quite apart from their impact on Felice – Kafka proposed next that they write to each other less frequently, once a week, saying that, as it was, her letters threw him into too much confusion. There was, in addition, a 'sad, sad reason' why he could not cope with the emotionally draining effect of the letters: 'My health is only just good enough for myself alone, not good enough for marriage, let alone fatherhood.'[47] What on earth could Felice have thought of this extraordinary statement from her lover, who seemed to be advertising to his potential bride an utter incapacity for normal family life and marriage? He welcomed her use of the familiar form of address, '*Du*', but said that he could not think of signing off, '*Dein Franz*'. 'No, I am forever fettered to myself, that's what I am [*das bin ich*], and that's what I must try to live with.'[48] This reads more like a suicide note than a love letter, and even Kafka himself subsequently realized that he had gone too far, trying to atone by sending her flowers, wrapped around an abject note, for her birthday on 18 November.

Felice was so distressed at Kafka's 'anguish and madness'[49] that she visited Max Brod to seek an explanation for his behaviour. Brod had been in Berlin and had telephoned Felice, an intervention for which Kafka was grateful: 'you surely said everything one could possibly say out of goodness, understanding and sensitivity, but even if an angel had taken your place and spoken into the telephone he would not have been able to prevail against my venomous letter'.[50] Brod secretly wrote to Felice, asking her to 'make allowances for Franz and his often pathological sensitivity. He responds entirely to the mood of the moment. Altogether he is a man who wants nothing but the absolute, the ultimate, in all things. He is never prepared to compromise.'[51] Brod shrewdly observed that Kafka, when he wanted to be, was 'very clever and sensible in practical matters' but 'when it comes to ideals he cannot take things lightly; in such matters he is terribly severe, above all with himself'. It was a plea for understanding towards a man whose writing 'puts everything I know in the way of literature in the shade'. Felice would now be in no doubt about the nature of her lover. He was beginning to express tentative references to 'your beloved eyes'[52] and her beloved lips. In heartfelt terms, he insisted, 'you have given me a gift such as I never dreamt of finding in this life'. But was this enough to quash her doubts?

In an attempt to interest her in what mattered to him most, literature, he sent her a copy of Flaubert's *L'Éducation sentimentale*, 'a book that for many years has been as dear to me as are only two or three people; whenever and wherever I open it, I am startled and succumb to it completely, and I always feel as though I were the author's spiritual son, albeit a weak and awkward one'.[53] Kafka, in all his voluminous letters and journals, never wrote a more eloquent tribute than this to another writer. To demonstrate exactly what the influence might have been in measurable terms is far more difficult. The admiration of one writer for another – a point not always grasped by some literary critics – does not in every case entail imitation or even identifiable influence. The response of Felice to Flaubert is not known, but she was probably more concerned about Kafka's angst. She suggested that he speak to his mother about his worries. By chance (and it is an insight into the claustrophobic mutual surveillance that took place in the Kafka apartment and so vexed her son) Julie Kafka found and read that very letter. She secretly wrote (everyone was practised in tiptoeing around Kafka's sensitivities) to Felice, saying, 'I have no words to describe the love I feel for my son, and I would gladly give several years of my life if this could ensure his happiness.'[54] There is no reason to doubt this.

But the rest of the letter is more well meaning than perceptive ('Anyone else in his place would be the happiest of mortals') and fails to appreciate that the outward terms of Kafka's life were not the pertinent ones. 'Her love for me is as great as her lack of understanding of me,'[55] Kafka claimed. Her reference to his writing as a 'pastime' has been noted above and, with her naïve decency, she observed that writing 'would not harm his health if only he would sleep and eat like other young people of his age'. She hoped that Felice, by quizzing her son about his eating habits, would turn him into a sensible boy again. But it did not work: he was still struggling against the office – though it is not every misunderstood writer whose boss (Dr Robert Marschner) reads Heine with him in the office[56] – and with the rollercoaster nature of his emotions towards Felice. 'We are lashing each other with all these letters,'[57] he told her. And if Felice's desire was to marry and have children, here may not have been the right man. 'When children are around I prefer to close my eyes,' he told her, in a complaint about family life in general. 'I have always looked on my parents as persecutors.'[58] He claimed that he had never found in any family 'as much coldness and false friendliness as I have always felt obliged to show towards my parents'.[59]

Yet, in spite of everything, he was in love with Felice, clinging to her, wanting her, and needing her. On 23 November Kafka wrote to her: 'Dearest, oh God, how I love you!'[60]

II

Late in November – in that extraordinary year 1912, when so much happened in his writing and in his emotional life – Kafka began to mention to Felice a 'little story'.[1] *The Man Who Disappeared* having been laid aside somewhere around the sixth chapter, Kafka was now at work on his second major story, *Die Verwandlung*, which is generally translated as *Metamorphosis* or *The Transformation*. Like *The Judgement*, this story grew directly from personal experience – though, also like that earlier story, it would be limiting and untrue to its originality and imaginative range to think of it as 'autobiographical'. The close atmosphere of the Kafka apartment and the strange distress of one of its inhabitants, his apparent mutation into something less than human, surrounded by an uncomprehending family, is the raw material transformed in the alembic of Kafka's art in *Metamorphosis*. If Ottla thought that *The Judgement* was set in the flat in Niklasstrasse, she would certainly have recognized the domestic setting of the new story. And if *The Man Who Disappeared* was set in an imagined United States, the product of a fictive leap into another larger and brighter world, *Metamorphosis* was a return to the closed, fearful world of Kafka's interior Prague.

Kafka sat down to write it, he told Felice, 'with an overwhelming desire to pour myself into it, which obviously springs from despair. Beset by many problems, uncertain of you, quite incapable of coping at the office . . . all but total insomnia for the last few days and nights, as well as some minor but nevertheless worrying and irritating things going around in my head.'[2] These were not the preconditions for a sunny tale, and Kafka himself admitted that the new story was 'exceptionally repulsive'.[3] He wanted to read it to Felice, but while doing so 'I would have to hold your hand, for the story is a little frightening. It is called *Metamorphosis*, and it would thoroughly scare you, you might not want to hear a word of it, for alas! I scare you enough every day with my letters.'[4] He worried that he was too depressed 'and perhaps I shouldn't be writing at all', but he also saw it as a way of exorcizing his demons: 'who knows, the more I write and the more I liberate myself, the cleaner and worthier of you I may become, but no doubt there is a great deal more to be got rid of, and the nights can never be long enough for this business which, incidentally, is highly voluptuous'. The use of the word 'cleaner' ('*reiner*') suggests that he felt he was evacuating something dark from himself in the writing (he hinted to Brod that the last sentence in *The Judgement* was analogous to an ejaculation), and the reference to the 'voluptuous' ('*wollüstige*') experience of writing implies a sexual subtext to the writing here which Felice may well have noticed and added to her store of evidence of the oddity of her lover. Although one could not describe Kafka's attitude to sex as 'puritanical', neither could one say that he ever represented it as a particularly joyful experience. Writing remained for him the most intense form of gratification.

On the Sunday morning of 24 November Kafka read the first part of *Metamorphosis* to his friends Oskar Baum and Max Brod.[5] It was the last literary triumph of a highly productive year (though *The Man Who Disappeared* was still only partially written). Probably the most familiar of Kafka's stories to readers, its dramatic qualities have been recognized by such actors and playwrights as Steven Berkoff, who memorably put Gregor Samsa on the London stage in 1969 at the Roundhouse and again at the National Theatre in 1976, with later revivals around the world. As Berkoff put it: 'What is so haunting about Kafka's vision is that it is the vision of the condemned man who views every fragment of his universe with unconcealed intensity, even if the mood is sometimes cool and austere.'[6]

Like Kafka, Gregor Samsa lives with his parents, hates the office, entertains impotent dreams of escape, and speaks softly, as if his family life has caused in him a traumatic aphasia. When Gregor is chased away by his father: 'No plea of Gregor's availed, indeed none was understood; however meekly he twisted his head his father only stamped the harder.' The story is characteristic of Kafka's ability to sustain a weirdly non-naturalistic situation by means of vivid particularity, a kind of hyper-realism that carries the strangeness on its back. The senses of horror, self-disgust, anguish and claustrophobia are vividly and dramatically present. And they are Kafka's emotions at this time.

Metamorphosis begins with a characteristic directness: 'When Gregor Samsa awoke one morning from troubled dreams he found himself transformed in his bed into a monstrous insect.' Gregor is a commercial traveller in a business that sounds like Hermann Kafka's wholesale drapery. He has often contemplated giving notice, but his loyalty to his parents and their needs holds him back. Otherwise: 'I'd have gone to the chief and told him exactly what I think of him.' The story immediately establishes Gregor's deadening routine in a task in which he has no interest, his sense of being trapped in the family, and his impotent dreams of escape. He is an adult, yet dependent on the whims of his parents and his boss. In his newly transformed insect state he hears a knock on the door which is the chief clerk himself. The latter makes common cause with his parents in policing him: 'What a fate, to be condemned to work for a firm where the smallest omission at once gave rise to the gravest suspicion!' In a neighbouring room Gregor's sister begins to sob while the representatives of the twin tyrannies of work and family begin to parley in another adjacent room. This recalls the disposition of forces in the Kafka household, with Ottla the sympathetic ally. The chief clerk starts to reprimand Gregor and to find fault with his work in the presence of his parents, stressing the infantile dependency of his situation.

Like Kafka, Gregor is overwhelmed by a sense that he cannot make himself understood by his family, even though his words 'seemed clear enough to him', and he struggles to achieve normality, hopeful at first that he managed to do so: 'He felt himself drawn once more into the family circle.' His resolve to try to open the door of his room – to cross the symbolic space between his private world and the shared world of family commonality which Kafka found so painful a space to negotiate in his own life – should have been welcomed: 'They should all have shouted encouragement to him.' But they did not. His discovery that he can manage to walk insectwise, his attempt to move towards his repelled family, is greeted with horror by them and his father actually chases him away, as Hermann so often repulsed Kafka's attempts at intimacy: 'No entreaty of Gregor's availed, indeed no entreaty was even understood, however humbly he bent his head his father only stamped on the floor more loudly . . . Pitilessly, Gregor's father drove him back . . . hissing . . . like a savage.' Hermann Kafka is standing behind this portrait – implacable, unforgiving, accusing, determined not to understand. Gregor's conviction that he is responsible for what has happened to him and that he is letting down his family reflects Kafka's guilt about his failure to meet his family's expectations – there is even a reference to the collapse of the father's business which expresses Kafka's self-reproach at not having been more supportive of the shop and the factory. As in *The Judgement*, the father is angry, overweening, and the son's principal enemy. The slamming of the door at the end of the first section of the story symbolizes the finality of rejection.

The second section begins with Gregor's sister setting out some milk for him (his parents refuse to participate in his feeding). He is no longer the family provider but a recipient of its charity. There is now a sense that he is a burden, and he begins to submerge himself in guilt. Gregor received no thanks for saving the family after the business collapse – 'With his sister alone had he remained intimate' – yet even she is appalled by the transformation, and with her mother tries to move the furniture in Gregor's room in order to make space. Gregor, however, clings to his old furniture, especially a writing desk (the central piece of furniture in Kafka's own room). Then his father returns, 'at once angry and exultant', and although Gregor is feeling stronger, he cannot confront his father in any adequate way: 'But Gregor could not risk standing up to him, aware as he had been from the very first day of his new life that his father believed only the severest measures suitable for dealing with him.'

The third and final section of the narrative, after Gregor's father's furious attack on him with flying apples – one of which remains embedded in his flesh, a symbolic wound – signals a further development of mood. The injury makes even the father recollect that 'Gregor was a member of the family, despite his present unfortunate and repulsive shape, and ought not to be treated as an enemy'. The fact of 'family duty' demanded that patience be exercised. Now that the door to his room is left open, Gregor can watch his family, and in particular register his father's perverse obstinacy which forces the women of the house to drop everything in order to attend to his needs. 'Who could find time, in this over-worked and tired-out family, to bother about Gregor more than was absolutely needful?' The theatrical lamentations of the family express a growing hopelessness at the burden which has been imposed upon them by the inconsiderate Gregor, 'the belief that they had been singled out for a misfortune such as had never happened to any of their relations or acquaintances'. When three curious lodgers arrive and encourage the violin-playing of his sister Grete, the sound of the music has some of the salving quality of art: 'He felt as if the way were opening before him to the unknown nourishment he craved.' But there is to be no salvation. 'If he could understand us . . . then we perhaps might come to some agreement with him,' his father suggests, but this one-way channel of understanding is not open, and Gregor, who 'thought of his family with tenderness and love', eventually dies from his suppurating wound, the apple lodged in his side. The family, having finally got rid of him, finds itself renewed and rejuvenated. They make a trip out to the country and resolve to make a new life and change the apartment 'which Gregor had selected'. They have escaped him and subtly made him the scapegoat for their ills.

Increasingly, from Kafka's letters, Felice was hearing more about his mode of life, his vegetarianism and fondness for sleeping with the window open whatever the weather. He told her that he wished she too could have been there to hear him read the story, which he explained had lost some of its 'natural spontaneous flow'[7] because of the need to write in the intervals of office work. There was no way around this problem: 'So one has to do the best one can, since the very best has been denied one.' Her letters were still a great consolation to him. He would pick them up in a state of trembling excitement as if they were living things, and yearned for constant confirmation from Felice that she loved him. 'I feel I shall never have the strength to do without you,'[8] he told her, as if her letters were curative – or addressing symptoms – rather than evidence of a spontaneous delight in being in love. When she told him that her company also manufactured gramophones, his first thought was the paranoid one that a neighbour would purchase one of the machines and furnish a new threat to his calm (though he confessed he had admired the Pathé showroom in Paris, where one could listen to coin-operated gramophones). He was ready to concede that this obsession with quiet solitude was not always desirable: 'I have noticed that my self-imposed isolation may perhaps have made me imperceptibly (imperceptible to me, not to you, my dearest) quite unpalatable . . . Once I enjoy a person, that joy knows no bounds. I can never have enough physical contact with that person.'[9]

But, on the other hand, the paramount need to write possessed him, even if the results were unsatisfactory: 'Can you understand this, dearest: to write badly, yet feel compelled to write, or abandon oneself to total despair! . . . to see the pages being covered endlessly with things one hates . . . that nevertheless have to be written down *in order that one shall live* [my italics].[10] The third partner in this relationship – writing – was becoming ever more intrusive. Could Felice ever match up to her rival? Yet Kafka also needed her. 'The extent to which I cling to you, dearest, frightens me . . . If I were with you I'm afraid I should never leave you alone – and yet my craving to be alone is continuous – we would both suffer, though of course it would mean a happiness well worth any amount of suffering.'[11] Even as he feared the intrusion into his writing solitude, he clung to her, but already had premonitions that the raft would sink: 'Dearest, I have you still, I am still happy, but for how long?'[12] His happiness was only about eight hours away by train – a railway journey between Prague and Berlin that could so easily have been made but which both seemed reluctant to undertake – 'yet impossible and unthinkable'. He began to imagine what her unvoiced thoughts might be, such as this: 'Almost every day [Kafka at this point was sometimes sending two letters a day] comes a letter tormenting me to death, but then of course there comes another which is meant to make me forget the first; but how can I forget it? He always talks in riddles; one can't get a candid word out of him . . . he ought to stop tormenting me and making me so miserable with his love.'[13] But Kafka did not cease to be her 'tormentor' ('*Plagegeist*'), and it seems that

Felice, protesting gently, had told him that, although he professed not to want to torment her, he was doing just that. This forced him to declare, 'you are my innermost, my most delicate self which, more than anything, I should like to protect and preserve in perfect peace'.[14] Yet it was a vain hope.

And so the letters kept on coming – a staggering fifty-four in December 1912 alone. Small wonder that Kafka was struggling to complete his novel. But the drama enacted in these letters was one that possessed him entirely. It was as if the struggle to write, the war against those forces (of which Felice must now be beginning to sense she was one, however passionate the declarations of love were becoming) that seemed to obstruct it, was the subject of his writing itself. He was trapped in a mad labyrinth, spinning around in agony, writing and living hardly distinguishable from each other, and with Felice, however much he said he wanted and needed her to complete himself, increasingly being seen as superfluous to this intense *pas de deux*. Yet he could not let her go. 'I am basically a very feeble and unhappy man [*ein sehr armer und unglücklicher Mensch*] . . . the things that are unusual about me are largely bad and sad . . . don't talk about the greatness hidden in me . . . Dearest, please hold me close.'[15]

In the middle of December, not long after the publication of a review of *The Judgement* (which Kafka always referred to as 'your story' when mentioning it to Felice) in the magazine *Bohemia*, in which Paul Wiegler (who had heard the then unpublished story delivered at a public reading in Prague on 4 December) called it the mark of 'a great, surprisingly great talent, passionate and disciplined, which already has the strength to go its own way'.[16] In addition, the collection of stories – some of them eight to ten years old – *Betrachtung*, had just appeared at the end of November. Nevertheless, looking out on the wider literary world into which his little book had been launched, Kafka noticed that his friend the young author Franz Werfel had become everything he was not – a precocious man of letters, living by his pen in Leipzig, where he worked as a reader for Kafka's publisher, Rowohlt. Werfel had 'got his reward' and had 'complete freedom to live and write. Imagine what he will produce!'[17] Kafka continued to believe, as writers often forgivably do, that if only he could concentrate on writing alone to the exclusion of all else, then great things would result. So often they do not, but this still became Kafka's sustaining myth.

Brod, who knew Kafka more closely than anyone else, allowed himself to speculate about what might have happened to Kafka had he been given the exit-key from his labyrinth. His parents could have afforded to grant him some respite, some opportunity, for example, to go and study abroad, but Kafka himself would never have pushed for this.[18] Towards the end of December, when the vacation started and some time for himself was in the offing, Kafka seems not to have relished the prospect: 'I am bewildered by these first two free days and in my haste don't know where to begin.'[19] The tussle with his opponents and tormentors had started to become necessary. In fact, he did not know anything else. After a week in which he had failed to write anything, he asked Felice: 'Dearest, what will happen when I cannot write any more? . . . if I am not going to write for myself, I shall have more time to write to you, to enjoy the nearness of you . . . but you, you will not be able to love me any more. Not because I am not going to write for myself any more, but because this not writing will turn me into a poorer, more unbalanced, less secure being, whom you could not possibly like.' This reasoning shows that Kafka was an expert at closing off all possible avenues of escape, all means of assuagement, all ways of taking an optimistic view of the perspectives opening up at any given time.

Given his lack of productivity at the year's end, he asked himself: 'haven't I every reason to stick to the office, work like the wind through all arrears, and become a keen, methodical official whose whole head is on the job?' He had found himself yawning at the Institute, and resolved never to start writing any later than 10 p.m. and to stop at 2 a.m. at the latest. Kafka was now one of three assistants to the head of department, Dr Robert Marschner, in a department employing seventy clerks. The Institute itself insured 200,000 employers, who were in turn responsible for three million workers. Kafka was still having to travel occasionally – to Leitmeritz (Litoměřice), for example, in early December – where he visited the widow of his uncle, Heinrich. Yet, in spite of all the disappointments that flowed from not being able to point to greater success with literary work carried out in those limited hours of freedom that a full-time job granted him, he could never quite banish the thought that great things were just around the corner: 'forces so close, so indispensable to me are at work; I marvel at the mystery of it all'.[20]

Felice seems not to have been very impressed by *Betrachtung*, and Kafka tried to play down her reaction by saying it was 'largely old stuff',[21] though he added that it was 'nevertheless still a part of me, hence a part of me unknown to you' (a discreetly barbed comment). He would prefer it if she came out and said she disliked it or even couldn't understand it; after all, it was 'full of hopeless confusion, or rather there are glimpses into endless perplexities, and one has to come very close to see anything at all'. He was clearly upset by her *indifference*. He claimed that 'the trouble the spendthrift publisher took and the money he lost, both utterly wasted', preyed on his mind, and it was only 'by chance' that it was published at all and not from any initiative by Kafka himself. He was presumably crediting Brod the impresario with its publication. All of this might justify an 'uncertain opinion' on Felice's part, but he was receiving no opinion at all from her.

This seems to have marked a turning point in their relationship. Kafka later recalled how, that Christmas of 1912, Brod had been in Berlin (a journey that he made fairly frequently but, as mentioned above, that seemed to defeat Kafka, in spite of his ardent expressions of desire to be near to Felice). Brod had spoken to Felice and had warned her of the opening cracks in the relationship, to which she replied (we have it only at the furthest remove, in Kafka's paraphrase of Brod's report of Felice's analysis): 'It is very strange, we write to each other quite regularly and very often, I have had a great many letters from him, I would like to help him, but it is very difficult, he makes it very difficult for me, we never seem to get any closer.'[22] Her summation was astute.

The book to which Felice was indifferent, *Betrachtung*, was published by Ernst Rowohlt at the end of November 1912 (though it bore the publication date of 1913) in a print-run of 800 copies (half of which would still be unsold five years later). It was dedicated to Max Brod and consisted of eighteen short pieces, some of which had already been published in such journals as *Hyperion* and *Bohemia*. These pieces, some barely a few lines long, are not exactly prose poems – a formulation that seems to do justice to neither poetry nor prose – but, rather, beautifully exact exercises in the fictional imagination that exhibit Kafka's love of precise detail and infinite suggestibility. 'Longing to be a Red Indian', for example, comprises just one sentence, rapid as the gallop it describes, expressive of a desire to get the instinctual life on a proper harmonious basis, to be as 'instantly prepared' ('*gleich bereit*') as the natural man who is adumbrated. In many of the other pieces the figure of the solitary, socially awkward, not at all '*bereit*' individual predominates. 'Whoever leads a solitary life and yet now and then feels the need for some kind of contact . . .' begins one piece. Another starts: 'It seems so dreadful to remain a bachelor . . .' and another: 'I am standing on the platform of the tram and am entirely uncertain as to my place in this world, in this town, in my family.' This is the world of Kafka at the age of twenty-nine, uncertain and anxious as an adolescent, envious of those who move in the world with spontaneous animal energy and vigorous confidence. The opening sketch of 'Children on a Country Road' injects an odd tone of unease into what appears at first sight a slight, impressionistic piece about children playing on a summer evening. Their games and their song evoke a sense of communion and shared high spirits from which the child-observer is excluded: 'When you mix your voice with others you are caught like a fish on a hook.' In 'Unhappiness', which closes the volume and is the longest and most complex piece in it, we are once again in a claustrophobic domestic interior (the diametric opposite of the open plains across which the free Native Americans race on horseback). Out of the windows brief possibilities are glimpsed, or sudden excursions are made into the street for unsatisfactory and fleeting encounters. In this story the solitary narrator encounters 'the small ghost of a child', who bursts into the room in an abrupt, dramatic gesture of a kind familiar in these stories, which echo the striking dramatic effects used in the Yiddish theatre or more widely in expressionist literature. There is also, as so often in Kafka's early fiction, a vaguely disturbing sexual dimension. The young man in the room suddenly, and for no apparent reason, tells the child: 'If you were a girl it would hardly be right to lock yourself into a room with me like this.' In part this is a story about the unhappy person's need to invent the possibility of companionship, in part a projection of a vague sense of unease, of threat. The narrator tells a neighbour on the stair after the ghost has gone: 'The real fear is the fear of what caused the apparition.'

Disappointed though Kafka was by Felice's lack of interest in his book, he continued to protest that he was in love with her. He did so, however, in his usual fashion, against a background of gloom. He told her how his father's illness – hardening of the arteries – was 'ever-threatening',[23] though, because of the efficiency of Hermann's domestic tyranny, 'The family's harmony is really upset only by me, and the more so as the years go by; very often I don't know what to do, and feel a great sense of guilt towards my parents and everyone else.' He told her that on more than one occasion he had contemplated suicide: 'But that is long past, and now the knowledge of your love has made me a more confident person than I have ever been before.' His New Year's Eve greeting on the last day of 1912 involved mentioning a collection of Napoleon's sayings into which he had been dipping, especially the *mot* 'It is terrible to die childless.' He told Felice – and, yet again, one wonders if he put much thought into some of the things he said to her – that this was the fate marked out for himself, 'for apart from everything else I would never dare expose myself to the risk of being a father'.[24] Lying in bed alone as the hour of midnight approached 'like a lost dog', listening to the New Year revellers in the Prague streets, he comforted himself with a recent remark of hers: 'We belong together unconditionally.'

The following year, however, their relationship would sail into turbulent waters that would test her resolve to the limit and lead to their first crisis.

12

After the excitement of 1912, the year of literary breakthrough for Kafka, he wrote little for the next eighteen months – though his letters to Felice, pouring out with the same rushing abundance as before, amounted, in their total number of words, to a decently sized novel. This was very much the point. He was channelling into this epistolary love affair, with a woman he had met only once, so much energy and nocturnal writing time that there was little left to spare for completion of *The Man Who Disappeared*. In January, when he was still managing to do some work on the novel, he urged Felice not to envy her rival: 'If the people in my novel get wind of your jealousy, they will run away from me; as it is, I am holding on to them only by the ends of their sleeves.'[1] He told her that he could not detach himself from his novel, 'for it is through writing that I keep a hold on life [*denn durch mein Schreiben halte ich mich ja am Leben*].'[2] He added, 'once I lose my writing, I am bound to lose you and everything else'.

Felice must have reflected on the order of these propositions. It was clear that his writing came first, that it was the source of his being, and that she must accommodate herself to this fact, of being second, unable to displace writing as his primary inspiration and support. The tragedy of this relationship is inscribed here, but both would struggle on for another four years, inflicting pain and anguish on themselves, until they could do so no longer.

Franz Kafka's father, Hermann (1852–1931), and his mother, Julie Löwy (1855–1934). Both outlived their son. *(Archiv Klaus Wagenbach, Berlin)*

The infant Franz.
(Archiv Klaus Wagenbach, Berlin)

Kafka aged about ten, with his sisters Valerie (known as 'Valli') (1890–1942) and (centre) Gabriele (known as 'Elli') (1889–1941).
(Archiv Klaus Wagenbach, Berlin)

school photograph at the German Gymnasium in Prague taken around the turn of the ntury. Kafka is second from the left on the back row. *(Archiv Klaus Wagenbach, Berlin)*

Kafka around 1901 as a new undergraduate at Prague's Charles Ferdinand University, the eighteen-year-old already displaying his elegant sartorial taste. *(Archiv Klaus Wagenbach, Berlin)*

Kafka's maternal grandfather, Jakob Löwy from Osek in northern Bohemia (1824–1910). *(Archiv Klaus Wagenbach, Berlin)*

Kafka's three sisters (from left to right): Valli, Elli and, his favourite, Ottilie (known as 'Ottla') (1892–1943), photographed around 1898. *(Archiv Klaus Wagenbach, Berlin)*

One of Kafka's earliest loves: Hedwig Weiler, a student whom Kafka met on holiday in Triesch. *(Archiv Klaus Wagenbach, Berlin)*

Kafka in a bowler hat as a student at a time when he frequented the winebars of Prague's Old Town. *(Archiv Klaus Wagenbach, Berlin)*

Kafka sent this photograph to his fiancée Felice Bauer in 1912, commenting, 'I don't actually have a twisted face, I only have a visionary gaze when taken with a flash.' *(Archiv Klaus Wagenbach, Berlin)*

The Worker's Accident Insurance Institute in Prague where Kafka worked from 1908 to 1922. *(Archiv Klaus Wagenbach, Berlin)*

Kafka in a holiday picture taken in the Prater in Vienna in 1913; Kafka was attending a conference on accident prevention. From left to right: Kafka, the writers Albert Ehrenstein and Otto Pick and the Zionist Lize Kaznelson. *(Archiv Klaus Wagenbach, Berlin)*

The writer Max Brod (1884–1968), Kafka's closest friend, first biographer, and enabler of Kafka's posthumous reputation. *(Archiv Klaus Wagenbach, Berlin)*

The Yiddish actor, Yitzhak Löwy, whose arrival with his theatre troupe from Poland in 1911 was pivotal in Kafka's rediscovery of his Jewish heritage. *(Archiv Klaus Wagenbach, Berlin)*

Kafka's friend the writer and critic Oskar Baum (1883–1941) was blinded as a schoolboy in an anti-semitic attack. *(Archiv Klaus Wagenbach, Berlin)*

The writer Felix Weltsch (1884–1964), editor of the Zionist paper *Selbstwehr*. Weltsch, Baum, Brod and Kafka formed a close Prague literary circle. *(Archiv Klaus Wagenbach, Berlin)*

The frontispiece of *Metamorphosis*, the most famous of Kafka's shorter works, published in 1916.
(Archiv Klaus Wagenbach, Berlin)

Kafka and Ottla at Zürau in north-west Bohemia where they both lived 1917–18 and where Kafka wrote his famous aphorisms.
(Archiv Klaus Wagenbach, Berlin)

Kafka and Felice Bauer in an engagement photograph taken in 1917, shortly before the cancellation of their second engagement. Felice, Kafka recalled on his deathbed, 'was not beautiful'. *(Archiv Klaus Wagenbach, Berlin)*

Grete Bloch, a friend of Felice. *(Archiv Klaus Wagenbach, Berlin)*

Julie Wohryzek (1891–1944) to whom Kafka was briefly engaged in 1919, eventually abandoning her for Milena Jesenská. *(Archiv Klaus Wagenbach, Berlin)*

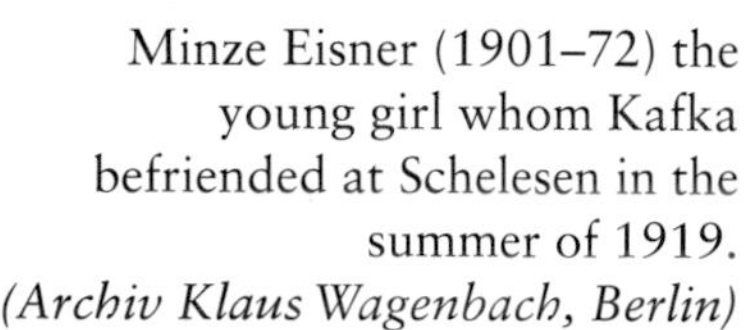

Minze Eisner (1901–72) the young girl whom Kafka befriended at Schelesen in the summer of 1919. *(Archiv Klaus Wagenbach, Berlin)*

The passionate Czech writer and translator Milena Jesenská (1896–1944) with whom Kafka had a brief but intense affair in 1920–21. *(Archiv Klaus Wagenbach, Berlin)*

afka and fellow guests at the sanatorium at Matliary in the High Tatra Mountains in 920 or 1921. Standing at the centre rear is the Hungarian medical student Robert lopstock (1899–1972) who nursed Kafka in his final illness and became a close friend, orming with Dora Diamant, his 'little family'. *(Archiv Klaus Wagenbach, Berlin)*

Dora Diamant (1892–1952), Kafka's partner in the last months of his life. *(Archiv Klaus Wagenbach, Berlin)*

The last photograph of Kafka, taken in 1923 or 1924. *(Archiv Klaus Wagenbach, Berlin)*

ragueʼs Old Town Square today. The house ‘At the Unicorn’ on the far right housed the
ılon of Berta Fanta which Kafka attended in his student years around 1902. *(Author)*

he tiny house (first in full view from the left) in Alchemists’ Street or Golden Lane, where afka lived in 1916, writing many of the stories in *A Country Doctor* and which is now a afka postcard shop. *(Author)*

All that remains of Kafka's birthplace today: the doorway of the house on the north-east side of Old Town Square on the edge of the old Jewish ghetto where the writer was born on 3 July 1883. *(Author)*

Kafka's grave in the New Jewish Cemetery in Strašnice in Prague. His parents are buried in the same grave, which also contains at its base a memorial to his three sisters who died in Nazi death camps. *(Author)*

However, the question remains – it is not asked frequently enough of Kafka – why were the stakes raised in such a way? Kafka had a secure, well-paid job and a routine that allowed him to write freely in his own room at night, after an afternoon of rest and recuperation, without interruption (apart from the family bustle of the apartment, about which he regularly complained). He was being published and enjoying a tiny *succès d'estime* with *Betrachtung*. He had an admiring and supportive circle of literary friends in Prague and an enthusiastic publisher in the shape of Kurt Wolff of Rowohlt. Many young writers in their late twenties would consider these things as matters for celebration rather than the occasion of lamentation.

The answer clearly lies in Kafka's state of inner anxiety, which had been with him since childhood, his fear of others' intrusion into the self's domain, his hatred of compromise with the outer world. Sitting at his *Schreibtisch* in the early hours, with his manuscript notebooks in front of him, he was fully in command of his own world. Intuitively, he feared that Felice would encroach on that well-defended territory and all would be lost. But at the same time he was passionately attached to her. Although there seems little evidence of any powerful sexual attraction, he was determined to hold fast to her: 'whether you like it or not, I belong to you'.[3] He told her of a very old bet he had made with a friend for ten bottles of champagne that he would not get married. The bet was made in his 'far-off, so-called gadabout days, when I spent many a night sitting in taverns, without drinking',[4] in such Prague nightspots as the Trocadero and the Eldorado. Then he promptly shared with her a dream in which he had become engaged to her ('It looked terribly, terribly improbable').

What exactly did Kafka want? To judge from one of his letters, Felice was in the habit of saying to him: 'Now, Franz, what am I to do with you?'[5] His answer was that 'you must really know me at my worst as well as at my best'. He felt that he was being honest with her, even if it meant tormenting her with his 'obstinacy . . . Yet how else but through obstinacy can the obstinate make sure of his incredible good fortune which, sent from heaven, came to him on a certain August evening?'

There were lighter passages between them. He gave her a locket photo of himself. He revealed that in the office he was known as 'a great laugher' ('*grosser Lacher*')[6] and he told her a story of how, when the Institute's president, Otto Příbram, formally listened to Kafka's speech of thanks for a recent promotion, the latter fell into a fit of giggles at the pompous demeanour of his boss. He quizzed her about her own office routines, which involved writing sales letters about the Parlograph. Like a fogeyish writer of today deprecating the computer, Kafka joked that a living typist was much less intimidating than a machine: 'A machine with its silent, serious demands strikes me as exercising a greater, more cruel compulsion on one's capacities than any human being.'[7] He also claimed to be 'afraid of the telephone',[8] yet wrote a remarkably detailed letter to Felice full of ideas about how the Parlograph could be marketed by installing the machine, which was at the cutting edge of 1913 office-information technology, in hotels, post offices and other public places. He also suggested combining the telephone and the Parlograph. Kafka may thus have been the unacknowledged progenitor of the modern hotel 'business centre' or 'fax bureau'. His own office life was less stressful than that of Felice, who worked sometimes until 7.45 p.m. with no break for lunch. He spent a whole day writing eight pages of an official report which would be torn up and started again the next day: 'apart from my office work I do practically nothing, and . . . owing to my neglect of the factory I hardly dare cast a glance at my father, let alone say a word to him'.[9]

But, in spite of the attempts at levity, the underlying travails could not be ignored. Two simultaneous engagements – those of his sister Elli and his best friend, Max Brod – made him suffer in an inexplicable way, 'as though an immediate and direct disaster had befallen me'.[10] He imagined going to the synagogue for Elli's wedding 'wearing my old tailcoat, cracked patent-leather shoes, a top hat far too small for me' and acting as an usher. The solemnity of the Jewish rituals annoyed him, and he considered that most of the assimilated Jews only bothered to go to the synagogue for weddings and funerals: 'these two occasions have drawn grimly close to each other, and one can virtually see the reproachful glances of a withering faith'. As ever Kafka felt alienated from all the family joshing that took place around the wedding, though touched by his father's suddenly breaking into Czech to describe Elli in her wedding-dress looking like 'a princess'.

Nothing could dull the pain of not being able to get on with his writing. Felice told him that she wanted to sit beside him while he wrote, but he told her, with more unsparing honesty, that this was impossible:

> For writing means revealing oneself to excess; that utmost of self-revelation and surrender, in which a human being, when involved with others, would feel he was losing himself, and from which, therefore, he will always shrink as long as he is in his right mind . . . Writing that springs from the surface of existence – when there is no other way and the deeper wells have dried up – is nothing, and collapses the moment a truer emotion makes that surface shake. This is why one can never be alone enough when one writes, why there can never be enough silence around one when one writes, why even night is not night enough . . . I have often thought that the best mode of life for me would be to sit in the innermost room of a spacious locked cellar with my writing things and a lamp. Food would be brought and always put down far away from my room, outside the cellar's outermost door.[11]

In these conditions Kafka would write without effort – 'for extreme concentration knows no effort' – but even he realized the limitations of these absolutist demands for perfect writing conditions. At the first failure he would be plunged into 'grandiose fits of madness'. Once again, Felice was presented with an image of exclusion – this time the locked door of an anchorite's cell – in place of a generous welcome from her lover into his innermost world.

Yet the anchorite did get out from time to time. He attended a lecture on 'Myth in Judaism' by the great Jewish thinker Martin Buber (1878–1965) on 18 January 1913, not because he was enamoured of the 'dreary'[12] speaker, but because the latter was followed by the actress Gertrude Eysoldt: 'I am completely under the spell of her personality and voice.' He went to the theatre to see the Ballets Russes. The dancers Nijinsky and Kyast were magnificent, 'two flawless human beings; they are at the innermost point of their art; they radiate mastery as do all such people'.[13] He was also rereading, yet again, Flaubert's' *L'Éducation sentimentale*, which left him speechless with admiration, and trying to interest Felice in the book. His own work, however, was making no progress at all, and he was tortured by the fear that he might be losing his capacity to write. 'Don't you know how weak and wretched and dependent I am on the moment?' he implored Felice. He worried that he was inflicting pain on her: 'Have I the right to do this?' And then, in a remarkable confession – one can never accuse Kafka of not being candid with Felice – he warned: 'you must realize that you will never get unadulterated happiness from me; only as much unadulterated suffering as one could wish for, and yet – don't send me away. I am tied to you not by love alone, love would not be much, love begins, love comes, passes, and comes again; but this need, by which I am utterly chained to your being, this remains.'

Could Felice bear this burden of need? Might her unease now be growing? The absence of any of her letters to Kafka means that such questions may be answered only by reasoned speculation, but he was certainly not making life easy for her, or lessening his personal demands on her. He did concede that his 'wretched disposition which knows but three possibilities: to burst forth, collapse, or pine away'[14] was hard for her, but: 'I belong to you entirely; this much I can say as a result of surveying my 30 years of life.'

Kafka at this time was reading the letters of the German dramatist Friedrich Hebbel (1813–63), and, drawn to the 'ancient, heart-stirring, expectant Germany of the middle of the last century',[15] he admired the clarity of Hebbel's mind and his ability to bear suffering 'because he felt secure in his innermost being'.[16] Kafka was self-aware enough to know that he was not as strong as Hebbel: 'How far removed I am from men like these!' Hebbel, Kafka felt, 'touches my weaknesses directly with his fingers . . . [His] thinking is very precise and contains none of the subterfuges in which one tends to seek refuge when in despair . . . When I try to follow all this in detail, the beneficial human effects of his letters cease at once, and he simply crushes me.'[17] It is as if Kafka feared Hebbel's powerful clarity, or feared that it was a resource from another epoch not available to the modern sensibility.

The intensely literary quality of Kafka's letters to Felice (they were, after all, usurping his normal creative writing time) seems to have made him feel, if not uneasy, then aware of a certain tendency to embellish for effect his miseries. 'I always feel 10 times better than I say; it's just my pen that runs away with me, that's all,'[18] he frankly told Felice. Another time he said she would get used to his 'overstating, uncontrolled writing'.[19] As well as Hebbel, Kafka was rereading another book almost as elevated in his personal pantheon as *L'Éducation sentimentale*, Heinrich von Kleist's famous novella *Michael Kohlhaas* (1810), a story of a man's obsessive pursuit of justice told with Kleist's characteristically powerful narrative energy. Kafka was reading it, he guessed, for the tenth time – 'it carries me along on waves of wonder'[20] – and, were it not for an unsatisfactory ending, 'it would be a thing of perfection, the kind of perfection I like to maintain does not exist. (For I believe that even the greatest works of literature have a little tail of human frailty which, if one is on the lookout for it, begins to wag slightly and disturbs the sublime, godlike quality of the whole.)'

On 3 February 1913 Kafka was sent on business by the Institute to Leitmeritz for a court case. He told Felice that he would far rather have paid a visit to Berlin to see her, followed by a trip south to the French Riviera, where Max and Sophie Brod were enjoying their honeymoon. The thought of the newly-weds increased Kafka's sense of loneliness (especially as Sophie had recently met Felice in Berlin), and he sent them a couple of postcards, urging them to keep a journal to compensate him for their absence. Ottla accompanied her brother to Leitmeritz, both rising at 4.30 a.m. to catch the early train from Prague. While her brother was in court, Ottla visited their relatives, Emil Kafka being a merchant in the town.[21] It was a welcome break for her from long hours serving in the shop, but it seems merely to have exhausted Franz, who, fond as he was of Ottla, hankered to be alone. Explaining this to Felice, he said: 'There are times, dearest, when I am convinced I am unfit for any human relationship.'[22] Meeting an occasional acquaintance, Lise Weltsch, who 'nauseated' him with her complaints of life but who, later at supper, sparkled contrastingly in someone else's company, Kafka reflected glumly: 'I must emanate an aura of unhappiness.'[23] He was worried that his misery would prove contagious to her, but nevertheless described a dream in which they were both in a Berlin which resembled Prague's Old Town Square, walking together arm in arm. In his letter he sketched the way their arms were linked and boasted facetiously: 'I was once a great draughtsman, you know, but then I started to take academic drawing lessons with a bad woman painter and ruined my talent.'[24] In fact, Kafka's expressionist pen-and-ink drawings, which can be found in his notebooks, display considerable skill.

There seemed, however, little chance of the two lovers walking arm in arm together, for, in addition to the writing block that was beginning to possess him (though the letters did not slacken), his health was deteriorating. He had permanent headaches, which made him decline an apparent suggestion from Felice that they meet at Dresden – roughly halfway between Berlin and Prague – where she had some business. He blamed the state he was in, 'which even here at home among my family assigns me to my dark room rather than to the brightly lit living room'[25] and made 'this kind of journey in itself an immense undertaking'. Dreaming of the opposite to this sickly gloom, Kafka asked Max and Sophie, while in the Riviera, to seek out some hot place 'where one can live as a vegetarian, where one feels permanently well . . . in short, a beautiful, impossible place'[26] for the autumn. It is hard to determine whether this was a serious proposal or a whimsical fantasy. One cannot help feeling it would have been a healthy move.

Felice now started to be offered, in addition to the previous portraits of the solitary Kafka, monastically dedicated to the art of writing, a new picture of the ailing hypochondriac, but one who continued to profess his unshakeable love. Reading the proofs of *The Judgement*, which was due to appear in May, he referred to it as 'your book' (he would continue to refer to it in this way throughout their relationship). Citing the proposed dedication, '*für Fräulein Felice B*', he urged her to see this as 'an unquestionable sign of my love for you, and this love exists not by permission, but from compulsion'.[27] Once again he was stressing *need* rather than *love*. He himself was worried that the outpourings of his letters (Felice had just discovered that her mother had secretly been reading them) would distress her, and that, 'considering the moods and states of weakness making up my existence, [they] easily may appear repulsive, artificial, superficial, coquettish, false, malicious, incoherent, or rather not appear, they undeniably are so'.[28] He told her that her love for him made him happy but not safe, 'for you might be deluding yourself; with my letters I may be performing some kind of trick that deludes you. After all, you have hardly seen me, hardly heard me talk, hardly suffered from my silences, know nothing about the accidental or inevitable unpleasantness my presence might cause you.' Yet, at the same time, he claimed that his love for her was invincible: 'this love has become integrated with my nature as though it had been born with me, but had only now been recognized'. But was this communication by letter 'the only kind of communication in keeping with my wretchedness'? No sooner had he expressed these negative apprehensions than he began to regret having gone too far – 'the wrong sentences lie in wait about my pen' – and was forced to conclude: 'When I look into myself I see so much that is obscure and still in flux that I cannot even properly explain or fully accept the dislike I feel for myself.'[29]

Kafka was now beginning to fear that actual contact and constant companionship with Felice – for example, if they went to the south of France together – would endanger the relationship. It was as if he were beginning to write himself off in her eyes, stressing the futility of his life, the irreducibility of his nature ('we have no powers other than those with which we were turned out into the world'[30]) and the fact that eventually she would see him for what he was: 'How long will it take you to see through it all, and once you have done so, how long will you stay?' He told her that he had reflected on the number of his current real and imaginary ills and had reached a total of six. He does not say what they are, but it is possible to guess: ill-health, difficulty with Felice, difficulty with writing, difficulty with his family, difficulty with work, and difficulty with being stuck in one place but unable, apparently, to do anything about it. He thought seriously during the early months of 1913 of leaving home (he was nearly thirty) and taking a room. He had planned to do so before, but he let his parents persuade him out of it. He always blamed his family for much of his predicament, but he had become fatally dependent: his meals were provided, his domestic arrangements taken care of, he did nothing in the apartment but retire to his room at night to write. Looking after himself was becoming an increasingly remote possibility. It is highly unlikely that Franz Kafka could boil an egg.

The emergence of some troubles of Felice's own – her family, as indicated above, was riven by problems, responsibility for whose solution seems to have devolved largely to her – intensified Kafka's sense that trouble was the inevitable signature of this relationship. Although he was now becoming obsessed with the relationship, to the exclusion of other social life and progress with his writing, he was still anxious at what would happen if it were jolted into a more defined reality than that established by correspondence. He told Felice that if an unexpected telegram arrived telling him to go and meet her at Prague station he would experience 'nothing but shock – like suddenly being torn out of a long night's sleep'.[31] Lethargy – 'this dreadful lethargy that turns the entire apartment, in fact, the entire city, into one big bed for me' – was taking hold. At least one of his friends, Felix Weltsch, was aware of this, and took him for a walk, in the course of which he tendered some unsolicited advice to Kafka to snap out of it. Another friend, Hans Kohn, a law student at the Ferdinand Karl University in Prague, tried to interest Kafka in a Zionist meeting, but was equally unsuccessful. Kafka was repelled by his activist zeal: 'my indifference to him as a person, or to any form of Zionism, was immense and inexpressible'.[32] Kafka was now speaking to hardly anyone at home, his relationship even with Ottla was wearing thin, he rarely saw a soul and passed his time on lonely evening walks. This was in marked contrast to Felice, who was at the centre of a busy web of business activity and family life. In spite of being promoted on

1 March to the position of vice-secretary at the Institute, work for Kafka was 'as irrelevant as I am: we suit each other'.[33]

He was now at some sort of dead end. The businesslike Felice asked him what his plans and prospects were. He replied that he had none: 'I cannot step into the future; I can crash into the future, grind into the future, stumble into the future, this I can do; but best of all I can lie still.' When things were going well he was 'entirely absorbed by the present'. When things went badly 'I curse even the present, let alone the future!' Only in literary get-togethers with friends such as Brod could he escape from this inertia. On Saturday 1 March he 'read myself into a frenzy' at Max's with the concluding section of *Metamorphosis*, the whole of which would not be published until 1915. At last he let himself go and indulged in laughter with his friends. 'If one bolts the doors and windows against the world, one can from time to time create the semblance and almost the beginning of the reality of a beautiful life.'[34]

Unfortunately, the world could not so easily be screened off and he now explicitly asked Felice, 'do you still care for me as much as you used to?'[35] It was not so much her letters as his own anxieties that had prompted this. He alluded vaguely to having been 'in the grip of something' indefinable for the past fifteen years (that is to say, since adolescence), from which writing furnished a temporary escape, one which enabled him to have 'the courage to turn to you'. It was like a 'rebirth' that gave him the confidence to 'accept the entire responsibility for my attempt at drawing you, the most precious thing I have ever come across in my life [*Dich, das Liebste, was ich in meinem Leben gefunden hatte*], over to me'.[36] But in view of the way he had conducted himself recently, how could she continue to stay with him? She had a compassionate nature which might make her stay with him even it were detrimental to her, and he could not bear that. She was a 'kind, active, lively self-assured person' who should not sacrifice herself to 'the confusion or rather the monotonous blur of my personality'.

It was as if he were trying to push her into rejecting him by these displays of keen self-loathing. 'I am now a different person from the one I was during the first two months of our correspondence,'[37] he claimed. This was not a transformation into a new state but a relapse into an old one. 'If you felt drawn to that person, you must, you must inevitably abhor this one.' The problem was that he was not at peace with himself. He went on 'fluttering around myself like a bird kept from its nest by some curse'[38] and came to the inevitable conclusion: 'Why, instead, don't I try to find a way of gently helping you to free yourself from me?'[39] She shouldn't allow herself to be deluded into thinking he was improvable: 'Not for two days could you live beside me.' Was this genuine or was it an artful stratagem? Was it mere self-pitying rhetoric? In any case, Felice did not rise to the bait. She said briskly of his litany of complaints: 'I don't believe them, and you don't believe them either.'[40] She told him not to entertain 'the feeling that you might be taken from me'.[41] He, in turn, confessed that his letters to her could be 'brutal'[42] and wondered if he should send her copies of his diary entries instead.

After a night at the cinema with Felix Weltsch – Kafka was fond of films and fascinated especially by movie posters[43] – when he had watched *The Other* by Paul Lindau, he reflected on his inability to emulate the quiet strength of his immediate boss at the Institute, Eugen Pfohl, and on his own generally sorry state: 'I sleep little, fitfully, and badly; I don't take much exercise, am utterly dissatisfied with myself, all of which makes me collapse quite helplessly into the armchair . . . I walked home like a sick man, with the idea of the distance still to be covered constantly before me. But I am not ill; in fact, I don't look any different, except that I have one line above my nose, and an ever-increasing, by now fairly noticeable quantity of grey hair.'[44]

Two days later he declared: 'If only I deserved you . . . as much as I need you.'[45] The conflict in him, however, was not just between his need for Felice and his sense of unworthiness. It was also, as ever, between the conditions of his life and his aspirations as a writer. After telling Felice that his family was, as he wrote, 'quarrelling in the kitchen about a stolen sausage' – once again, he relished the chance to dramatize the circumstances of the composition of his letters – he explained that this was as nothing compared to the real tensions within him: 'It is not only they who distract me, inside I am exulting with forces that are distracting.' Yet he did not seem able to share that 'exulting' ('*in mir jubelt es*')[46] with Felice. She remained outside his writing, which appears not to have interested her at all.

Towards the end of March, Kafka made the first tentative steps towards proposing a visit to Felice in Berlin, though he drew back from the idea of seeing her relatives. Both of them realized that if the relationship were to have a future it must consist of more than the exchange of copious letters. 'Writing to you and living have drawn very near to each other,'[47] he admitted. Yet he was finding that words did not always work in saying what he wanted them to say, and therefore Berlin was necessary: 'I am going to Berlin for no other reason than to tell and to show you – who have been misled by my letters – who I really am . . . Presence is irrefutable.'[48] Right until the last minute he dithered, envisaging unnamed obstacles, worrying that work meetings scheduled around Easter might require him to cancel, but, at last, he took the train from Prague to Berlin, arriving on 22 March 1913, to check in to the Askanischer Hof Hotel in Königgrätzerstrasse. Seven months after first meeting Felice Bauer in Prague, and with tens of thousands of words having been written to her in the small hours, Kafka at last was preparing to come face to face with his beloved for only the second time in their already tortured relationship.

13

It was not to be expected that Kafka's first meeting with Felice since August 1912 would be a smooth affair. On the morning of 23 March 1913, Easter Sunday, he sat bewildered in a Berlin hotel lobby, wondering where Felice had got to. He had sent an express letter announcing his arrival on Saturday night, but somehow it had not reached her. He now scribbled a letter from the hotel and sent it by messenger, saying that he was waiting at the Askanischer Hof. He urged her to telephone because he had to leave Berlin late that afternoon.

Eventually they made contact and took a walk together in the Grunewald, sitting on a tree trunk to talk. They may also have visited the grave of Heinrich von Kleist.[1] They spoke again on the hotel telephone before Kafka's departure (delayed until Monday now) for Leipzig, where he had a meeting with his publisher, Kurt Wolff (to whom he had promised to send the manuscript of *Metamorphosis*), followed by a business trip for the Institute to Aussig.

It is not easy to establish what transpired between the two lovers in Berlin, but when Kafka eventually returned to Prague on 28 March, thoroughly exhausted by his travelling and work assignment, he wrote: 'How close I came to you by my visit to Berlin! I breathe only through you.'[2] While this clearly implies that it was a successful tryst, he felt it necessary to add, 'you do not know me well enough, you dearest and best one', which confirms also that the underlying script was unchanged. Accordingly, he wrote what he told Brod was his 'great confession'[3] to Felice on 1 April.

His one fear was that 'I shall never be able to possess you.'[4] If this were true, 'then surely I had good reason to want with all my might to part from you six months ago, and moreover good reason to fear any conventional bond with you, since the consequences of any such bond could only be the severing of my desire from the feeble forces that still sustain me – who am unfit for this earth – on this earth today.' Kafka told Brod that Felice was 'a real martyr and it is clear that I am undermining the entire basis on which she previously used to live, happy and in tune with the whole world'.[5]

In any conventional relationship this would have signalled the end, but the couple appeared ready to continue; both had their reasons to want to persist. Both seemed to see marriage as a goal to be pursued whatever the cost. Kafka dismissed Felice's suggestion that they were becoming 'estranged' by insisting that he did nothing but 'die of longing'[6] for her and by stressing that his need for writing to her had its roots in the very centre of his existence. A hint was dropped that they would meet again at Whitsun. Meanwhile, as a change from his usual complaints about his family, he reported a strangely touching moment when his mother had come into his room and offered to kiss him goodnight, something which had not happened for many years. 'That's good,' he said, and his mother replied: 'I never dared, I thought you didn't like it. But if you do like it, I like it very much, too.'[7] This little incident speaks volumes about the emotional culture of the Kafka household.

Whether at Felice's instigation or on his own initiative, Kafka decided to try to combat his poor health, sleeplessness and generally addled spirit by trying to adopt a healthier and more active lifestyle. Instead of sleeping after lunch, he started to put in two hours' labouring with a market gardener in the Prague suburb of Nusle (Troja), working 'in nothing but my shirt and trousers'[8] in the cool April rain. He explained to Felice that this was done 'to escape self-torture for a few hours – in contrast to my work at the office, which virtually flies away from me each time I try to grasp it (*real hell is there in the office, no other can hold any terror for me*)'.

In the weeks leading up to their third meeting at Whitsun, Kafka continued to play the same role of the tortured lover who keeps insisting that he is trying to free his beloved of him, but who also could not countenance that happening. He continued to complain – as Canetti puts it, 'complaint takes the place of writing as his integrating factor'[9] – that Felice had not properly grasped the fact that writing 'is the only thing that makes my inner existence possible. No wonder I always express myself so badly; I am awake only among my imaginary characters.'[10] As the date of their meeting approached, Felice began to voice some complaints or her own. She accused him of wanting to hurt her, a charge which gave him 'a jolt as though I had been put back into the world, after having been outside it for a long time'.[11] In spite of his frequently deployed rhetoric of self-accusation, Kafka was always taken aback when others reproached him. He buried himself in work, preparing a lecture for the Institute on the topic of 'Methods for the Prevention of Accidents'. The prospect of visiting Berlin again, and seeing Felice's family, filled him with nervous apprehension.

On 1 May Kafka told Felice that 'a very short book of mine'[12] was to be published in June in a new young writers' series from Wolff called *Der jüngste Tag/The Day of Judgement*. He considered the title 'somewhat ludicrous' and 'a useless contrivance of unity that isn't really there', but on the other hand he was indebted to Wolff for his enthusiasm – he had 'practically wormed the story out of me' – especially as the latter was promising to publish 'The Stoker' ('*Der Heizer*'), the first chapter of *The Man Who Disappeared*, later. In March Kafka had sent

Wolff a copy of *Metamorphosis* (the publisher called it 'the bedbug story'[13]) and had responded to a request for 'The Stoker'. He tried unsuccessfully to persuade Wolff to publish these two, together with *The Judgement*, as a book called *The Sons*, emphasizing the unifying theme of father–son conflict and calling it a 'secret'[14] connection (presumably because it was rooted in Kafka's relationship with his own father, but also because Felice was intimately involved in *The Judgement*). The appearance of 'The Stoker' as a forty-eight-page book with the usual print-run of a mere thousand copies was some compensation for the fact that Kafka was not producing any new material at this precise moment.[15]

At the beginning of May he resumed his diary, explaining to himself the necessity of doing so: 'The uncertainty of my thoughts, F., the ruin in the office, the physical impossibility of writing and the inner need for it.'[16] This was a succinct inventory of his travails. He had started one of the famous 'blue octavo notebooks', the seventh, for this diary and, when it was finished early the following year, he noted that it had begun with Felice 'who on May 2nd 1913 made me feel uncertain'.[17] The brevity of some of these resumed diary entries highlights their bleakness: 'The terrible uncertainty of my inner existence,'[18] runs one. Physical and psychological symptoms worked on each other: '1. Digestion. 2. Neurasthenia. 3. Rash. 4. Inner insecurity,'[19] ran another list of woes. For the first time he was prepared to admit that, given his sorry state, 'in the long run my parents put up with more from me than I from them'.[20] On 11 May another set of parents, the Bauers, were given the opportunity to see what their potential son-in-law was like when he arrived for his second visit to Berlin.

Kafka entered Berlin in characteristic mood. He sent a note to Felice: 'The journey has made me realize that there is no way of recognizing things except in each other's presence . . . we still have a number of terrible things to discuss.'[21] He added that, while packing for Berlin, he had said to himself repeatedly – and this, in the plainest possible terms so far, defines the essence of his relationship with Felice Bauer – 'I cannot live without her, nor with her [*Ohne sie kann ich nicht leben und mit ihr auch nicht*]'[22]. On meeting Felice's parents, Kafka considered that he made 'a very nasty impression on them'.[23] He told her afterwards that her family 'presented an aspect of total resignation so far as I am concerned. I felt so very small while they all stood around me like giants with such fatalistic expressions on their faces.'

Things do not appear to have been much better in their personal encounter. He apologised to Felice for 'the craziness of my behaviour during those two days in Berlin'[24] and tried to explain by saying: 'I feel there is one too many of us; the separation into two people is unbearable.' This gives a glimpse into Kafka's inability to formulate a mature relationship with another person. The give and take, the trade-offs, the allowances, the tolerances – and the reciprocal rewards – of two people negotiating each other's intimate space seem to have been beyond him, to have frightened him. He could not bear to leave the bright, white cell of his self and put himself in another's hands, even though he longed for that consummation: 'You don't know, Felice, you don't know what it is that imprisons me and makes me the unhappiest of men, in spite of seeming to be very close to you – you, my sole purpose on this earth.' Why didn't he seize her? 'Why instead do I squirm on the forest ground like one of those animals you are so frightened of?' He was worried by the fact that this canny, self-assured, decisive young woman, who knew her own mind, nevertheless became evasive and uncertain in his presence: 'when you are with me, you flag, turn your head or stare at the grass, endure the silly things I say as well as my many well-founded silences, do not seriously wish to know anything about me [but did she not, on the contrary, know in one sense quite enough?] but simply suffer, suffer, suffer.' She told him that he should not be so analytical and instead simply trust her blindly.

In spite of the two meetings in Berlin and the myriad ill omens, however, the couple persisted with their epistolary love affair. Continuing to declare his love for her, Kafka announced that he would be writing to her father, presumably with the intention of making a formal proposal of marriage. He told her about his earlier relationships, in the briefest of terms, implying that they were superficial and meaningless, except for the girl he met in the summer of 1905 or 1906 at Dr Schweinburg's sanatorium in Zuckmantel. Since those days, however, he had increasingly withdrawn into his shell, helped along by his 'wretched physical state' until 'when I had almost reached the end'[25] he met Felice. Perhaps to keep both their spirits up, he sent her a draft of a letter from September 1912, written soon after they had first met. But even that letter seemed already to be sounding the characteristic note of complaint.

The letter to her father, which he was struggling to compose, was much more serious. He felt constrained to tell Herr Bauer the truth about his poor constitution, which he explained to Felice in this way: 'For about 10 years I have had this ever-growing feeling of not being in perfect health; the sense of well-being that comes with good health, the sense of well-being which in most people is the source of constant cheerfulness, and above all unselfconsciousness – this sense of well-being I lack.'[26] It was not due to any specific serious illness, for he had never really suffered any, but was more a general condition which 'prevents me from talking naturally, eating naturally, sleeping naturally, so it prevents me from being natural in any way'. He could not live intimately with Felice and successfully disguise this rather vaguely expressed condition, and he was already worried that whenever they met she – who was normally so strong and vivacious – now seemed cowed into a 'dull indifference' by him. On this point he wanted from her 'a heart-to-heart talk', the need for which was 'burning me up because I have kept silent about it for so long'. His own family and friends could give him no advice and so he would confront Herr Bauer and ask him to nominate a doctor who would examine the prospective son-in-law. This searing example of Kafka's self-lacerating honesty was clearly a shock to Felice and she failed to answer him for more than a week. Kafka was in despair. He thought it was 'the end'[27] and the final cancellation of 'the only kind of happiness I am capable of in this world'. He even conquered his reluctance and picked up the telephone but thought he detected only more indifference when Felice came on the line. He told her to stop writing to him: 'you don't want me, nothing could be more obvious'.[28] The situation looked very bad indeed.

A welcome respite from all this angst was provided by the arrival in Prague of Löwy, who on 2 June performed an evening of Yiddish recitations and songs, organized by Kafka at the Hotel Bristol. His friend Otto Pick wrote an advertisement for the performance for the *Prager Tagblatt* at Kafka's instigation after the two had taken a walk together. Kafka also received some consolation from his inner conviction that 'The Stoker', just published, was good. On 24 May he read it to his parents, reflecting wryly that 'there is no better critic than I when I read to my father, who listens with extreme reluctance'.[29] And eventually Felice did reply, saying she was satisfied with him, a fact that did not satisfy Kafka, who could still see that he also made her suffer. Once again, this taught him that 'there is no doubt that we are immensely different'.[30] Shortly afterwards, she told him that she was not writing to him out of any sense of compassion. *The Judgement* had been published at the end of May in the annual *Arkadia*, edited by Max Brod. Kafka asked Felice if she could discover any meaning in it, affecting to say that he could not, even as he set to work explaining the connections with her – the verbal echoes of her name – that were inscribed in it. He remained, however, dissatisfied with her responses and silences. He waited two hours for a telephone connection to Berlin to speak to her and wrote a letter 'in the miserable waiting room of some miserable post office'[31] to her mother seeking to find out if she were ill. He sent her a telegram which prompted a reply that he could see was produced under duress: 'What do I want from you? What makes me persecute you? . . . On the pretext of wanting to free you of me, I force myself upon you.'[32]

In spite of all this distress, pain, uncertainty and reproach, Kafka resolved to go forward. Between 10 and 16 June he drafted a letter which would be his proposal of marriage, ten months after their first meeting, and after they had seen each other only three times. Setting aside the verdict of the doctor, which was still to come, he asked the 'criminal'[33] question – 'will you consider whether you wish to be my wife?' – then proceeded to deal with her recent objection that he was 'further ahead in every way' than she was. Kafka insisted that he had never in fact come across anyone who was more 'hopeless' than he was in ordinary human relationships and everyday life. He had no memory and knew less about most things than the average schoolboy, he was unable to reason or to tell a story – 'in fact I can hardly even talk' – so how could she possibly say she was not equal to him? 'All I possess are certain powers which, at a depth almost inaccessible under normal conditions, shape themselves into literature, powers to which, however, in my present professional as well as physical state, I dare not commit myself, because for every inner exhortation of these powers there are as many, if not more, inner warnings. Could I but commit myself to them they would undoubtedly, of this I am convinced, lift me out of my inner misery in an instant.' Besides, intellectual equality was not necessary for a happy marriage, what mattered was 'personal harmony, a harmony far deeper than that of opinions, a harmony that cannot be analysed but only felt'.

Felice's next objection was that he might not be able to stand life with her. This was true only in the sense that he was 'lost to all social intercourse' and 'quite incapable of conducting a prolonged, vigorously developed conversation with any individual'.

Even with Max Brod, in all their years of close friendship, this had not been accomplished. He was happiest in a room with two or three friends. In a larger group or in unfamiliar surroundings, 'the whole room presses on my chest and I am unable to move, my whole personality seems virtually to get under their skins, and everything becomes hopeless'. This was precisely what happened at Whitsun in the bosom of Felice's family. Solitude in his own room might seem the perfect state for Kafka, 'but then I can't even cope with myself, except when I am writing'.

Given all these frankly stated facts, what would be the profit and loss account for both of them were they to marry? 'I should lose my (for the most part) terrible loneliness, and you, whom I love above all others, would be my gain.' Felice, on the other hand, would lose a life with which she was 'completely satisfied' – Berlin, the office she enjoyed, her girlfriends, the small pleasures of life, 'the prospect of marrying a decent, cheerful, healthy man, of having beautiful, healthy children for whom . . . you clearly long'. Evidently Kafka had concluded, without offering any evidence, that the latter was not a prospect for them in spite of his frequently stated desire to raise a family. In place of all these 'incalculable' losses, Felice would gain 'a sick, weak, unsociable, taciturn, gloomy, stiff almost hopeless man [*einen kranken schwachen, ungeselligen, schweigsamen, traurigen, steifen, fast hoffnungslosen Menschen*] who possibly has but one virtue, which is that he loves you'.[34] And finally, she would face a drop in income because this self-designated hopeless case earned only 4,588 kronen a year, had little prospect of a salary increase, had nothing to expect from his parents, and certainly no prospects from literature (in his lifetime this would prove to be an accurate assessment). Having begun with the conventional question, Kafka ended with a more pertinent one: 'Would you really do this and stand it for my sake, for the sake of the man described above?' On the night of 16 June Kafka left the shop late (his parents were away and he had been forced to spend some time there in their absence) and walked to the station to mail the letter. The platform ticket machine (a ticket was required to gain access to the post office on the station for night mail) was empty, but a stranger appeared who offered to take the letter for him: it was a final touch of the surreal: what if the letter never reached its destination?

Characteristically, Felice was slow to reply. It is worth remembering that she was probably far busier than he was and had family problems to resolve about which he would be unaware (her brother's misdemeanours and her unmarried sister's pregnancy – of which the rest of the family knew nothing), but even so, he had given her a great deal to consider. Her answer was a long time coming, but Kafka, in spite of having attempted to paint the most discouraging picture of himself that he could, was eager to hear her response: 'I want to get married and am so weak that as a result of a little word on a postcard my knees begin to shake.'[35] Eventually Felice replied, but without responding to the specific points in his letter, describing his self-indictment merely as 'too harsh'.[36] She was untroubled by the unresolved issue of Kafka's medical examination and said he would make 'a good, kind husband'. He was worried that she had not considered with sufficient care what she might be risking. Gloomily he told his diary: 'The anxiety I suffer from all sides.'[37]

The examination by the doctor was intrusive and unpleasant and he was tormented by a vision of what he wanted to achieve in contrast to the miserable reality into which he had been pitched: 'The tremendous world I have in my head. But how free myself and free it without being torn to pieces. And a thousand times rather be torn to pieces than retain it in me or bury it. That, indeed, is why I am here, that is quite clear to me.' He told Felice this, that his writing was 'actually the good part of my nature'[38] and that if she could not come to love it, then there would be 'absolutely nothing to hold on to' and she would be 'terribly lonely'. Just now he was 'slowly being pulverized between the office and my writing' and had written nothing for five months. Could she live with his routine? He reminded her that he returned from the office at 2.30 or 3 p.m., ate, lay down to sleep until seven or eight o'clock, hurriedly ate his supper, took an hour's walk, and then started writing until 1 or 2 a.m. Moreover, his desire to get away from people would mean living on the outskirts of Prague, whereas Felice liked a lively social life. In short, Kafka feared that Felice was not registering all the warnings he was issuing: 'You have to believe what I say about myself; which is the self-knowledge of a man of 30 who for deep-seated reasons has several times been close to madness, thus reaching the limits of his existence, and so can see all of himself and what can become of him within these limits.'

He then decided to raise another objection (Kafka's skill in setting out an unattractive stall for himself was incomparable). This time, the problem was his position at the office, which was said to be insecure, and he had been on the verge of handing in his notice several times. If he did so, they would end up being poorer than Elli or Valli, or friends such as Max Brod and Oskar Baum. It was becoming clear, however, that his doubts were stronger than any lingering misapprehensions on the part of Felice. Nevertheless, he had yet another self-deprecating card to play.

Kafka chose at this point to refer to the 'nauseating'[39] spectacle of his father fussing over Elli's baby Felix in an adjoining room. The previous day, while again playing with the child, the whole family 'lost themselves in the nethermost regions of sexuality. I felt as revolted as if I'd been condemned to live in a sty.' The bawdy vulgarity of the scene can be imagined, and in acknowledging his 'exaggerated sensitivity' in this regard Kafka may have been, consciously or not, sending a warning signal to Felice about his sexual fastidiousness. He followed this with some appalled comments on his sister's and his mother's loss of shape after childbirth, a curiously inopportune moment to raise such matters.

The wait for a definitive 'yes' to his proposal went on. He repeated to Felice that his attitude to his writing and to people couldn't be changed; it was part of his nature and he wasn't sure that she realized this. He needed seclusion for his writing, but not merely that of a hermit: 'that would not be enough, but like the dead'.[40] With delicate understatement, Felice admitted that this might be 'rather difficult' for her. He warned: 'I have always had this fear of people . . . their intrusion on my weak nature; for even the most intimate friend to set foot in my room fills me with terror.' Troubles at the Institute continued to haunt him, especially the fear that he might be sacked for incompetence (he would never have the courage to resign). He knew that this meant his letters were becoming 'intolerable'[41] and that 'I am beginning to lose my perspective.' He had been eating very little and Ottla and his mother were starting to worry about him. Yet still the definitive, considered consent from Felice that indicated she had answered every objection did not come. She must, at this point, have been paralysed with uncertainty about what to do, as torn apart as Kafka was.

But, by the start of July, it seemed that Felice was ready to say 'yes', or to 'take up the cross',[42] as her prospective fiancé rather disconcertingly put it. He insisted – in the teeth of Felice's claim that all his objections were in reality 'tiny' – that 'I have not come to the end of my counter-arguments,' but he acquiesced. On 3 July 1913, his thirtieth birthday, Kafka finally told his mother that he was engaged. She took it 'with remarkable calm',[43] and insisted only on one thing. It was common at this time for prospective spouses to be investigated through the use of detective agencies, and Kafka was persuaded to allow his parents to secure such a report on Felice from Berlin. In the end it merely yielded the information that she was a good cook. Her parents (who can be presumed to have had greater grounds for anxiety) commissioned their own report.[44] What it said about Kafka is not known.

Although Kafka now went as far as walking around the district of Prague which the couple had selected as a possible place to live together after they were married, he was still wretched: 'I am absurdly afraid of our future and of the unhappiness which, through my fault and temperament, could develop from our life together . . . I am basically a cold, selfish, callous creature [*ich bin im Grunde ein kalter, eigennützziger und gefühlloser Mensch*].[45] He agreed to write formally to Felice's parents (whom he feared) and to speak again to his own, whom he approached with almost equal trepidation – 'fear, next to indifference, is the basic feeling I have towards people'. He could not bear his family at this moment; they left him 'choked with loathing',[46] as if, at a moment when he was on the verge of letting go his solitude, they conspired to torment him with a vision of noisy sociability: 'I cannot live with people . . . I cannot abide communal life . . . happier in a desert . . . than here in my room between my parents' bedroom and living room.' He felt life was so terrible that 'I doubt whether I am a human being' – the whole scene reminiscent of the world of *Metamorphosis*.

As the reality of formal engagement approached, Kafka became inflamed with anguish – 'squirming before you like something poisonous'[47] – and full of fear that marriage would turn him into 'a dangerous lunatic'. He told Felice: 'You have no idea . . . what havoc literature creates inside certain heads.' 'Literature' here is doing service for something more than the composition of prose fiction; it is a label for the world of Kafka's inner self which he had protected so assiduously for thirty years and was now about to be breached by he knew not what. Kafka, therefore, continued to fret, and to acknowledge 'my *dread of the union* even with the most beloved woman'.[48] In spite of her constant reassurances, 'I have a definite feeling that through marriage, *through the union, through the dissolution* of this nothingness that I am [*dieses Nichtigen, das ich bin*], I shall perish, and not alone but with my wife, and that the more I love her the swifter and more terrible it will be . . . there surely isn't a girl who has been loved as I love you, and been tortured as I find it necessary to torture you.' Only a desperate fantasy could close off this fearful prospect: 'the best plan would probably be . . . to go south with you for ever to some island or lake. In the south I feel everything is possible. And there lead a life of seclusion, feeding on grass and fruit.'[49]

Towards the middle of July Kafka joined his parents at their summer home in Radešovic, where this idyllic scenario was drafted. He was in a better mood, and began to discuss practicalities for the flat he and Felice would occupy in May 1914, a co-operative building society scheme of which he had just become a member. He decided to postpone writing to Felice's parents about firm marriage plans until the end of the year or early 1914: 'You will get to know me better; there are still a number of horrible recesses in me that you don't know,' he warned Felice.[50] He also planned to do some writing during the autumn.

Kafka's mood may suddenly have improved with the country air, but Felice had much to digest, and for the rest of the month, until just before the start of her August holiday at Westerland on the Isle of Sylt, he hardly heard from her, which may have indicated that she wanted time to consider everything that he had flung at her in recent weeks and months. The long silence did not bode well.

14

Kafka's letters to Felice were explicit enough about his fears and apprehensions as the reality of marriage came nearer, but in his private diary he drew up a formidable 'Summary of all the arguments for and against my marriage'[1] in which the noes decisively had it, and which ended with the desperate ejaculation: '*Miserable creature that I am!*' The first argument for marriage was 'inability to endure life alone . . . I am incapable, alone, of bearing the assault of my own life'. Marriage might 'give my existence more strength to resist'. On the other hand, all his intuitions about the married state were negative, down to 'the sight of the nightshirts on my parents' beds, laid out for the night' and hadn't everything he had accomplished so far, small as it was, been 'the result of being alone'? Moreover, he hated 'everything that does not relate to literature' and could not bear the idea of becoming a social animal, a family man and, above all, a conversationalist: 'Conversations take the importance, the seriousness, the truth out of everything I think.' In the end, it was simple terror of 'passing into the other' after which 'I'll never be alone again.' He conceded that in the presence of his sisters (not his mother and father) he had been known to blossom. A couple of weeks earlier he had noticed the 'fire' with which he had described a comic movie to Ottla during one of those special conversations they used to have together in the bathroom of the Niklasstrasse apartment, safely out of earshot of their parents. That incident had made him wonder why he could never do the same in the presence of strangers.[2] Marriage, perhaps, might draw out this sparky side of him. But then would it not be at the expense of his writing? 'Not that, not that!' And finally, he could just about conceive the possibility of giving up work if he remained a bachelor, but it would be impossible if he married. Of the seven charges drawn up against marriage by Kafka, only one stood a chance against the prosecuting counsel: the fear that, alone, he could not bear 'the demands of my own person, the attacks of time and old age, the vague pressure of the desire to write, sleeplessness, the nearness of insanity'.

Yet, in spite of this summing-up, less than a week later Kafka was writing to Felice to say 'we belong together and shall be together'.[3] He told her he was dreaming about her every night and said that he wanted his father to pay a visit to Berlin to see her father, with May clearly envisaged as a date for marriage. He casually mentioned that the doctor had dismissed those fears about his physical condition which had earlier seemed to form a potential obstacle to marriage. He revealed that he had poured out his troubles to his uncle Alfred Löwy in Madrid and in doing so realized how close his letter to his uncle came to *The Judgment*. Uncle Alfred, jumping too quickly to conclusions, sent the couple a premature telegram of congratulations.

A possibility of the two seeing each other in Prague when Felice was on a business trip receded, and Kafka announced that he was going to spend some time in September at the sanatorium at Riva. Outwardly purposeful in preparing the following next May's wedding, Kafka was growing frustrated with Felice's tardiness in replying to his letters and her emotional restraint. He was not impressed by the analysis of his handwriting carried out by a graphologist in Felice's holiday pension in Westerland, especially his finding that Kafka had 'artistic interests'.[4] This was preposterous: 'I have no literary interests, but am made of literature, I am nothing else, and cannot be anything else.'[5]

A curious entry in Kafka's diary at this time reads: 'Coitus as punishment for the happiness of being together. Live as ascetically as possible, more ascetically than a bachelor, that is the only possible way for me to endure marriage. But she?'[6] He and Felice could not conceivably have had sexual relations by this point. They had met each other only briefly, three times, in specific circumstances. Nothing is known of Felice's history, but Kafka was certainly sexually experienced. The meaning of this entry, its suggestion that sexual relations between them might be problematic, is opaque and merely adds to the oddity of the whole courtship. He also seemed to believe that he was now responsible in some way for Felice, having brought her this far and, in effect, having pushed her into a 'blind alley' which made it an 'unavoidable duty' to see through the whole thing. And so, in spite of sporadic suicidal thoughts and a frank statement by his mother that she did not understand him, Kafka persisted, discovering 'possibilities in my ever-increasing decisiveness and conviction which may enable me to pass the test of marriage . . . and steer it in a direction favourable to my development'.[7]

Apparently for the first time, he read Kierkegaard in an anthology of his writings. Like Kleist, here was another writer whose case 'is very similar to mine . . . He bears me out like a friend.'[8] Kafka was referring to Kierkegaard's struggle over marriage to Regine Olsen which resulted in a decision to break off the engagement because marriage was not compatible with his sense of his vocation as a writer and thinker. Kafka sent Felice another of his favourite writers, Flaubert – he did not say which book but, as noted earlier, *L'Éducation sentimentale* was the one of which he was most fond – saying: 'What life there is in that book! If one clings to it, this life seeps into one, whoever one may be.'[9] He told her that writing was more important to him than speaking and that the life which awaited her was not that of the happy couples she could watch strolling at Westerland but 'a monastic life at the side of a man who is peevish, miserable, silent, discontented, and sickly'[10] and a man 'chained to invisible literature by invisible chains' who screams when approached because, so he claims, someone is touching those chains. Once again, 'literature' was being asked to perform work for which, perhaps, it was never intended. Felice was rebuked for referring with unacceptable casualness to his 'bent for writing [*ein Hang zum Schreiben*]'.[11] 'Not a bent for writing, my dearest Felice, not a bent, but my entire self.' He warned her that living with him would be like living with a monk who could offer her only one hour a day with him away from his writing.

Incredibly – though credible perhaps, given the strange half-life that Kafka lived within the bosom of his family – it was not until 24 August that Kafka uttered his first words about Felice to his father. Hermann, he explained to Felice, was 'my enemy' but at the same time 'my admiration for him as a man is perhaps as great as my fear of him'.[12] As always, Kafka found himself forced to admire his father's robust strength and vigour. Interrupted in his customary post-prandial game of cards with Julie, Hermann accordingly gave his shrewd, businessman's assessment – which was that the marriage was economic non-sense – and briskly offered to go to Berlin and say so. If his 'irrefutable objections' were ignored in Berlin, then he would stand aside. He did not want to have to worry about a financially burdensome Franz and Felice in addition to his two sons-in-law, who weren't impressing him. Franz, who had not much financial acumen, was inclined to take his father's advice seriously in this sphere. Julie Kafka, on the other hand, begged her son to get married, perhaps fearing that this would be the only chance for the thirty-year-old bachelor.

Kafka resolved to write to Carl Bauer, Felice's father. It was an extraordinary letter in its candour, its unflinching determination to outline his unsuitability. He stressed that 'my whole being is directed towards literature', that he had followed this direction 'unswervingly until my 30th year, and the moment I abandon it I cease to live'.[13] In an earlier draft Kafka had made his famous assertion that his only calling was literature: 'I am nothing but literature [*Ich nichts anderes bin als Literatur*] . . . and can and want to be nothing else.'[14] He now claimed to Carl Bauer that he was 'taciturn, unsociable, morose, selfish, a hypochondriac, and actually in poor health' and, in a rare stroke of the portentous, said that this was no more than 'the earthly reflection of a higher necessity'. His family life was virtually non-existent: 'In recent years I have spoken hardly more than twenty words a day to my mother and I exchange little more than a daily greeting with my father . . . And is your daughter, whose healthy nature has destined her for a happy married life, to live with this kind of man?' For any father with his daughter's best interests at heart, this question might be considered all too readily answerable. Kafka also hinted again that it might be 'a relationship of love and friendship rather than a real marriage', echoing his earlier comment to Felice about living 'ascetically'.

It would appear that this letter was sent to Felice, who did not at first give it to her father and, in fact, may never have done so. However, if her mother had been reading Kafka's letters in the past, confidentiality may have been hard to preserve. Irrespective of whether they were aware of the letter's contents, the Bauers gave their consent to the marriage. Perhaps they were anxious for Felice to marry (she was now twenty-six) and may have been persuaded by their daughter to discount Franz's hyperbolic self-condemnations. The suspicion that Kafka may have deliberately been raising the stakes in order to release himself is heightened by his reaction to Felice's 'dear, suicidal letter'[15] following the letter to her father – 'suicidal' because in it she consented to marry him. He implored her – at just this point – to 'push me aside; anything else means ruin for us both'. A few days later he was still in a state of high anxiety and self-reproach: 'This is the law by which all weaklings are governed, insisting on extreme atonement and extreme radical measures [he had just shared a rather harsh punishment fantasy with her]. The desire to renounce the greatest human happiness for the sake of writing keeps cutting every muscle in my body. I am unable to free myself.'[16] In another famous passage Kafka then referred to 'the four men I consider to be my true blood-relations (without comparing myself to them either in power or in range) Grillparzer, Dostoevsky, Kleist and Flaubert'. Of this quartet, Dostoevsky was the only one to marry, 'and perhaps Kleist, when compelled by outer and inner necessity to shoot himself on the Wannsee, was the only one to find the right solution'.

Kafka had wondered if it would be best for him to meet Felice in Dresden or Berlin, but now he had to go with his boss to an International Congress for First Aid and Hygiene in Vienna. Afterwards, he planned to go on to a sanatorium at Riva. He urged her to use this fortuitous cooling-off period for 'regaining your peace of mind'. He would stop writing and just send some occasional diary entries. There was no more talk of a wedding in May.

On 6 September Kafka travelled with his director, Robert Marschner, his immediate boss, Chief Inspector Eugen Pfohl, and Otto Pick to Vienna, where they stayed at the Hotel Matschakerhof. For Kafka, this was 'out of sympathy with Grillparzer who always dined there',[17] according to W. G. Sebald in *Vertigo* ('Dr K Takes the Waters at Riva'). Miserable, in poor health and suffering from terrible headaches, Kafka tried to come to terms with his unhappy courtship. The next day he sent Felice a postcard with a picture of the famous Ferris wheel from the Prater in Vienna, and complained to her of 'relentless insomnia'.[18] He was reading Heinrich Laube's 1884 life of Grillparzer and gloomily tolerating the tedium of the conference, the torrential rain in Vienna, the awful noise in the hotel and unsettling dreams. He tried his best to avoid all human contact and sat at meals 'like a ghost'. He visited Theophil Hansen's nineteenth-century Imperial Parliament building but the sights of Vienna could not neutralize the increasingly irritating effects of his companion, Otto Pick, and his 'inane literary gossip'.[19] Debating with Pick, Kafka reflected that it was 'Impossible to lead the only possible kind of life i.e., to live together, each one to be free, each one for himself, not to be married, neither outwardly nor actually, simply to be together and by so doing to have taken the last possible step beyond the friendship between men, right up to the limit set for myself.' He met Felix Weltsch's cousin, Lise Weltsch, and went with Pick to see the Austrian expressionist poet Albert Ehrenstein (1886–1950), whose poems he did not understand, and later went out on the gondola pond and visited a fairground shooting-gallery and a vegetarian restaurant. He also met the writers Felix Stössinger (1889–1954) and Ernst Weiss (1884–1940), both of whom were slightly more sympathetic. On 8 September he attended the 11th Zionist Congress, which happened to be taking place in the city, but was not impressed by the 'permanent uproar' of the proceedings. 'I have no real contact'[20] with the Zionists, he told Felice. He told Max Brod that it was 'useless' and 'totally alien to me'.[21] (It was not until the 1920s that Kafka began to treat Zionism at all seriously.)

Duty done, Kafka travelled on 14 September to Trieste and from there made a short sea crossing, in a gale which provoked slight sea-sickness, to Venice, where he checked into the Hotel Sandwirth. From there, he tried to explain to Felice why he could not bring himself to write to her father: 'I am here alone, talk to hardly a soul except the hotel staff, am overflowing with unhappiness, and yet think I feel this condition to be appropriate to myself, assigned to me by some superhuman justice, a condition not to be transgressed but borne by me to the end of my days.'[22] He denied that the reason he was resistant to marriage was because it entailed giving up too much of himself. It was rather that 'I am prostrate, like an animal that one cannot get at . . . either by coaxing or persuasion.' He told her bluntly: 'We shall have to part.'

From Venice, he travelled to Verona, where he wrote another miserable postcard to Felice while sitting in the Church of Sant' Anastasia, and went to a cinema where he wept quietly alone. From there, he went on to Desenzano on Lake Garda, where he lay on the grass and felt 'empty and futile in every corner of my being . . . like a great stone at the very centre of which there flickers a tiny soul',[23] and thence by lake steamer to Riva, where Dr von Hartungen's sanatorium and hydrotherapy centre took him in from 22 September to 13 October (there are echoes of his arrival by steamer in 'The Hunter Gracchus', begun around this time). It was Kafka's second visit to Riva, still an Austrian possession at that time, but his first to the sanatorium.[24] It had the usual range of fresh-air and water therapies, with sixty rooms and a colony of twenty 'open-air huts' ('*Lufthütten*'). Insomniac, prone to headaches, generally run-down, Kafka's physical debility on arrival at Riva was easily matched by his spiritual condition. He would address no letters to Felice from the sanatorium, and he had apparently meant it when he had said that they should part. He enjoyed the solitude of his *Lufthütte* by the lake, even if it was 'a miserable shack' and he enjoyed sunning himself on the diving-board that projected from it over the lake.[25] He went swimming every day in Lake Garda and his health quickly started to improve. At table he found himself between an old general, Ludwig von Koch (who, one morning, failed to appear at Kafka's breakfast table: he had shot himself), and 'a small Italian-looking Swiss girl'[26] with a low-pitched voice.

This was Gerti Wasner,[27] who was not actually Swiss but from Lübeck. Kafka later decided that this was a very important episode for him: 'For the first time I understood a Christian girl and lived almost entirely within the sphere of her influence.'[28] He was touched by her excitement at hearing stories and wished he could write some for her (he was still writing nothing). They communicated at night in a language of taps on the ceiling, spoke to each other from their windows, and once Kafka snatched at a ribbon she let down. He lay awake listening to her singing before she fell asleep. None of this stopped him speculating that another sanatorium guest, a young Russian woman who was fond of telling people's fortunes with cards, might have let him into her room at night (she was diagonally opposite and Kafka felt that what he imagined could easily have happened). Gerti left before he did, by steamer: 'Too late. The sweetness of sorrow and love. To be smiled at by her in the boat. That was most beautiful of all. Always only the desire to die and the not-yet-yielding; this alone is love.'[29] A few days, a few lines, produced a more genuine sense of the joy of love than the entire bulk of the letters to date poured out to Felice.

Marriage, as opposed to fleeting dalliance, remained as unwelcome as ever: 'The idea of a honeymoon trip fills me with horror. Every honeymoon couple, whether or not I put myself in their place, is a repulsive sight to me, and when I want to disgust myself I have only to imagine placing my arm around a woman's waist.'[30] Such comments have sometimes been taken as evidence of suppressed homosexuality in Kafka,[31] but they need to be balanced by plentiful contrary evidence, such as the almost contemporaneous comment in the diary about the 'pleasures' of the Russian woman's bedroom that were missed only because of his dalliance with Gerti. He also told Felice, from Venice, how the sight of honeymoon couples showed that 'I am capable of enjoying human relationships but not experiencing them.'[32] In other words, it was a sense of failure, of exclusion from normal married life, rather than disgusted sexual recoil from its reality, that saddened him.

Certain passages in Kafka's diaries (deleted by Max Brod but now restored in the critical edition) show that Kafka had at least an awareness of the sexuality of other men. In 1912 in the Jungborn sanatorium Kafka refers to 'two beautiful Swedish boys with long legs whose shape and posture are such that one could really stroke them with one's tongue'.[33] Some critics, taking such comments at face value, identify a 'discrepancy between "disgusting", "animal-like" heterosexual intercourse on the one hand and seductive, eroticised fantasies about powerful men on the other'.[34] Also in this context is an oft-quoted comment by Kafka (who had been reading the work of the Freudian Otto Gross at the time): 'in a recent dream of mine I gave Werfel a kiss'.[35] If that had been a record of homoerotic desire, it would probably not have been expressed so casually in a letter to Brod, and there is no other corroborative evidence. Much more interesting is the fact that Kafka would have been exposed to certain trends in early twentieth-century German culture, such as the inclination to associate in a male group – the *Männerbund* – and the Wandervogel movement. In 1899 Adolf Brand founded the world's first gay journal, *Der Eigene*, which celebrated 'manly culture' as a specifically German, or 'Greek-German', phenomenon, and which was anti-feminist and anti-Jewish. Its underlying assumption – that a healthy culture was inherently masculine, aristocratic and racist – was the sort of proto-Nazi twaddle that Kafka would have deprecated, open as he was to certain health, dietary, 'reform clothing' and personal fitness trends that bordered on the 'cranky'.

Likewise, the writings of Hans Blüher, first historian of the Wandervogel movement, and his theories of 'male society' and the role of homoeroticism in the formation of the state, were known to Kafka. (It is hard not to dissociate one's responses to the photographs of naked men in massed, serried ranks doing their prescribed exercises, in some of the advertising brochures of the sanatoria used by Kafka, from those provoked by Nazi propaganda images.) Some of Kafka's early aestheticized male friendships (with Oskar Pollak, Franz Werfel and even Yitzhak Löwy, though it has never been suggested of his closest friend, Max Brod) may have had a certain *frisson*, but the notion that he was either a practising (or repressed) homosexual or a misogynist with a hatred of heterosexual sexuality is not persuasive. Kafka's difficulty with marriage was of a different order, and when he struggled with his own courtships he turned exclusively to women for support and understanding.

That difficulty, however, was real. Kafka told Brod that, though 'it is all over' and he wrote no more letters to Felice, 'still, still, I cannot free myself'.[36] He repeated the mantra 'I cannot live with her and I cannot live without her', adding: 'I ought to be whipped out into the desert.' To Felix Weltsch, he protested: 'things will not get better, things will never get better for me'. Kafka returned to Prague around the middle of October, with Felice still not out of his system. On 29 October he ended his six-week silence and wrote to her. He told her of 'that day at Desenzano'[37] when he had felt that the relationship was truly at an end, that it was necessary for him to tear himself away if she were not to reject him. He began by saying that it was family life – his own dysfunctional one, the prospect of becoming involved with hers, the challenge of establishing one of his own – that gave him pause for thought, made him feel that he could possibly 'share the pleasures but never the life of others', no matter how hard he tried. It would be false to pretend that he could happily insert himself into the Bauer family and, for him, 'living together permanently without lies is as impossible as it is without truth'. Yet – in spite of the six-week silence, in spite of Gerti and the Russian woman, in spite of the perpetual torment – he was still gripped by a 'longing for you'. He alone, he said, was to blame for 'the despair we are in' and all her letters to him amounted to 'an expression of amazement that a man such as I could possibly exist'. Felice had said a number of things – that her mother's love for her would be transferred to Kafka, that the net result of her parents' deliberations on the outward pros and cons of marriage was for it to be seen as no more than a love-match – but none of this could surely be true, Kafka insisted, if she were to think of him as a normal husband.

And now a new woman enters the story. Grete Bloch, another young businesswoman in the office machines trade, was sent by Felice from Berlin to be her intermediary with Kafka. Grete and Kafka probably met at the end of October. The most extraordinary aspect of this encounter was the claim, made by Grete long after Kafka's death (in a letter to a friend in Palestine, Wolfgang Schocken, written on 21 April 1940), that she had given birth in 1914 to an illegitimate child who had died seven years later in Munich. Grete's friends greeted the claim with incredulity, and posterity has judged the allegation likewise. Nothing in the correspondence with her suggests such a level of intimacy with Kafka – though the tone of the letters does change over the year in which they corresponded. The child could hardly have been kept a secret from Felice, yet she never mentions it, and no death certificate in Munich has ever been produced. The story therefore remains rather unlikely, if not utterly implausible.[38] A remark of Kafka's to Felice on 31 August 1916 about some burden being borne by Grete is the nearest to a sliver of evidence for the child's existence. Grete herself died in Auschwitz in 1944.

Kafka agreed to meet Grete in Prague after warning her that in his case discussion rarely clarified matters and probably had the opposite effect. Expecting some sort of 'elderly spinster',[39] he was rather taken aback to discover 'a slim, young, undoubtedly rather unusual girl' who, far from being an old and trusted friend, had known Felice for only six months, and who managed to make him feel that he had said more than he ought. Which he undoubtedly had. They met at a coffee-house several times – Grete was staying at the Hotel Schwarze Ross – and appear to have visited the Kunstgewerbe Museum. Afterwards, either at Grete's prompting or his own, Kafka decided that he must make another visit to Berlin. He knew that he must do so, but he was not hopeful, since previous meetings had served only to augment Felice's doubts.

So, on Saturday 8 November, Kafka checked into the

Askanischer Hof in Berlin for one night. As usual, his trip went far from smoothly. Felice did not respond to Kafka's letter saying he would be arriving at the hotel at ten-thirty on Saturday evening and she was at neither the station nor the hotel when he arrived. On Sunday morning at eight-thirty he sent a bicycle messenger to her (he was worried that he had to catch his train back to Prague at four-thirty) and Felice sent back the message that she would telephone in fifteen minutes. He finally heard from her (his inability to use the telephone himself remains a mystery) at 10 a.m. They went for a walk together in the Tiergarten, but this had to be interrupted at noon because Felice had to go to a funeral. Kafka lunched, then hurried back to the hotel to await her call. It did not come. Depressed at sitting in the hotel watching the rain, Kafka decided to pay a call to the writer Ernst Weiss, who lived in Schöneberg, but he tore himself away at 2.45 p.m. in order not to miss the call. Again, it did not come. He packed his bags, hung around the lobby for as long as he could, but left at four to catch his train. He did not see or hear from Felice. Once again he felt excluded and humiliated. He left Berlin 'like one who had no right to be there'.

Neither Kafka nor Felice wrote to the other about this episode, but Kafka confided to his diary: 'I intentionally walk through the streets where there are whores. Walking past them excites me . . . This uncertainty is surely the result of thinking about F.' [40] He also wrote to Grete, having rapidly established an intimate fluency with her. It was she, not Felice, who was told about the upheaval caused by the Kafka family moving from Niklasstrasse (where they had lived for six years) to a six-roomed apartment in the Oppelthaus on the Old Town Square, another of those luxurious buildings built on the ruins of the eradicated old Jewish ghetto. The new flat had a good view, he told Grete: 'Immediately opposite my window on the 4th or 5th floor is the great dome of the Russian church with its two towers, and between the dome and the neighbouring apartment house a distant view of the Laurenziberg [Petřín Hill] with a tiny church. On my left I can see the Town Hall with its massive tower rising sharply and foreshortened in a perspective that perhaps no one has ever truly observed.'[41]

Although he frequently asserted he was 'nothing but literature', Kafka had produced no serious literary work since February and would not do so until July 1914. This was in spite of the discreet and respectful reviews he had received for 'The Stoker', published back in May. The anguish of his relationship with Felice and the thousands of words he poured out to her in the late evening and early hours of most days had put a stop to any sustained creative writing. He felt himself bereft of confidence: 'Everything appears to me to be an artificial construction of the mind . . . I am more uncertain than I ever was, I feel only the power of life. And I am senselessly empty.'[42] Not even a letter from Löwy, saying how good Kafka had been to him, could raise him from this slough of despond. His reply said that he was 'in great confusion, and work, without myself or anyone else getting much out of it'.[43] Only the cinema seems to have provided him with any satisfactory diversion as the winter began. He was 'tremendously entertained'[44] by a film called *Lolotte*. Less successful was a reading in Toynbee Hall in Prague of the first part of Kleist's *Michael Kohlhaas*. Although this *Novelle* was one of Kafka's favourite pieces of prose, he considered that he read 'wildly and badly and carelessly'.[45] Normally he relished reading aloud and had been trembling with eagerness all day to do so.

Still hearing nothing from Felice, receiving no replies to four letters he had posted, he asked Grete for news of her. At the end of December, he wrote directly to Felice, reproaching her for her silence and saying, 'at the merest word from you I would write to your parents at once'.[46] No sooner had he finished his letter than one from her finally arrived. It contained what Kafka described as the 'terrible' comment: 'Marriage would mean that we should each have to sacrifice a good deal; let us not try to establish where the excess weight [*Mehrgewicht*] would be. It is a good deal, for each of us.'[47] Having bombarded Felice with so many reasons why marriage was difficult for him, Kafka could hardly have objected – but he was now doing precisely that – when Felice also indicated that there were potential costs on her side. He also took a new tack: he said that she was wrong to think that he held back from marrying her because of 'the thought that in winning you I would gain less than I would lose by giving up my solitary existence'. It was rather the fact that 'complete isolation' was an 'obligation' for him. This had now all changed as a result of his recognition of the fact that 'I cannot live without you . . . not for the sake of finding solace, nor for my own gratification, but so that you should live with me here as an independent human being.' She was unaware of an earlier diary entry in which Kafka had set out his impossible ideal: 'In me, by myself, without human relationship, there are no visible lies. The limited circle is pure [*Der begrenzte Kreis ist rein*].'[48]

And then, as his final shot of breathtaking candour to close the long and difficult year of 1913, Kafka suddenly announced that at Riva he had been in love with Gerti Wasner, ' a girl, a child, about 18 years old . . . still immature but remarkable and despite her illness a real person with great depth'. Although Kafka, in a reference to her non-Jewishness ('by blood as alien to me as can be'), made a slight concession to Felice, the confession is otherwise unsparing of her feelings: 'we meant a great deal to each other, and I had to make all kinds of arrangements to prevent her bursting into tears in front of everyone when we said goodbye, and I felt much the same'. He claimed that 'paradoxical as it may seem', this affair 'helped to make my feelings about you clearer to me'. Whether Felice shared this unvarnished Kafka logic is unclear. When they resumed their correspondence in the new year no further mention was made of Gerti. The struggle went on.

15

Kafka had now entered a new phase in his relations with Felice which began with a belated realization by him that he was not the only one who was making calculations of possible loss and gain in the proposed marriage. On his side, he feared the intrusion of another into his creative solitude, perceived as a threat to the thing which he claimed was constitutive of his very being: literature. One might note in passing that, in spite of his constant invocation of this personal deity, he had written very little *Literatur* in comparison with his four personal exemplars – Grillparzer, Dostoevsky, Kleist and Flaubert – at the age of thirty. Kafka had published one short collection of prose pieces (*Betrachtung*), four brief magazine pieces, a short story (*The Judgement*) and the first chapter ('The Stoker') of what would be the posthumous *The Man Who Disappeared*. Moreover, he had not written anything substantial for nearly a year. Even safe from the distraction of matrimony, Kafka was having difficulty in realizing his potential as a writer.

Writing to Felice on New Year's Day 1914, Kafka told her that it was the first time that she had spoken of the losses that *she* would suffer by leaving Berlin and marrying him. But he then claimed, rather boldly, that this is 'just what I have been trying to convince you of for an entire year'.[1] Coming to live with him in Prague could spell the end of her successful business career. To her, he predicted the city would seem no more than 'a provincial town with a language unfamiliar to you'. And, by entering into 'an official's, moreover not even a fully fledged official's, inevitably petty-bourgeois household, you would not be short of worries . . . and instead of social life and instead of your family you would have a husband who, more often than not . . . is melancholy and silent, and whose infrequent personal happiness lies solely in an occupation that, as an occupation, would inevitably continue to be alien to you'. Kafka didn't like the now more assertive Felice's notion of an 'excess weight', the idea that there would be disproportionate losses if they married. He claimed that it was never a question of 'loss' on his side and that 'I love you so much that I should have wanted to marry you even if you had made it perfectly clear that you had but a faint liking for me'. He was emphatic that the only kind of marriage he wanted was a union of equals where there was no question of loss sustained on either side. So he challenged her either to abandon the idea of their marriage or to have confidence in him. She had told him that he should 'live more in the real world' and 'take things as you find them', a clear indication that she was not blind to his shortcomings. He replied that you have to take people as they are, as a whole: 'I love you, Felice, with everything that is good in me as a human being, with everything in me that makes me deserving of being astir among the living.'

Kafka was taking refuge from his personal troubles in reading the life of Goethe and Wilhelm Dilthey's *Das Erlebnis und die Dichtung/Poetry and Experience*. And then – it is not clear what prompted it, though it may have been in response to Brod urging his Zionism on Kafka with too much enthusiasm – he recorded on 8 January in his diary a much-quoted observation: 'What have I in common with the Jews? I have hardly anything in common with myself and should stand very quietly in a corner, content that I can breathe.'[2] Given Kafka's steady exploration of (and reconnection with) his Jewishness, especially since the encounter with the Ostjuden in 1911, this can hardly be taken at face value as a rebuff to his inheritance. It is more in the nature of a writer's anxiety to clear a space for himself, to think and create freely beyond the constraints of particular allegiance, and is analogous to the declared aim of his almost exact contemporary, James Joyce, articulated by one of his characters in *A Portrait of the Artist as a Young Man* (1916), of flying past the nets of language, religion and nationality. But Kafka never chose (it is tantalizing to consider what the result would have been had he done so) Joyce's path of 'exile and cunning', remaining grounded in Prague, the flight of Icarus never undertaken. (When Kafka arrived in Trieste in September 1913, Joyce was there teaching English, but there could not have been the remotest possibility of either being aware of the other's presence or even existence.) 'There are possibilities for me, certainly; but under what stone do they lie?'[3] he asked himself.

These aimless days were given some shape and purpose by the arrival of the proofs of *Metamorphosis*. Kafka was less enamoured of the story now that he looked at it again: 'Unreadable ending. Imperfect almost to its very marrow. It would have turned out much better if I had not been interrupted at the time by the business trip.'[4] Furthermore, in spite of his sense of isolation, the world of letters was aware of him, and around this time the great Austrian novelist Robert Musil approached him to see if he wished to contribute to a literary magazine he was launching. Kafka was angry with Brod for giving Musil his address and turned down the offer.

Stepping out of the lift at the Oppelthaus apartment building one morning, Kafka was struck by the fact that his life 'resembled that punishment in which each pupil must according to his offence write down the same meaningless ... sentence ten times, a hundred times'.[5] Always there is the sense that he is being punished – precisely but unaccountably – for some unspecified misdemeanour. This is the world of *In the Penal Colony* and *The Trial*. Felice was continuing to make him suffer, in part because she had breached his monopoly of self-punishing angst, but also because she had not replied to his renewed request for her hand. He had seen a great deal of Ernst Weiss over the Christmas holidays in Prague and had sent him as a messenger to Felice in Berlin with instructions to report back on her appearance and demeanour. Weiss did this, but still she remained silent. To some extent Kafka displaced some of his anxiety on to Grete Bloch, who became his surrogate correspondent. As in the early letters to Felice, he deluged her with detailed questions about what she was doing with herself. When Felice, however, finally broke her silence with a postcard early in February, 'it was again as on the first day'.[6] He was faint with joy, so much so that he dropped the apple he was eating. Nevertheless, he was still tormented by the earlier phrase 'excess weight', which he would continue to quote back at her repeatedly, as he had done to Grete Bloch. Felice had written the card from Berlin's Anhalt Station on 8 February. It was very brief and said with studied casualness: 'One of these days you will be hearing more from me.'[7] She added, ' I had to write this postcard,' but the more Kafka handled the pencil-written card, the more he began to doubt that it signalled an upturn in the fortunes of their relationship. He told Grete that it was only because of her intervention that the card came at all, and that it was humiliating to have had to force it out in this way. Humiliation was to be the keynote of the relationship from now on.

The announcement that his friend Felix Weltsch was engaged to be married was not calculated to restore Kafka's spirits. He told Grete that it amounted to 'losing a friend, for a married friend isn't a true one',[8] The precious one-to-one intimacy that Kafka valued was now to be replaced by the awesome face of 'a partnership'. On the other hand he was relieved that the 'bachelor fraternity' of which he and Felix had been a part was now dissolved: 'I am free; alone everyone can be what he wants to be and is.' He was a little more candid in his diary, where he admitted that he was angry with Felix for getting married: 'I remain alone, unless F. will still have me after all.'[9] Another friend, Brod, had told Kafka that he was dedicating his new novel, *Tycho Brahe's Way to God*, 'To my friend Franz Kafka', a gesture which was 'the first unalloyed pleasure I have had in a long time . . . I am raised up and placed on the same level as Tycho, who is so much more vital than I.'[10]

In reality, as he ached for Felice to respond to him, Kafka was so far from being raised up that he began to entertain thoughts of suicide. He fantasized about the scene, rushing to the balcony, disentangling himself from all the restraining hands, leaping, and leaving behind a letter which would say 'that I was jumping because of F., but that even if my proposal had been accepted nothing essential would have been changed for me. My place is down below, I can find no other solution. F. simply happens to be the one through whom my fate is made manifest; I can't live without her and must jump, yet – and this F. suspects – I couldn't live with her either.'[11]

By 27 February Kafka had had enough. With most uncharacteristic spontaneity, he took a day's leave and caught the train to Berlin on the Friday night, not even sure that Felice would be there (once again, the telephone was a bafflingly unused resource). Next morning he went to her office and asked the receptionist to take up a note to Felice. While he waited he gazed at the switchboard, 'which in my case had never proved to be of use'.[12] Felice, not too put out by his surprise arrival, came down to reception and at lunchtime took him to a nearby teashop where they spent an hour together. He went back to her office and saw her room, and when she left work they spent another two hours walking together. That night Felice was obliged to attend a ball for business reasons, but on Sunday morning they had another three hours together, walking in the Tiergarten and visiting a coffee-house. Once again, she was too busy with family affairs to come to the station and see him off that afternoon, but this time she later apologized by telegram.

The upshot of this weekend seemed to be that Felice 'quite likes me', but not enough to marry Kafka as 'she has insurmountable fears about a joint future; she might not be able to put up with my idiosyncrasies'. She told him she didn't do things by halves. He insisted that, even if she didn't love him as much as she felt she needed to if she were to risk marriage, she should still say 'yes' because 'my love for you is great enough to make up the insufficiency'.[13] Kafka knew that he had always suppressed certain forebodings and fears that Felice did not love him enough. He even wondered whether she did not actually feel 'a certain disgust for me'. When they said goodbye in the entrance hall of her house, he insisted on opening her glove in order to kiss her bare hand, but was rewarded with a 'quite hostile grimace'. Kafka, in turn, was rather put off by the excessive dental work that had been carried out on the mouth of his beloved. In addition to these falterings of desire, Felice was not sure how ready she was to penetrate the atmosphere of literary Bohemianism, and face the prospect of life in Prague. She would miss her Berlin and her nice clothes and would not relish third-class railway compartments, cheap theatre seats and other privations. She was a material girl.

At the same time, she was friendly enough (even though, as a conversationalist, she didn't quite satisfy Kafka; in the seven hours they spent together, he claimed, she hardly finished a sentence). She walked arm in arm with him, addressed him with the familiar '*Du*' form, even in the presence of others, showed him his picture in her locket, said she wanted to keep his letters and photographs, and was happy to go on corresponding. But marriage was clearly now out of the question. Kafka delivered his verdict to Grete on a postcard scribbled in Dresden station on the return journey: 'It couldn't have been worse. Next thing will be impalement.'[14]

One consolation from Berlin was a second meeting with Martin Buber. Kafka looked back on this encounter as 'the purest memory I have of Berlin, a memory that has often served me as a kind of refuge'.[15] Otherwise the whole expedition had been a disaster. To avoid complete collapse, he made a firm resolution that, if he could not marry Felice, he would resign his post at the Institute (or ask for a prolonged period of absence), go to Berlin and try to live as a literary journalist. The Berlin to which he would have moved was that of the painter Ernst Ludwig Kirchner, whose famous *Potsdamer Platz* was painted in this year. 'You have to realize what Berlin meant to us back then in Vienna,'[16] the Austrian novelist Flesch von Brünningen had written the year before. 'For us, Berlin was crazy, debauched, metropolitan, anonymous, gargantuan, futuristic. It was literary and political and artistic (*the* city for painters.) In short: an infernal cesspool and paradise in one.' In not choosing this frenetic metropolis and remaining in Prague, Kafka closed off another avenue of escape, though the idea of Berlin stayed with him, until, in the last year of his life, he finally moved there. But for the present, in the early part of 1914, he felt hemmed in and needed to escape the overwhelming fact that 'I am completely lost in F.'[17]

Kafka tried to set down in writing the full extent of his predicament; the form he used was a sort of dialogue with himself. For as long as he remained in Prague he would never forget Felice and, because he was stuck in his usual routines, having 'a more than ordinary inclination towards a comfortable and dependent life', he would never break out and marry. 'But you wanted that sort of life for yourself, didn't you?' His answer was that an official's life could benefit him if he were married, 'But I cannot live out such a life as a bachelor.' So why didn't he marry? Because, 'much as I always loved F.', it was chiefly 'concern over my literary work that prevented me, for I thought marriage would jeopardize it. I may have been right, but in any case it is destroyed by my present bachelor's life. I have written nothing for a year, nor shall I be able to write anything in the future; in my head there is and remains the one single thought, and I am devoured by it.' Kafka added that 'as a result of my dependence, which is at least encouraged by this way of life, I approach everything hesitantly and complete nothing at the first stroke'. This was certainly true and, as Elias Canetti points out, this exquisite hesitancy was central in the writing of Kafka: 'For a good part of his work consists of tentative steps towards perpetually changing possibilities of future. He does not acknowledge a single future, there are many; this multiplicity of futures paralyses him and burdens his step.'[18]

Grete Bloch briefly entered the post-Felice vacuum in the role of confidante by becoming the recipient of the letters Kafka could not write to Felice. He offered her (brazenly, one might have thought) advice on family life, urged vegetarianism on her, sent her copies of his recently published stories, and suggested she move from Vienna to Prague in order to resolve her problems at work. He pointed out that 'although our respective relationships with F. cannot be eliminated . . . they at least no longer form the most important part in our own relationship'.[19] Small wonder that Felice, who knew Grete well in spite of the brevity of her acquaintance with her, and who would soon be recruiting her for a special role in this affair, had felt constrained to observe crisply: 'Frl Broch seems to mean a great deal to you.'[20] Kafka began to propose a meeting with Grete in either Vienna or Prague, apparently experiencing none of the difficulty in making travel arrangements which invariably overcame him in relation to Felice. He felt now that he had to leave Prague – 'I cannot see F. more and more slipping from my grasp, and myself more and more unable to escape'.[21] In addition, he felt that by doing so he would 'Counter the greatest personal injury that has ever befallen me with the strongest antidote at my disposal.' The job and its security meant nothing to a bachelor without commitments. In practical terms, as an Austrian lawyer, he could work only in Prague and Vienna (but he hated the latter city). So, with employment in Austria thus ruled out and with no talent for languages, that left only Berlin, where he would try to write and where 'I think I know definitely that from the independence and freedom I should have in Berlin (however miserable I otherwise would be) I should derive the only feeling of happiness I am still able to experience.' His needs were minimal – 'a room and a vegetarian diet' – but of course Berlin was still home for Felice. 'If our being together will help me to get F. out of my blood, so much the better, it is an additional advantage Berlin has.' With all questions thus decisively answered, Kafka's course of action was clear. Naturally, he did not follow it.

On the other hand, Kafka could not leave Felice alone. And, in spite of her declaration in Berlin that the affair was over, she was writing to him again by the middle of March. She revealed that there were problems within the Bauer family, but also, with this letter, she succeeded in reviving with a 'shock'[22] the former intensity of feeling between them. Kafka now talked to her of making progress, of the need to talk, of a possible meeting in Dresden, and then proposed another visit to Berlin. Truly, he 'could not live without her'. Felice also wrote to Kafka's mother, who, having seen the distress caused by Felice's silence, had secretly urged her to reply to Kafka's letters (Kafka, in a state of complete turmoil, had written to Felice's parents to ask if she were ill). Eventually, Felice phoned Kafka at the Institute, where at the sound of her voice 'a passionate longing to see you came over me again'.[23] She then wrote to say: 'Let us draw a line right through those discussions in the Tiergarten.' Her subsequent comment – 'You told me you were content with the love I have for you' – seemed to him to imply that she was merely prepared to sacrifice herself to him, which was completely unacceptable.

Running in parallel with this anxious set of exchanges, Kafka was writing more expansively (and more intimately) to Grete, who claimed to be surprised that he should want to go and see Felice. It was now clear that Grete was jealous of Kafka's stubborn devotion to her friend. Meanwhile, Felice continued to agonize over Kafka. She said she still had apprehensions about life with him, but he could not answer these, even if he were at her side as he had been in the Tiergarten, 'on the point of prostrating myself . . . humiliated, more deeply than any dog'.[24] Once again, Kafka was using an animal metaphor for his sense of self-loathing, of being used and humiliated, senselessly, a metaphor which recurs in so many of his stories. He told her: 'I do not know myself completely.' He was aware of his 'immaturity', of his lack of understanding of his own fluctuating nature, but he still loved her, and everything in his life had changed as a result of contemplating the possibility of marriage. 'I have quite definitely reached a dead end. I am not likely to forget that it was you who made me realize this. Never in my life have I had such definite signs to prove the absolute need for decision. I must tear myself out of my present life either by marrying you, or by giving notice and going away.' The 'decision' that did not come easily to Kafka was now showing itself in an application for a 'minor' job in Berlin and an attempt to climb 'the lowest rungs of journalism'. Felice suggested that he should come to Berlin to see her parents, but only after they had spoken to each other first.

But she then resumed her silence, driving Kafka to distraction. He saw her lack of correspondence in the same light as her silences and withdrawals when they walked together in the Tiergarten. Once again he was transformed into a maltreated animal, thoughts of happiness with Felice tinged with the recollection of her 'dull hatred and antagonism'[25] in the Tiergarten: 'Surely no human being can ever have been more profoundly humiliated at the hands of another than I was on that occasion by you, though certainly no one could have asked for it more than I did.'

On 4 April Kafka managed to get to the telephone to speak to Felice, proposing that they meet in Berlin after Easter. He hated the instrument, and to use it in the office he had to descend two floors from his desk to the Institute president's anteroom, where the speaker was invariably surrounded by a crowd of noisy, laughing people. 'I find that even in ordinary telephone conversations I can say nothing owing to my total lack of quick-wittedness, and my preoccupation with this inability makes it almost impossible for me to understand anything (it is not so very different when talking face to face).'[26] The result of this technophobia ('this invention which is new to me and which I hardly know how to deal with') was that on a long-distance call Kafka could understand practically nothing, 'and in any case [had] absolutely nothing to say'. When Felice heard him on the line she thought he sounded cross, but it was in reality his being distracted by a senior colleague who was 'tactfully pointing out that my mouth rather than my eyes should be on the receiver'.

Kafka persisted, in spite of a realization that, after eighteen months' running to meet each other, they were still far apart. He made his trip to Berlin on the weekend of 12–13 April 1914. While there, the engagement of Franz Kafka and Felice Bauer was finally announced. Julie Kafka immediately sent Felice (losing no time in addressing her as 'Dear Daughter'[27]) her congratulations and, as soon as he was back in Prague, Kafka told his fiancée that 'I have never at any time taken a step which has left me as firmly convinced of having done the right and absolutely necessary thing as when we became engaged'.[28] He added, 'The fact that I asked questions, and will go on asking them, is due less to any need of the heart than to a craving for logic.' The round of family visits meant that the couple could hardly snatch a kiss, and Kafka felt that the business of an engagement was seen as 'a couple putting on an act'. On the same day he told Grete, 'Our relationship, which for me at least holds delightful and altogether indispensable possibilities, is in no way changed by my engagement or my marriage.'[29] She, however, started to demand that he destroy all her letters to him. Grete was starting to cover her tracks.

The prospect of marriage meant the cancellation of Kafka's plans to go to Berlin and work as a journalist, but there was no cessation of his habit of obsessive analysis of the relationship. He didn't like Felice's mother, whom he found a little 'sinister'[30] (probably, he felt, reciprocated after he had 'quite unnecessarily flaunted my vegetarianism'). He told Felice that 'we do seem to be outwardly diametric opposites, so we must be patient with each other, must have almost godlike perception . . . of the other's needs, truths, and sense of belonging'.[31] For her part, Felice thought he looked 'terribly ill' when he was in Berlin. She was also slow to tell him all about her brother's unspecified troubles and about a former male friend from Breslau whose picture hung in her room. But the plans went ahead. Felice was to quit her job in August, flat-hunting began, an engagement notice appeared on 21 April in the *Berliner Tagblatt*, and Kafka wrote to his prospective mother-in-law (addressing her as 'Dear Mother') to say that, though she 'may have detected certain shortcomings in me . . . none of us is perfect',[32] and she was giving her daughter 'to a man who certainly loves her no less than you do'. Plans were also in train for the Bauers to visit Prague.

Kafka looked at some apartments in his city and found a beautiful one in the suburbs, surrounded by greenery, with three rooms and a terrace. However, its rent was far more than they could afford. Moreover, as he explained to Felice, there was a further defect: 'You would be surrounded by Czechs.'[33] This quite untypical prejudice was probably caused by Kafka searching for a demerit with which Felice would concur. The distinction between them – a Prague German and a metropolitan German – had occasionally been mentioned in their correspondence, with Felice pulling Kafka up on the odd linguistic point. Kafka clearly did not want Felice to think she was being enticed into a provincial backwater. He had looked at a much cheaper inner-city apartment behind the museum at the top end of Wenceslas Square, but his description of its urban squalor seemed calculated to fill Felice with horror. In the end, Kafka's parents intervened and found a place, reminding him of how much he depended on them for life's practicalities: 'I wonder whether they will lay me in my grave too, after a life made happy by their solicitude.'[34]

But even this flat proved too expensive and in early May, after Felice had gone back to Berlin, the couple were forced to look at ways of reducing the cost of the flat, which Felice had left too early to see. One plan was for Grete to share the apartment with them. This was a surprising solution for several reasons, not the least of which being that Kafka's chances of solitude and silence would surely be diminished by it. Sitting alone at his desk, he admitted to Felice that he was 'less dependent on you than when I am with you',[35] a rather ominous comment that was followed by the fear that 'We may be holding each other firmly by the hand at present, but the ground under our feet is not firm; it keeps shifting endlessly and chaotically. At times I don't know whether our firm holding of hands is enough to keep the balance.' Kafka's need to reassure Grete that 'nothing has changed'[36] in their relationship implies that uncertainty was growing in the latter's mind also.

Back in Berlin on 1 June, the official engagement party was thrown. Kafka's mother and sister Ottla went on ahead, leaving Kafka with his father alone in the apartment. There was a faintly uncomfortable atmosphere, probably occasioned by Hermann's private coolness about the impending marriage. Kafka noted in his diary that night: 'How Father acted when I touched F.'[37] On 30 May he left for Berlin, 'In spite of insomnia, headaches and worries, perhaps in a better state than ever before.'[38] It was, however, only to be expected that the engagement party would be an ordeal for Kafka, because he was the focus of attention, and was required to jump through the conventional hoops of a family gathering. On his return to Prague he recorded in his diary: 'Was tied hand to foot like a criminal. Had they set me down in a corner bound in real chains, placed policemen in front of me and let me look on simply like that, it could not have been worse. And that was my engagement; everybody made an effort to bring me to life, and, when they couldn't, to put up with me as I was. F. least of all, of course, with complete justification, for she suffered the most.'[39]

Kafka returned from Berlin to Prague with the idea that 'it is not the most important thing for me to write in Prague.'[40] He had recently begun to put pen to paper again after a year's inactivity, with a short sketch, 'Temptation in the Village', which points towards *The Castle*, written eight years later. At this point in time, though, 'the most important thing is for me to get out of Prague'. In a letter to Grete – again, with her he was more emotionally easy, more likely to share literary ideas and responses, than he ever was with Felice – Kafka allowed his doubts to struggle to the surface: 'At times – and for the moment you are the only one to know – I really don't know how I, being what I am, can bear the responsibility of marriage.'[41] Significantly, he expressed himself with more warmth and fluency to a woman than to any of his circle of male friends, who seemed shut out of this current phase of his life. 'You, after all, are my adviser on both major and minor issues,'[42] he told Grete. As marriage neared, all his anxieties gathered like the 'ghosts' which he described to Grete and which had always haunted him: 'huge, bony ghosts they were, nameless in their multitude . . . If one were writing, they were all benevolent spirits; when not writing, they were demons, and pressed so close that all one could do was raise a hand to declare one's presence.'[43] Nothing better illustrates the way in which Kafka had to live to write but also write to live; it was only in the moment of writing that all these tensions were resolved, these ghosts banished. As a prospective husband, he saw himself as 'a typical case' in the following terms:

> Owing to circumstances, as well as to his own temperament, a completely antisocial man [*gänzlich unsocialer Mensch*] in an indifferent state of health hard to determine at the moment, excluded from every great soul-sustaining community on account of his non-Zionist (I admire Zionism and am nauseated by it), nonpractising Judaism; the most precious part of his nature continually and most agonizingly upset by the forced labour of his office – a man of this kind, certainly under the deepest inner compulsion, decides to get married – to undertake, in other words, the most social of acts. For a man of this kind, that strikes me as no mean venture.[44]

Kafka's health – or his perception of his state of health – was worsening. He could not sleep properly, he was irritable, and he acknowledged his 'enormous hypochondria'.[45] He told Grete: 'If I were healthier and stronger, all difficulties would have been overcome, I would have left the office long ago, I would be quite sure of F. and sure of the whole world.' His state of health was strategic, it was being called upon as an ally whose auxiliary forces might soon be required. But still he told himself he was doing the right thing: 'Convinced that I need F.'[46]

That conviction, however, was not shared. Kafka's closest confidante at this time, Grete – whether from jealousy or, more likely, from a judgement about the lack of wisdom of this union – had begun to work against the marriage, and with some justification. In the letters Kafka had written to her about his doubts, the evidence had been mounting up. At the beginning of July Kafka planned to go to Berlin again. He could not have foreseen what would greet him there. It is clear that Grete's apprehensions and fears about Kafka as a husband for her friend had been growing. He had written to her in the same spirit as he had always written to Felice, with unflinching, self-critical candour, holding nothing back, elaborating the indictment of himself with endless detail. Grete may also have felt guilty at having 'betrayed' Felice by allowing Kafka to write to her so affectionately and intimately, and because of what she called in a draft letter to Kafka, 'my ridiculous, irresponsible weakness when answering your previous letters'.[47] On the eve of his trip to Berlin, Grete finally told him: 'I suddenly see the situation so clearly, and am in despair. The fact that I was determined, at all costs, to see your engagement as a stroke of good fortune for both of you, and considered it your destiny, undoubtedly creates an infinite responsibility in me to which I no longer feel equal.'[48] She added that she almost wanted him *not* to come to Berlin 'if you don't feel clear in your mind, firm within yourself, and *full* of enthusiasm'. She hardly dared look Felice in the eye, because she felt that she had not acted early enough in sounding the warning bell about Kafka's weakness, indecision, self-doubt and plain unsuitability for her friend.

Kafka's reply, written on his thirty-first birthday, 3 July 1914, declared – obtusely, one cannot help but feel – 'It looks as though I have convinced you at last.'[49] He claimed that the sole object of his relationship with Grete had been to 'convince' her of the truth about himself. Evidently he felt this was enough; as if, in possession of it, everyone would fall into line. He was what he was, and 'These conditions cannot be improved deliberately; the human fabric is not like water that can be poured from one glass into another.' Kafka was either being deliberately unresponsive to the gravity of Grete's letter or simply knew no other way to act. Telling the truth about himself was the only thing he knew how to do well. But he was riding for a fall.

Julie Kafka the next day wrote a friendly letter to Felice's mother, fussing about bedlinen and furniture for the couple and reporting cloyingly that she had just surprised Franz working as usual in his room and 'blissfully contemplating dear Felice's photograph'.[50] On 11 July Kafka travelled to Berlin, unaware of the full extent of what was waiting for him the next day at the Askanischer Hof. He may have had an inkling – 'there is nothing definite to say about the question or about me'[51] he told Ottla enigmatically the night before he left – but surely he could not have anticipated Felice, her sister Erna and Grete Bloch trooping into his hotel room like a prosecution team entering a courtroom. Ernst Weiss followed them in as Kafka's half-hearted and unconvinced defence lawyer. Everyone was engaged in the trial of Franz K. He called it later 'the tribunal [*Gerichtshof*] in the hotel'[52] and recalled 'F.'s face. She patted her hair with her hand, wiped her nose, yawned. Suddenly she gathered herself together and said very studied, hostile things she had long been saving up.'

It was the end (or so it seemed). Kafka offered no defence, for he did not understand the charges. What crime had he committed? He sat mutely as the quartet, who had arrived together by cab, started to repeat a funny story told by the cab-driver, which fell like lead in the tense atmosphere of the room. Felice, angered by Kafka's sullen silence, read out extracts, underlined in red, from the letters supplied by Grete. He later claimed that his silence – he merely 'stammered some inconsequential words'[53] – was not due to spite. He could understand, in view of the letters, why Grete had been brought along, but could not comprehend why Erna, whom Kafka liked, had been dragged into the show. He did not have anything decisive to say because 'I realized that all was lost . . . I loved you then as I do now [three months after the event]. I knew that though innocent you had been made to suffer for two years as even the guilty ought not to suffer; but I also realized that you could not understand my position . . . I was continually trying to explain my position to you – and what's more you obviously understood it, but couldn't bring yourself to accept it.' That 'position' was that, within Kafka, there were 'two selves wrestling with each other'. One could have been made to be what she wanted; the other was the one that thought only of work and was able to suffer for it. The two selves were in conflict but symbiotic. 'This is how it is, Felice. And yet they are locked in combat, and yet they could be yours; the trouble is that they cannot be changed unless both were to be destroyed.' Kafka told Felice bluntly that she should have accepted this state of affairs 'completely'. He realized that what was going on in this struggle 'was also happening for you'. Everything that looked to her like 'obstinacy and moodiness' was 'nothing but an expedient', partly forced on him by the unsympathetic circumstances of his life, given what he considered his vocation to be. Also, her idea of setting up a home characterized by its 'bourgeois orderliness' was not what he needed. In fact, 'it actually frightens me', and the conditions of such a life would be 'antagonistic to my work'.

Kafka allowed that Felice too might have felt threatened, that 'your fears were as fully justified as mine', but he wasn't convinced. Passages such as these are why many people find the letters to Felice hectoring. His determination to pursue logic relentlessly to its bitter end – what we might call the rabbinical side of Kafka – was not always welcome to those who preferred certain things not to be remorselessly spelled out. Nor did it seem that Felice was to be granted those allowances to which he thought *he* was entitled: 'I don't believe this was the case. For I loved you in your true nature, and feared it only when it met my work with hostility.' He even risked asking if she did not *want* to be 'endangered'. This implacability in Kafka must have been what ultimately broke the string of Felice's tolerance. In the end, it was what put Felice, Erna, Grete and Ernst in the cab from Charlottenburg to the Askanischer Hof.

After the trial, everyone adjourned to the Bauers', where Felice's mother wept and her father 'sat there in his shirt sleeves'.[54] Both parents resigned themselves to the fact that 'there was nothing, or not much, that could be said against me. Devilish in my innocence.'

If Kafka was inclined to blame anyone, it was Grete, who had been the agent of his downfall in spite (because?) of all the confidences he had shared with her. Kafka went back to the hateful hotel – hot, noisy 'as a boiler factory', with bad smells and even a bedbug. 'Crushing it a difficult decision,' Kafka observed bitterly. That evening he sat 'alone on a bench on Unter den Linden', then 'suffered through a horrible night'. The next day he had lunch at the Restaurant Belvedere on the Strahlau Brücke with Felice's sister Erna, also in tears, who tried to cheer him up. Kafka didn't visit the Bauers again, merely sending a letter saying: 'Don't think badly of me.' He left that night for Lübeck.

Julie Kafka was utterly baffled by what had happened. She told Frau Bauer that when an explanatory letter from Berlin from Kafka had arrived she had 'frozen into a pillar of salt'.[55] She asked to see 'the letter that was so disastrous' – a reference to the letter to Grete, with passages underlined in red, which Felice had read out at the 'tribunal'. Julie identified the problem as being her son's long-standing inability to show affection: 'I am firmly convinced that he loves me most tenderly, and yet he has never shown me, his father, or his sisters, any particular affection.' This was in spite of the fact that he was 'the kindest person imaginable', who even gave money to his less well-off colleagues at the office because he considered he did not need it for himself. In a simple but accurate verdict, Julie Kafka summed up: 'Perhaps he is not made for marriage, since his only endeavour is his writing, which is the most important thing in his life.'

Terrible as the experience of the 'tribunal' had been, it was to precipitate one of the most famous works of modern European literature.

16

In August 1914, a month after the events at the Berlin hotel, the First World War proper began, Austria-Hungary having already declared war on Serbia in July. The war would have immediate consequences for the Kafkas because the husbands of Elli and Valli immediately signed up. This resulted in a family game of musical chairs. Elli and her two children moved into the Oppelthaus apartment, occupying Franz's room. He moved out to Valli's apartment in Bilekgasse (Bílková ulice), then later into Elli's in Nerudagasse (Polská), then back to Bilekgasse, and eventually, in March 1915, found his own place on Lange Gasse (Dlouhá). 'Things are very gloomy here in Prague,'[1] Julie told Frau Bauer (she still hoped that the two lovers would be reunited and wanted Frau Bauer to keep her promise to come to Prague, regardless of the war).

The shop remained open but trade had collapsed as a result of the war, and six months' advance rent on the Oppelthaus was due. Interrupted mail services had left Elli and Valli in ignorance of where their husbands had been posted. Kafka himself, exempted from military service through being in what was considered essential civilian work, would willingly have signed up but would almost certainly have been declared physically unfit. He realized, however, that not being caught up in the general mobilization would mean that he would have to spend his afternoons at the asbestos factory, as well as moving out of the family home, but he was firm in his resolve: 'I will write in spite of everything, absolutely; it is my struggle for self-preservation.'[2] He went to the station to see off Karl Hermann, and was clearly not indifferent to the war, in spite of a much-quoted diary entry for 2 August: 'Germany has declared war on Russia. Swimming in the afternoon.'[3] This merely emphasizes the nature and purpose of Kafka's diary, which was more a sketchbook of ideas and self-analysis than a record of world events, only rarely touching on the latter. Even the reference to going swimming is untypical. He continued to follow the war's progress, expressing anguish at its progress and the incompetence, as he saw it, of the generals. A few days later he watched an artillery regiment across the Graben (Na Příkopě) and noticed a 'rigidly silent, astonished, attentive black face with black eyes'.[4]

The war had given Kafka yet another reason to feel like an outcast: 'I discover in myself nothing but pettiness, indecision, envy and hatred against those who are fighting and whom I passionately wish everything evil.'[5] He was repelled by the patriotic parades through Prague – 'I stand there with my malignant look' – and considered them 'one of the most disgusting accompaniments of the war'. Moreover, they were 'originated by Jewish businessmen who are German one day, Czech the next'.[6] Against this background, and out of the wreckage of his marriage plans, Kafka tried to make an assessment of where he stood:

> What will be my fate as a writer is very simple. My talent for portraying my dreamlike inner life [*meines traumhaften innern Lebens*] has thrust all other matters into the background; my life has dwindled dreadfully, nor will it cease to dwindle. Nothing else will ever satisfy me . . . But the strength I can muster for that portrayal is not to be counted upon; perhaps it has vanished for ever . . . Thus I waver . . . Others waver too . . . But I waver on the heights; it is not death, alas, but the eternal torments of dying.

This may have been the beginning of a kind of death-wish in a thirty-one-year-old who had less than a decade left to live. Kafka would naturally now feel at a low point, but this was something more: a sense that the game could be up, that the life lived only for literature might not, ultimately, be liveable at all. It needed greater resources than he could muster. Someone like Strindberg had the strength and was 'tremendous. This rage, these pages won by fist-fighting.'[7]

Before returning to Prague, Kafka had drafted a letter to his parents from the Danish Baltic resort of Marielyst, where he was staying. Having travelled from Berlin to Lübeck, he had found himself in another dreadful hotel and had met Ernst Weiss, who was no doubt anxious about his friend. He had then taken an excursion to the beach at Travemünde, where he bathed, before going with Weiss and his companion Rahel Sanzara to Marielyst. He had been in a state of despair in the immediate aftermath of Berlin. He wrote in his diary: '*I am more and more unable to think, to observe, to determine the truth of things, to remember, to speak, to share an experience; I am turning to stone, this is the truth* . . . If I can't take refuge in some work, I am lost . . . I shun people not because I want to live quietly, but rather because I want to die quietly.'[8] He told Brod, 'I have put aside my apparent stubbornness, which has cost me my engagement, and eat almost nothing but meat.'[9] This rebellion merely gave him an upset stomach and renewed his insomnia, with the result that he woke, like Gregor Samsa, 'feeling my abused and punished body in the bed like something alien and disgusting'. The first time in months that he had felt 'any life stir in me in the presence of other people' was on the train back from Berlin when he sat opposite a Swiss woman who reminded him of Gerti Wasner, whom he had loved so simply. At the end of July, in a fictional fragment scribbled in his diary, for the first time emerged a character called 'Joseph K'.[10]

In the letter to his parents from Marielyst – a precursor of the

Letter to the Father – Kafka put it to them that he had perhaps 'had it too good'.[11] Until now he had 'grown up wholly in dependency and comfort', which was not good for him, and it was time he made the experiment of breaking out on his own, as he had earlier thought of doing when his first engagement to Felice broke down in 1913. He rejected the idea that he was too old for such a breaking out ('I am younger than I seem') and insisted that he must escape from Prague. 'Here everything is arranged so as to keep me, a person basically craving dependency, in it.' The Institute, though a nuisance, was basically easy and gave him more money than he needed. 'I am risking nothing and have everything to gain if I give notice and leave Prague. I am risking nothing because my life in Prague is leading to nothing good.' His practical plan was to take his savings of 5000 kronen and live off them in Berlin or Munich – he loathed Vienna: its 'provincialism and hopelessness',[12] its atmosphere of a 'decaying mammoth village'[13] – for two years. During that period, through literary work, he would bring out of himself what in Prague he could not achieve 'in such clarity, fullness, and unity'[14] because he was 'hampered by inward slackness and outward interference'.

Kafka acknowledged that he could be deluding himself with this plan: 'But an argument against it is that I am thirty-one years old and such delusions at such an age cannot be taken into the reckoning, for otherwise all reckoning would be impossible.' And besides, he had already written 'several things, though little, which have met with some degree of appreciation', a suitably modest (and accurate) assessment of his literary profile at that time. He wasn't lazy and he was quite frugal, so the plan could work, but he wanted his parents' approval before taking it any further. Either they did not give that approval or, more likely, the letter was never sent and he sank back into his grimly resigned existence in Prague.

By the middle of August, however, he was able to report that he had been writing for several days – 'may it continue'. He was now at work on *The Trial* and felt that, in contrast to two years before when he had written *The Judgement* and had begun *The Man Who Disappeared*, he was 'not so completely protected by and enclosed in my work'[15] and could 'once more carry on a conversation with myself'. In other words, his 'monotonous, empty, mad bachelor's life has some justification'. For the rest of the summer and early autumn Kafka pushed ahead with *The Trial*. He was battling against his old apathy and despair and wondered if the Austrian defeats in the war explained his general feelings of anxiety: 'The thoughts provoked in me by the war resemble my old worries over F. in the tormenting way in which they devour me from every direction.'[16] Looking back on the beginnings of his relationship with Felice, he realized that he had allowed himself to be supported by his writing only in the early stages – 'henceforth I will never allow it to be taken from me'. In early October he took a week's leave in order to advance the novel – a clear sign that it was working out – but this tactic didn't yield results at first, forcing him to ask himself whether he were 'unworthy of living without the office'.[17] He took another week and this time the writing came.

An unexpected letter from Grete Bloch, two months after the Berlin fiasco, revived his old fears: 'I know that it is certain I shall live on alone (if I live at all which is *not* certain), I also don't know whether I love F.'[18] He tried to recall certain moments when she had repelled him ('dancing with her severe eyes lowered, or when she ran her hand over her nose and hair in the Askanischer Hof before she left'), but in spite of everything 'the enormous temptation returns again'. He told Grete that he didn't, as she said, hate her and that although she had sat in judgement over him in Berlin, 'in fact I was sitting in your place, which to this day I have not left'.[19] Kafka worried that this letter to Grete had seemed too unyielding, for he was not sure that he did not want to yield. He had lived for two months without Felice (although he had corresponded with her sister

Erna) and she was to all intents and purposes dead. Now suddenly she was the centre of everything again and was probably interfering with his work even though she still seemed paradoxically remote to him.

By the end of October progress on *The Trial* was grinding to a halt and Kafka decided to write to Felice: The result was the longest letter he ever wrote to her. He had been silent for three months, he told her, because there was no reason to write and because the 'tribunal' at the Askanischer Hof had rather exposed 'the futility of letters and the written word in general'.[20] It was clear that nothing had changed. He repeated the point that 'You were unable to appreciate the immense power my work has over me . . . you were not only the greatest friend, but at the same time the greatest enemy, of my work, at least from the point of view of my work. Thus, though fundamentally it loved you beyond measure, equally it had to resist you with all its might for the sake of self-preservation.' He wasn't silent at the hotel out of spite but because he simply had nothing to say: 'I realized that all was lost . . . I loved you then as I do now . . . but I also realized that you could not understand my position.' He gave her a glimpse of how he was living in Prague in the first few months of the war, alone in Valli's apartment. He worked at the office until two-thirty in the afternoon, had lunch at the Oppelthaus, spent an hour or two reading newspapers, writing letters or doing work for the office; he went to his apartment to sleep; then, at 9 p.m. he walked back to his parents' for supper, catching the tram back to Bilekgasse at 10 p.m. 'and then to stay awake as long as my strength, or fear of the following morning, fear of headaches at the office, permits'.

During the two weeks' leave he stayed at his desk until five in the morning, and in one case until seven-thirty. This was the way of life that was an obstacle to Felice and which was non-negotiable. He thought he had detected in the past something like a 'fear' or even 'hatred' in her letters in relation to this modus vivendi of his. 'It was my duty to protect my work, which alone gives me the right to live, and your fears proved . . . that here lay the gravest danger to my work.' Kafka knew that the same arguments as ever obtained, and the night before he wrote this letter he thought he had 'crossed the borderline of madness' with thinking about them. In spite of this, however, he was 'extremely impatient' for an answer from Felice.

The renewed contact with Felice wrecked Kafka's current writing project and threw him once more into turmoil. He felt that he had come up 'against the last boundary, before which I shall in all likelihood sit down for years, and then in all likelihood begin another story all over again that will again remain unfinished. This fate pursues me.'[21] He believed he had become cold and insensible again but wanted to try win back Felice: 'I'll really try it, if the nausea I feel for myself doesn't prevent me.' When her father suddenly died of a heart attack he thought it was further proof that he had brought ruin on the Bauers.

Kafka's remark about the fate of producing endless unfinished stories is telling. None of his three major posthumous novels was finished, though that has never seemed to prove an obstacle to readers. He had started *The Trial* in July, before having finished *The Man Who Disappeared* – though the final part of the latter as we know it was completed in October 1914. In that month he also wrote *In der Strafkolonie/In the Penal Colony*, reading it to Brod and Otto Pick at the start of December in spite of its 'glaring and ineradicable faults'[22] and in December he wrote the story '*Vor dem Gesetz*/ Before the Law' and finally 'finished' *The Trial*. It had been, in spite of the constant complaints, an astonishingly productive six months. 'One has no hesitation in calling these latter five months of 1914 the second great period in Kafka's life as a writer,'[23] Canetti argues. The first was two years earlier in the autumn of 1912. At the end of December he wrote yet another story, '*Der Riesenmaulwurf*/ The Giant Mole' – 'almost without knowing it'.[24] Kafka felt that 'the beginning of every story is ridiculous at first', as if it couldn't possibly survive, but 'one shouldn't forget that the story, if it has any justification to exist, bears its complete organization within itself even before it has been fully formed'. 'The Giant Mole' explores, among other things, the country and city theme, which was often on Kafka's mind.

On New Year's Eve 1914 Kafka summed up this great creative period since August as 'working . . . in general not little and not badly, yet neither in the first nor in the second respect to the limit of my ability, especially as there is every indication (insomnia, headaches, weak heart) that my ability won't last much longer'.[25] The origin of Kafka's intuition that he was now in some form of terminal decline is not clear. There is no mention of illness, doctors, leave of absence from work. It is hard not to banish the thought that he was willing himself into such a state. Certainly, self-punishment was a leading theme of his writing at this time.

Der Verschollene, the novel that is now known as *The Man Who Disappeared* (the German word is suggestive of 'missing person'), was first published in 1927, three years after Kafka's death, with Brod's title, *Amerika*. The first chapter, 'The Stoker', as we know, was published separately by Kurt Wolff in May 1913. The novel has rightly been called, by one of its most recent translators, 'the Cinderella among Kafka's three novels'.[26] Less well known than *The Trial* and *The Castle*, and at a superficial glance less obviously 'Kafkaesque', it is nevertheless a very characteristic piece of work. Most of the novel was completed in the vigorous period of Kafka's creativity in the wake of the breakthrough composition of *The Judgement* in September 1912, but after putting it aside to work on *Metamorphosis*, he more or less abandoned it during the long barren period that ended in the summer of 1914, only resuming in the autumn of that year. When he offered 'The Stoker' to Wolff in April 1913, Kafka suggested putting it in one volume with *Metamorphosis* and

The Judgement under the title *The Sons*. The reason for this suggestion is obvious: all three stories concern the fate of young men, exiled, threatened or sent to their deaths by their fathers. The relationship of Franz and Hermann Kafka lies behind all of them (though they are not mimetically 'autobiographical'). Their relationship was permeated by a powerful sense of guilt on the part of the son, and *The Man Who Disappeared* is shot through with the characteristic themes which that guilt engendered. Kafka himself called the novel 'Dickensian', which in one sense is reasonable – the young innocent leaving home to make good is in *David Copperfield* and other Dickens novels – but it is a much more complex, unsettling and *modern* novel than that comparison might suggest. Kafka was thinking in particular of the first chapter, 'The Stoker'. 'It was my intention, as I now see,' he wrote in the autumn of 1917, 'to write a Dickens novel, but enhanced by the sharper lights I should have taken from the times and the duller ones I should have got from myself.'[27] This is nicely put, for it draws attention to the contemporaneity of the novel and the personal element in it. Actually, although he was immersed in Dickens and his life story when he started to write the book, Kafka had reservations about the 'awful insipidity' of Dickens, the 'heartlessness behind his sentimentally overflowing style' and the 'rude characterizations'. He admired his 'opulence and great, careless prodigality' (so different from Kafka's own careful, controlled exactness) but in the end felt there was a 'barbarism' in Dickens' art that he hoped he had managed to avoid.

The modernity in Kafka's novel is partly a product of its moment: the mass emigrations to America, its extraordinary imaginative grip on the huddled masses of Eastern Europe who dreamed only of getting there. It also drew on the Kafka family tradition of members – the kin, or *mishpocheh* in Yiddish – who had made good there, such as Otto Kafka, one of the Kafkas from Kolin, his younger brother Franz, and also Emil, the son of

Heinrich Kafka, a merchant in Leitmeritz, whom Kafka sometimes visited on his business trips into northern Bohemia.[28]

But, however much Kafka drew on these sources, the novel's peculiar mixture of precision and imaginative strangeness was entirely his own. His America is an imagined one – he never set foot on its soil – and it is permeated with actual or studied small errors, which may signal this counter-factual temper. We have become accustomed to these 'post-modernist' tricks in the contemporary novel, but in *The Man Who Disappeared* they seem to point to deeper thematic concerns. One need look no further than the novel's first paragraph to identify these features. Seventeen-year-old Karl Rossmann arrives in the United States, having been thrown out of his parental home because he allowed himself to be seduced by a servant girl. Like all those immigrants bearing down on Ellis Island, he glimpses the Statue of Liberty: 'The sword in her hand seemed only just to have been raised aloft, and the unchained winds blew about her form.' There is, of course, no sword (the instrument of vengeful justice) in the hand of the real statue, but rather a torch of liberty. And are those 'unchained winds' ironic in their suggestion of freedom? Karl, innocent but declared guilty, may not be coming to a land of promise and freedom, but to a place where he will have to struggle to expiate this arbitrary and unsought guilt in order to justify a series of unsuccessful bids for freedom.

The opening chapter, where Karl takes the stoker's side in pursuit of justice for him against arbitrary power, echoes Kafka's own attachment to a politics of social justice quite different from the authoritarian mindset of his father. Karl also possesses Kafka's ambivalent attitude to the father figure, at once fighting him and seeking approval from him, half in love with his despotic mastery, needing his love. 'If only his father and mother could see him now, fighting for justice in a strange land before men of authority . . . Would they revise their opinion of him?' Karl is searching for an adequate father figure – there will be many such in the book, all programmed to disappoint – someone to be loyal to, someone to trust.

In the next chapter there is a picture of the modern workplace – which seems to resemble a giant call centre and may reflect Emil Kafka's stories of working for the retail giant Sears-Roebuck – which emphasizes newness and gigantism and includes a description of a strikers' demonstration. The next false-father figure is Mr Pollunder, who takes Karl to his country house near New York. During dinner there is a subtle dramatization of family dynamics and tensions, the narrative proceeding with precision and clarity, but with the strange ever present. Kafka is always meticulous in describing *processes*, and, as in his previous fictions, sets many scenes in confined spaces (a ship, a dining room, a hotel) which emphasize the characters' sense of being trapped and enclosed. The disapproval of Karl's uncle for this visit, the fact that 'everything cramped him here . . . all round him was a vague fear', culminates in the latter's letter – absurd and arbitrary but characteristic of the bold dramatic lines of this narrative – cutting off his nephew. This expulsion, an ironic reversal of the American myth of promise, constitutes Karl's first rebuff by the materialistic Eden. In the next phase of fending for himself Karl fetches up as a lift boy in the Hotel Occidental, but eventually he is arbitrarily dismissed. These situations into which Karl Rossmann falls are always the result of a failure of trust towards him on the part of the powerful, a deliberate misprision. The theme of the novel is, as ever, power and its abuses, the baffling way it plays with the life of the individual.

The final chapter, or final fragment, of the book, which describes the 'Nature Theatre of Oklahoma',[29] has continued to baffle critics. After the qualified naturalism of the pacy tale so far, the rich and strangely imagined makes a comeback. Is the nature theatre – women dressed as angels on pedestals and blowing loud trumpets are its recruitment team – an allegory of the palace of art? Or of the social democratic welfare state? The ending, finally, is abrupt. The fate of Karl, like that of his creator towards the end of 1914, remains hanging in the balance.

There is a striking surface contrast between the flowing vivacity in the story of Karl Rossmann and the sheer horror of the story *In the Penal Colony*, which Kafka broke off from *The Trial* to write in October 1914 after *The Man Who Disappeared* was 'completed'. But the underlying thematic connections between the two fictions (and of course between them and the suspended second novel) are also very real. Kafka's preoccupation with guilt and punishment, with the mystery of how the individual, seemingly through no identifiable fault of his or her own, is suddenly arraigned and made to pay the price for unidentified crimes and misdemeanours, is universal in his work and in his life. Writing to Kurt Wolff the following year, he proposed a new collective title for his recent stories – now to include *In the Penal Colony* – to replace his earlier suggestion of *The Sons*. The new title was *Punishments*.[30]

There is an undoubted sado-masochistic streak in Kafka's writing and nowhere is it more apparent than in the brutal *In the Penal Colony*. He began writing it at a time when his attempts to marry were apparently frustrated, when his health seemed set on a permanently downward course, and when his country was at war. In spite of the fact that his writing was going well at this time, it is hardly to be expected that any fiction produced in these conditions would be sunny in temperament.

The story recounts the visit by an 'explorer' or 'voyager' ('der Reisende') to a tropical penal settlement where an officer is keen to demonstrate his instrument of punishment, called 'the harrow' ('die Egge'). 'Whatever commandment the prisoner has disobeyed is written upon his body by the harrow,' the officer explains. Punishment is determined without fuss; there is no trial and the sentence is decided arbitrarily: 'My guiding principle is this: guilt is never to be doubted.' The condemned knows neither the sentence nor even the fact that it is to be carried out. 'There would be no point in announcing it to him. You see, he gets to know it in the flesh.' The long-standing debate about whether Kafka foresaw the fate of the Jews in Nazi Europe is revived by this story. The Officer's cold, calm description of his hideously efficient machinery of death cannot now be read without calling to mind the existence of the Nazi death camps. His casual observation about those who are stripped naked and laid out on the bed in preparation for the name of the commandment they have transgressed to be written on their body by the needles of the machine – 'Enlightenment dawns on the dullest' – can stir memories of the camp-gate maxim at Auschwitz: '*Arbeit macht frei.*' The whole apparatus is a symbol of man-made justice, the endemic failures, the fallibility of its upholders. The references to the former commandant of the colony who, unlike the current incumbent, devised and eagerly participated in the punishment, has been interpreted by some critics as suggesting an analogy with Old Testament ethical harshness. Certainly, there are traces of religious metaphor in the story. '*Schrift*', used to describe the lethal writing on the prisoner's back, is also the German word for 'Scripture'. And when the Officer finally puts himself on the machine and it fails to work, he is mangled. For his corpse: 'It was as it had been in life: no sign of the promised deliverance could be detected.' The idea of punishment as atonement, of human suffering as meaningful redemption, is thus dismissed. Kafka's narrative method is often starkly dramatic – sources such as the early cinema, the work of expressionist painters and writers and Yiddish theatre have variously been seen as contributing to this – but there is a stark, savage brutality about this story which is unique.

In December Kafka finished – once more, one hesitates to use this misleading word, for it never was definitively completed – his second novel, *Der Prozess/The Trial.* It was first published – again posthumously, again in an incomplete form and edited by

Max Brod – in 1925, the year after Kafka's death. It is perhaps this novel which is most associated in the minds of the reading public with the notion of 'Kafkaesque' (though the adjective is used liberally by those who have never read Kafka's work) for it begins with an arbitrary and meaningless arrest, and takes its protagonist through an intricate labyrinth of futile protocols. There is a clear connection between Kafka's state of mind when he began this novel and its content. The conclusion one derives from the long tussle with Felice – and it is still not yet over – is that Kafka felt himself to be a victim, like Joseph K, of some nameless, malignant authority or Law (a term he uses in the story and one which adumbrates the Judaic tradition) who had marked him out to be punished for faults that he could not identify with precision. Kafka felt lifelong guilt in relation to his father, who, even if the later *Letter to the Father* judged him unfairly, certainly never went out of his way to show love or encouragement to his son. Kafka always *wanted* to please and impress his father and to equal him in his strength, resilience and sheer competence in the business of living. His persistent failure to make an accommodation with the world, to come to terms with his job, to secure a proper marital relationship, to find (in spite of all those sanatoria, diets, naked exercises at the open window, boating and swimming sessions) decent health, sleep, proper rest and renewal of a body with which he was never comfortable, seemed to him to proceed from no fault of his own. And finally, the writing, which he saw as the only means of escape, the only means of fulfilment, the only goal of his life, did not always deliver him from a sense of failure and guilt. At the end of his life he even requested that it be destroyed so that nothing could remain of his failed attempts, through writing, to live adequately in the world.

By comparison with Kafka, Joseph K responded on the day of his arrest with a certain equanimity. The keynote was bafflement. The low-key opening sentence, familiar to English-speaking readers for many years in the translation by Edwin and Willa Muir as 'Someone must have been telling lies about Joseph K . . . [*Jemand mußte Josef K verleumdet haben* . . .]' and now generally rendered more accurately as 'Somebody must have made a false accusation against Josef K',[31] introduces the central situation at a stroke. Joseph K, without violence or outward fuss, suddenly finds himself under arrrest without ever learning why. It is impossible not to think of Kafka at the Askanischer Hof, mutely resigned to his arraignment, baffled at its taking place at all, wondering what on earth he could have done to deserve this confrontation, this gradual battery of accusations. If *The Trial* is to be taken in some measure also as an allegory of Kafka's difficulties with parental authority, then the preliminary reactions of Joseph K, the initial confidence that he can tactically outwit those who have come to arrest him, are analogous to the ultimately ineffective strategies designed to appease his father described in *Letter to the Father*. There are also parallels in the fact that Joseph K did not pick this predicament where authority held all the cards. At the same time, and this is the dominant characteristic of Kafka's style, the realization of the story is extremely concrete and vivid, however abstract its underlying meaning.

The scene of the arrest at Joseph K's lodgings is sharply etched – the Inspector playing with matches or examining the length of his fingers – and the cramped domestic interior is the familiar one of Kafka's home life in Prague: gloomy corridors, strips of light under the door, sounds from neighbouring rooms. Joseph K is arrested but allowed to go on working – one is indicted by one's family but goes on living within it and its irksome routines. His first interrogation takes place in an outlying suburb of the city – significantly, he is informed of it at work (a workplace that sounds very much like the Institute) by telephone, the instrument Kafka so loathed. The poor people of the *banlieu* whom Joseph K sees on his way to his interrogation are those whom Kafka would have seen through his work or at the asbestos factory. The manner of the first interrogation seems to inscribe a political analogy in its galleries and in the separated right and left sections of the chamber, but then he discovers that they are all wearing badges, they are part of the same conspiracy against him, and not taking separate parts at all (just as Grete, who had seemed to be taking his side, was suddenly revealed in the *Gerichtshof* to be one of the prosecutors).

At first Joseph K's tone is confident, rather haughty, self-satisfied in its put-downs, but his unease grows with further evidence that everyone is against him. 'Most of these accused men are so sensitive,' someone remarks, and the atmosphere of paranoia is constantly growing. Joseph K is suffocated by the foul air of the interrogation rooms, unlike the officials whom it sustains and who cannot take fresh air. The strange episode of 'The Whipper', where Joseph finds Franz and Willem, the two warders who arrested him, being flogged because he had complained about them to the examining magistrate, intensifies the sense of complicity, of confused allegiances and arbitrarily distributed guilt.

If there is a sado-masochistic undertone to this scene, then sexuality in general in the novel is often out of control, unmeasured, threatening and unsettling. Leni, for example, is typical of the women in Kafka's novels in her strident and open sexuality. Throughout the novel, women are a desired but unsuccessful means of salvation for the male protagonist. There is, of course, no salvation, no escape from guilt, even if its sources, its occasions, are opaque.

In the penultimate chapter, when in the Cathedral and summoned by the priest in the pulpit, Joseph K says: 'But I am not guilty . . . It's a mistake. How can a human being ever be guilty? We are all human beings here, after all, each the same as the other.' The priest replies: 'Everyone who is guilty talks like that.' He adds that Joseph K has been misunderstanding the facts:

'Judgement does not come suddenly; the proceedings gradually merge into the judgement.' The priest also warns him against looking for outside help with his predicament, especially from women, but Joseph K dissents: 'Women have great power. If I could persuade some of the women I know to work together to help me, I would be bound to succeed.' Then the priest introduces a parable (which first occurred in Kafka's diary in December 1914 under the title 'Before the Law') aimed at showing how Joseph K is deceived about the law. The parable tells of a man who is constantly denied access to the law by a doorkeeper, growing old as he waits to be admitted. Close to death, he asks the doorkeeper why, since everyone strives for the law, in all the years of waiting, nobody but he has asked for admittance. The doorkeeper replies: 'Nobody else could gain admittance here, for this entrance was meant only for you. I shall now go and close it.' After a long and sophistical argument about the meaning of this parable, the priest concludes that 'one does not have to believe everything is true, only has to believe it is necessary'. Joseph K finds this a depressing thought: 'It makes the lie fundamental to world order.' The parting remark of the priest is that he is the prison chaplain and thus belongs to the court, so there is nothing he wants from Joseph K: 'The court asks nothing of you. It receives you when you come and it releases you when you go.'

Joseph K is taken away by his executioners, passing Fräulein Bürstner on the way (given Kafka's fondness for making initials and patterns of letters signify, we cannot dismiss the hint of Felice Bauer here) and reflecting, 'the only thing I can do now is preserve my logical understanding to the end'. As the knife that will despatch him is produced, he glimpses a far-off light in a casement window and wonders if it were a friend or someone who could still help. Might there be some arguments left? 'Logic is of course unshakeable, but it cannot hold out against a man who wants to live. Where was the judge he had never seen?

Where was the high court he had never reached?' Joseph K's final cry – 'Like a dog!' – echoes Kafka's sense of himself when he was rejected in Berlin. 'It was as if the shame would outlive him. [*Es war, als sollte die Scham ihn überleben.*]'

But still Kafka had not abandoned the idea that there were 'some arguments left' for him. He would see Felice again.

17

After the extraordinary creative activity of the second half of 1914, Kafka began 1915 with a burning desire to continue writing but he was defeated, once again, by circumstance: 'It is all pointless. If I can't pursue the stories through the nights, they break away and disappear.'[1] He was now having to go to the asbestos factory regularly and, after Valli's husband joined up, this would become a requirement every single afternoon. The factory was struggling and his father tried to blame Franz for having embroiled everyone in the project when in truth he was the last person now who wanted to be concerned with it. This duty would put a stop once and for all to any writing: 'The thought of the factory is my perpetual Day of Atonement.' He decided he was incapable of doing any more work on *The Trial* and that he really must start to sleep less in the afternoon in order to sleep better in the small hours when his writing stint was over. This would involve starting earlier in the evening, around nine, rather than eleven.

In January or February 1915, Kafka wrote a story that he never finished called '*Blumfeld, ein älterer Junggeselle*/Blumfeld, an Elderly Bachelor', whose resemblance in the opening pages to his creator might be said to lie in their occupation of the usual claustrophobic domestic interior. Blumfeld is employed in a linen factory (Kafka was invariably precise about the economic underpinning of his characters) where he is an indispensable employee, but in his solitary flat he is visited by 'two small white celluloid balls with blue stripes jumping up and down side by side'. Perhaps these symbolize the unavoidable intrusion of the outside world into the lonely bachelor's existence. The story then moves to an office setting which probably reflects Kafka's sense of the absurdities of his own workplace. Like Blumfeld, he could not conceive of leaving his office.

Kafka's only consolation in these bleak winter months of early 1915 was Fanny Reiss, a young woman from Lemberg whom he had met at a lecture on world literature given by Max Brod at a school for refugee Jewish children from Galicia. He could never bear to live very long without a young woman in his life, without the promise of some kind of immediate happiness which 'resembles the hope of an eternal life'.[2] This didn't, however, stop him making plans to see Felice in late January, to gauge whether she still loved him: 'I do not deserve it. Today I think I see how narrow my limits are in everything, and consequently in my writing too. If one feels one's limits very intensely, one must burst.'[3] Kafka felt that he had already forgotten the arguments he had previously marshalled 'to defend and assert myself against F.', which did not sound auspicious.

The factory continued to wreak havoc on his writing, creating the usual situation of several stories being started then left unfinished like circus horses standing on their hindlegs in front of him. He felt as if he had been transported back to the days of his first job at the Assicurazioni Generali, where work completely negated his creative powers: 'Immediate contact with the workaday world deprives me – though inwardly I am as detached as I can be – of the possibility of taking a broad view of matters.'[4] Being unable to write left him in a rather bad state to go and meet Felice, because without the clear centre writing normally gave him he immediately became clumsy and confused in his thinking.

Kafka and Felice met (for the first time since the Berlin catastrophe of July 1914) on the weekend of 23 and 24 January

1915, on neutral ground, at the border town of Bodenbach (Podmocly), just on the Bohemian side of the railway from Prague to Berlin, like two diplomats anxiously avoiding contentious territory. Brief as the meeting was, Kafka managed to find time to read some of his recent work to Felice. When he returned to Prague, however, he had very confused and mixed feelings: 'I think it is impossible for us ever to unite, but dare say so neither to her nor, at the decisive moment, to myself.'[5] He felt that he had stupidly held out hope to her again and that they could not start to torment each other again with letters. But Kafka suspected himself: 'is it that I believe I shall win freedom here, live by my writing, go abroad or no matter where and live there secretly with F.?'

Once again, the tantalizing – for Kafka hopeless – chimera appeared and vanished. He would never take that sunny route of escape. More to the point, the Bodenbach meeting reaffirmed the obduracy of each of them: he wanted a life arranged solely in the interests of his work; she wanted a solid bourgeois existence with bed at eleven, central heating, her 'personal touch' (a phrase that grated with him) on all the furnishings, and good order. Not merely did she demand to reset his watch, which had been an hour and a half fast since the beginning of October; she corrected his provincial German when he spoke to a waiter and told him his two eldest sisters were 'shallow', and didn't even mention his favourite sibling, Ottla. Most grievous of all: 'she asks almost no questions about my work and has no apparent understanding of it'. He wasn't much better – 'incompetent and dreary as always' – managing to experience only 'boredom and despair' during the two hours they sat together in a room. Kafka seemed determined not to read the writing on the wall, however plain the facts of their life together were: 'We haven't yet had a single good moment together during which I could have breathed freely. With F. I never experienced (except in letters) that sweetness one experiences in a relationship with a woman one loves, such has I had in Zuckmantel and Riva – only unlimited admiration, humility, sympathy, despair and self-contempt.' When he read to her she could manage only a 'lukewarm' request to borrow the manuscript, though when he read to her the 'Before the Law' parable from the end of *The Trial* he found that 'the significance of the story dawned upon me for the first time; she grasped it rightly too'. Kafka considered that the difficulties he had in carrying on a normal conversation with anyone arose from the fact that 'my thinking, or rather the content of my consciousness, is entirely nebulous . . . yet conversation with people demands pointedness, solidity, and sustained coherence, qualities not to be found in me'. Felice had made a considerable effort to get to Bodenbach, obtaining a wartime passport to travel, and losing a night's sleep in the process, all for this dubious prospect. 'Does she feel it to be the same sort of calamity as I do?' Apparently not. 'After all, she has no sense of guilt.' Kafka, of course, had enough of this commodity for both of them.

One striking feature of the long relationship of these two was the relative lack of involvement of Kafka's friends, except at certain fixed points, such as Brod's occasional approaches to Felice. Kafka always gives the impression that his battles were fought alone. Almost certainly, his circle of friends in Prague decided very early on that this was a futile affair. Ernst Weiss, in particular, was convinced that Kafka should abandon Felice, which earned him her cordial enmity.

After Felice returned to Berlin a letter from Kafka was not long in coming. He was all too conscious that they got on better in letters than in person and took the opportunity to state the unvarnished truth: 'We have established the fact that our time together was not pleasant. And that's putting it mildly. We may not have spent a single minute together entirely free from strain.'[6] Felice, it seems, was moody, unwilling to respond to his conversational overtures, or even catch his eye; and he was as he had described himself. 'Each of us is merciless towards the other.' It might even have helped had they been able to conduct a decent row. Instead, 'all the time tremors keep running between us as though someone were continually cutting the air between us with a sword'. In spite of the harsh nature of Kafka's summing up – and in spite of these obdurate facts of incompatibility that make this relationship such a mystery – he could still end with a lovely passage in which he asked her to wake him by appearing to him in a dream: 'But try to arrange it in such a way that the dream, before waking me, continues right through to the truly happy ending which, let us hope, may still await us somewhere.' This was a resolution that could happen only in the land of dreams.

If the relationship with Felice could not be made to work, then Kafka's writing must. But it, too, was assailed by the usual obstacles: the factory, the office, noise, headaches and insomnia, and the need to change apartments, all of which nearly brought his writing to a standstill. On 10 February he moved into his own room in another apartment in the same building in Bilekgasse where he had previously been occupying Valli's rooms, and immediately began to contend with the noise. He had just been reading Strindberg again, his novel *By the Open Sea*, and was intrigued by the hero's special earplugs. Kafka had to make do with ordering from Berlin some called Ohropax, a kind of wax wrapped in cotton wool. He was, however, aware that, at this time of war, 'many people are suffering nowadays and the cause of their suffering is something more than whispers in the next room'.[7] He felt that the war was making him suffer because he was not taking part in it, and he had not ruled out the possibility that he would eventually be called up. But it was not just that the new room was much noisier than the old. Kafka's sense of isolation was growing: 'I live entirely alone, spend every evening at home.'[8] This wasn't strictly true, for he had attended some meetings at the instigation of Max Brod with some of the growing number of Ostjuden in Prague, displaced by the war. He observed 'the matter of fact Jewish life'[9] of these people but had to record his 'confusion' in relation to it. Nevertheless, he felt out of place in Prague now: 'not that I am in conflict with my surroundings . . . I am in conflict only with myself . . . In Prague it seems impossible for me to escape from this predicament.'[10]

At the same time, he had just received a substantial pay rise and was trying to take a positive attitude towards Felice, promising her a registered letter every two weeks, sending her the letters of Flaubert and Browning, and even talking about doing some travelling with her in the summer. He was reading Gogol and Herzen and recoiling in horror from the latter's picture of married bliss. It was also now spring, with weather that enabled him to take walks at last, especially in the Chotek Park, which he considered the most beautiful place in Prague. When Felice started to speculate about a life with him again in Prague, Kafka decided that they should try to meet at Whitsun, at Bodenbach, and spend a couple of days in Switzerland. He himself took a brief trip to Hungary in late April with Elli to see her serving husband, feeling all the time that his self-absorption rendered him 'apathetic, witless, fearful'.[11] They went to the hated Vienna, and Budapest. Signs of the war and its impact were evident in every railway carriage and every street.

In his moody isolation Kafka was back to reading Strindberg obsessively to keep his spirits up and give himself strength. At one low ebb he reflected on other people's relationship to him: 'Insignificant as I may be, nevertheless there is no one here who understands me in my entirety. To have someone possessed of such understanding, a wife perhaps, would mean to have support from every side, to have God.'[12] Ottla understood him well. Max Brod and Felix Weltsch, Felice's sister Erna (whose correspondence with Kafka, unfortunately, does not survive; it would have been most illuminating) understood many things. But

Felice, he considered, understood nothing. Just at this time he met again Angela (or Alice) Rehberger, a young woman he had met on his Swiss trip in August 1911, and whose beauty had faded rapidly – 'we are continents apart'.[13]

Kafka's sense of isolation was growing, and he told Felice – who had surpassed herself by sending *him* a book, Flaubert's *Salammbô* – that 'misunderstandings'[14] still existed between them in advance of their projected Whitsun meeting. He also believed that he might be called up, if his health would permit it, before the end of May. Kafka did not resent this and seems rather to have been keen to serve in the war. He and Felice did meet, eventually in June, and at Karlsbad not Bodenbach, where the only difficulty seems to have been a failure of their holiday snaps to come out! Later, from 20 to 31 July, driven away from Prague by insomnia, Kafka went on his own to a sanatorium at Rumburg (Rumburk) in northern Bohemia, where he admired the 'huge beautiful woods'.[15] Not long after his return he resumed the struggle with Felice, telling her (just at the point when she was starting to think that she could live in Prague with him) that he could not remain in the city, and that this fact was 'the most definitive thing I know',[16] and thus he could not have her. He then informed her with his usual lowering relish that he felt he was being 'crushed by these torments on every side. But my present suffering is not the worst. The worst is that time passes, that this suffering makes me more wretched and incapable, and prospects for the future grow increasingly dismal.' For weeks on end he had dreaded being alone in his room and had been 'in the grip of a kind of imbecility'. He was also aware that writing to Felice sometimes made matters worse for him. Starting a new diary early in September, he promised himself that he would depend on it less and not become too excited: 'how can one heart, one heart not entirely sound, bear so much discontent and the incessant tugging of so much desire?'[17] It was in the diary, however, that he recorded a fascinating insight into the heroes of, respectively, *The Man Who Disappeared* and *The Trial*: 'Rossmann and K., the innocent and the guilty, both executed without distinction in the end, the guilty one with a gentler hand, more pushed aside than struck down.'[18] Kafka clearly felt that Joseph K was 'guilty' in the sense that he himself had declared himself guilty and Felice innocent.

On 11 September Kafka, Brod and the Prague Jewish mystic Georg Mordechai Langer went to see the so-called 'wonder-rabbi' from Galicia who was holding court in Žižkov. The rabbi wore a silk kaftan, underneath which his trousers showed, and he struck Kafka, who inspected him closely in the crowded, filthy room, as 'dirty and pure, a characteristic of people who think intensely',[19] An outing such as this was apparently not unusual, so, in spite of his frequent references to his isolation and social dysfunction, Kafka was clearly far from a total social outcast. He was also preparing for the publication of *Metamorphosis* in November. In an anxious letter to his publisher, Kurt Wolff, he expressed alarm that the frontispiece illustrator, Ottomar Starke, would choose to represent Gregor Samsa as an insect: 'Not that, please not that!'[20] Kafka was most insistent that 'The insect itself cannot be depicted. It cannot even be shown from a distance.' He was clearly trying to say that the deformity, the transformation, was more metaphorical than literal, an important clue to the way in which Kafka's stories, in which the tale is always told from the point of view of the principal character, can be thought of as *almost* existing inside their creator's head for all their vivid, dramatic realism. Kafka's suggestions for the illustration were the parents and the head clerk in front of the locked door, 'or even better, the parents and the sister in the lighted room, with the door open upon the adjoining room that lies in darkness'. Starke's eventual cover design goes some way towards the latter, showing a man with his hands clasped to his face in front of the open door.

Kafka also fussed with Wolff about typefaces and bindings.

The publisher told him, in addition, some interesting news: the winner of the 1915 Fontane Prize, Carl Sternheim, who was a millionaire, had decided to offer the prize money to Kafka. The latter was baffled and confused by this gesture. The least materialistic of writers, Kafka did not want the money, as he had enough for his solitary needs, and accepted the gesture – itself revealing of how Kafka's literary standing was judged by his eminent contemporaries – only for the honour of taking a share in the prize rather than for the cash.

By the end of the year, Kafka's complaints about his incapacity, illness and general stultification were once again filling his diary. He told Felice: 'I don't want a man in this state to be thrust at you, you mustn't see me like this . . . I do believe that even the true voice of an angel from heaven could not raise my spirits, so low have I sunk.'[21] But he indicated that 'I shall want to reorganize myself after the war. I want to move to Berlin, despite the official's notorious fear for his future, for here I cannot carry on.' He then confessed for the first time to a realization that was surely just: 'I should have left in 1912.' Kafka went to see his boss just before Christmas, determined to speak frankly (the imminence of the confrontation permitting him only two hours' sleep the night before). He set out for Eugen Pfohl four options: to let everything go on as it had 'and end up with brain fever, insanity or something of the like';[22] to take leave, which he was reluctant to do out of a sense of duty, nor would it really help; to give notice but, because of his parents and the factory, that was impossible; and to consider military service as the only viable course. Pfohl responded decisively with the suggestion that Kafka should take a week's leave and a course of blood treatment. It turned out that Pfohl was sick himself and proposed to join Kafka in the treatment. Kafka's frankness in mentioning the word 'notice' had caused 'an official convulsion in the atmosphere of the office'.

This end-of-year moral and physical accounting did not,

however, solve anything. On 18 January 1916 it was the same wretched thing who wrote once more to Felice, saying that the man who would come to Berlin after the war would be one 'consumed by insomnia and headaches'.[23] His first task would be to 'crawl into some hole and examine myself . . . I have no right to you until I emerge from that hole, emerge from it somehow'. When Felice now reproached him for not writing to her, he replied (it is hard to disagree): 'Are not my letters more terrible than my silence?'[24]

Throughout the first months of 1916, Kafka's health was poor, consisting of raging headaches and insomnia that made him feel 'like a caged rat'.[25] He told Felice: 'To be free from the office is my only possible salvation, my primary desire.' The Institute told him that he was (like Blumfeld, the elderly bachelor) indispensable (and he was working extra hours to prove it), and it was this and the factory rather than the fact that he was 'afraid of life outside the office' that was holding him back from moving to Berlin. Yet Felice wanted to keep him in Prague. He recalled the time they went looking for furniture when they were first engaged, furniture whose monumental solidity terrified him, as if it were his tombstone being manoeuvred into position. He wanted to escape: 'I am so hemmed in by ghosts from which the office prevents me freeing myself.' Yet if the complaints were familiar, there was a new tone in the letters to Felice. Kafka seemed stronger (at a period of self-declared weakness in all other respects) and more assertive. Canetti calls this new phase one of 'rectification'.[26] Kafka still wanted to see Felice and tried to get a passport to Waldenburg in Silesia, where Max and Sophie Brod were staying, so that they could meet, but it was refused because of wartime travel restrictions. He did take two business trips – in April with Ottla to Karlsbad and in May to Marienbad – and in between he was visited by Robert Musil, in his military uniform. Musil had invited Kafka to contribute to his magazine, *Die Neue Rundschau*, and had reviewed

Betrachtung and 'The Stoker' in the magazine in August 1914. Kafka visited a nerve specialist but was unimpressed by both his diagnosis of cardiac neurosis and his proposed treatment: electric therapy. Kafka's hatred of conventional medicine and his preference for holistic or natural therapies was behind this rejection of the latest medical opinion.

He continued in his bid to escape the Institute, and in May asked its director either for a long leave later in the year (if the war had ended by then) or, if it had not, for his exemption from military service to be cancelled. The director immediately took this for a gambit by Kafka to procure the three weeks' leave which exempted staff were denied, and he promptly gave it to him. Kafka couldn't get across his wish to join the army, 'a wish I've suppressed for two years'.[27] He felt that if he did receive a long period of leave, it should be without pay, 'because it is not a matter of an organic illness that can be established beyond a doubt', but the director treated the idea of an extended leave as nothing more than a joke. Kafka was frustrated by the fact that he was not managing to be honest with his boss about his reasons: 'I can only cope with the simplest practical tasks by staging outrageously sentimental scenes.'[28]

The stay in Marienbad in mid-May was a relief, for it was 'unbelievably beautiful' with its woods, mineral springs and a peace that even tempestuous spring rain could not spoil. There may also have been some of the usual amorous encounters, for on 2 June Kafka told his diary: 'What a muddle I've been in with girls, in spite of all my headaches, insomnia, grey hair, despair. Let me count them: there have been at least six since the summer. I can't resist . . . With all six my guilt is almost wholly inward.'[29] Even if this implies that they were non-sexual encounters, such a passage does go some way to countering the conventional view that Kafka was disgusted by the reality of sex. Unaware of these liaisons, Felice now proposed that they both go to a sanatorium in the summer, a suggestion which surprised him, as he claimed to have finished with sanatoria: 'sick people, among whom I now seriously count myself, should give sanatoria a wide berth'.[30] Besides, 'they waste too much of one's time and thoughts'. In the end, after some business in Tepl, near Marienbad, Kafka met Felice at the Hotel Schloss Balmoral & Osborne at Marienbad, where they stayed together in separate rooms (though adjoining, with keys on both sides of the connecting door) between 3 and 13 July. After Felice left, Kafka stayed on for another ten days. All his headaches and insomnia vanished on arrival, but the proximity of Felice – they had never spent so long in each other's company – caused problems. Two days after checking in, he wrote in his diary the sad and laconic: 'Poor F.'[31] It was the old story: 'Impossible to live with F. Intolerable living with anyone. I don't regret this; I regret the impossibility for me of not living alone.'

In a postcard to Ottla, Kafka claimed, 'Things have gone much better for me than I could imagine and perhaps better for F. too than she imagined,'[32] but the diary seemed to tell another story. The night before Felice left he wrote the plaintive: 'Receive me into your arms, they are the depths, receive me into the depths; if you refuse me now, then later.'[33] But by this time the pair had written a joint letter to Frau Bauer. In Kafka's section of it he wrote that he and Felice had 'met' (as if it were by chance) and 'discovered that years ago we tackled things in the wrong way . . . Many things have changed . . . but one of the few is the relationship between Felice and me and its assurance for the future.'[34] Felice added her wish that 'I hope you will interpret Franz's words the way they are intended.' Nothing could be clearer: the mother was being informed that the engagement was alive again. On 13 July Kafka and Felice paid a visit to his mother and Valli, who happened to be staying at Franzensbad, to share the news with them. Kafka was surprised to find that his happiness and ease with Felice made him at ease with his mother, too.

After Felice's departure, and in spite of some difficulties with noise in the hotel (as a result of the management assigning him to Felice's vacated room), Kafka enjoyed the rest of his stay, taking plenty of rest and eating, by his standards, a great deal. He even considered – it is not easy to imagine – that he was getting fat. He went for walks and seems to have confined his reading, back at his section of the hotel, the 'Balmoral Castle', to the Bible. There were cafés, and good vegetarian food at the Neptune Hotel, and all the latest Berlin newspapers in the Reading Room of the Town Hall. Kafka, having been tipped off by Max Brod, also eagerly went to see the famous Rabbi of Belz, one of the leading Hasidic Jews, who had arrived in Marienbad. Brod claimed that Kafka always felt drawn towards everything connected with the Hasidic movement, 'with a curious mixture of enthusiasm, curiosity, scepticism, approval, and irony'.[35]

Kafka explained to Brod that after a series of 'frightful days spawned in still more frightful nights'[36] at the start of the stay, Felice had gradually got through to him 'and we arrived at a human relationship of a kind I had so far never known and which came near in its meaningfulness to the relationship we had achieved at the best periods of our correspondence'. Recalling those two past cases when he had really been at ease with a woman's love, he confessed, 'now I saw the look of trustfulness in a woman's eyes, and I could not fail to respond. Much has been torn open that I wanted to shield for ever . . . and through this rent will come, I know, enough unhappiness for more than a lifetime, but this unhappiness is nothing summoned up, but rather imposed, I have no right to shirk it, especially since, if what is happening were not happening, I would of my own accord make it happen, simply to have her turn that look upon me.' The extraordinary way in which this is expressed – its grim fatalism, its automatic premonition of disaster, its final surrender – explains why Kafka could only be tortured in love.

He seems not to have possessed the capacity for simple joy in another's love. He told Brod, 'I did not really know her up to now,' and admitted that 'When she came towards me in the big room to receive the engagement kiss, a shudder ran through me . . . I have never feared anything so much as being alone with F. before the wedding.' Miraculously, all that had now changed, and the couple were making eager plans to marry soon after the end of the war, to rent a two- or three-roomed apartment in a suburb of Berlin such as Karlshorst, and each to pursue their independent career.

Brod's own career was clearly taking off, with nearly 14,000 copies of his novel *Tycho Brahe* sold, but Kafka remained a special taste for the reading public. He was retreating from the idea of the three *Novellen* being brought out as *Punishments* but had a number of discussions with Kurt Wolff about future plans. Kafka's instinct was to 'keep quiet'[37] unless he could produce a genuinely new work, something he hardly felt capable of doing: 'In the past three or four years I have squandered my forces . . . and am now suffering the consequences.' He even felt too tired to travel to Leipzig to confer with Wolff. The latter then conceived the idea of publishing *In the Penal Colony* and *The Judgement* in one volume, but Kafka wanted them to be issued separately. His argument for treating the latter on its own was that 'The story is more poetic than narrative and therefore needs open space around it if it is to exert its force. It is also my favourite work and so I always wished for it to be appreciated if possible by itself.'[38] Wolff was pleased with *In the Penal Colony*, though he did not publish it until 1919, instead bringing *The Judgement* out in October 1916. Kafka agreed with him that there was a painful element in the deferred book, and asked him: 'Have you noticed how few things are free of this painful element in one form or another?'[39] He said that the painfulness was not peculiar to his work alone, but 'our times in general and my own times as well have also been painful and continue to be, and my own even more consistently than the times. God knows how much farther I would have gone along this road had I written more or better, had my circumstances and my condition permitted me, teeth biting lips, to write as I long to. But they did not.' This sense that he had not achieved enough in his writing did not prevent him welcoming the success of others or trying to help them. He urged Wolff to publish the poems of Ernst Feigl (1887–1957), a Prague Jewish writer, whom he had met the previous year and had invited to come and see him in his office at the Institute.

Not long after his return from Marienbad, Kafka started to urge Felice to take an interest in the Jewish People's Home in Berlin, which they had discussed together. This was a centre for Jewish relief work founded by Siegfried Lehmann (1892–1958), a prominent figure in Jewish education in Berlin and later in Israel. Kafka became almost obsessive about this project and Felice's involvement in it, constantly badgering her for news about her practical activity there. 'What matters to me (as it will to you)', he told her, 'is not so much Zionism as the thing in itself, and what it may lead to.'[40] He himself was reading Samuel Lublinski's *The Origins of Judaism* (1903). Despatching to her an article by Brod about the home, he said that it had 'a strange Zionist atmosphere . . . Through the Jewish Home other forces, much nearer to my heart, are set in motion and take effect. Zionism . . . is but an entrance to something far more important.'[41] Eventually Felice paid a visit, and Kafka – whose enthusiasm was quite out of the ordinary for him – offered to pay her expenses so that he could feel he was getting involved himself. He realized that he wasn't capable of doing practical charity work – 'I would lack the necessary dedication'[42] – but felt that the joint endeavour would form a closer spiritual bond between them. He considered that the children should be educated to 'the standard of the contemporary, educated, West European Jew, Berlin version', but preferred, as he always had done, 'the simple East European Jews'. He felt that Zionism gave the home 'a youthful vigour . . . and . . . where other means might fail it kindles national aspirations by invoking the ancient prodigious past . . . How you come to terms with Zionism is your affair; any coming to terms with it (indifference is out of the question) will give me pleasure.' Nevertheless, Kafka declared roundly, 'I am not a Zionist.'

As regards any children Kafka and Felice might have themselves (throughout the summer and early autumn of 1916 they seemed to be communicating more easily on a whole range of matters), Felice seems to have tried to raise the question but Kafka replied that it was 'insoluble. It actually plays the most important part in my fits of despair.'[43] Yet her reports from the home filled him with pleasure: 'It is almost as though the girls were my children and had acquired a mother (belatedly?) . . . or as though I were sitting somewhere in peace, and much-needed rain was pouring down upon my land.'[44] He felt this institution and Felice's involvement with it was bringing them together and told her that she should, in answering the girls' questions, 'let the dark complexity of Judaism, which contains so many impenetrable features, do its work'.[45] He was increasingly preoccupied with that 'dark complexity': 'I wouldn't think of going to the synagogue,' he told Felice. 'I still remember how as a boy I almost suffocated from the terrible boredom and pointlessness of the hours in the synagogue; these were the rehearsals staged by hell for my later office life. Those who throng to the synagogue simply because they are Zionists seem to me like people trying to force their way into the synagogue under cover of the Ark of the Covenant, rather than entering calmly through the main door.' He added that 'owing to my origin, my education, disposition, and environment I have nothing tangible in common with their [the East European Jews'] faith'– an empathy which Felice herself might just be able to deploy. He continued to send her suggestions for reading matter for the young people and to derive pleasure from her accounts.

In part because of this shared project, Kafka was apparently more at ease with himself now – or at least less ill at ease. He was enjoying the Prague summer, discovering places on the edge of the city where he could lie in the grass, listening to children playing, or taking walks with Ottla, in the course of which he would read Plato to her and she would teach her unmusical brother to sing. He considered that he was almost turning from a city dweller into a countryman.

In his diary, however, he was still addressing himself harshly: 'What seems a sense of responsibility on your part . . . is at bottom the official's spirit, childishness, a will broken by your father.'[46] He urged himself to do something about this: 'And that means, not to spare yourself (especially at the expense of a life you love, F.'s), for sparing yourself is impossible; this apparent sparing of yourself has brought you today to the verge of your destruction . . . One cannot spare oneself, cannot calculate things in advance. You haven't the faintest idea of what would be better for you.' Kafka concluded this ammunition-round of brisk good advice with the order: 'Mend your ways, escape officialdom, start seeing what you are instead of calculating what you should become.' He told himself that the 'nonsensical' comparisons he was always making between himself and Flaubert, Kierkegaard or Grillparzer (all writers, as noted above, who sacrificed themselves to art or put it above personal considerations such as marriage or worldly success) were 'simply infantile'. This was especially true with respect to Flaubert and Kierkegaard, who were after all 'men of decision' who did not calculate but acted. By contrast, Kafka did nothing but make 'calculations' ('*Berechnungen*') endlessly, 'a monstrous four years' up and down'. Grillparzer was perhaps the nearest relevant example, but who would want to imitate him, 'an unhappy example whom future generations should thank for having suffered for them'?

Kafka no doubt felt much better after having given himself

this vigorous talking-to. However, he did not act upon it, and went on 'calculating' as before. In particular, the reality of married life, of intimate sharing, seemed to horrify him. Writing to Felice several weeks later, prompted by her candid admission (a candour he was not sure he relished – this kind of ruthless plain-speaking was, after all, his forte) that she did not look forward to sitting at table with his family, he explained how much he hated family life and the threat it posed to individual freedom: 'the sight of the double bed, of sheets that have been slept in, of nightshirts carefully laid out, can bring me to the point of retching . . . it is as though my birth had not been final, as though from this fusty life I keep being born again in this fusty room; as though I had to return there for confirmation . . . something still clings to the feet as they try to break free, held fast as they are in the primeval slime.'[47] At the same time he knew that he was bound to his parents, that they were 'essential strength-giving elements of my own self, belonging to me, not merely as obstacles but as human beings. At such times I want them as one wants perfection; since from way back and despite all my nastiness, rudeness, selfishness, and unkindness I have always trembled before them . . . and since they, Father on the one hand and Mother on the other, have – again quite naturally – almost broken my will, I want them to be worthy of their actions.'

Reading passages such as this, one is reminded that Kafka was an Austrian contemporary of Sigmund Freud, even if he had little time for Freudianism as a science. Something in the spirit of the times and the intellectual climate led both men along these dark, labyrinthine paths. Ottla, he thought, would have been his perfect mother, but he was saddled with the parents he had and, because he 'cannot rebel against the laws of nature without going mad', he was left with 'hatred, and almost nothing but hatred'. He particularly hated the idea that his family would incorporate Felice and begin to use her against him: 'But you belong to me, I have made you mine; I do not believe that the battle for any woman in any fairy tale has been fought harder and more desperately than the battle for you within myself – from the beginning, over and over again, and perhaps for ever. So you belong to me.' With Felice, Kafka felt that his life was in two parts: one 'feeds on your life'[48] but the other was 'like a cobweb come adrift'. It would soon be two years since this second – writing – self had done any work 'and yet it consists of nothing but the capacity and longing for this work'. Felice rather shrewdly observed: 'You are a man who sees so clearly that being alone is bound to make you more depressed than you are otherwise.'[49]

On 10 November 1916 Kafka travelled to Munich to take part in a literary reading at the Kunst-Salon Goltz. He read from *In the Penal Colony*, and Felice came to listen to him. He also met several now-forgotten writers such as Gottfried Kölwel, Max Pulver and Eugen Mondt, and possibly the poet Rainer Maria Rilke. Reviews of the reading suggested that it was not an unqualified success, though neither a 'grandiose failure',[50] which is how Kafka afterwards described it. His time with Felice offered little comfort: they quarrelled in a 'ghastly pastry shop',[51] the haste and distraction of the reading causing an inevitable tension.

On his return to Prague two days later, Kafka busied himself trying to find a quiet and peaceful apartment that would allow him to get down to some proper creative work. While this search was going on Ottla allowed him to use (during the day – he returned to his own flat to sleep) a little house she had rented in the walls of Prague Castle in the charmingly (though inaccurately) named Alchemists' Street, Alchimistengasse (now Zlatá Ulička). Ottla had been renting the house, unknown to her parents, since November – possibly as a place to rendezvous with her lover Josef David, a non-Jew of whom her parents disapproved – and she had cleaned it up after the large family which had been crammed into it vacated. She installed some bamboo furniture which Kafka found particularly comfortable. This tiny house, which today boasts a small and reasonably tasteful Kafka souvenir shop, was inhabited in the reign of Rudolf II (1576–1611) not by the tribes of alchemists who came to seek their fortunes at the eccentric Holy Roman Emperor's court, but by castle functionaries. The street's name is redolent of that city of alchemists, golems and wonder-working rabbis that is explored so vividly in Angelo Maria Ripellino's wonderful, sprawlingly erudite book *Praga Magica*.[52] This magic Prague, in its sometimes garish excess, is not, however, the Prague of the exact, rational and precise Kafka. Alchemists' Street nowadays, especially in the summer season, is swamped with visitors clutching their compulsory entry tickets – mass tourism having proved a more secure way of generating wealth from nothing than the *lapis philosophorum*. But in early December 1916 Kafka had found a truly peaceful spot.

At the back of the house, No. 22 – which is hardly bigger than a room and appears from the street to have the dimensions of a doll's house – there is a view of the Stag Moat, above which fraudulent alchemists were sometimes, on the orders of the mad Rudolf, suspended in iron cages to die a lingering death from starvation. Kafka left the house reluctantly in the middle of the evening to return to his own flat: 'A strange feeling, locking up one's house on a starlit night in this narrow street.'[53] On 6 December, the feast day of St Nicholas, when children were given presents, his neighbour, Dr Knoll, stood in the middle of the empty street with a bag of sweets, waiting for the children to appear.

This should have been a special period in this old, tranquil, beautiful place, but the anxieties would not leave Kafka. Shortly before Christmas, he wrote to Felice: 'The other day you mentioned some kind of solution to our main problem. Is there nothing you can add to that?'[54] This enigmatic question probably concerned their continuing anxiety about having children, an issue which showed no signs of disappearing, although the precise nature of the problem is not clear. If the question were not one of impotence, it might simply have been Kafka's fear of accepting responsibility for a child, especially given his powerful critique of the damage done by the family to the individual, which he drew from his own experience. His mother, in a new year message to Frau Bauer, expressed both the wish that the Almighty might 'bring this terrible war to an end' and her disappointment that Felice had not, after all, made a Christmas visit to Prague. In spite of these formal pieties, however, the couple's troubles were not over.

18

Taking advantage of his new writing-space in the little house in Alchemists' Street, Kafka wrote throughout the winter of 1916–17, in a series of notebooks scholars have christened the 'blue octavo notebooks' (today they are in the Bodleian Library at Oxford). In this period he also wrote '*Der Kubelreiter*/The Coal-Scuttle-Rider', published in 1921, and stories such as '*Der Schlag am Hoftor*/The Knock at the Manor-Gate', parts of '*Beim Bau der chinesichen Mauer*/The Great Wall of China', '*Der Gruftwächter*/The Warden of the Tomb', '*Die Brücke*/The Bridge' and '*Der Jäger Gracchus*/The Hunter Gracchus', works that would not be published in his lifetime.

'The Great Wall of China', like the shorter piece 'The Knock at the Manor-Gate', is concerned with the ineluctable nature of power and the powerlessness of the individual. Glancing perhaps at Prague's 'Hunger Wall' (Hladová zed), started in the 1460s by Charles IV as employment for the city's destitute, it is another story about *organization*; about the intricate procedures that govern how things get done; about work. 'Almost every educated man of our time was a mason by profession and infallible in the matter of laying foundations,' the narrator explains, reflecting the story's theme of the dominance of work in the modern world, our obsession with its all-absorbing futility. It describes the piecemeal construction of the wall, individual segments unconnected and built in the absence of any overall view of what was happening, as if it were a symbol of the fragmented modern consciousness: 'We . . . did not really know ourselves until we had carefully scrutinized the decrees of the high command, when we discovered that without the high command neither our book learning nor our human understanding would have sufficed for the humble tasks which we performed in the great whole.' The narrator's phrase 'our leaders know us', like the reference to the high command's having existed 'from all eternity', seems to combine an idea of human helplessness with divine providence, to admit the timelessness of the world and of power. The wall-builders' refusal to prosecute their enquiries further into why it is being built seems to point to the impossibility of transcending the historical condition of man, of deflecting the power of history.

'The Hunter Gracchus', which exists in several fragments, was written between December 1916 and April 1917, and is realized with the same precise accumulation of detail – another wonderfully original, strange invention, like a fairy tale or fable of death, its immanence. It is unusual in being set in a specific location, Riva on Lake Garda, which Kafka had twice visited. The army officer whom Kafka met in Riva in 1913, and who has been identified as Ludwig von Koch,[1] was a retired major-general in the Sixth Regiment Hussars of the Austrian Army. He shot himself on 3 October when Kafka was in Dr von Hartungen's sanatorium with him and his body was laid out in the mortuary chapel of St Anna at Riva. It is very likely that Kafka was influenced by this suicide when he wrote his story of Gracchus, who died 1500 years ago yet exists in a halfway state between death and life. He arrives in a drifting barge at Riva, a soul who can find no permanent rest, like a suicide in traditional moralities.

Another story written at the end of 1916, '*Ein Traum*/A Dream', appeared in a 1917 anthology called *Das jüdische Prag* and featured the first public appearance of 'Joseph K'. It is a wonderfully vivid dream narrative set in a cemetery, where Joseph K meets an artist who is lettering a gravestone in gold. Slowly, Joseph K becomes aware that the grave is his own and steps into the grave while 'up above his name went racing with mighty flourishes across the stone'. Another beautiful suicide.

This dream had been written while Kafka was still spending the nights in his hellish flat at Lange Gasse, plagued by noise, musical instruments and crashes from the kitchen and all sides of the concrete building. The pleasant walk up to Alchemists' Street and the silence were a balm. He took his evening meal up there and stayed till around midnight, enjoying the late-night walk home. He loved having a real front door to close behind him and to step straight out into the snow and the quiet street. It was not expensive (twenty kronen a month), and he was looked after by Ottla and 'a little flower-girl'[2] called Růženka, whom Ottla had taken under her wing.

Shortly after he had arrived in the house at the end of November 1916, Kafka had written in a book left lying on the table for Ottla, 'To my landlady',[3] and even in his hermit's cell he was still at the centre of a web of dependency, the hunch-backed Růženka taking care of him when in March he left Lange Gasse and moved into a new apartment in the Schönborn Palace (today the US Embassy) in the Castle district – Hradčany. In spite of his new accommodation, he continued to work at Ottla's small house. The new apartment was on the second floor and had been furnished 'with a girlish touch' by an old countess, but the landlord removed the furniture. It had two rooms, electric light, but no bathroom, and Kafka envisaged it as a place where he and Felice could live after their marriage, at least initially. He tried to entice her by describing the beautiful adjacent park to which he would have access. Another pleasant piece of news in March was the final closure of the hated asbestos factory.

Not long after, Kafka sent twelve of the new stories that had been set down in the blue Octavo notebooks to Martin Buber for possible publication in his Zionist periodical *Der Jude.* He told Buber that they would eventually be published in a book to be called *Responsibility* (the title had been changed to *Ein Landarzt/A Country Doctor* when the book appeared in 1919). Buber took two 'animal stories',[4] 'Jackals and Arabs' and 'A Report to an Academy', which were published in the autumn under Kafka's instructions that they should not be described as 'parables'. Kafka was in a much better mood and content with the flow of all this new work. Kurt Wolff was equally pleased and praised the thirteen manuscripts Kafka sent him in July, though the latter still claimed it was 'a far cry from what I would really like to do'.[5] He said that after the war he planned to marry and leave Prague for Berlin, which meant that he would have to abandon his customary indifference to royalties. He even went as far as to ask Wolff for some reassurance that he would continue to publish him once the war was over. The assurance came by return of post.

Also in July Felice came to Prague and, for the second time, the couple became formally engaged. It seemed as if the five-year epic struggle of anguished correspondence was finally to have a happy outcome. The couple went to Budapest and then to Arad to see Felice's sister. Kafka travelled back alone, via Vienna. He planned to spend ten days at the beginning of September with Ottla in Zürau (Siřem) in north-west Bohemia, where she was managing the farm that belonged to Karl Hermann, Elli's husband, who was at the front. The great attraction for her of Zürau was that it was a long way from Prague and her parents. She had become embroiled in frequent rows with them, especially her father, about her decision to abandon the shop. Unsurprisingly, during these altercations, Franz had taken his sister's side, and the bond between them seems to have been stronger than ever. No doubt he was looking forward to spending time in the countryside with her. But, when he was alone in his apartment on the night of 9–10 August 1917, a month before he was due to leave, disaster struck.

Kafka does not seem to have told anyone immediately. The first to know was Ottla, and even she was spared the news for a few weeks because her brother knew she was in the middle of the hop harvest. 'About three weeks ago,' he announced baldly to her on 29 August, 'I had a haemorrhage from the lungs during the night. It was about four o'clock in the morning; I woke up, wondering at having such a strange amount of spittle in my mouth, spat it out, but then struck a light, strange, it's a blob of blood.'[6] And then the flow began, bubbling up in the throat – he used the Czech word '*chrlení*', to spit or spew – so steadily that he thought it would never stop. He got up and walked around his room, looked out of his window, until eventually the flow stopped and he returned to bed, sleeping much better than he had in a long time. In the morning Růženka came in and exclaimed in Czech: '*Herr Doktor*, you won't last much longer!'[7] Later that day, during office hours, he went to Dr Mühlstein, who diagnosed bronchial catarrh and prescribed three bottles of medicine. Kafka didn't take to the doctor and doubted his diagnosis of a cold (Kafka didn't catch colds normally and it was high summer, but it is true the apartment was a 'cold, stale, ill-smelling place') and didn't agree with the doctor's dismissal of consumption ('all inhabitants of big cities are tubercular . . . you inject tuberculin and all's well'). Kafka was convinced, rightly, that he had tuberculosis, but it was not going to be any old tuberculosis. The struggle would be on an epic scale, and indeed he saw it as the culmination of the past five years' battling for a marriage. 'It is the greatest struggle that has been imposed upon me, or rather entrusted to me, and a victory (which, for instance, might present itself in the form of a marriage; perhaps F. is only representative of the presumably good principle in this struggle), I mean a victory with a halfway bearable toll of blood, would in my private world history have had something Napoleonic about it. Now it appears that I am going to lose the struggle this way.'[8] The immediate effect was that his insomnia, feverish conditions and headaches vanished and he slept well. It was like the eerie silence of a battlefield after a great conflict. To Ottla, Kafka described the tuberculosis as 'this mental disease'. He was in no doubt about the intellectual and moral significance of the illness, its intimate connection with his private dramas.

Kafka's first step was to give notice on the Schönborn Palace apartment (and to accept the notice which had just been given at the little house in Alchemists' Street, in which he had been writing during the day). He left the apartment for the last time at the beginning of September ('how much like dying this must be'[9]) and moved back in with his parents (whom he had still not told of his illness), to sleep in Ottla's room, which was next to the bathroom and its unwelcome music of splashing and flushing. On 3 September he went to see Dr Mühlstein, who recommended plenty of food and air, two compresses on Kafka's shoulders at night, and monthly visits. Injecting tuberculin was kept in reserve for the time being.

Kafka continued to see the illness as part of fate's plan for him: 'There is undoubtedly justice in this illness; it is a just blow, which, incidentally, I do not at all feel like a blow but as something altogether sweet in comparison with the average course of these last years; so it is just, but so coarse, so earthly, so simple, so hammered into the most convenient slot.'[10] On 4 September, at Brod's urging, he went to see a specialist, Professor Friedl Pick, who was director of the Laryngological Institute of the German University in Prague. Pick (who confirmed Mühlstein's diagnosis of 'pulmonary apicitis' or infection of the apex of the lung), ordered a stay in the country. In a letter to Brod, Kafka described Mühlstein's initial reluctance to diagnose the worst as the action of a man who 'wanted to shield me with his broad back from the Angel of Death which stood behind him, and now he gradually steps aside'.[11] Kafka asked Ottla if it could be at Zürau, though Brod wanted him to go to Switzerland, where doctors would be on hand. He approached his boss, Eugen Pfohl, to request either retirement or three months' leave, in a scene he described as 'a sentimental comedy'.[12] He joked that Pick's report read like 'a passport to eternity', though the specialist he had said that there might be some improvement in the long term. Still shielding his parents from the truth, Kafka said the leave was the result of his nervous condition. Retirement with a pension was ruled out by the Institute, which continued to treat its vice-secretary as a valued employee. 'Once I've attached myself anywhere, I stick like something distinctly repellent,' Kafka observed wryly.

On 12 September, having finalized arrangements with Kurt Wolff for the publication of *A Country Doctor*, Kafka set off for Zürau. 'You have the chance, as far as it is at all possible, to make a new beginning,' he wrote in his diary soon after arriving. 'Don't throw it away . . . If the infection in your lungs is only a symbol, as you say, a symbol of the infection whose inflammation is called F. and whose depth is its deep justification; if this is so then the medical advice (light, air, sun, rest) is also a symbol. Lay hold of this symbol.'[13] All that remained now was to resolve the question of Felice.

On 9 September, following some earlier (now lost) letters to her which Kafka thought had probably been 'monstrous'[14] (it may have been that Kafka was moving anyway towards a rejection of Felice before the discovery of the illness, which seems to be confirmed by what he told the Prague poet Rudolf Fuchs when he met him in Vienna on the way back from Hungary) and exactly four weeks after the *Lungenblutsturz*, he had written to tell her about the haemorrhage. 'That I should suddenly develop some disease did not surprise me . . . ultimately my maltreated blood had to burst forth; but that it should be of all things tuberculosis, that at the age of 34 I should be struck down overnight, with not a single predecessor anywhere in the family – this does surprise me.' On 20 or 21 September Felice made the arduous thirty-hour journey from Berlin to see him. 'I should have prevented her. As I see it, she is suffering the utmost misery and the guilt is essentially mine . . . I myself . . . am as helpless as I am unfeeling . . . she is an innocent person condemned to extreme torture; I am guilty of the wrong for which she is being tortured, and am in addition the torturer.'[15] As ever, Kafka's analysis was ruthlessly honest – though his honesty sometimes had the faintest trace of a rhetorical strategy – but he seems not to have asked himself the question: why did I not do something about it? Knowing he was torturing her, why did he persist in it? Wouldn't it have been kinder to make a decisive break earlier and more cleanly?

If the letter written before Felice's visit hinted at what the implications might be for both of them, his next, written from Zürau on 30 September, after she had been and gone, finally removed any doubt. It has been called 'the most disagreeable letter he ever wrote'[16] and in it Kafka formulated a faintly self-serving myth about his illness:

> As you know there are two combatants at war within me. During the past few days I have had fewer doubts than ever that the better of the two belongs to you. By word and silence, and a combination of both, you have been kept informed about the progress of the war for five years, and most of that time it has caused you suffering . . . You are my human tribunal. Of the two who are at war within me, or rather whose war I consist of – excepting one small tormented remnant – the one is good the other evil . . . The blood shed by the good one (the one that now seems good to us) in order to win you serves the evil one . . . For secretly I don't believe this illness to be tuberculosis . . . but rather a sign of my

> general bankruptcy. I had thought the war could last longer, but it can't. The blood issues not from the lung, but from a decisive stab delivered by one of the combatants.[17]

There is something unsatisfactory about this equation of the blood of the battlefield and the haemorrhage (which at this stage was not fatal; Kafka was in a reasonably good condition), as if he is trying to overdramatize in order to reach the letter's real conclusion: 'I will never be well again.' Kafka had already decided that Felice was lost to him, or he to her, and was now looking for an effective way of writing the postscript to the affair, but it is not at all clear that she was as ready to end it as he was: throughout September a series of her letters had arrived which in their calmness and equanimity were a marked contrast to the blow he felt he had to deliver. 'I don't grasp her. She is extraordinary.'[18]

One more letter exists from Kafka to Felice, written on 16 October, in which he recalls her visit to Zürau. She had been unhappy about the apparent pointlessness of her journey, about his 'incomprehensible' behaviour, about everything. He claimed that, though 'tormented', he was not unhappy, because: 'I did not *feel* the whole tragedy as much as I saw it, recognized it, and diagnosed it in its immensity which surpasses all my strength (my strength as a living man at least); and in this knowledge I remained relatively calm, my lips shut tight, very tight.'[19] Kafka's fatalism, his neat summation, might have seemed to Felice a little too pat, after what they had gone through together, after what she had been put through. As her carriage had pulled away from the farmhouse at Zürau, it had circled the pond, and Kafka had cut across and come close to her again, looking at her for what he planned to be the last time, conscious that he was losing her, and already acting out his part in a shakily directed tragedy. And then she vanished with Ottla, trotting towards the station.

It seemed that it was all over, but there would be one final meeting, two months later, in Prague at Christmastime. Kafka had righted himself a little and now saw clearly what was happening. 'The days with F. were bad,'[20] he confessed to Ottla. 'But of course, it would have been much worse, or impossible, if I had had the least shred of doubt as to the rightness of what I was doing.' The formal dissolution of the second engagement seemed to him a great wrong done to Felice, 'and became all the more wrong by the calmness and especially by the kindness with which she received it'. On 27 December, when the decisive break was made, Kafka 'wept more than in all my years after childhood'. He went to see Brod at his office, on his way back from seeing off Felice at the station, and was more visibly upset and uncontrolled than his friend had ever seen him. He sat down on a small chair provided for visitors and declared, between sobs: 'Is it not terrible that such a thing must happen? [*Ist es nicht schrecklich, daß so etwas geschehen muß?*]'[21]

After a quarter of a million words and five years, it really was now all over.

In March 1919, little over a year later, Felice married a well-off Berlin businessman and had two children. In 1931 the family moved to Switzerland and then in 1936 to the United States, where Felice died on 15 October 1960. In 1955 she had sold the letters she had kept from Kafka to Schocken Books of New York. The correspondence – lengthy, anguished, sometimes rather hard to bear – constitutes a major document, in some sense a classic of epistolary love.

In spite of the end of his engagement and the onset of his illness, Kafka's stay at Zürau – he remained there until April 1918 – was pleasant. Naturally, there were farmyard noises, squawking geese on their way to the pond, and a hammering tinsmith across the way to provoke him, but Ottla's loving care was 'literally bearing me up on her wings through the difficult world'.[22] She had provided him with an airy and warm room and was trying to tempt him to eat the country produce. But what he felt most was 'freedom, freedom above all'. The disease had, in a sense, liberated him, ended the torment and the doubt. It was inevitable that he should attribute a moral rather than a physiological character to it. Nevertheless, he told Max Brod that he was constantly seeking an explanation for the disease, for he had not sought it: 'Sometimes it seems to me that my brain and lungs came to an agreement without my knowledge. "Things can't go on this way," said the brain, and after five years the lungs said they were ready to help.'[23] The price of freedom, however, was the loss of the 'made-up marital bed as the reward and meaning of my human existence'. He informed Brod that living in Zürau with Ottla was like 'a good minor marriage'[24] and that they ran 'a fine household'. He did what he could to facilitate the movement of farm produce back to his friends and colleagues in Prague in exchange for items that were hard for the villagers to acquire in wartime. He loved the country people, 'noblemen who have escaped into agriculture . . . True dwellers on this earth',[25] and recorded a 'Homeric' image of two heavy horses bathed in a fleeting ray of sunshine in their stable. He was putting on weight, having arrived weighing 61.5 kilos, and gaining a kilo in the first week.

He wondered if he were destined to become a country recluse like his uncle, Siegfried Löwy, the country doctor – or even the village idiot. 'But have I the right to expect something good, at the age of thirty-four, with my highly fragile lungs and still more fragile human relationships?'[26] He wrote in his diary that he could still gain passing satisfaction from works like *A Country Doctor*, 'provided I can still write such things at all (very improbable). But happiness only if I can raise the world into the pure, the true and the immutable [*Glück aber nur, falls ich die Welt ins Reine, Wahre, Unveränderliche heben kann*].[27] The fact that the world is rarely pure, true and immutable did not dissuade him from this task. He had articulated an aesthetic ambition which he would struggle, for the remaining years of his life, to fulfil.

Less loftily, but in a more shrewdly self-perceptive way, he told his diary in his first weeks of illness: 'You have destroyed everything without having really possessed it.'[28] Still, he harboured ambition: 'I haven't yet written down the decisive thing, I am still going in two directions. The work awaiting me is enormous.'[29] He was reading mostly in Czech and French, and nothing but autobiography and correspondence. When Brod (who was rewarded with a partridge) sent him some Hasidic stories from the *Jüdische Echo* he said they were 'the only Jewish literature in which I immediately and always feel at home'.[30] Kafka was sinking ever further into village life, sunning himself, doing no work, not writing at all, determined never to be prised away from this rustic idyll (in spite of the mice which gave him a great deal of trouble and anxiety) and fearing the noisy cabarets of Prague that he used to frequent.

Around the middle of October, Kafka started to compose, in his blue octavo notebooks, a series of short pieces that has become known as the 'Zürau aphorisms' (some older editions of Kafka's writing print these separately as *Reflections on Sin, Suffering, Hope and the True Way,* but recent editions restore them to their context among longer, more reflective passages). They have the weaknesses and strengths of all aphorisms – occasional portentousness balanced by occasional terse insight – and are highly regarded by some readers of Kafka, especially those who see him as a religious thinker. A few representative examples (using a numbering devised by Kafka himself when he selected them from his original notebooks) would be: '38. A man was amazed at how easily he went along the road to eternity; the fact was he was rushing along it downhill' and '62. The fact that there is nothing but a spiritual world deprives us of hope and gives us certainty.'[31]

The aphorisms and longer reflections show that Kafka at this time had the leisure for contemplation and was conducting, quite understandably, given the outward circumstances of his life, a profound metaphysical enquiry into himself and his relationship to the world. He was reading Kierkegaard again, the only philosopher in whom he took a sustained interest. 'How pathetically scanty my self-knowledge is compared with, say, my knowledge of my room,'[32] he wrote in October. 'Why? There is no such thing as observation of the inner world, as there is of the outer world . . . The inner world can only be experienced, not described.' He realized how he needed to garner his forces at this point, even more so as a result of the illness: '[How] even to touch the greatest task . . . if you cannot collect yourself in such a way that, when the decisive moment comes, you hold the totality of yourself collected in your hand like a stone to be thrown, a knife for the kill?'

In a long letter to Brod in mid-November Kafka explored his sense of having failed in some sense in relation to the normal, everyday world, of not having 'acquitted myself well'.[33] He had always cherished Flaubert's phrase about people who are *dans le vrai*, that is to say, people whose lives are in some very vital way authentic, true and naturally right. Kafka described to Brod his earlier thoughts of suicide and his later notion that 'what lay before me was a wretched life and a wretched death', quoting the concluding words of *The Trial* that 'the shame of it must outlive him'. Then he claimed that he had discovered 'a new way out' which consisted in saying 'that I not only privately, by an aside, as it were, but openly, by my whole behaviour, confess that I cannot acquit myself properly here. This means I need do nothing but continue to follow with the utmost resolution the lines of my previous life. As a result I would assume a coherence, not dissipate myself in meaninglessness, and keep a clear-eyed view.'[34] This sounds more like a determined effort of will than an intellectual breakthrough, an acceptance of a rather limited view of his future potential, and may have been an attempt to brace himself for a return to the Institute, as the doctors were recommending that course to him.

Kafka's attempt in December to persuade the Institute to allow him to retire was again unsuccessful. In Prague for that purpose and to see Felice for the final time, he had another consultation with Dr Pick, who agreed that retirement on a pension was a reasonable request and approved of Kafka's decision not to marry. The official reason for cancelling the engagement was the onset of the disease, but this clearly masked some more awkward and undeclared issues. At home Kafka had to listen to his father fulminating against Ottla and complaining that it was all very well for her to be in the country with plenty to eat; let her have some experience of real hunger as he had done. Kafka told Ottla that they were right to do what they had done but that their father was right in one respect only: 'that we have everything too easy . . . He knows no other test except that of hunger, money worries, and perhaps sickness.'[35] Kafka conceded some truth in his father's position, 'some goodness too', and realized that as long as he and Ottla depended on him financially, 'our conduct towards him remains constrained and we must yield to him in some way . . . In this realm something more than the father speaks with his voice, more than the merely non-loving [*nicht-liebende*] father.' Kafka was saying that their father was in fact the embodiment of the principle of patriarchy, of abstract power, which they were in no position to resist. The loving father, the real Hermann who either would not or did not know how to express his love, had been genuinely worried when, at the end of November, Ottla had made a brief visit to Prague and told him the truth about her brother's tuberculosis. She had to reassure Hermann that his son would have enough to eat in Zürau and that he was in no danger.

The time was approaching when Kafka could no longer resist the need to settle his accounts with his father in the only way he knew: by writing about it. The seeds of *Letter to the Father* are in this interchange with Ottla. Meanwhile, he was itching to escape from Prague and return to his rural village deep in snow which so much resembled the landscape of the village at the foot of the castle in his last novel.

PART III

Milena

19

A contemporary photograph[1] shows Ottla and her brother at the entrance to the farm in Zürau. In this and other photographs Ottla is sensibly dressed for the country, generally preferring a rough, dark dress with a leather belt around the waist. Franz, on the other hand, is immaculately turned out, like a man stepping out of an elegant café in the centre of Prague: highly polished shoes, formal overcoat, neat collar and tie and hat. Convinced as he was of the therapeutic qualities of the open-air life (he was sleeping with a window open in temperatures of eight degrees below freezing) and the dignity of physical labour, he seems to have passed his time at Zürau in more refined pursuits than agriculture and animal husbandry.

At the beginning of 1918 Kafka returned to the farm in the company of Oskar Baum, his old university friend, who was having problems in his seven-year-old marriage. It is worth noting, in passing, Oskar's inability to speak Czech (Kafka thought that this fact, in the Bohemian countryside, coupled with his blindness, would create difficulties for Oskar). Kafka's own fluency is all the more remarkable in not being shared by most of his Prague German circle – though Brod, of course, was another exception, who famously promoted the work of native Czech writers and composers such as Janáček. Oskar's marriage problems reopened the wound for Kafka: 'The impossibility of his marriage really comes down to the impossibility of marriage in general,'[2] he told Brod after Oskar had left. Deep in Kierkegaard again – this time his major work *Either/Or* – Kafka rhetorically judged it, because of his present mood, 'hateful, repellent . . . written . . . with the sharpest of pens' and a book that would 'drive you to despair'. Brod's own marriage was now also rocky, because of his involvement with another woman. Kafka was thus caught between these two failing marriages, writers' marriages with all the conflicts he understood (at least theoretically, as a non-combatant), and the intellectual wrestlings of Kierkegaard on the same topic. 'You are right in saying that the deeper realm of sexual life is closed to me; I too think so,'[3] he told Brod. Kafka knew about brief sexual encounters but, at the age of thirty-four, he had never been in a sustained sexual relationship. He continued with Kierkegaard, admiring his apparent ease and fluency in writing – 'He certainly cannot be called negative . . . affirmativeness becomes objectionable when it reaches too high'[4] – rereading *Fear and Trembling*, and awaiting his ordered copy of *Stages on Life's Way*. The first of these – the philosopher's portrayal of Abraham's apparently incomprehensible willingness to sacrifice his son, Isaac, and his discussion of its profound ethical implications – was a hard book to accept because of the gulf between 'the ordinary man' and 'this monstrous Abraham in the clouds' who sacrificed his son 'on the strength of the absurd' out of an implacable faith in God which permitted him, again in Kierkegaard's words, a 'teleological suspension of the ethical'. Idealist that he was in relation to marriage, Kafka did not appear to subscribe to this absolute 'affirmativeness' of the Danish philosopher, though he would have admired his emphasis on individual ethical choice.

Kafka had initially been given exemption from military service until the end of 1917, which would mean a further visit to Prague early in 1918 to see the military authorities. He went on 19 February without apparently resolving anything. He was also worried about his relationship with the Institute, which showed no signs of wanting to let him go or to accede to his request for retirement. Kafka felt reasonably healthy at the farm and had no desire to leave. He was passing his time, as well as reading Kierkegaard, with books by Martin Buber and others, and was continuing to produce his aphorisms or the longer reflections which surrounded them. Particularly interesting were those on art: 'The point of view of art and that of life are different even in the artist himself. Art flies around truth, but with the definite intention of not getting burned. Its capacity lies in finding in the dark void a place where the beam of light can be intensely caught, without having been perceptible before.'[5] These are not necessarily propositions that one would have deduced from reading Kafka's own comments on life and art to date. More recognizable is: 'Suffering is the positive element in this world, indeed it is the only link between this world and the positive.'[6] Kafka felt, in the silence of the countryside, and in its stillness, a reminder of his incapacity: 'The stillness keeps impoverishing my world,'[7] he told Brod. 'I have always felt it my special misfortune that I (the symbols take a physical form) literally do not have the lung power to breathe into the world the richness and variety that it obviously has, as our eyes teach us.'

If, as seems likely, the aphorisms were Kafka's attempt in the new conditions of his life (that might now be lived in borrowed time) to draw up a sort of intellectual balance sheet, so there was another accounting to be done. He was thinking more about his relationship with his father. In January he had asked Kurt Wolff, when returning the proofs of *A Country Doctor*, if he could add a dedication page: 'To My Father'. He had an intuition that this would be his last book and he wanted to see it appear as soon as possible: 'Not that I could appease my father this way; the roots of our antagonism are too deep, but I would at least have done something; if I haven't emigrated to Palestine, I will at any rate have traced the way there on the map.'[8] This comment is enigmatic but suggests that his account with his father was somehow bound up with his reckoning in relation to Judaism. In a passage in the blue octavo notebooks he writes:

> It is not inertia . . . that causes me to fail, or not even to get near failings: family life, friendship, marriage, profession, literature. It is not that, but the lack of ground underfoot, of air, of the commandment . . . I have brought nothing with me of what life requires, so far as I know, but only the universal human weakness . . . I have vigorously absorbed the negative element of the age in which I live, an age that is, of course, very close to me, which I have no right ever to fight against, but as it were a right to represent . . . I have not been guided into life by the hand of Christianity – admittedly now slack and failing – as Kierkegaard was, and have not caught the hem of the Jewish prayer-mantle – now flying away from us – as the Zionists have. I am an end or a beginning. [*Ich bin Ende oder Anfang*].[9]

This is one of the more fascinating passages of self-analysis in Kafka's writing. It expresses his powerful sense of modernity, of being at a certain very precise epoch in the development of art, the human spirit and religious belief. He registered the full pressure of the contemporary. He knew that the conventional forms of religious belief – Christian or Jewish (the latter in the process of being revitalized to some extent by the Zionism that fascinated him but which couldn't boast him as a signed-up member) – were faltering, had possibly exhausted themselves (his residual Nietzscheanism), but he knew that something must follow them: either complete dissolution or a rebirth. Insofar as he was a representative artist of his time, he was especially destined to find out what was in store. He was either an end or a beginning.

The delightful spring weather in Zürau in April tempted Kafka away from his books and notebooks and out into the garden, but all the signs were that the stay was drawing to a close. He could no longer put off the return to work, and on 30 April he finally left. Two days later he was back in the office. During the summer, however, he tried to keep up his interest in gardening and did some work in his spare time at the Pomological Institute at Troja, where he had laboured before, in April 1913. It was one of the largest nurseries in Bohemia, mostly for trees. Kafka enjoyed talking to the nurserymen, for he was always interested in the conditions of working people, not least because it was his professional duty to examine factories and other workplaces to assess their health and safety provisions.

In one of his notebooks, while he was still at Zürau, he had drafted an interesting Utopian socialist programme, probably deriving from some of the ideas he had explored while a student or had heard expounded as a young man in Prague sitting silently at the back of political meetings. It was a manifesto for a 'Brotherhood of Poor Workers'[10] who would choose a monastic poverty with no possessions except what they required for their immediate needs. 'Everything else belongs to the poor.' The brotherhood would get their living only by working for it, would work only two days a week for just those wages necessary to support life, to live in moderation and simplicity, and eat little. They would also enjoy a relationship with their employer based solely on mutual trust, with no intervention by the courts, and would have a full range of welfare services provided by the state. Numbers would be limited to 500 and, like the self-governing anarchist communes he would have heard so much about, each council would negotiate when necessary with the central government. All inherited wealth would go towards welfare provision. This progressive-sounding scheme had its limits: the 500 Utopian bachelors would permit no wives or women of any kind into their experimental egalitarian commune.

Max Brod, glad to have his friend back from the country backwater, visited Kafka in the afternoons at Troja in the summer of 1918. Their two chief topics of conversation, according to Brod, were the war and learning Hebrew. Kafka had started to learn the language in May 1917, had shelved it in Zürau, but back in Prague had taken it up again. Brod felt, nevertheless, that Kafka was withdrawing into himself a little at this stage, as if he were protecting his declining powers and concentrating simply on those things that 'one is absolutely master of'[11] – even if that meant seeming to exclude his friends from his life. 'The test of the writer is in his works,'[12] Kafka had told Brod, 'a world is conceivable to me that is governed by a living idea, a world in which art has the place it deserves, which in my experience it never has had.' Kafka was once again setting himself an exacting standard in art. It was as if, having reconciled himself to failure in ordinary life – symbolized by marriage – he were going to spend what time was left to him in perfection of the work.

During the summer he made a few inspection trips into Bohemia and his health seemed reasonably good, according to Dr Pick, whom he was still seeing regularly. He visited, as an official rather than as a guest, a sanatorium for nervous diseases at Frankenstein near Rumburg in northern Bohemia, and told Felix Weltsch that the experience had stiffened his resolve never again to enter one. He did stay in September in a hotel at Turnau, sixty-five miles north-east of Prague (many such hotels were facing closure because of wartime shortages) and, in spite of the lack of butter and milk, he enjoyed the beautiful woods, 'quite as good as the woods of Marienbad', and the excellent local apples and pears.[13] Wartime privations even began to affect publishers, and Kafka was told that *A Country Doctor* would be delayed by a shortage of metal type. The war, however, was almost over.

Towards the end of November, now in peacetime, Kafka,

along with millions of others, was a victim of the Spanish influenza that was ravaging the world. His mother took him on the last day of the month with her to the Pension Stüdl in the northern Bohemian mountain village of Schelesen (Želízy) near Liboch, which was pleasant and very inexpensive. He stayed throughout December and, after a visit to Prague for Christmas, returned on 22 January 1919. In the course of his bout of flu the Habsburg Empire passed away. On 28 October a provisional post-war government was formed in Prague, and on 11 November the Austrian Emperor formally abdicated. Three days later the republic of Czechoslovakia was proclaimed, with Tomáš Masaryk as President. Franz Kafka was now a Czech citizen. His fluency in Czech would ensure that he would not fall victim, as many Prague Germans did in the new republic, to a backlash against those associated with the former imperial power. He kept his job at the Institute. In January 1919 the Great Powers started their peace conference at Versailles to determine the future of Europe. 'Here I am, having a second winter in the country,'[14] Kafka announced to Oskar Baum from Schelesen. His health was tolerable, with no fever, no shortness of breath and less coughing, but his stomach was upset.

One other person shared the veranda of the Pension Stüdl that January: Julie Wohryzek. She was the daughter of a Prague shoemaker and synagogue custodian and, on the evidence of surviving photographs, far prettier than Felice Bauer. Kafka described her to Brod as

> Not Jewish and yet not not-Jewish, not German and yet not not-German, crazy about the movies, about operettas and comedies, wears face powder and veils, possesses an inexhaustible and non-stop store of the brashest Yiddish expressions, in general very ignorant, more cheerful than sad – that is about what she is like. If one wanted to classify her racially, one would have to say that she

> belonged to the race of shop-girls. And withal she is brave of heart, honest, unassuming – such great qualities in a person who though not without beauty is as wispy as the gnats that fly against my lamp.[15]

This delightful, impromptu sketch – he added that she reminded him of Grete Bloch – makes it unsurprising that a romance quickly blossomed in the snows of Schelesen. Julie seems to have quickened and amused Kafka. He told Brod that in the last five years he had not laughed so much as he had done in these few weeks at the Pension Stüdl.

As the relationship developed, Kafka's parents were appalled. He had turned down the good, solid, sensible, bourgeois Felice Bauer for this vivacious trollop. From Kafka's point of view, Julie's enthusiasm for Zionism – her fiancé, killed in the war, had been a Zionist – was a significant point of interest. Ottla was having difficulties at this time with her parents over her plans to marry Josef David, a Christian, whose religion was anathema to them and whom they considered 'alien'.[16] Kafka, who had been trying to help Ottla with advice and suggestions about her agricultural career, tried to reassure her about her decision – which also disappointed Brod, who saw it as a loss of her Jewishness – by saying that, although what she was doing was 'extraordinary',[17] it was good to attempt the extraordinary and the difficult.

Eventually, Julie had to return to Prague, while Kafka himself won some extra concessions on leave from the Institute. Initially three weeks had been given, then two further extensions on 7 February and 6 March, but he finally followed Julie back to the city at the end of March. There are tantalizingly few details of Kafka's courtship of Julie Wohryzek in the spring and summer of 1919. Kafka made hardly any reference to her in letters and even fewer entries in his diary about his relationship with her. The apparent resignation to a life without marriage because of his illness seems to have been put on hold. He was back at the Institute, was apparently writing little at home – though *In the Penal Colony* was finally published in May in book form – and his health was stable. He was taking Hebrew lessons from Friedrich Thieberger, who remembered him as 'tall, slim, pale'[18] and with a very taut and serious expression. Thieberger also noticed his quiet, mild speech, his reserve and then his sudden enthusiasm in the middle of a conversation in response to an idea: 'his words came as if from another world and matched exactly what had been said'. Two things especially struck him: Kafka's vain endeavours to 'escape the loneliness of his personal destiny' and his storyteller's delight expressed in 'the joy with which he wove himself into small details' – a characteristic that is highly visible in his letters and diaries, as well as in the precision of the details in his fiction. Another pupil, Miriam Singer, was fascinated by Kafka's 'steel-grey eyes'.[19] She watched him entering every Hebrew word spoken into one of his small blue notebooks and noted how he made humorous associations with each word to help him remember it. He later signed a copy of his *A Country Doctor* for her with the words: 'You are so healthy, you will not understand it.' With that gesture, 'Instantly the joyful atmosphere of the room vanished.'

At the end of June Kafka was in Rieger Park (Riegrovy sady), promenading with Julie by some flowering jasmine bushes: 'False and sincere, false in my sighs, sincere in my feeling of closeness to her, in my trustfulness, in my feeling of security.'[20] He recorded that he had an 'uneasy heart', as he might well have, for the official reason for breaking off with Felice was an illness which, at this time, was generally considered incurable and therefore an impediment to any responsible prospect of marriage. And yet he now seemed prepared to go ahead and marry after all. A week later he was still torn between desire and anxiety: 'Yet calmer than usual, as if some great development were going forward the distant tremor of which I feel.'[21] They continued to walk together in the woods, in the evening streets of Prague, and went swimming in Cernosic (Černošice). During the summer – the date is unspecified – Kafka and Julie became engaged, though it seems that Kafka was more keen on marriage than she was. In November the banns were issued and a wedding was scheduled for the 2nd or 9th of that month, but it was postponed because they were having trouble finding an apartment.

Kafka took the opportunity to have another week at the Pension Stüdl with Brod. According to the owner of the hotel, Olga Stüdl, Kafka lost no time in making the acquaintance of 'a lively young girl'[22] called Minze Eisner. 'Strictly speaking I don't care for her at all,'[23] he told Ottla. 'She also has all the hysteria of an unhappy youth, but yet she's wonderful.' The relationship with Minze, a resident of Teplitz (Teplice), seems to have been more avuncular than amorous (Kafka was, after all, on the point of marrying Julie) and in their subsequent correspondence he lavished a great deal of improving advice on her. Younger women were always attracted to Kafka, and he seems, in spite of his reserve and shyness, to have been good at communicating with them.

On his previous visit, Olga Stüdl had been struck by how Kafka, who always made a fetching invalid, enjoyed sitting out on the veranda in the crisp winter air, swaddled in blankets, a cap drawn deeply down around his neck. Seeing him thus, one of the other guests described the hat as an airman's cap. 'More a recliner's than an airman's cap,' he replied with a laugh. On another occasion, a child was being told off for his forgetfulness and Kafka intervened, telling the company: 'Perhaps he has many interesting things in his little head and can occupy himself with those, while instructions bore him and mean nothing to him. Let adults speak for adults!' There are other recorded anecdotes of this kind which show both Kafka's fondness for children and his innate sense of justice. There was only one other convalescent in

November 1919 at the pension, Hermine Beck, who occasionally shared a balcony with Kafka and helped him with his Hebrew vocabulary. She recalled his once getting very angry with her for swatting a fly and, to her amazement, exclaiming: 'Why don't you leave the poor fly in peace, what has he done to you?'

Stung by his father's opinion of Julie and by the resistance his parents were showing to Ottla's marriage, and conscious of how much his present situation derived from his family predicament, Kafka, in his spare time at the pension, started to write his *Letter to the Father*, and let Ottla know that he was doing so. For those who locate the source of Kafka's evident metaphysical pain or angst in the relationship with his father, and for the Freudians who see this as a classic father–son Oedipal scene, the letter supplies much support. But it is a document which needs to be handled with some care. Kafka himself warned of its rhetorical construction, its 'lawyer's tricks' of argument, as has already been noted. In many ways it is unfair and a little shrill.

Nadine Gordimer's brilliant monologue, imagined as being from Hermann Kafka in response to his son, 'Letter from His Father' (1984),[24] puts its finger on the rather too insistent note of grievance, and its lack of generosity towards other people's failings: 'It was the sound of live people you didn't like,' Gordimer has Hermann say. In particular she makes a convincing case that Hermann's great crime in his son's eyes – leaving the book he gave him unread on a side-table – may simply have been due to his father's lack of education and his being no great reader. Kafka's fictions, which were emanations of the early twentieth-century European avant-garde, were after all perhaps not the best place for such a man – who worked twelve hours a day in a shop while his son sat in his room with his nose in a book – to start his bookish journey. Gordimer also presents a rather bizarre criticism: that Kafka was anti-Semitic because he never wrote about contemporary attacks on Jews in his diaries and letters. (In fact, he did.)

There is a sense in which, in this letter, the indictment is all one way.[25] Kafka is silver-tongued prosecuting attorney, judge and jury in his own case, never doubting the truth of his great reproach. Even his concessions – the typical rhetorical strategy – are cancelled out by his skill in manipulating their consequences. The opening two sentences embody the entire dilemma of the letter: 'You asked me recently why I maintain I am afraid of you. As usual, I was unable to think of any answer to your question, partly for the very reason that I am afraid of you, and partly because an explanation of the grounds for this fear would mean going into far more details than I could even approximately keep in mind while talking.' In other words, the fear which needs to be explained is such a powerful and all-embracing reality that it cannot adequately be explained without the victim collapsing under the sheer weight of the difficulty of articulating his pain. Hermann, the bluff, ebullient, self-made man, who got where he was today by hitting all obstacles for six, is being asked to understand the strange phenomenon of one of his own flesh and blood whose sensibility is utterly foreign to him: anxious, unbearably aware of all the obstacles that lie in the path of the hyper-sensitive individual in an insensitive world, weak where the father is strong, indecisive where the father is swiftly and uncompromisingly resolute, hesitant where the father is forthright, unwell where the father is vigorous. If Kafka was angry and resentful at his own condition, Hermann must in turn have been vexed and perplexed. His anger would be that his son had not made better use of his talents, justified his investment in him, made a good marriage, shaken himself out of this self-pitying lethargy, established himself as a man of property and position in Prague's professional class.

All over Europe intellectual sons were having this debate with their fathers at the start of the twentieth century (one thinks of Walter Benjamin), as indeed they had done in the preceding century. By not making a decisive break, by remaining, in relation to his father, a complaining child at the age of thirty-six, Kafka had no choice but to sit on his balcony at Schelesen, in a brief week of reprieve, drawing up his long litany of complaints and getting nowhere. For it is in the nature of these conflicts that, once they have reached a certain point of rancid maturation, they cannot be resolved. Kafka should simply have walked away from the situation described in the long letter – which was never delivered but which, from his remarks to Ottla, clearly was written with the intention of being sent. Instead, he remained trapped in a half-admiration/half-fear of his father's strength, and was almost defeated by its example, no matter how eloquently he seems in the *Letter* to be challenging Hermann and asserting his freedom from his dominion.

As Kafka's reputation started to grow after the Second World War, the father–son theme was often seen as the key to understanding his work. Edwin Muir, Kafka's first translator into English, for example, wrote in a 1949 introduction to *Amerika*: 'To trace back the inspiration of Kafka's stories to his relations with his father is not to belittle them or to give them a merely subjective validity. The extraordinary thing in Kafka was the profundity with which he grasped that experience and worked it out in universal terms, until it became a description of human destiny in general, into which countless meanings, at once ambiguous and clear, could be read.'[26] This is a nicely judged comment. Even if one declines to accept Kafka's account of his family life as the definitive, completely secure interpretation (there is less doubt about the accuracy of the *facts*, but facts are not quite the pivotal issue), there is no doubt that the theme of power and the individual's struggle against it and its overwhelming, generally inscrutable purposes are at the heart of Kafka's writing. The descriptions in the *Letter* of the capricious exercise of patriarchal power ('I, the slave, lived under laws which had been invented only for me') may or may not have been the 'source' of Kafka's nightmare visions of dark power, but the parallels and correspondences cannot be ignored. Muir, however, is right to warn against reductive interpretations.

Written at the precise point it was, when Kafka's terminal illness had begun, it was a last attempt to draw up the balance sheet. 'All his life Franz was overshadowed by the figure of his powerful and extraordinarily imposing father – tall and broad shouldered,'[27] claimed Max Brod. He confirmed that Kafka admired his father's strength and capacity for hard work, his success: 'His admiration for his father in this respect was endless – it had a touch of the heroic in it . . . something of an exaggeration too. Anyhow it was fundamental in Franz's emotional development.' In the *Letter* Kafka writes movingly about how he felt himself to be puny and insignificant in his father's presence: 'I remember, for instance, how we often undressed together in the same bathing-hut. There was I, skinny, weakly, slight, you strong, tall broad. Even inside the hut I felt myself a miserable specimen, and what's more not only in your eyes, but in the eyes of the whole world, for you were to me the measure of all things.' This scene in the swimming-pool, interpreted less bleakly, returned in the heartbreaking last letters Kafka wrote to his father when he was dying. Kafka's father, in spite of his inability to show it, almost certainly loved his son, and in spite of the constant complaints it is equally clear that the son desperately sought his father's love. There was, after all, no physical chastisement or abuse – just a slow leaking away of self-esteem: 'I was so uncertain of everything that I really only possessed what I already held in my hands or had in my mouth . . . I had lost my self-confidence where you were concerned, had traded it for a boundless sense of guilt.' Hermann objected to Kafka's friends, which then 'became in me distrust of myself and a perpetual fear of everyone else'. His aversion from Kafka's writing was at least a guarantee that it would become a protected space, a zone of freedom. But even that was a delusion, for: 'My writing was all about you; all I did there, after all, was to bemoan what I could not bemoan upon your breast. It was an intentionally long-drawn-out leave-taking from you.' But perhaps the most immediately pertinent complaint in November 1919 was about marriage and founding a family, which Kafka felt was 'the utmost a human being can succeed in doing at all'. He took his father's bitterly dismissive comment about Julie – 'She probably put on some specially chosen blouse, the thing these Prague Jewesses are good at, and straight away, of course, you made up your mind to marry her . . . Isn't there anything else you can do?' – as a derisive suggestion that it was better to visit a brothel if he needed sexual satisfaction rather than to marry a tart of a cobbler's daughter.

Whether because of his parents' opposition or for some other reason, the marriage to Julie was not destined to be realized. Back in Prague from Schelesen in late November, Kafka wrote a very long letter to Julie's sister. He described his early courtship of Julie at the start of the year, how she must have found him strange, their mutual reserve – that laughter not perhaps so light and spontaneous as it at first seemed – their unnatural closeness at the Pension Stüdl, 'the literally enchanted house in which we two were almost alone and to which we were restricted because of the wintry conditions outside'.[28] He represented the two lovers as being 'brave' in overcoming their ill-health and taking on marriage. In spite of this: 'It was established between us that I regarded marriage and children as the most highly desirable things on earth in a certain sense but that I could not possibly marry.' So they had parted, without ever having used the intimate '*Du*' form of address, and with no more than a briefly extended holding of each other's hands on taking their leave.

But that was not the end, of course. After exchanging no letters during the three weeks he stayed on in Schelesen, on his return to Prague 'we flew to each other as if driven'. Kafka had explained that he wanted it to be 'a love-marriage, but even more a marriage of prudence in the highest sense'. He had brushed aside some reservations about Julie's circle of acquaintances and was fortified rather than the reverse by his father's opposition. He had admitted to some anxieties about marriage, asking himself reasonably enough: 'You who can barely manage to bear the responsibility for yourself from moment to moment now want to add on the responsibility for a family? What reserve of strength do you have to draw on?' The reality of what Kafka was proposing could be expressed as 'a civil servant, moreover excessively nervous, one who long ago fell prey to all the perils of literature, with weak lungs, exhausted by the meagre scribbling in the office' wanting to make happy a 'trustful, yielding, incredibly unselfish girl'. They would even have done so by now if the apartment hadn't slipped through their fingers. The fact that it did so had acted as the trigger to a series of warnings in Kafka's head. He had confessed them to both Julie and Ottla. He now considered that he should not marry but still wanted to keep hold of Julie in some sort of relationship, which he described as 'fidelity or love outside marriage'.

In his latest doomed attempt to uproot himself from Prague, Kafka announced that he was planning to go and live in Munich early in 1920. He seemed disposed to follow the example of his publisher, Kurt Wolff, who was relocating there from Leipzig. In the autumn his collection of stories, mostly written between September 1916 and June 1917 in Alchemists' Street and the Schönborn Palace, finally appeared. *A Country Doctor* was published by Wolff, and, in spite of everything that had occurred since it was first proposed by Kafka, it carried the planned dedication: to '*Meinem Vater*'. The dreamlike title story, like most of those in this volume, is as mysterious, if not hallucinatory, as anything previously written by Kafka, and has defied attempts by critics to offer a definitive interpretation. Kafka establishes an atmosphere of moral anxiety through the story of a doctor called out at night (he has no horse of his own but two emerge from nowhere to take him to his patient) to a young boy. In taking the horses and abandoning his maid to the violence of the groom who had brought them, the doctor is filled with guilt. The boy's open wound – described with Kafka's usual unflinching relish – is incurable, in part because of his extreme sensitivity, and in part because he lives in a community which has lost its beliefs, an observation that suggests that it is to be seen as a spiritual wound, like Kafka's transformation of his bleeding lung (after these stories were written) into a metaphysical punishment. Kafka's view of medicine – the shortcomings of conventional doctors and the need for natural therapy where the spiritual is as important as the material in the process of healing – is entwined in this tale, which also draws on Kafka's reading of Hasidic tales, where some of its themes are echoed.[29] Perhaps more than anything it is about the collapse of moral and cultural authority in the modern world.

Another of the stories, '*Schakale und Araber*/Jackals and Arabs', finds a traveller in the desert being addressed by a group of jackals which has gathered in sight of the camp fire. It has a clearer intention of satirizing attitudes of the Jews towards their identity, and in particular those, like the Western Jews, who live at the margins of their societies and shirk the Zionist challenge to take practical steps towards improving their condition – in this case the jackals who rely on others to provide their food and want the traveller to cut the Arabs' throats and solve their problems for them. 'A Report to an Academy' satirizes the assimilation strategy of many Western Jews, while Kafka satirizes himself in 'Eleven Sons'. He told Brod that the latter was meant to represent eleven of his stories, each of the sons being gifted in his way but unlikely to impress the father, who perceives in each 'a kind of inability to develop to the full the potentialities of his nature which I alone can see'.[30] The father, like the conscience of a high-minded artist, is never satisfied. Many of the other shorter pieces, such as 'A Message from the Emperor', reflect Kafka's search for meaning and certainty, his sense that it will never be found, that the message destined for him will not arrive in time.

Towards the end of 1919, Kafka's plans to go to Munich remained in place. He knew that Julie also wished to escape Prague, proposed that she accompany him to Munich in the new year, telling his sister, 'We could see another part of the world; some things might undergo a slight change; many a weakness, many an anxiety, will at least change its form, its direction.'[31] But Kafka had recently received a letter from a young woman who wanted to translate some of his work into Czech. Her arrival on the scene now meant that those plans for 1920, the pursuit of a new life with Julie in Munich, would gradually disappear.

20

On 1 January 1920 Kafka received yet another promotion, from vice-secretary to secretary at the Institute. His official title was now *Anstaltsekretär.*[1] His absences in the previous year, his clearly identified illness, his requests for early retirement had done nothing to lessen the confidence of his employers in him. They would not, of course, be aware of his private thoughts on the office, and saw only the outwardly diligent 'civil servant', or *Beamte*, who was too useful to them to be allowed to leave. In his diary for the first two months of 1920 – between 6 January and 29 February – Kafka wrote a series of aphorisms known collectively as *He*, after the pronoun used in each, beginning: 'Everything he does seems to him extraordinarily new.'[2] The aphorisms explore Kafka's senses of opportunity and constraint, the realization that progress is possible, but that he is at the same time a prisoner: 'He has the feeling that merely by being alive he is blocking his own way. From his obstruction, again, he derives the proof that he is alive.'

If the 'he' of these aphorisms is not necessarily the historical Kafka, much of the detail, the angst, the world-view, is familiar: 'He feels imprisoned on this earth, he feels confined . . . But if he is asked what he actually wants he cannot reply, for – this is one of the strongest arguments – he has no conception of freedom.' Kafka's feeling of being trapped – by his situation in Prague, by his family and his work, and now by an illness that he must have started to sense was terminal and which was an obstruction to his means of escape (one of those means being marriage) – comes out in many of the aphorisms: 'He has two antagonists; the first presses from behind, from his origins, the second bars his road ahead. He struggles with both . . . it is not only the two antagonists that are present, but himself as well, and what his own intentions are who can really say?' In one passage written in mid-February he recalled a day years previously when he was sitting sorrowfully on the slopes of the Laurenziberg (Petřín Hill), examining the wishes that he had for his life: 'What emerged as the most important or the most attractive was the wish to gain a view of life (and – this was certainly a necessary part of it – to be able to convince others of it in writing), in which life, while still retaining its natural, full-bodied rise and fall, would simultaneously be recognized no less clearly as a nothing, as a dream, as a hovering.'

These beautifully exact, measured, though ultimately tragic reflections are a key to Kafka's mood at this time, a mood of resignation and clear-sightedness, less angry and accusatory than the mood of *Letter to the Father*, preternaturally calm. They also exhibit as ever his powerful grasp of the concrete allied to a sense of the strangeness of the imagination, the 'dream', the 'hovering'. And, above all, they are overshadowed by the thought of death: 'One develops in one's own way only after death, only when one is alone . . . It becomes apparent whether his contemporaries did more harm to him, or whether he did more harm to his contemporaries; in the latter case he was a great man.'

A lighter diversion in these first months of 1920 was a correspondence with Minze Eisner, the nineteen-year-old (little more than half Kafka's age) whom he had met at Schelesen. It was not a love affair; more a case of Kafka giving the rather unhappy and directionless young woman some sense of purpose. He advised her about her education and offered his own nuggets of wisdom: 'It is good to pursue one's dreams but bad, as it mostly turns out, to be pursued by them.'[3] She responded with some mild flirtation, sending him photographs of herself (and later a drawing which reminded him of his childhood album of pictures of Shakespearean heroines, his favourite being Portia) and telling him his eyes were 'clear, young, tranquil'.[4] The reality, he replied, was different: 'here they are dim enough and ever more unsure, with little flickerings from being open these thirty-six years'.

Brod recalled a conversation with Kafka of around this time in which the latter said: 'We are nihilistic thoughts that came into God's head.'[5] Denying, however, the Gnostic view that the universe was a sin of God's, Kafka said that it was merely the product of one of God's moods: 'He was having a bad day.' Brod suggested that there was therefore hope outside our world. Kafka smiled: 'Plenty of hope – for God – no end of hope – only not for us.' This recalls Kafka's aphorism from the recent sequence, on the theme of original sin, 'the ancient wrong committed by man', which consists in 'the complaint that man makes and never ceases making, that a wrong has been done to him, that it was upon him that original sin was committed'.

Kafka continued to advise Minze, especially in relation to her going to a gardening school, and urged her to get out of her home town because 'for any halfway restless person the home town, even when he willingly deceives himself about it, is highly unhomelike, a place of memories, of dolefulness, of pettiness, of shame, of being misled, of misuse of energy'.[6] Kafka had not deceived himself about his Prague. He pointed out to her (and he would know) that 'everyone has his sharp-toothed sleep-destroying devil inside him, and this is neither good nor bad, but is life . . . This devil is the material (and basically what wonderful material) that you have been endowed with and with which you are supposed to make something.'[7]

Towards the end of February Kafka's health was poor and he was wondering about taking some recuperative leave. He didn't want to have any medical treatment, preferring the formula of 'sunlight, air, country, vegetarian food',[8] and he would rather not have to visit a sanatorium to find these, but at this time of year he might have no choice. One possibility was Kainzenbad in the Bavarian Alps, but there were visa problems in the unsettled post-war period, so he eventually settled for Merano in the Italian province of Alto Adige, in the southern Tyrol, having been given two months' sick leave. Initially, at the beginning of April, he stayed in the Hotel Emma (where he noted with disapproval the behaviour of the rich, assimilated and baptized Jews) but soon he moved to the cheaper Pensione Ottoburg, just south of the town at Untermais. His sickness had caused the cancellation of his projected trip to Munich with Julie Wohryzek, to whom no letters survive, and no sooner had he settled in the Tyrol than he began a correspondence with another woman who would drive poor Julie from his consciousness.

This was the remarkable Milena Jesenská, the first non-Jewish woman with whom Kafka had ever become seriously involved. Her extraordinary life story, which ended in the Nazi camp of Ravensbrück in 1944, has been told in Margarete Buber-Neumann's *Milena*.[9] Aged twenty-five, unhappily married to the Prague writer Ernst Polak and living in Vienna as a Czech translator, Milena had led a rebellious youth in Prague and was a strong and fiery woman who was the first of Kafka's lovers truly to grasp the significance of his writing and to meet him on appropriate terms as a literary partner. She also had some knowledge from her own experience of what it meant to do battle with a powerful father. 'She is a living fire,'[10] Kafka told Brod, 'of a kind I have never seen before.' Too much of a fire, in retrospect, for Kafka's ailing physical and spiritual condition, which meant that he could not, in the end, answer her needs, though she understood him as a writer profoundly.

He had met her the previous year in a Prague café, though he claimed not to be able to recall her face in any precise detail:

'Only how you finally walked away between the tables of the coffee house, your figure, your dress, these I can still see.'[11] It was clear from the very first letter to Milena where this correspondence was heading. Kafka, when he saw her translations, was impressed, feeling that there was 'hardly a misunderstanding' in them. He read Czech fluently and wanted her to write to him in the language. He always replied in German. 'I have never lived among German people,' he confessed to her, 'German is my mother tongue and therefore natural to me, but Czech feels to me far more intimate.'[12]

The weather in the Tyrol was sufficiently good in April and May for Kafka to sit out on a balcony in the evenings, and to indulge in his usual health-giving nudity. He could look out on to flowering shrubs, darting lizards and a variety of birds. The air was purer and the sunlight stronger than at Schelesen. In the first month his weight went up from 57.4 kilos to 59.55 kilos. In the dining room he asked for a separate table where his vegetarianism and careful chewing (Kafka was a devotee of the fad of 'Fletcherizing', a method of diligent mastication) would attract less attention. Nevertheless, two military men (one a general) staying at the pensione summoned Kafka to the communal table, where everyone's place was marked by their own napkin ring, and proceeded, for social sport, to analyse his accent. They knew Prague and wanted to know whether he was Czech. Unhesitatingly, Kafka said no. Around the table further suggestions were made. The tall, thin young man was German-Bohemian or from Prague's Malá Strana, or Little Quarter (the area across the Vltava from the Old Town captured so beautifully in the stories of Jan Neruda). The general would not let the bone go and started to examine Kafka's face as well as his accented German. Kafka put him out of his misery by explaining that he was Jewish. The whole company then got up and left the table – contrary to their usual habit of lingering – a resolution that left Kafka feeling that he was 'a thorn in their flesh'.[13]

In a letter to Brod at the beginning of May Kafka exclaimed, in response to the former's reports on the situation of the Jews in Munich, where he was staying: 'What a terribly barren preoccupation anti-Semitism is, everything that goes with it, and Germany owes that to her Jews.'[14] His argument was that the Jews had 'forced upon Germany things that she might have arrived at slowly and in her own way, but which she was opposed to because they stemmed from strangers'. At the pensione, Kafka had managed to pacify the general by employing his great skill – 'I am an excellent listener' – but he could not staunch the flow of 'I am not prejudiced' anti-Semitism at the table. Meanwhile, he marvelled at Milena's devotion to her unworthy husband: 'she is extremely tender, courageous, bright, and commits everything she has to her sacrifice . . . what kind of a man must he be, who could evoke that?'

Kafka himself was not without his commitments. In an early letter to Milena in April he referred to his past engagements (showing in the process that he was aware that Felice, now married, had given birth to her first child, a boy) and his present one to Julie, which he characterized as 'still alive but without any prospect of marriage, so that it actually doesn't live or rather it lives an independent life at the expense of human beings'.[15] He added that in such cases 'men suffer perhaps more'. If that was true, Kafka, in spite of his suffering, was making every effort to persuade Milena to come to the Tyrol from Vienna for a while. He was a little less callous and a little more honest when he admitted to Brod that: 'I have done the worst possible harm to this person and perhaps in the worst way.'[16] Julie, unaware of her potential rival, had just opened a hat shop in Prague.

Anti-Semitic military men aside, Kafka was enjoying himself in the Tyrol. But he realized that his sick leave would expire at the end of two months, so he asked Ottla to go and see the new Czech director of the Institute, Dr Bedřich Odstrčil, on his behalf, in order to seek permission to add on a further five weeks from his annual leave allowance. Ottla, whose Czech was slightly better than her brother's, could also look over his letter for spelling mistakes. She was given another errand: to buy at the bookseller Borový's in Malá Strana twenty copies of the Czech magazine *Kmen*, which contained Milena's translation of 'The Stoker'. Ottla was just about to marry Josef David, and her brother joked, 'I am remaining single for the two of us.'[17]

Abandoning a plan to meet Julie at Karlsbad and then see his parents, who were on holiday at Franzensbad, Kafka went instead on 28 June to Vienna to see Milena. 'I have done perhaps the worst possible thing to her,'[18] he wrote to Ottla about Julie, shortly before this excursion, 'and it is probably over. That is the way I play with a living human being.' In truth, from early May, his letters to Milena had been of an intimacy that confirmed Kafka's harsh judgement on himself.

The correspondence to Milena invites comparison with that to Felice. Mercifully shorter, it is equally, as a whole, a literary work, full of artifice – that is not to say it is insincere – and of a lighter spirit. There is more spontaneous and freely expressed love in these letters, and there is more intellectual equality between the two correspondents. Milena wrote for the newspapers *feuilletons*, or sketches, and Kafka declared after first reading some of her efforts: 'I have almost as much confidence in your writing as I have in your person. I know in Czech only one music of language, that of Božena Němcová [author of the Czech classic *The Grandmother*, which Kafka had loved since childhood], here is another music.'[19] Kafka's Jewishness was something they discussed. He talked of 'the insecure position of the Jews',[20] their 'anxiousness', which fits the case of isolated Jews, 'but these most poignantly, for instance myself'. But his real anxiety lay in the state of his health, which he began to link directly and explicitly to his mental condition. Explaining on one occasion that he would not be coming to see Milena in Vienna because of 'the mental strain',[21] he went on: 'I'm mentally ill, the disease of the lung is nothing but an overflowing of my mental disease.' By expressing it in this way, Kafka was confirming the role that the disease was playing now in his life. It was a nemesis. It was a judgement. It was more than just an infection of the lung; it confirmed his sense of having been marked out and arraigned. He told Milena that he had been ill since the four or five years of his first two engagements (both to Felice) and that he felt the gap between her youth and health (Kafka was unaware of the hardships and struggle of Milena's life in Vienna, as described by Margarete Buber-Neumann) as a woman of twenty-four and his older years. 'I'm 37, almost 38, almost a short generation older, almost white-haired from the past nights and headaches. I won't spread out before you the long story with its veritable forests of details of which I'm still afraid, like a child, only without the child's power of forgetting.' To his credit, Kafka confessed that the failure of the two engagements to Felice and the third to Julie were 'all my fault, quite undoubtedly my fault. Both girls I made unhappy.'

Kafka was reluctant to discuss Julie – whose name he never mentioned in Milena's presence – ostensibly because she was 'sensitive, and any word, even the kindest, would be the most appalling offence to her',[22] but in reality because the relationship was clearly at an end and he had done nothing to bring it to a proper conclusion. Again without mentioning her name, he said that with Felice he couldn't have made a lasting marriage, 'although I had repeatedly and quite voluntarily assured her of it, although I sometimes loved her desperately, although I know nothing more desirable than marriage in itself. Almost five years I battered at her (or, if your prefer, at myself) – well, fortunately, she was unbreakable, Prussian–Jewish mixture, a strong invincible mixture. I wasn't all that robust, after all she only had to suffer, whereas I battered *and* suffered.' Milena was 'a strong invincible mixture', every bit as formidable as Felice, and she was in an unhappy marriage. Kafka's words would therefore have the effect of warning her about who and what he was. Either consciously – in his current mood of fatalism – or unconsciously, this must have been his intention. It is also interesting to note that the victim of the 'tribunal' at the Askanischer Hof had now subtly changed his plea from one of bewildered innocence to one of guilty as charged.

As for Julie, she would now be told by wire, with a slippery explanation, that the planned meeting at Karlsbad was off: 'This is the way I play with a living human being.'[23] Julie was referred to in the correspondence with Milena only as 'the girl', not even dignified with a name. Kafka even argued that Milena, by offering him a way to transfer his affections, had 'rendered this girl the greatest service . . . I can think of no other way but this by which she could have become free of me.'[24] He recalled sitting with Julie in a one-room apartment in Prague, the one they had found the previous November. On this sofa in this room he could glimpse the beginnings of their married life together and it terrified him, as marriage always did when the reality of it was imminent rather than an idea in the mind. He blamed himself: it was 'exclusively me who had urged this marriage, she had only complied, frightened and resisting, but gradually of course had lived herself into the idea'. He still thought it could have been 'a marriage of reason in the best sense of the word', another compromise like that which seemed to offer itself towards the end of the five-year affair with Felice. It was handsome of Kafka to shoulder the blame, but an unkind critic might say that he always did so too readily and too easily, and that something more was needed. By the end of May 1920, the tone and content of the letters to Milena were unambiguously those of a man in love. It was only a matter of time before the engagement with Julie was formally dissolved.

Kafka kept returning to his awareness of the age gap between himself and Milena: 'my 38 Jewish years, faced by your 24 Christian ones'.[25] And, as with his previous love letters, he plunged enthusiastically into accounts of his woes. He told her he was 'afraid to take a step on this earth, bristling with mantraps as it is' and that he had to tell himself, 'you're a Jew, and know what fear is'. For the first time, to anyone, he confessed that the best time of his life had been the eight months at Zürau, from September 1917 to April 1918, when he had thought he had 'finished with everything', when he had confined himself only to that which within himself was 'unquestionable', when he had been free, without letters, without the five-year 'postal connection to Berlin' and Felice and in the 'shelter' of his illness. In Zürau Kafka did not have to change much of himself but only to 'retrace more firmly the old narrow outlines of your nature (after all, your face under the grey hair has hardly changed since your sixth year)'. In his youth Kafka had been influenced by progressive political ideas and by Darwinist and neo-Darwinist thinking about development and progress in the organism and in human affairs, but his illness had now confronted him with the prospect of stasis. Things were not going to improve, and would certainly worsen. He had 'honestly' fought for marriage to Julie in the autumn of 1919, but against the odds, realizing that he 'could hardly have dragged another human being, a good dear girl extinguishing herself in selflessness, deeper down with you, no not deeper; without any way out, not even towards the depths'. Against that background, he told Milena that she called to him 'with a voice which penetrates your reason and your heart with equal intensity'. He was about to run the risk of destroying a third young woman. He shrank from going to Vienna because all this would be confirmed when she saw the 'long thin creature [*ein langer magerer Mensch*]' standing there, doomed, with a friendly smile (which he considered he had inherited from an old aunt and which signified, in both of them, nothing more than embarrassment).

'Sometimes I have the feeling that we're in a room with two opposite doors and each of us holds the handle of one door, one of us flicks an eyelash and the other is already behind his door, and now the first one has but to utter a word and immediately the second one has closed his door behind him and can no longer be seen,'[26] he told Milena. 'Agonizing misunderstandings' came out of this situation of fragile communication. He urged her also to consider the kind of person he was: 'the 38-year journey lying behind me (and since I'm a Jew an even much longer one) and if at an apparently accidental turning of the road I see you, whom I've never expected to see and least of all so late, then, Milena, I cannot shout'. He warned her not to expect sincerity from him because everything seemed to elude him now: 'I'm on such a dangerous road, Milena . . . I can't listen simultaneously to the terrible voice from within and to you, but I can listen to the former and entrust it to you, to you as to no one else in the world.' Kafka kept circling back to this anxiety, as if, this time, he really did believe it was his last chance, perhaps beyond his last chance, and, having 'destroyed several human relationships'[27] in the past (not just with women: he instanced Ernst Weiss) 'from a logical disposition of mind that always believed more in an error of the other person than in miracles', he feared that he was about to do it again. She had appeared as his salvation, but was it right to accept her offer of redemption? 'A man lies in the filth and stench of his deathbed and there comes the angel of death, the most beatific of all angels, and looks at him. Can this man so much as dare to die?' The rhetoric is a little inflamed here: Kafka was in a couple of weeks to return to work after his stay in the Alps and was thus not quite on his deathbed.

Meanwhile, Kafka came up with an idea: that Milena should leave her husband in Vienna and say she was going to some peaceful part of Bohemia for the sake of her health. Kafka would fund the expedition and she could pay him back later. This would have the additional benefit of giving him some reason to earn his money – 'my job, incidentally, is ridiculous and pathetically easy, you can't imagine it, I don't know what they pay me for' – and he would briefly be transformed into 'a rapturously working clerk'. Presumably 'the girl', Julie, would not be informed of this scheme. Milena, however, replied that she would prefer yet another solution, a period on her own somewhere in solitude.

Kafka continued to be thrown into confusion by the affair and tormented by the sudden arrival of hope and a new direction precisely at the time when his powers were failing: 'My world is tumbling down, my world is building itself up . . . I deplore my lack of strength, deplore the being born, deplore the light of the sun.'[28] Feeling his age and debility, he called Milena 'a girl', and one to whom he dare not offer his hand, 'this dirty, twitching, clawlike, unsteady, uncertain, hot–cold hand'. Yet, from mid-June 1920 onwards, he started to use the familiar '*Du*' in his letters to her. He tried to explain that he felt 'used up' ('*Verbrauchtsein*') in contrast to 'your youth, your freshness, your courage'.[29] The contrast, what it portended, filled him with fear, a fear which kept increasing, 'for it signifies a withdrawal from the world, thus increase of its pressure, thus further increase of fear [*Angst*]'. Her letters frightened him: 'I cannot after all keep a storm in my room; in these letters you must have the magnificent head of Medusa, for the snakes of terror hiss around your head and indeed around mine the snakes of fear hiss even wilder.' After Kafka's death, in an obituary written for the Czech paper *Národní listy* – the most eloquent short summation of Kafka ever written by anyone[30] – Milena stressed this element of fear: 'he was a man who let his illness bear the whole burden of his fear of life'. She also believed that though he was being treated for the lung disease, 'he also deliberately cultivated it and encouraged it psychologically'. Kafka felt that he had accumulated a 'monstrous dust which 38 years [gloomily, he had added over a year to his age here] have kicked up and which has settled in me'[31] and, if she really wanted to know 'what my early life was like', he offered to send her 'the gigantic letter I wrote my father about six months ago, but which I've not yet given him'. He was afraid of 'this inner conspiracy against myself [*diese innere Verschwörung gegen mich*]'[32] which the *Letter* tried to convey and which derived from the fact that 'I, who in the great Game of Chess am not even Pawn of a Pawn, far from it, yet now, against all the rules of the game and to the confusion of the game, even want to occupy the place of the Queen'. Given this context, his proposal that he help her to leave Vienna was 'at the moment, the only thing that is unquestionable, free of morbidity and making me completely happy'.

On 28 June Kafka finally left the Tyrol and travelled by train to Vienna, where he checked into the Hotel Riva near the South Station. The old curse of noise fell on him here and he hardly slept for two nights. On 30 June he met Milena, for the first time since Prague the previous year. They walked together in the Vienna Woods, and a letter written to her on Kafka's return to Prague suggests strongly that they were intimate on this occasion.[33] Accompanying this letter was a copy of Grillparzer's *The Poor Musician*, which Kafka chose because it has a Viennese setting, 'and because he was in love with a girl who was good at business'. He also promised again to send her *Letter to the Father*. There is a rapturous tone in these letters wholly absent from those to Felice, in which so often Kafka's love was asserted rather than *felt*. 'Please stay with me always [*Bleib immer bei mir*],' he pleaded.

The only shadow over this love affair was cast by Julie, who was still in the dark about it. Kafka went to see her soon after his return to Prague on 4 July and Julie 'didn't say one even remotely angry word about you or me'.[34] Kafka felt that nothing had changed between them and that what he was being compelled to carry out in relation to Julie was 'an executioner's job'. He was also worried about Julie's health and knew that he would have to keep seeing her. The two of them sat together on the Karlsplatz (Karlovo náměstí) with Julie's body trembling beside him. 'I can't leave you,' she said, 'but if you send me away, then I'll go. Are you sending me away?'[35] Kafka answered: 'Yes.' Julie then blurted out: 'But I can't go after all.' She said she couldn't understand what was happening, claimed that Milena loved her husband, and fell into abuse of her rival. Overcome by remorse, Kafka acceded to her request to be allowed to write to Milena – he asked the latter to be 'severe but kind' to Julie – and agreed to meet her for one last time the next day, the Czech national holiday of Jan Hus Day, with the idea of taking a steamer excursion on the Vltava. Not feeling too well in the morning, Kafka sent Julie a 'pneumatic' letter (a form of express-mail delivery), putting her off and saying that she should not send the letter to Milena. Grasping at the straw of this apparent reprieve by Kafka, Julie, who had already posted the letter, dashed off to the main post office in Prague and managed to retrieve it at the cost of giving an official all the money she had with her and which she could ill afford. In the evening she brought the letter to Kafka, who now had no idea what to do. Resisting the temptation to read it, he decided that it must be sent to Milena after all. She replied to Julie (neither letter has survived) and finally Kafka reported on 19 July, 'I'm turned down'.[36] Julie was never heard from again. A few years later she was admitted to a mental home in which she probably died.

It must have seemed to Kafka that his last chance of marriage had disappeared with Julie in that Prague summer of 1920.

21

On his return to Prague, and after his four-day break in Vienna with Milena, in July 1920 Kafka stayed briefly with his parents and then moved into Elli's apartment in Nerudagasse to allow his uncle Alfred Löwy from Madrid to be put up at the Oppelthaus. Kafka liked the large, empty feel of the apartment and considered it a fair trade for the noisy street outside: 'To be alone in a room is perhaps the condition for living.'[1] His first letters to Milena from Prague seem a little overexcited, possibly due to his condition, for although he was judged well enough to return to work (where he stayed until the end of the year), he was by no means in a good state of health. He told Milena that the 'brief physical closeness and the sudden physical separation'[2] had confused him – he was, after all, more used to conducting his love affairs by post. He concluded this letter by asking her to receive 'the flow of everything I am and have and everything that is blissfully happy'. Felice had never received letters like this.

In an odd outburst he compared the pleasant calmness of his apartment with the busy communal living spaces more typical of Prague: 'the noise, the lechery, the incest of the dissolute, uncontrolled bodies, thoughts and desires'. Kafka's habitual self-control seemed under pressure and sexual excitement was evidently an element in his unsettled condition. He was also worried about the fact that there was a third person to consider in the relationship (there had been four, of course, but Julie was no longer a rival), Milena's husband Ernst Polak, but Kafka was averse to 'the thinking out of the possibilities'[3] until he really had to. 'The only thing to fear at the moment is, I think, your love for your husband,'[4] he told Milena. He even suggested writing to Polak, an offer that scared Milena at this stage and which was consequently soon withdrawn. Kafka, who was now coughing a little (something he put down to the air of Prague), claimed that he was 'essentially less shattered than I have been, perhaps, during the whole of the last seven years, with the exception of that year in the village [Zürau]',[5] implying that the reason was the 'life-giving power' of 'Mother Milena'. The latter's strength and vitality – as well as her intelligence – were intoxicating to Kafka as he felt his own powers ebb. But the dilemma remained, in Milena's words: 'Yes, you're right, I love him. But Franz, I love you, too.'[6]

On 13 July Kafka went to see the doctor, who found him in much the same condition as before his visit to the Alps: 'the disease sits in the apex of the left lung as fresh as ever'.[7] Although the doctor considered this, and the failure to put on weight, 'a fiasco', threatening a course of injections in the autumn if there was no improvement, Kafka was content. He considered that all he needed was 'a special kind of quiet, or, if one looks at it from another angle, a special kind of disquiet'. It was clear that Milena did not feel able to agree to his request that she come to Prague. But he said he trusted her: 'Until recently I thought I couldn't endure life, couldn't endure people, and was very ashamed of it, but you confirm to me now that it wasn't life that seemed unendurable to me.'[8] Nevertheless, her absence unsettled him and caused sleeplessness and a reacquaintance with the fear or *Angst* which 'deprives me of my will . . . I have no one, no one here but the *Angst*, locked together we toss through the nights . . . this *Angst* is after all not my private *Angst* – this is only part of it, and terribly so – but it is as much the *Angst* of all faith since the beginning of time'.[9] Repeatedly, Kafka kept coming back to this word, '*Angst*/fear', which may in some measure have been, in addition to his customary anxieties, a fear of taking on something beyond his current capacity – though it perhaps ought to have been a fear of wrecking another life.

Having to attend Ottla's marriage to Josef David at Prague Town Hall – and the wedding breakfast at which, myrtle in his buttonhole, he sat between David's two sisters – served only to intensify his desire to see himself more deeply involved with Milena: 'What an easy life it will be when we are together.'[10] The more Kafka insisted on such an outcome, the more the fault line in this relationship became evident. Milena was less able to contemplate leaving her husband than Kafka imagined her to be. Although he said that for her to come to him would be to 'renounce the whole world in order to step down to me',[11] there was in this correspondence none of the abasement that entered into – often rhetorically – the letters to Felice. But he continued to insist on the omnipresence of fear in his life which she alone could assuage: 'I don't know its inner laws, I know only its hand at my throat, and this is really *the most terrible thing I've ever experienced or could experience.*'[12] As a consequence of this fear, 'we are now both married, you in Vienna, I to my *Angst* in Prague'.

It gradually became clear to Kafka during his first month back at the Institute – where, on his own admission, he did very little work in spite of being presented with a backlog of documents – that Milena was not going to leave her husband. 'So we have drifted apart completely, Milena,' he wrote at the end of July, 'and the only thing we appear to have in common is the intense desire – that you should be here and your face somewhere as near mine as possible. But of course the death-wish we also have in common, this wish for a comfortable death.'[13] Although Milena had an unidentified illness at this time (she appears to have mentioned some bleeding to Kafka), she was normally in vigorous health, in contrast to him, and while both were in love, the 'death-wish' may have been a little melodramatic. Kafka may also have underestimated both Milena's readiness to abandon her life in Vienna for him and her powerful independent spirit. Such a spirit would not necessarily see its vocation as the exclusive tending of Kafka's fear – he had been in the habit of describing her as his 'saviour'. He, too, had constraints on his actions and could not, in turn, visit Vienna. He tried to make Milena understand that the office was 'not just any old stupid institution . . . but it has been my life up to now, I cannot tear myself away from it, though perhaps this wouldn't be so bad . . . I can treat it shabbily, work less than anyone else (which I do), botch the work (which I do), can in spite of it make myself important (which I do), can calmly accept as due to me the most considerate treatment imaginable in an office',[14] but he could not lie in order to be free to travel to Vienna. The Institute – like his school, university and family – was to Kafka 'a living person who looks at me wherever I am with his innocent eyes, a person with whom I'm connected in some way unknown to myself, although he's stranger to me than the people whom at this moment I hear crossing the Ring [Old Town Square] in their automobiles'. He did, however, concede that getting away from his parents would be good for him. Wryly pointing out the possibly unheroic nature of his struggle with the domestic tyrant, he observed, 'one man fights at Marathon and the other in the dining room'.[15] There was no real hiding-place from essential conflict. He compromised by making arrangements to obtain a passport so that, if it became necessary, they could meet. And then, in early August, they conceived the idea of meeting halfway at the border town of Gmünd (the station was in Czech territory; the town was Austrian).

As the meeting drew nearer, Kafka confessed to Milena he was a person 'watching your life intensely and with a beating heart and almost to the exclusion of everything else'.[16] This intensity may have been too much for Milena, who at the last minute tried to cancel the meeting, saying that she was not coming because she was 'waiting for the day when it's necessary for *you* [Kafka] to come'.[17] He was reading at this time Milena's fashion journalism in the Czech paper *Tribuna* and confessed, 'to my shame',[18] that he had been reading her articles secretly before she officially encouraged him to do so, anxious for any way of experiencing proximity to her. Kafka was full of anxiety about the difficulties they appeared to be in: 'Where did all this trouble between us come from? . . . I could have stopped it long ago, the eye was clear enough, but the cowardice was stronger.'[19] Equally, he was dissatisfied with Milena's reasoning about her husband's dependency on her. He told her the story (described earlier) of his sexual initiation, in order to convey – it must be said a little opaquely – his current sense of finding her physical proximity 'quieting–disquieting' and his recoil from what he called 'obscenity' ('*Schmutz*'). He confessed that in the Tyrol he had made plans to seduce the chambermaid and had encountered 'a very willing girl' towards the end of his stay, but the 'fear' he had expressed about spending a night in Gmünd was his usual *Angst* and not – this is presumably what he is driving at – sexual anxiety. In one of his most beautiful letters to Milena, just before they met again, Kafka said he loved her (underlining the words) '*as the sea loves a pebble in its depths, this is just how my love engulfs you*',[20] and strongly implied that sex (which Milena had dismissively termed that 'half-hour in bed') played no part in his love. He also told her that the *Angst* to which he constantly referred was 'part of me and perhaps the best part. And as it is my best, it is also perhaps this alone that you love. For what else worthy of love could be found in me?' By her side, he said, 'I'm most quiet and most unquiet, most inhibited and most free.'

For less than twenty-four hours across 14 and 15 August, Kafka and Milena met at the border at Gmünd. Kafka sent a picture postcard to Ottla, saying that he was feeling well, 'not coughing at all'.[21] But the letter had been dictated to Milena, who added a postscript: 'He was not able to finish.' The journey had probably exhausted him. And it is clear that things were said about the impossibility of their affair surviving. The meeting, in short, was a disaster.

On his return to Prague, Kafka anxiously awaited the letters that would clarify what had been said. Milena was away for two weeks, which prolonged his agony but enabled him to set out on paper 'several inexpressible, unwritable things'[22] that would 'help you understand profoundly how things are with me, so that you won't be frightened away from me'. Gmünd had been a turning point. The rapturous expressions of love which were without precedent for Kafka would now increasingly be replaced by the familiar extended analyses of what was wrong as the affair slowly began to fall apart. 'I sometimes feel as though I were carrying such weights of lead that I must at any moment be dragged down into the deepest sea and the person trying to seize or even "rescue" me would give up, not from weakness, not even from hopelessness but from sheer annoyance,' he told Milena. He begged her not to allow herself to be frightened away from him 'even if I disappoint you once or a thousand times'.

Eventually Milena replied and he told her: 'I'm dirty, Milena, infinitely dirty, which is why I make so much fuss about purity. No people sing with such pure voices as those who live in deepest hell.'[23] Kafka brooded over her letters – in his new regime of resumed afternoon sleeping and retiring late – and confessed that: 'All day long I was preoccupied with your letters, in torment, in love, in worry, and in quite an indefinite fear of something indefinite, whose indefiniteness consists largely in the fact that it goes beyond the bounds of my strength.'[24] It was clear that this affair was draining him of his already sapped energies. His cough would not abate and he mingled his illness with hers, saying that as he lay, unsleeping, in the night he dreamed that he was nursing her, living for her.

But it was Kafka who was truly in need of care. On 30 August he went to see the doctor, who noted no improvement and thought he should visit one of the sanatoria in Lower Austria. The prospect of these places, devoted solely to lung patients, appalled Kafka: 'houses which in their totality cough and shiver with fever day and night, where one has to eat meat, where ex-hangmen dislocate one's arms if one resists the injections, and where beard-stroking Jewish doctors, as callous towards Jew as Christian, look on.'[25] Even such visitors as the writers Paul Adler and Franz Blei were almost too much for Kafka in his present fragile state. He now realized that there was to be no future for him with Milena: 'Few things are certain, but this is one of them: we shall never live together, in the same apartment, body to body, at the same table, never, not even in the same town.'[26] He envisaged himself lying on a bed crushed by the weight of 'a heavy cross', an odd image which suddenly mutated into 'a corpse', and was exhausted by the thought of yet another failure. Milena seems to have reproached him for his earlier references to being 'dirty', but he insisted: 'why shouldn't I go on displaying it [the dirt], my sole possession?' She also said that the thought of death frightened her, but Kafka, in his mood of hopeless resignation, oppressed by the dead weight of existence, declared: 'I'm terribly afraid only of pains. This is a bad sign. To want death but not the pains is a bad sign. But otherwise one can risk death. One has just been sent out as a biblical dove, has found nothing green, and slips back into the darkness of the Ark.'

With Milena now lost, Kafka was thrown back on himself and his pains, and was leafing through the prospectuses of a couple of sanatoria, but he really wanted to stay in Prague and 'learn some craft'. All his life he was drawn to this idea of working simply with his hands or performing some ordinary task – a nurseryman, a bookbinder in Palestine, even, at the end and half-sardonically, a waiter in a restaurant. He was bitter about the indignities of the sanatorium, about having to put himself into the hands of the despised medical profession, which paid no heed to his notions of natural healing and holistic medicine. He envisaged the senior physician taking him between his knees so that he would 'choke on the lump of meat he stuffs into my mouth with his carbolic fingers and then forces down my throat'. Kafka felt himself to be physically and figuratively weightless – on the scales he weighed fifty-five kilos – in a world that was crushing him with its alien counterweight. He seemed to be looking on his own life from some disembodied state: 'You don't seem to realize, Milena, that we're standing side by side, watching this creature on the ground which is me; but I, as the spectator, am then non-existent.' He feared that he had allowed himself to become too dependent on her: 'there's certainly something blasphemous about building so much on one person, and this is also the reason why fear creeps round the foundations. It's not, however, so much the fear about you as the fear about daring to build like this at all.'[27]

At eight o'clock on the evening of 6 September, Kafka looked from the street into the banqueting room of the Jewish Town Hall, where more than a hundred Russian Jewish émigrés were queuing for their American visas. Around half past midnight, he looked through the illuminated windows again. In this building he had once read aloud his favourite *Novelle*, Kleist's incomparable *Michael Kohlhaas*, and on another occasion had introduced Löwy's readings with his own lecture on the Yiddish tongue. The electric light shone all night long on the sleeping forms stretched out on chairs, and Kafka looked longingly on these people – hungry as they were, prone to disease, victims of anti-Semitic threats hurled at them through the windows – and confessed that 'if I'd been given the choice to be what I wanted, then I'd have chosen to be a small Eastern Jewish boy in the corner of the room, without a trace of worry'.[28] Their soon-to-be-realized dream of escape, their concentrated purpose, their risk of everything for a certain goal, the fact, above all, that 'they are *one* people', moved him with its simple manifestation of something from which he felt himself to be totally excluded. Instead he was going nowhere, except to his death.

'Sometimes when one wakes,'[29] he told Milena, 'one believes Truth to be close . . . to be more exact, a grave with a few wilted flowers, open, ready to receive one . . . Milena . . . am I really such an evil creature . . . when I do write I'm torn to pieces by restlessness and fear . . . What do I want?' He offered her a parable of himself as an animal of the forest ('*Waldtier*') in a dirty ditch who perceived her 'outside in the open – the most wonderful thing I'd ever seen' and who came across and basked in her attention, losing his fear and tasting unfamiliar freedom: 'I was so happy, so proud, so free, so powerful, so at home.' The elusive idea of being 'so at home [*so zuhause*]' was at the heart of Kafka's longing. 'So at home – but fundamentally I was still only the animal, belonged still only in the forest, lived here in the open only by your grace, reading without realizing it . . . my fate in your eyes.' Here, as so often, Kafka translated his anxieties into animal fables and metaphors, coupled to fantasies of self-loathing, of metamorphosis into something repellent to normal human beings. 'It grew more and more clear to me what an unclean pest, what an obstacle I was to you, hindering you everywhere . . . I remembered who I am . . . I had to return to the darkness, I couldn't stand the sun, I was desperate, really like a stray animal.' His last words in this letter were: 'You ask how I live: this is how I live.'

Milena had told Kafka that some people 'haven't got the strength to love'. His displays of weakness, his self-portrayal as a frightened animal, were not what this strong, vigorous woman wanted and needed, however much she understood his writing and his intellectual being in ways no previous lover had been able to do. But Kafka went on trying to explain the roots, the manifestations, of his *Angst*. He referred to what tormented him as 'an attack' or 'an outbreak' which eventually passed, 'but the powers that call it forth are trembling within me all the time, before and after – indeed, my life, my existence consists of this subterranean threat. If it ceases I also cease, it's my way of participating in life; if it ceases I abandon life, as easily and naturally as one closes one's eyes.'[30] Wedded to his *Angst*, he saw no possibility of escaping its embraces, 'for I will always be frightened, above all, by myself'.

Milena was shrewd enough – in these last few letters which threw handfuls of earth into the grave of their relationship – to realize that what was happening was simply the latest in a long line of failed relationships with women. 'I can after all only be the same and experience the same,' Kafka confessed, adding that he could almost see the punishment coming, 'so over-alert has my conscience become'. But with Milena, he believed, it had the potential to be different: 'To you as to no one else one can tell the truth for one's own and for your sake; in fact, from you one can actually find out one's own truth.' The truth, however, was that they could not stay together. Conscious of this, Kafka relapsed into a kind of oppressive stasis – he admitted that he was using the word 'heavy' ('*schwer*') too much to describe this condition – but he refused to blame Milena: 'I live in my dirt, that's my business . . . the terrible thing is . . . that through you I become much more conscious of my dirt.'[31] As if to confirm his self-punishing interpretation, he drew one of his expressionist pen-and-ink sketches for her in the letter which showed a man being torn apart by an instrument of torture, watched by the insouciant inventor of this cruel *Apparat*. 'Aren't we human beings pathetic to the point of farce?'[32] he asked Milena two weeks later.

Kafka and Milena continued to correspond through the autumn of 1920, even though these were no longer love letters, more opportunities for Kafka to explore his *Angst* with an understanding other. Except that neither Milena nor anyone else could really understand what was the problem. 'Try to understand it by calling it an illness,'[33] he suggested, although he didn't like psychoanalysis's claim that it had uncovered such illnesses: 'I consider the therapeutic part of psychoanalysis to be a hopeless error.' Kafka had long ago acknowledged Freud as an influence on *The Judgement* and he had taken an interest in another Austrian psychoanalyst, Otto Gross (1877–1919), an early follower of Freud, whom Kafka had met at a party on 23 July 1917 at Max Brod's. At this party Gross had launched an idea for a new magazine to be called *Journal for the Suppression of the Will to Power*. His father had had him committed to a psychiatric clinic because of his drug addiction, and Gross was a possible catalyst for *Letter to the Father*: he was an advocate of revolution against patriarchy, which would be replaced by matriarchal power.[34] In spite of these influences, Kafka felt that attempts to explain away religion by psychoanalytic means ignored its innate hold on human nature; he could not agree that it was merely a symptom and could be 'cured': 'All these so-called illnesses, sad as they may appear, are matters of faith, efforts of souls in distress to find moorings in some maternal soil.' Kafka's personal theory was much more straightforward. He asked Milena to imagine three circles, an innermost one A, then B, then C. A explains to B why B has to torture and to distrust himself, why he has to renounce, and why he may not live. C is the active person to whom nothing is explained; he merely takes orders from B and acts under pressure in a cold sweat of fear. 'Thus C acts more from fear than from understanding; he trusts, he believes that A has explained everything to B and that B has understood and handed on everything correctly.'

In November 1920 in Prague anti-Semitic riots broke out repeatedly, an ugly feature of the new republic brought over from the old imperial epoch, whipped up by Czech papers such as *Venkov*, the organ of the reactionary, anti-Semitic Agrarian Party. Although Kafka did not discuss such outward political events a great deal in his diaries and letters, they would have coloured his general reflections on the Jews. He told Milena that he was one of the most typical examples of the Western Jew. 'This means, expressed with exaggeration, that not one calm second is granted me, nothing is granted me, everything has to be earned, not only the present and the future, but the past too – something after all which perhaps every human being has inherited, this too must be earned, it is perhaps the hardest work.'[35] In comments such as this one glimpses the absolute centrality of Kafka's Jewishness in the formation of his views about his relationship to the world. Whatever exasperated comments he might have thrown out from time to time about Judaism or political Zionism, he believed that the task of carrying the world on his shoulders in this way was so great that he hadn't the strength for it: 'On my own I can't go the way I want to go.' It was as if each time he went out into the street he had to make himself afresh, 'sew his clothes as well, make his shoes, manufacture his hat', only to run into 'a mob engaged in Jew-baiting in the Eisengasse'. He was drawn towards a kind of resigned quietism, and told Milena that she was utterly wrong when she said, 'it is against me that he broke'.[36] But nor was it his fault: 'It's just that my home is in the quietest quiet, this is what is right for me.'

In October Ottla, alarmed at her brother's state of health, had gone against his will to see the Institute's director to persuade him to grant a further period of sick leave. Kafka was told to come in himself and he did so. Leave was granted. He began to explore the possibilities of such sanatoria as Grimmenstein and Wiener Wald, respectively eighty and sixty kilometres south of Vienna, both of which would have made it possible to visit Milena. Kafka agonized about whether he should go: 'I haven't the strength to travel; the idea of standing before you I can't bear in advance, can't bear the pressure on the brain.'[37] He despaired that no one, not even Milena, could understand his situation: 'To live a human life in my surroundings is impossible; you see it, and yet you don't want to believe it.' He even despaired of his letters to her, which produced nothing but 'misunderstandings, humiliation, almost perpetual humiliation',[38] and which increased his sense of powerlessness, seeming to speak to him with an '*irrresistibly strong voice, as it were your voice*, which begs me to be silent'. The letters were, in the end, 'nothing but torture, *born of torture, create only torture, incurable torture*, what's the good of it . . . To be silent, this is the only way to live.'

Yet when he went out into the streets of Prague, 'wallowing in the Jew-baiting',[39] hearing the cry of 'filthy rabble' directed against the Jews, he asked: 'Isn't it the natural thing to leave the place where one is hated so much? (For this, Zionism or national feeling is not needed.) The heroism which consists of staying on in spite of it all is that of cockroaches which also can't be exterminated from the bathroom.'

The use of the word 'exterminated' ('*auszurotten*') is another reminder of the long-standing debate in Kafka studies about how far he can be said to have 'foreseen' or 'predicted' the Shoah. At a superficial level, common sense says he could not have done so, but the superficial level is not the place where we should be looking. He understood his time and its darker side. His machines of experimental death, his nightmare visions of totalitarian cruelty, his deep understanding of the fate of the Jewish people, cannot now be read – for we are different readers, readers with unwelcome knowledge – innocently, and so we cannot answer properly. In the end the conundrum is futile, but at the same time it cannot be put out of one's mind. On that day in mid-November 1920, Kafka looked out at the real rabble, the mounted police, the *gendarmerie* ready for a bayonet charge, and from his upper window in the Oppelthaus felt acutely 'the loathsome disgrace of living all the time under protection'. Where would he ever find a home, a place that would allow him entry?

22

On 13 December 1920 Kafka was granted a further three months' sick leave. He decided to take it at the tuberculosis sanatorium of a Mrs Jolan Forberger in Tatranské Matliare, the High Tatra mountains, in Slovakia. He had been given an official residency permit for Grimmenstein but changed the venue to Matliare and set off on 18 December, expecting to return on 20 March 1921. He had told Milena in November that one of the reasons for his apprehension about a possible journey to Vienna had been his coughing, which started at about 9.45 p.m. and went on till eleven. Then, after an hour's respite, it resumed and continued until 1 a.m. For this reason he felt he could not take a sleeper compartment. However, in spite of the travelling difficulties this presented, the journey from Prague turned out to be not so bad, the only vexation being a delayed trunk.

At Tatra Lomnitz Kafka was met by a sleigh, which took him on a beautiful ride in the moonlight through the snow-covered forest. On arrival at Matlárháza, the sanatorium at Matliare, a 'distinctly dark, dubious-looking lodge',[1] there was no one in the freezing-cold lobby and the driver had to stamp about and shout for some time before a maid appeared and took Kafka up to his two rooms on the first floor of the lodge known as 'Tatra', a fussily half-timbered building 900 metres above sea level. He had a room with a balcony, and the one next door was intended for Ottla, who would shortly be joining him. Entering his room, he was horrified by the stench of the stove, the iron bed with no bedcover, a broken wardrobe door, and the fact that there was only a single-paned door on to the balcony. The maid did her best to put an optimistic gloss on everything, but as far as Kafka was concerned it was a poor substitute for the Pension Stüdl at Schelesen.

Frau Forberger then appeared, lowering the temperature a little further: 'a tall woman (not Jewish) in a long black velvet coat, unpleasant Hungarian-German, saccharine but hard'. Kafka was very rude to her, provoked by her bland reassurances, and decided that, first thing in the morning, he would decamp by sleigh to the sanatorium of Dr Miklós von Szontagh in Nový Smokovec, about an hour's walk away. At this point the maid suggested that he take Ottla's room instead, which turned out to be much more attractive in every respect; 'So I stayed.'

Next day, when Kafka started to explore the other buildings, he was satisfied with what he saw and with the mostly Hungarian guests ('few Jews,' he thought initially, but later discovered that they were in the majority) who would allow him to remain 'nicely in obscurity'. His balcony at the Tatra was sunny, and meals could be brought over from the main building. It was much quieter, and there was a doctor, Leopold Strelinger, 'a handsome, red-cheeked, strong man',[2] three doors down. Even the fearsome Frau Forberger seemed less frightful in the bright December morning sunshine. Special vegetarian meals were prepared for Kafka and the doctor visited him daily at six crowns a time, though his offer of an arsenic cure was politely declined. Kafka struggled to meet his prescribed targets of milk five times a day and cream twice. Everything seemed outwardly satisfactory. 'There remains only the enemy inside my head.'

In the end Ottla did not come, and Hermann Kafka was also deterred from paying a visit. Kafka would be alone with his ghosts and demons as he sat half-naked, sunning himself on the balcony. He kept himself to himself, making only one friendship at the start, with a twenty-five-year-old Hungarian Jew called Herr Szinay (nicknamed *Der Kaschauer* – the man from Kaschau), a socialist and student of the Talmud, one of those moody, enthusiastic, clever but slightly directionless young people whom Kafka liked to take under his wing. Another of these was Gustav Janouch, son of one of Kafka's colleagues at the Institute, who had started to visit him at the office in March 1920 at the age of seventeen. Janouch, who had literary ambitions, kept notes of his meetings with Kafka and later published them as a book, *Conversations with Kafka* (1953). Scholars have always been uneasy about this collection, worried about its authenticity (often this is a Kafka who doesn't sound at all like Kafka, though Brod insisted otherwise) and, according to one critic, so unreliable is this Bohemian Boswell that it has resulted in the 'virtual removal from the canon'[3] of the book as a biographical source. It has not been drawn on for this biography.

Kafka felt that if he could endure the regimen at Matliare, physically and mentally, for three months, he would 'come very close to health'.[4] As usual when arriving at sanatoria, he initially gained weight – 1.6 kilos this time – but 'I always come on like a lion in the first week of a cure'. The old demon of noise, however, was soon plaguing him. A guest on the balcony above sang and chatted to Szinay, which caused a 'nervous shock'[5] that prevented him from sleeping and forced him to consider moving again. The management headed off this possibility by moving 'a quiet lady' into the room above instead of the jovial youths.

Kafka joked to Brod that his condition was like that of the old Austrian Empire, where some small political tremor alone was needed 'to begin to make the throne in Vienna begin to sway'.[6] Three years into the new post-Habsburg political world of Mitteleuropa, Kafka seemed as unaffected by the empire's departure as he had been by its presence. He was also pleased to be able to prove that he could be cured without being forced to eat meat, as at Zürau and Merano. 'To be sure the Enemy intervened, but eating meat doesn't fend him off or not eating meat bring him on. He comes in any case.'[7]

Kafka was increasingly referring to his inner demon or *Angst* as 'the Enemy' or as 'ghosts', building up an independent antagonist, with whom he must fence in order to preserve his life and sanity. In a discussion with Brod about the latter's affair with a Berlin woman called Emmy Salveter (who may have contributed to the drawing of the character Pepi in *The Castle*) Kafka said that the difference between them was that 'You want the impossible, while for me the possible is impossible.'[8] Brod had evidently told Kafka that it was his friend's striving for perfection that made the attainment of women impossible for him. Kafka replied, 'The striving for perfection is only a small part of my huge Gordian knot.'[9] In other words it created difficulties in every department of his existence, not just relationships with women. Kafka admired Brod for the way he had overcome his deformation of the spine, which gave him a hunch-backed look, and compared his triumph to that of the skiers he could see from his window at the Tatra, flying over all obstacles. Kafka realized that he had not achieved such a triumph over the odds. To Brod's demand to know exactly what Kafka was afraid of, the latter replied, 'Of so much, but on the earthly plane above all fear that I will not suffice, not physically, not mentally, to bear the burden of another person. As long as we are almost united, it is merely a groping fear . . . And when this fear has done its work, it becomes an absolutely irrefutable, unendurable fear.'

Kafka was *becoming* his fear. No one could get between it and himself. But he insisted to Brod that he was not crossing the line into clinical paranoia: 'I have learned from experience that no place remains unoccupied and if *I* do not sit high on my horse, the persecutor will be sitting there.'[10] He added that he was a person 'who returns from supper to his quiet room trembling almost physically from the painful after-effects of mere contact with someone at table'. In this case the provocation was 'an elderly spinster, repulsively powdered and perfumed . . . also unhinged by nervousness', a Czech, and a bigoted devotee of the anti-Semitic paper *Venkov*. He was biding his time for a confrontation with her, though later he grew to feel sorry for her.

Kafka, since his declaration to Milena in November that they could not share a life together, had not written to her and had asked her not to write to him. The state of febrile sensitivity he describes in the early weeks at Matliare demonstrates how ill equipped he must have been to deal with the passion she had unleashed in him and in herself. Observers at the time, like Max Brod, had been alarmed: 'I saw that his health, already shattered by his grave disease, was deteriorating alarmingly under this inward stress.'[11] Sometimes he even stayed at the Institute, with Brod for company, waiting for a telegram from Milena. She herself had written to Brod in the second half of 1920, expressing her worries about Kafka, and was perplexed by his seeming incapacity to deal with life's practicalities. She had been with him to a post office and seen him almost unable to complete a basic transaction or tormented at the discovery that he had been given too much change. 'This world is and remains mysterious to him,'[12] she told Brod. With her typical passion, Milena declared: 'But Franz cannot live. Franz does not have the capacity for living. Franz will never get well. Franz will die soon.' She said that he was incapable of getting drunk because 'He possesses not the slightest refuge. For that reason he is exposed to all those things against which we are protected. He is like a naked man among a multitude who are dressed.'

What Kafka interpreted as a 'last letter' from Milena arrived in late January in spite of his request that she should not write. 'She is strong and unalterable,' he told Brod.[13] Milena wrote again to Brod, distraught at the implacable nature of Kafka's rejection of her: 'I simply don't know what to do . . . It seems to me that during these last months something utterly horrible has happened to me.'[14] She kept returning to Kafka's letter from Tatra, which said calmly: 'Do not write and let us not see each other; I ask you only quietly to fulfil this request of mine; only on those conditions is survival possible for me; everything else continues the process of destruction.' Milena told Brod she was 'on the verge of madness'. She wanted to know 'whether I am the kind of person who has made Franz suffer the way he has suffered from every woman, so that his sickness has grown worse, so that he has had to flee from me, too, in his fear, and so that I too must get out of his life – whether I am at fault or whether it is a consequence of his own nature'.

Milena eventually calmed down and wrote again to Brod with calm insight: 'What his terror is I know down to the last nerve . . . In the four days he was with me [in Vienna, at the beginning of July 1920], he lost it . . . I know for certain that no sanatorium will succeed in curing him . . . no psychic strengthening can overcome this terror [Kafka's *Angst*] because the terror prevents the strengthening . . . The flesh is too exposed; he cannot bear to see it.'[15] Milena recalled how, during those four days, she had dragged him over the hills on the outskirts of Vienna in his white shirt, his throat now tanned, tramping determinedly in the sun. He had not coughed, he had eaten a lot and slept like a log, his illness reduced to nothing more than a minor cold (a fact he himself confirmed). Milena's powerful life force had dragged him into health. She saw herself as the only person who could have healed him, but she was unable to leave her husband. More than this, however, she knew that her nature could not stand the 'strictest asceticism for life', which a life with Kafka would entail, and her 'raging desire' was for an altogether different kind of life, 'for a life with a child, for a life that would be very close to the soil'. Kafka saw this struggle going on in her 'and that frightened him off'. She added: 'The women who were with him in the past were ordinary women and did not know how to live except as women. I rather think that all of us, each and every one of us, is sick and that he is the only well person, the only person who sees rightly and feels rightly, the only pure person. I know that he does not resist *life*, but only *this kind of life*: that is what he resists. If I had been capable of going with him, he could have lived happily with me . . . That terror of his was right.'

Milena's biographer, Margarete Buber-Neumann, who walked with her subject twenty years later between the huts at Ravensbrück and listened to Milena's story from her own lips, concluded that Kafka ended the affair because 'He was very sick, and Milena's vitality weighed on him. She wanted all his love, including the physical love he dreaded.'[16] Although he had expressed a desire never to see her again, they continued to see each other from time to time later in Prague, but the affair was over.

Meanwhile, at Matliare, the continuing problems from noise being picked up by Kafka's 'fear-sharpened ears' prevented him from attaining a proper calm. Nevertheless, his weight continued to increase – by 4.2 kilos in five weeks – and he began to make arrangements to extend his stay. This involved writing to the Institute to soften them up, in preparation for a direct approach about an extension of leave, especially if a doctor's report could be brought in support, and he knew that the request must be framed in the proper official style. His Czech was not quite up to it so he sought help from Ottla's husband, Josef David (nicknamed 'Pepa'). He told Ottla that 'Everything depends on its being classical Czech.'[17] Pepa did his best and the result was a letter to the director of the Institute, posted on 27 January 1921, in which Kafka explained that he had been at Matliare for five weeks, was well housed, and was recuperating: 'My body weight and external appearance have significantly improved.'[18] His fever was less frequent and usually milder when it came and his coughing was lighter, but he spent most of the day in bed and avoided all exertion. Kafka left it there and thanked Pepa, explaining that 'Here I am trying to live quietly. A newspaper hardly ever comes my way.'[19]

One morning while out walking Kafka met a young man who was carrying in his hand a copy of Kierkegaard's *Fear and Trembling*. Since Kafka himself was carrying a copy of the same book they naturally broke into conversation – notwithstanding Kafka's expressed wish to keep himself to himself. The young man turned out be a twenty-one-year-old Hungarian medical student called Robert Klopstock.[20] Kafka told Brod the next day that Klopstock was 'a Budapest Jew, very ambitious, intelligent, also highly literary; incidentally he greatly resembles Werfel in appearance, though somewhat coarser on the whole. He has a hunger for people, the way a born doctor does. Is anti-Zionist; his guides are Jesus and Dostoevsky.'[21] The fact that Kafka knew the great Max Brod was a significant draw as far as Klopstock was concerned.

The young man was very solicitous to Kafka both at Matliare and in his final illness. He regularly prepared compresses for him. Klopstock had been primed for a possible meeting with Kafka by Szinay, who told him he must meet this amazing man who 'smiles like I have never seen anyone smile'[22] and was a sympathetic and understanding listener. When Klopstock asked about Kafka's profession, Szinay said he had told him he was 'an official in an insurance office [*Beamter in einer Versicherungsgesellschaft*]'. Klopstock found Kafka's nature 'all-embracing and overwhelming' yet not at all oppressive. He noted that Kafka followed every detail, every small change in the progress (or decline) of another guest nicknamed 'the Czech' as if he were watching his own future as a TB sufferer unfold before his eyes.

When Klopstock met Kafka he had no idea his fellow guest was a writer. The former, whose correspondence with Kafka was recently offered for sale and may soon enter the public domain,[23] received guidance from his new friend on a literary translation from the Hungarian, and Kafka later tried to help Klopstock in his literary career by persuading his publisher to give him the rights to translate Kafka's works into Hungarian. In the course of their conversations Kafka told Klopstock that he was disappointed by his friend Franz Werfel's failure to take seriously his role as a leading Jewish-German author. Werfel, the great hope of the early twentieth-century Prague authors, worked for Kurt Wolff's publishing house, where he promoted the work of the expressionist generation of writers. Kafka admired Werfel's ability to provide intellectual leadership, to play roles he himself could not play, but increasingly he felt that Werfel was not living up to early expectations. His play *Schweiger*, for example, keenly disappointed Kafka because of its fictionalized and, in his view, trivializing portrait of Otto Gross.

These literary conversations gave Kafka some respite from his life as a patient, sucking his thermometer seven times a day and writing down the results, and sitting endlessly on the sofa or on his sunny balcony: 'I lie for hours in the reclining chair in a twilight state, like that of my grandparents, which I used to marvel at when I was a child.'[24]

By early March, with his sick leave running out, Kafka did not feel well: 'I never had such coughing, such shortness of breath, never such weakness.' He felt, however, that he ought to leave Matliare because he was becoming too settled. The weather was improving and he was at last able to sun himself naked on the balcony and in the pavilion in the woods. He had even agreed, with great reluctance, to eat meat (thought it exacerbated his haemorrhoids) and came to the conclusion that it was a mistake in the past not to have lived with consumptives, for 'as yet I have not looked the disease straight in the eye'. He told Ottla (who was extremely concerned about his health and had warned him, having seen the detrimental effect of the tempestuous affair with Milena, to keep away from women) that one of the gains of being with sick people is that 'one takes the disease more seriously'.[25] He also asked her to send books for Klopstock[26] – Plato's *Symposium*, Hoffmann's life of Dostoevsky, and Brod's *Death to the Dead*. Klopstock was thrilled with the books when they arrived.

The imminent return to Prague, however, continued to cast a menacing shadow over this languid life. Kafka's intermittent dream of finally quitting his job and going to Palestine flared up but he admitted to Ottla that it was 'the stuff of dreams'.[27] The security of a life he knew was something he could not let go: 'To me the Institute is a featherbed, as heavy as it is warm. If I were to crawl out from under it, I would at once risk catching cold; the world is not heated.' Kafka had the measure of his own dependency. He was in a real dilemma about the return to Prague just as spring had reached the High Tatra, making the region beautiful, 'But I am tired of the asking-for-leave, tired of the thanking-for-leave.' Convinced that his disease was not contagious, Kafka was still worried that, in the city, where 'nobody is entirely healthy', infection might be possible. 'So for that reason too I am reluctant to return to my place in the domestic nest, where all around the little beaks are opening wide, perhaps to receive the poison that I disseminate.'

The doctor at Matliare took a tougher line and warned Kafka of 'total collapse'[28] if he returned to Prague. Kafka therefore resolved to try to extend his sick leave. He had left it so late that there was no time for the normal procedures and it was thus 'all but indecent extortion' suddenly to bounce the Institute into granting an extension. He commissioned Brod to go to the office, taking with him a medical certificate from Dr Odstrčil, and plead on his behalf. Kafka, who had a bad conscience about all the sick leave he had taken, was seeking just another two months at first and was prepared to take a cut in salary, though 'I also want them to wait a while before retiring me on pension'. He said the director of the Institute was a 'good, kindly man', though probably from political motives because it enabled him to say to the Germans 'that he had treated one of theirs with exceptional kindness, even though the man was only a Jew'. Kafka admitted that he was impressed by the director's creative use of language, and 'first learned to admire the vitality of spoken Czech through him'. He told Brod to mention this. Such advice to Brod on presentation shows how astute a civil servant Kafka had become. As it turned out, Ottla, in spite of her pregnancy, made a confidential visit to the director and won the two-month extension of sick leave.

Kafka's plan was to go to Dr Guhr's sanatorium in Polianka, also in the mountains, but ultimately he remained at Matliare. He agreed with his uncle Siegfried's suggestion that he should really be doing some light gardening work in a health resort rather than sitting around, but he was still not well enough, and indeed, from the end of March until early April, he fell quite seriously ill with a fever and intestinal catarrh.

The new extension ran until 20 May, but what then? Kafka was forced to resubmit an application for yet another extension, and on 13 May he was granted another three months, expiring on 20 August. His letter of thanks to the director explained that his condition had hardly improved, but he did say that he was not suffering so much from fever and coughing, probably as a result of the beautiful weather. The willingness of the office to carry Kafka for so long is a testament to how much they valued him as an employee. Kafka himself claimed it was 'nothing but a form of alms and it is a disgrace that I accept them'.[29] He told Brod that he now had three wishes: to achieve 'approximate recovery',[30] to go to 'a foreign land in the south' (not necessarily Palestine) and to practise 'a modest handicraft'. None of the three wishes would be granted.

In the middle of April Kafka had received a letter from Milena in which she told him that, uncharacteristically, she was unwell at the time of writing. Because he saw her as healthy and energetic,

Kafka could not conceive of Milena ever being ill, and he asked Brod to warn him if she were planning to come anywhere near the High Tatra so that he could flee: 'For a meeting would no longer mean that desperation tears its hair, but that it scratches bloody welts on head and brain.'[31] Kafka had received a shock from the hurricane impact of Milena and could not possibly withstand a second blast. He tried to diagnose his failure in love:

> It's an illness of instinct, a product of the age; depending on vitality there are ways to deal with it one way or the other. But in accord with my lack of vitality I cannot find any such ways, or at most the way of fleeing . . . the fact was that the body of every other girl tempted me, but the body of the girl in whom I placed my hopes (for that reason?) not at all. As long as she withheld herself from me (F. [Felice]) or as long as we were one (M. [Milena]), it was only a menace from far away . . . but as soon as the slightest thing happened, everything collapsed. Evidently on account of my dignity, on account of my pride (no matter how humble he looks, the devious West European Jew!), I can love only what I can place so high above me that I cannot reach it . . . She is unattainable for me; I must resign myself to that.

In these painful self-dissections, Kafka showed that he knew the reasons for his failure to marry. Later, he instructed Brod, who was due to meet Milena: 'When you speak to her about me, speak as you would of someone dead.'[32] The expressionist poet Albert Ehrenstein, who paid a visit to Kafka at Matliare, told him that 'in effect in Milena life was reaching out its hand to me and I had the choice between life and death. That was somewhat too magniloquent . . . but in essence it was true.'[33]

Kafka's note at Matliare in mid-summer was one of resignation. Tormented by noise again (the whistling and hammering of a man installing stoves in adjacent rooms), he concluded that 'it isn't the noise here that's at issue, but rather the noise of the world, and not even this noise but my own noiselessness . . . This by and large out-of-the-world life which I lead here is not in itself worse than any other.'[34] But, neither writing nor reading, Kafka could not continue to live like this. In the second half of the previous year, from the summer of 1920 onwards, he had started to write again after three years of inactivity, but just now he was marking time. It was important that he return to work and to ordinary life if there were to be any possibility of his getting well. 'I have continued on here, unable to move, as though I had put down roots,'[35] he told Brod, adding that he feared most of all the Institute, from which he had never been away so long. 'My debt to the Institute is so enormous, so unpayable, that it can only go on increasing.'

On his balcony at Matliare, Kafka, as always, was continuing to ponder on his Jewishness. He was fully aware of the psychoanalytical father complex but said that he preferred 'another version, where the issue revolves not around the innocent father but around the father's Jewishness. Most young Jews who began to write German [he had just been discussing Yiddish with Brod] wanted to leave Jewishness behind them, and their fathers approved of this . . . But with their posterior legs they were still glued to their father's Jewishness and with their waving anterior legs they found no new ground. The ensuing despair became their inspiration.' The problem with this was that the result 'could not be German literature' and the writers – the case, of course, is Kafka's – faced a triple dilemma: 'The impossibility of not writing, the impossibility of writing German, the impossibility of writing differently.'

Kafka had thus not yet given up the idea that he would go back to Prague, and his writing, again. Beautiful as Matliare was in summer, he knew that he must be back in the city by 20 August. He could not continue in this artificial indolence. But at the very last minute he had an attack of fever. This mortified him as he must yet again write to the office to explain the delay. One more time Pepa was pressed into service to ensure that Kafka's draft letter to the director was put into perfect Czech. Nine days late, on 29 August 1921, Kafka returned to Prague and to his desk at the Institute.

23

Kafka's stay at Matliare had not been a complete success. He had gained only eight kilos in weight during his eight-month stay and was still far from cured. The Prague he returned to at the end of August 1921 had not changed. He was living at home with his parents and, although he kept in touch by letter with such new friends as Klopstock and such old ones as Minze Eisner, he was once again experiencing all the unwelcome features of family life. A letter written shortly after his return to his sister Elli, in response to her worries about a choice of school for her children, contained a sermon on the topic of parents and children. Kafka wanted her to avoid the fate of children of prosperous Prague Jews, which was to be infected by a 'small, dirty lukewarm, squinting spirit'.[1] Such comments by Kafka – which are by no means rare – exhibit what is sometimes called 'Jewish anti-Semitism', a characteristic of assimilated Jews. As one student of the phenomenon put it: 'To counter the inevitable accusation of divided loyalties, the Jews had only one option: to torment themselves with the same reproaches that the Christian majority used against them.'[2] Kafka was no stranger to the tactics of self-accusation.

In a series of letters to Elli, her brother declared that 'children are there to save their parents',[3] adding, 'Theoretically I do not understand how there can be childless people.' But he also quotes Swift: 'parents are the last of all others to be trusted with the education of their own children'. Kafka saw the family as 'an organism but an extremely complex and unbalanced one' in which the parents 'deprive the children of their right to personality' and which had room only for 'certain kinds of people who conform to certain kinds of requirements'. As far as Kafka was concerned – now back in the parental home at the age of thirty-eight with none of his problems with his family resolved – 'the selfishness of parents – the authentic parental emotion – knows no bounds . . . tyranny or slavery, borne of selfishness, are the two educational methods of parents . . . the love that parents have for their children is animal, mindless, and always prone to confuse the child with their own selves . . . Mistrust is a Prague failing.' Freshly reacquainted with it, Kafka denounced 'the oppressive, poison-laden, child-consuming air of the nicely furnished family room'. He was back in Prague with a vengeance. He even tried to deter Klopstock from coming to visit him there: 'To walk in the inner city on a warm afternoon, no matter how slowly, affects me as though I were in a long unventilated room and did not even have the strength to open the window and get some air.'[4]

It was in this disconsolate mood, in early autumn 1921, that Kafka drafted the first of two testamentary wishes that all his work be destroyed after his death. These are considered in more detail later (on pp. 347–8), but the post- Matliare mood of self-doubt, unease about his future and worry that his health would never improve undoubtedly contributed to that rather extreme form of stocktaking.

On 15 October Kafka, who had written little for months, resumed his diary, shortly after a sudden decision to give his earlier ones to Milena to read. It is possible that she met him on his return to Prague at his parents' home, where she would encounter him several times over the remainder of the year. He promised himself that the new one would be a different kind of diary, and would not be so obsessively concerned to document every minute change in his war against bachelorhood: 'I am not so forgetful as I used to be in this respect, I am a memory come alive, hence my insomnia.'[5] He used the diary to clear a space for himself, to see where he now stood in relation to what was obviously a permanent illness and surveyed the terrain ahead from a realization that there was so much unachieved. He felt 'the misery of having perpetually to begin', but was, to some degree, reconciled. Watching the young women in the park on one of his walks, he realized he was not envious and had 'enough imagination to share their happiness, enough judgement to know I am too weak to have such happiness, foolish enough to think I see to the bottom of my own and their situation'. He faced the weakness of his constitution but was determined not to yield to despair. Wryly he perceived that he had allowed himself to become 'a physical wreck' because he 'did not want to be distracted by the pleasures life has to give a useful and healthy man. As if illness and despair were not just as much of a distraction!'[6] Equally, he envied all married couples but 'the happiness to be found in any one marriage, even in the likeliest case, would probably plunge me into despair'. His condition seemed to him unique: 'I don't believe people exist whose inner plight resembles mine.' It struck him, further, that it was 'astounding how I have systematically destroyed myself in the course of the years'.

When Kafka was not in his room, drawing up this series of accounts with himself, he was trying to sustain the inadequate relationship with his family. One evening, as usual, his parents were playing cards. 'I sat apart, a perfect stranger; my father asked me to take a hand, or at least to look on; I made some sort of excuse. What is the meaning of these refusals, oft repeated since my childhood?'[7] In the same spirit of calm, resigned introspection, as if he had quietly stepped outside himself, Kafka considered that he could easily have played a more normal role in society or public life but for some reason had always refused:

> Judging by this, I am wrong when I complain that I have never been caught up in the current of life, that I never made my escape from Prague, was never made to learn a sport or trade, and so forth – I should probably have refused every offer, just as I refused the invitation to play cards. I allowed only absurd things to claim my attention, my law studies, the job at the office, and later on such senseless additional occupations as a little gardening, carpentry and the like . . . I always refused, out of general weakness, probably, and in particular out of weakness of will.

A few evenings later Kafka showed willing and agreed to keep score for his mother during the card game – 'but it begot no intimacy'.[8] He was simply bored and regretted the waste of time. 'I have seldom, very seldom, crossed this borderland between loneliness and fellowship, I have even been settled there longer than in loneliness itself. What a fine bustling place was Robinson Crusoe's island in comparison!' Another night, having returned from a performance of Molière's *Le Misanthrope*, he confessed to a 'feeling of complete helplessness'[9] and asked himself what it was that bound him to these human beings rather than to the inanimate objects on his desk. Was it because he belonged to the same species? 'But you don't belong to the same species, that's the very reason why you raised this question.' It was, he felt, a wonder, a riddle, that he had not perished already. 'Left to my own resources, I should have long ago been lost.' This unruffled ability to look deep into the heart of such bleakness echoes descriptions of Kafka by his friends who always noted his calm, equable spirit in company, whatever raged beneath the surface in the devil's workshop of his *Angst*.

At the beginning of December, Milena, who had been in Prague throughout the autumn, paid the last of her four calls on Kafka at his parents' house, before leaving the city the next day.

On these visits she seems to have brought him some peace where once she alarmed him with her passion. 'I feel no sorrow at her departure, no real sorrow,'[10] he wrote, but it is clear that she was still on his mind. Lately he had been thinking how 'as a little child I had been defeated by my father and because of ambition have never been able to quit the battlefield all these years despite the perpetual defeats I suffer'. These late reflections of 1921 all seem rooted in a sense that he was going nowhere because of his illness; that there would be no new beginnings. He was considering some of the avenues he might have taken, yet even these turned out to be blocked. Even writing and its use of metaphor made him despair, because metaphor showed writing's lack of independence of the world, a world ruled by its own laws: 'Only writing is helpless, cannot live in itself, is a joke and a despair.' Kafka consoled himself at the year's end with Tolstoy's sombre masterpiece *The Death of Ivan Ilych*.

January 1922 began badly for Kafka. His health had not seriously deteriorated, even if temperature and weight were not quite as good as they had been in Matliare, and his doctor had suggested that Kafka join him and his family at Spindelmühle, a snow-covered resort in the Reisengebirge near the Polish border, in late January. Kafka had been examined in October by a Dr O. Hermann, who, having diagnosed catarrh in the lung, prescribed a special cure which required yet another period of leave from the Institute. Three months' leave was granted on 29 October until 4 February 1922, and the cure, about which no further details exist, was administered during November in Prague.

Probably around this time Kafka wrote the story 'First Sorrow/*Erstes Leid*', which would be published in his last collection, *A Fasting Artist/Ein Hungerkünstler.* It is the tale of a trapeze artist who, as the only way of keeping his art at the pitch of its perfection, remains up on the trapeze permanently, day and night, with his needs supplied by attendants who haul up and down everything that is required. Like the lonely artist dedicated to his vocation, the trapeze artist was isolated from others who sometimes found his perfectionism a little trying – his presence was a distraction during other acts, for one thing – but he was tolerated because of his special gifts. The trapeze artist might have enjoyed this way of life for ever were it not for the need to travel from place to place (as Kafka the writer had from time to time to negotiate with the outside world and go to the office?). The story exhibits Kafka's fondness for pursuing every last detail of his madcap invention – the trapeze artist hangs upside down from the luggage rack, for example, in the special compartment assigned to him while the circus is on tour. Then he suddenly announces that he is in need of a partner, a second trapeze, which the manager immediately grants. But the trapeze artist bursts into tears and cannot be consoled even though his wish had been granted: he cannot face performing on the single trapeze while the second one is on order. He then sobs himself to sleep while the troubled manager watches him, thinking, 'he could see the first lines beginning to furrow the infant smoothness of the trapeze artist's brow'.

This is a typical Kafka short story: beautifully exact and told with the briskly straightforward pace of a realistic narrative, except that it is an utterly fantastic invention. It has that boldly dramatic, expressionist manner – as when the artist burst into tears and the manager 'stroked him and laid his cheek against him, so that he too was bathed in the trapeze artist's tears' – which is the hallmark of Kafka's fictional style. And it has the feel and suggestiveness of a parable, its rigorous and self-sustaining objectivity inescapably suggesting a symbolic purpose. In this case it persuades that it is about artistic maturity, the inability of the artist to find peace in the exclusive exercise of his art, in his solipsistic obsession.

Early critics of Kafka, guided in part by the preoccupations of Max Brod, who sought to turn his friend into a religious thinker, fastened on to the idea that Kafka's work was allegorical – that its structures and images mirrored specific religious readings of the universe. But it is much more satisfactory to see a story such as 'First Sorrow' as symbolist rather than allegorical, embodying its own imaginative truth rather than enacting a programmatic parallelism like *Pilgrim's Progress*. Even biographical interpretations like the above risk the same sort of reductiveness, of diminishing the imaginative richness of the symbol by worrying at the definitions and real-life parallels rather than dwelling imaginatively in the work of art as it is.

In the second week of January 1922, before going to complete his sick leave at Spindelmühle, Kafka seems to have had what he described to himself as a 'breakdown' ('*Zusammenbruch*') comparable in seriousness to his illness of early 1920 before going to Merano. 'Everything seemed over with,'[11] he wrote. He found it impossible to sleep and 'impossible to endure life', as if the inner and outer clocks were out of synchronization: 'the inner one runs crazily on at a devilish or demoniac or in any case inhuman pace, the outer one limps along at its usual speed'. He explained 'the wild tempo of the inner process' as being caused by introspection following on introspection in an endless sequence. His breakdown was also caused by his isolation from other people: 'The solitude that for the most part has been forced on me, in part voluntarily sought by me – but what was this if not compulsion too? – is now losing all its ambiguity and approaches its denouement. Where is it leading? The strongest likelihood is that it may lead to madness; there is nothing more to say, the pursuit goes right through me and rends me asunder.' He tried to persuade himself to be more resigned to his fate, 'to rest content in the moment',[12] to accept that it was only fear of the future that made the present moment appear so terrible. And he tried to confront the other major issue in his life, his failure to marry, asking: 'What have you done with your gift of sex?' He believed that this 'might easily have succeeded' and that it was only 'a mere trifle [*eine Kleinigkeit*]' that had prevented its being successful – though this is hardly how it appears to anyone confronting the evidence of his difficult relationships. He felt that 'sex keeps gnawing at me, hounds me day and night, I should have to conquer fear and shame and probably sorrow too to satisfy it'.

In spite of all Kafka's devastating critiques of family life, he was tormented by the idea of not being able to experience paternity – 'the infinite, deep, warm, saving happiness of sitting beside the cradle of one's child opposite its mother'[13] – and felt this lack terribly: 'Sisyphus was a bachelor.' Although any sort of renewed approach to Milena was impossible and her recent visits had been merely those of an old friend, he could not help noticing her manner on those occasions, which were 'like the visits one pays to an invalid'. He wondered if, having read his diaries, she had discovered 'some final proof against me'. Milena kept the diaries until after Kafka's death, when she handed them over to his literary executor, Max Brod. Kafka felt that she had understood him, and his refusal of consolation. He found himself comparing himself to his uncle Rudolf – 'young to the end of our days ("well preserved" is a better expression), both on the verge of insanity'. 'Madness' and 'insanity' were words that Kafka had not used before in such a way as to make them sound like real possibilities. He later told Brod that he *had* been on the verge of madness at this time, a fact which influenced Brod when he came to make his famous decision to ignore Kafka's request, written down not long before this time, that all his unpublished work be destroyed after his death.

Kafka was tortured by anxiety that his life had been 'merely marking time, has progressed at most in the sense that decay progresses in a rotten tooth. I have not shown the faintest firmness of resolve in the conduct of my life.'[14] He reviewed the many examples of his aborted starts in life: 'It was as if I, like everyone else, had been given a point from which to prolong the radius of a circle, and had then, like everyone else, to describe my perfect circle round this point. Instead, I was forever starting my radius only constantly to be forced at once to break it off. (Examples: piano, violin, languages, Germanics, anti-Zionism, Zionism, Hebrew, gardening, carpentry, writing, marriage attempts, an apartment of my own.)' Kafka was always a diligent archivist of his failures. The 'marriage attempts' ('*Heiratsversuche*') were the most bruising and the most desolating for him now: he noticed the happiness of the married men in his office and considered that what they had was the only thing that would appease his longing. Not merely had his life been a series of false starts (and his writing, too, is in large measure a corpus of unfinished work: several of the short stories may have been completed, but no novel was), but it was as if it had hardly left the blocks: 'If there is a transmigration of souls then I am not yet on the bottom rung. My life is a hesitation before birth [*Mein Leben ist das Zögern vor der Geburt*].'[15] Kafka's insight was extreme but it did not help him in his dilemma: the 'hesitation' was to be infinitely prolonged. Actually, he no longer wished to pursue any particular course of development; he wanted to live on another planet. '[I]t would be enough if I could exist alongside myself, it would even be enough if I could consider the spot on which I stand as some other spot.' He felt that his development had been a simple one: 'I have always been discontented, even with my contentment.'

On 27 January 1922 Kafka travelled to Spindelmühle, where he discovered that, in spite of earlier correspondence with the hotel, which had it correctly, his name had been written in the hotel register as 'Joseph K'. He threw himself into tobogganing and mountain-climbing, and even tentatively took to skis. However, he felt himself to be incapable of forming any human friendships and was 'full of endless astonishment when I see a group of people cheerfully assembled here'.[16] He continued at Spindelmühle with the extraordinary sequence of diary entries that had begun in early January, remorselessly analysing himself and his peculiar fate. He was thinking of his father again, and how he had made his son want to quit the world because he 'would not let me live in it, in his world'.[17] In a biblical metaphor he saw himself as a person exiled and displaced by his father's power from his rightful homeland – 'a kind of Wandering in the Wilderness in reverse'.

Although Kafka's picture postcards from Spindelmühle to such friends as Robert Klopstock – whom he had been helping to secure a passport to travel to Prague and work – and Minze Eisner were cheerful enough, the mood of the diary continued to be dark. He envisaged his situation in this world as 'a dreadful one, alone here in Spindelmühle, on a forsaken road, moreover, where one keeps slipping in the snow in the dark, a senseless road, moreover, without an earthly goal'. Deep snow, a perplexed arrival, uncertainty about the 'earthly goal' (with the suggestion that there is a more satisfactory other-worldly goal if only one can locate it) – these are also present in the opening pages of Kafka's last major novel, *The Castle*, which he had possibly begun to write on arrival at the snowy resort in January 1922. He told himself that 'I am fond of lovers but cannot love, I am too far away' and that 'I live elsewhere', though 'the attraction of the human world is so immense, in an instant it can make one forget everything' and 'those who love me love me because I am "forsaken"'. If Milena suddenly arrived it would be 'dreadful' because it would plunge him into a world in which he could not live.

Undoubtedly it was Kafka's illness that was intensifying these negative thoughts, making him think that his grasp on the 'human world' was slipping. He felt haunted by 'the Negative', which he saw as a force always ready to bring him down whenever he was making any positive progress in his life. It was 'a defensive instinct in me that won't tolerate my having the slightest degree of lasting ease and smashes the marriage bed, for example, even before it has been set up'. He was followed around by a persistent question: 'whether the cause of my downfall was not insane selfishness, mere anxiety for self . . . such that it would seem that I have despatched my own avenger from myself . . . In the Great Account of my life, it is still reckoned as if my life were first beginning tomorrow, and in the meantime it is all over with me.'[18] His failures in love meant that 'I have known only the expectant stillness that should have been broken by my "I love you", that is all that I have known, nothing more.'

Kafka left Spindelmühle some time after 18 February and returned to Prague, although his sick leave would not expire until 4 May, but he was no better either physically or spiritually. At the beginning of March he told Robert Klopstock, 'you are writing to a wretched little person possessed by all sorts of evil spirits',[19] wryly adding that it was to the credit of modern medicine that it had replaced possession by evil spirits with the 'comforting concept of neurasthenia'. His diaries are littered with references to 'attacks', 'fear' and 'the perpetually shifting frontier that lies between ordinary life and the terror that would seem to be more real'.[20] His *Angst* was rampant. Later in the month he described himself as a man hard to put up with, who was buried in himself 'and locked away from himself with a strange key'.[21]

But, more importantly, he was writing again 'in order to preserve myself from what is called nerves. From seven in the evening I sit awhile at my desk, but it is nothing, like trying to scratch a dugout with one's fingernails in the midst of the World War.' He knew that he would soon be back at work, so he was seizing the chance to write. As well as *The Castle*, he was at work on another story, 'The Fasting Artist'. The eponymous main character, who recalls the trapeze artist, is another extreme professional performer whose public fasts eventually bore his audience. This suggests that it is another parable of the artistic life and its troubled relationship with fame or reputation. He is soon eclipsed in popularity by more populist performers and decides to join a circus, where he has to contend with the rival attraction of a menagerie. The fact that the fasting artist would not have fasted had he found a food he liked suggests an analogy with Kafka's doubts about the artistic vocation, the way in which it makes a certain kind of dedicated artist sacrifice his life and happiness to its service. The panther who eventually replaces the fasting artist glows with 'the joy of life', which is what a successful creator of works of art should also do. The fasting artist felt it was impossible to explain his art: 'No one who does not feel it can be made to grasp what it means.' Something of the loneliness and despair voiced by Kafka in his letters and diaries at this time – his anxiety about ever being understood – comes through in his portrait of the fasting artist. 'How would it be if one were to choke to death on oneself?' Kafka wrote. 'I am not far from it at times . . . Mount your attacker's horse and ride it yourself. The only possibility.'[22]

On 15 March Kafka read the first chapter of *The Castle* to Brod. He would work on it for most of the remainder of the spring and through the summer, finally abandoning it, in the form which it has been handed down to readers, in late August 1922.

Not long after this reading Kafka resumed his correspondence with Milena, who had still not been put quite out of his life. He told her that he hated letters and that all the misfortune of his life derived from them, or from the possibility of writing them, making the odd (and of course untrue) claim that he had not written to anyone for years. He took up again with Milena his recent theme of being partly dead to the real world: 'It was as though, through all these years, I had done everything demanded of me mechanically, and in reality only waited for a voice to call me, until finally the illness called me from the adjoining room and I ran towards it and gave myself to it more and more.'[23] This is a striking confirmation of how the illness had in a sense given Kafka a way out, a reason to abandon his struggle with life. Immediately (in contrast to the letters he used to exchange with Felice) he plunged into literary matters with her. He was reading Charles-Louis Philippe's novel *Donadieu*, which couldn't hold a candle to anything by Flaubert, and he said that Chekhov was someone 'I love every much'. He also presented a very interesting theory to her: 'that living authors have a living connection with their books. With their existence they fight for or against them. The real independent life of the book begins only after the death of the writer, or, more correctly, some time after his death, for these eager men still go on fighting awhile for their book beyond their death.'

This was a long letter and it rekindled Kafka's anxiety – 'the evil sorcerer of letter-writing begins to destroy my nights' – such that he again suggested that they stop writing to each other. She visited him, however, on 27 April and again in early May, though they both agreed that that should be the last time: 'yet there is perhaps still a possibility whose locked door we both are guarding lest it open, or rather lest we open it, for it will not open itself'.[24] He told Klopstock that he had 'a fear of any indissoluble bond at present'[25] and dissuaded the enthusiastic young man from visiting him, now that he was in Prague, because of the need to protect his writing time. He then asked Klopstock why he was surprised at Kafka's angst: 'A Jew, and a German besides, and sick besides, and in difficult personal circumstances besides.'

Kafka was living with his parents at the Oppelthaus, working on *The Castle*, and maintaining the illusion that he would return to work on 4 May, but on 17 April he asked if he could extend his sick leave by adding on to it his normal five-week annual leave. The Institute agreed, which should have meant that he returned to work on 8 June, but his condition was so poor that, on 7 June, he finally decided to apply for retirement. On 30 June he was informed that he would be retired on a pension of

1000 crowns a month with effect from the following day. One long-entrenched battle position was thus finally abandoned. Much as Kafka had complained about his work, as something that robbed him of the energy he needed for his creative work, he knew that it had also helped him by giving him a hold on day-to-day life, and by according his existence some shape. However confused and inchoate his inner life, outwardly he was the punctilious, well-liked and competent senior official – he always called himself a civil servant rather than a lawyer – who went each day to the office, neatly dressed in his long coat and hat. The Institute, since he first began to take periods of sick leave in 1918, had shown remarkable generosity and forbearance to their much-valued secretary, Dr Kafka, but the point of no return had now been reached.

Kafka immediately resolved to go and stay with Ottla at the house she had rented for the summer in Planá, a village sixty miles south of Prague. Kafka would have been relieved to have finally resolved matters at the office, for he had a bad conscience about all the time off he had been granted. He knew that he was ill and perhaps at some level foresaw the truth: that he had less than two years to live.

24

Kafka quickly settled into his room at Planá, the attractive village on the River Luschnitz (Lužnice) where Ottla, Pepa and their one-year-old daughter were already in residence. The family had made considerable sacrifices to their comfort in order to give Kafka the best room in the house. Over the next four months he would write here the remaining nine chapters of *The Castle*. It was a beautiful spot, with woods, rivers and gardens, but – as ever – the farmyard noises, of haymaking and of a peasant youth playing his horn, tortured Kafka in spite of his ears having been stuffed with his trusted Ohropax earplugs. 'I feel like someone expelled from the world,'[1] he told Brod about these outbreaks of noise. But the world was not wholly absent. He was reading the *Prager Abendblatt*, thinking a great deal about the currently active anti-Semitic writer Hans Blüher and whether he should respond to him. Kafka was familiar with Blüher's earlier work and took him more seriously than he did other anti-Semites. He also asked Klopstock to send him a copy of Karl Kraus's famous satirical journal *Die Fackel* (*The Torch*). He did not want to deny himself 'this tasty dessert made up of all the good and bad instincts'.[2]

Before deciding to go to Planá Kafka had been planning a trip with Oskar Baum to Georgental (Jiřetín), a village in the Thuringian Forest, with medicinal springs. His reason for wanting to go, he told Baum, was his fear. If he stayed where he was the *Angst* would show itself in the tiniest movement, so he must school himself to incur all the anxieties of travel and change in order to keep on top of the fear. 'In the last or the next-to-last analysis, it is of course nothing but a fear of death. Partly also the fear of calling the gods' attention to me.'[3] In the end, though, the fear conquered him and he remained, explaining to Brod that one sleepless night he had seen 'on what frail ground or rather altogether non-existent ground I live, over a darkness from which the dark power emerges when it wills and, heedless of my stammering, destroys my life. Writing sustains me, but is it not more accurate to say that it sustains this kind of life?'[4] Kafka didn't mean that his life was better when he wasn't writing. 'Rather it is much worse then and wholly unbearable and has to end in madness . . . a non-writing writer is a monster inviting madness. But what about being a writer itself? Writing is a sweet and wonderful reward, but for what? In the night it became clear to me . . . that it is the reward for serving the devil . . . Perhaps there are other kinds of writing, but I know only this kind; at night when fear keeps me from sleeping, I know only this kind. And the diabolic element in it seems very clear to me.' He described the predicament of a writer who has 'a terrible fear of dying because he has not yet lived'. This was why he was staying with his fear and why he would not travel. No longer a *Beamte*, he was, for the first time in his life, nothing but a full-time *Schriftsteller*, a writer, whose existence was dependent on being at his desk if madness were to be kept at bay. 'The definition of a writer, of such a writer, and the explanation of his effectiveness if he has any: He is the scapegoat of mankind. He makes it possible for men to enjoy sin without guilt, almost without guilt.' Kafka genuinely felt that he would never again go outside Bohemia, even outside Prague, once he returned from Planá. In the short time left to him, however, Fate was to prove a little more forgiving.

Kafka stayed at Planá until September, contending with a

gathering storm of noise, including platoons of holidaying Prague schoolchildren whooping and shrieking, and continuing to write, 'less than average in quality, no more',[5] his last novel. He made a couple of trips back to Prague, one when his father was suddenly taken ill in mid-July and operated on for a hernia. Hermann was in great pain afterwards and made everyone well aware of it, especially his long-suffering wife. Franz himself was chased away. He tried to imagine how he would appear in his father's eyes:

> A son incapable of marriage, who could not pass on the family name; pensioned off at thirty-nine; occupied only with his weird kind of writing, the only goal of which is his own salvation or damnation; unloving; alienated from the Faith, so that a father cannot even expect him to say the prayers for the rest of his soul; consumptive, and as the father quite properly sees it, having got sick through his own fault, for he was no sooner released from the nursery for the first time when with his total incapacity for independence he sought out that unhealthy room at the Schönborn Palace.

Before returning to Planá Kafka had time to hand over to Brod his notebook containing parts of *The Castle*. Apprehensively, he awaited his reply. He started to write letters to his family from Planá which, no doubt because of the alarm over his father's illness, were more eager and family-friendly than in the past. After a second visit to Prague in August for four days he came back feeling 'gloomy and dull'[6] and 'somewhat saddened by my father's persistent suffering' and by that of his mother, who was 'destroying herself looking after him'. He was also concerned about Brod and seems to have involved himself in the latter's complicated affair with Emmy Salveter by drafting a letter to her, offering to meet her in order to help smooth over the difficulties in the couple's relationship, which may not in the end have been sent. One of his last letters to Brod from Planá revealed that he had had four separate breakdowns while in the village, sparked by various factors, and the last of them had made him shelve 'the Castle story' for good. This last breakdown was caused by anxiety over what would happen if he were to remain in Planá after Ottla returned to Prague, with his meals being supplied by the landlady of the inn. Kafka was tortured by the fear of the inevitable loneliness even though he realized that this was just what he had always claimed to be seeking. In the end he returned to Prague on 18 September, having advised Klopstock to seize his chance to go to Berlin, something Kafka could not do because he was 'not intellectually transportable'.[7] He told Klopstock that Prague was a medicine against Berlin and vice versa, 'and since the West European Jew is a sick man and lives on medicines, it is essential for him, if he is to move in these circles, not to pass up Berlin'.

Kafka's return to Prague was not that of a healthy man, in spite of all those walks in the woods and the occasional chopping of wood. By November he was so unwell that he took to his bed for most of the remainder of the year. In December he had a visit from Franz Werfel, the writer whom he and his circle had so much admired in his youth, when he was considered the most brilliant and talented of the Prague writers. Werfel arrived with Otto Pick and the visit, 'which otherwise would have given me pleasure, left me in despair'.[8] The reason was Werfel's recent play, *Schweiger*, a tragedy. Kafka was unable to conceal his loathing of it: he felt that the characters were 'not people' and that the whole was 'three acts of mud' through which Werfel had waded. Later, he was full of remorse at having repaid Werfel's 'charming friendliness' with a bout of disagreeable criticism. However, in an unsent letter to Werfel he said the playwright was 'one of the leaders of this generation'[9] but that *Schweiger* represented 'a retreat from leadership . . . a betrayal of the generation, a glossing over, a trivializing, and therefore a cheapening of their sufferings'. Convinced that he was unable to leave Prague now, in spite of being a free man at last with an adequate pension, Kafka declined Werfel's invitation to join him in Venice and retreated to his bed with Kierkegaard's *Either/Or*.

Some time in September Kafka had given a copy of the now abandoned manuscript of *The Castle* to Milena. It would be published after his death, like his other two novels, in defiance of Kafka's request that his work be destroyed. In an 'epilogue' to the 1925 edition of *The Trial* Brod explained why he had refused to carry out Kafka's request. Nearly everything that was published in Kafka's lifetime, claimed Brod, 'was rescued from him by dint of persuasion and guile on my part'.[10] Brod conceded that Kafka took great pleasure in his writings, in spite of referring to them as 'scribblings'. In particular he loved reading extracts to his friends. 'Anyone who had the privilege of hearing him read his own prose to a small circle, with a rhythmic sweep, a dramatic fire, a spontaneity such as no actor ever achieves, got an immediate impression of the delight in creation and the passion that informed his work.' Brod could have added that Kafka showed a keen interest in the arrangement and ordering of a book's contents, the choice of title and even the typeface. He was keenly aware of how a book should look and how it could be made more appealing than other publications.

Brod put Kafka's unwillingness to publish down to 'certain unhappy experiences that drove him to a kind of self-sabotage, and therefore to an attitude of Nihilism regarding his own work'. But he added a second reason – that Kafka 'applied the highest religious standards to all work of his' and, because he fell short, as all those who would judge their work *sub specie aeternitatis* must, he could not adequately discharge his role as a spiritual guide when he felt he had so palpably failed to set an example in his own life. This seems a very questionable argument, coloured by Brod's rather than by Kafka's assumptions.

Kafka was indeed a serious ethical thinker (and this aspect of his writing is not always given its due), but nowhere does he imply that his work was intended as a form of spiritual guidance. He was emphatically not a secular guru. It would be more accurate to say that he had the highest standards, the highest ambitions, for his art. He wanted to raise it, as noted above, to the level of the beautiful and the true. He was conscious, as are all serious artists, that the ambition and the failure are intertwined, that perfection of the work is not possible in this world, even if there is no choice but to persist in aiming for it.

Kafka's own sense of failure, as has already been noted, was potent at the start of October 1921, after he had returned from Matliare. He had gone back to work, in spite of not having been cured, and he had handed over his diaries to Milena, as if he had no desire to keep even those intimate personal testaments. Around that time he wrote his first testament – a scrap of paper written in ink – his *Tintenzettel* – addressed to Brod, telling his friend to destroy everything 'in the way of notebooks, manuscripts, letters, my own and other people's, sketches and so on to be burned unread and to the last page, as well as all writings of mine or notes which either you may have or other people, from whom you are to beg them in my name. Letters which are not handed over to you should at least be faithfully burned by those who have them.' This is both exactingly comprehensive and utterly unambiguous. Kafka at this time wanted to perform a kind of self-cancellation. Having declared that he was 'nothing but literature', he was now asking for every piece of 'literature', that he had created – and thus himself – to be annihilated. The *Tintenzettel* was discovered only after Kafka's death, among his papers, where there was also another, longer note, written again on return to Prague from convalescence, this time in Planá, in October 1922. In the second note Kafka speculated that 'this time I shan't recover, pneumonia is likely after the month of pulmonary fever I have had'. In a document he called 'my last will concerning all I have written' Kafka was strangely specific and ambiguous at the same time: 'Of all my writings the only books that count are these: *The Judgement*, *The Stoker*, *Metamorphosis*, *In the Penal Colony*, *A Country Doctor* and the short story: *A Fasting Artist*.' In addition, *Betrachtung* was virtually out of print. 'When I say that these five books and the short story ['A Fasting Artist', which had just been published in the *Neue Rundschau*] count, I don't mean that I want them to be printed again and handed down to posterity; on the contrary, should they disappear altogether that would be what I want. Only, since they do exist, I don't mind anyone's keeping them if he wants to.' Everything else – including letters and notebooks as well as occasional pieces published in newspapers or magazines – was 'without exception' to be burned. Kafka knew full well that published work cannot be rendered non-existent for posterity, and the wavering formulation 'should they disappear altogether' seems to concede this. If all that posterity had received was the titles mentioned, however, then it would have cause to be grateful, and Kafka's name would still have lived on. The list contains some of his most perfectly accomplished work (remembering that all three of the novels were, strictly, unfinished). But there is no ambiguity at all about the rest of the work earmarked for destruction. All of us who read and write about Kafka – especially biographers – do so in the calm consciousness that we have deliberately ignored his wishes.

Brod's main argument for ignoring Kafka's request was based on the fact that Kafka must have known that his friend would not carry it out because, after all, he had firmly rejected a similar request several years earlier. Furthermore, in 1921, when Kafka had hinted in conversation with Brod that he had penned the *Tintenzettel*, the latter had told him categorically that he would not fulfil it. And Brod later pointed to inconsistencies in Kafka's own position: he agreed to parts of *Betrachtung* being reprinted in a newspaper, and supervised on his deathbed the collection of stories with the title *A Fasting Artist*. At the very end of his life Kafka discovered a happiness, Brod claimed, that cancelled out his earlier self-loathing. Finally, whenever Brod had succeeded in persuading Kafka to publish anything, the latter had never regretted having done so.

The Castle appears to be the most complex and ambitious of Kafka's three novels (its characterization is richer), yet one may still be permitted to prefer *The Trial* for its tauter, more dramatic construction. *The Castle* also has its *longueurs*, and the ending is less satisfactory than that of the earlier novel. Kafka told Brod that it would have ended with the death of K, followed by the arrival of a messenger from the Castle with the news that, although K would not be accepted as official land surveyor, he would be allowed to remain in the village.

Since its first publication *The Castle* has been seen as a religious allegory, a purely poetic symbol, a figment of its narrator's imagination (with the puzzling events all taking place inside K's head) and countless other interpretations. The common tribute of all criticism of *The Castle* is to the novel's infinite suggestibility. Kafka was a master of protracting ambiguity and uncertainty, of allowing the reader to imagine an infinite series of possibilities. Yet this ambiguity is achieved with the most perfectly lucid prose. Even the reader without German can perhaps see this from the first two sentences: 'It was late in the evening when K arrived. The village lay in deep snow. [*Es war spät abend als K ankam. Das Dorf lag in tiefem Schnee*.]' There is no bravura linguistic firework display in the opening sentences such as one has come to expect from major works of modernist literature (Joyce at the time was starting to write *Finnegans Wake*). The calm, clear tone is intimately connected to Kafka's ability to project the strange and unsettling economically.

From the point of view of ambiguity, the opening page immediately sets up a reverberation with K's announcement of his profession: *Landvermesser*, or land surveyor. The German word carries overtones of someone who makes an error of measurement or who is guilty of presumption or boldness. It also puns on two Hebrew words, *mashoah* (land surveyor) and *mashiah* (Messiah), and it has been suggested that the whole book is 'deeply indebted to Kafka's knowledge of the Messianic tradition'.[11] Kafka was not uncritical of that tradition, and it is possible to see in K's aggressive attitude and his determined ambition a critique of Messianic figures. The novel has often been read as a symbol of the Jew seeking acceptance in Gentile society, and while always being alert to the dangers of such single-thread explanations of Kafka's writing, Kafka's progressively deeper involvement with Judaism cannot be ignored. His Hebrew studies had continued throughout 1922 and at the end of the year he started to take lessons from a female teacher, Puah Menczel-Ben-Tovim, who was of the opinion that the teaching he had been receiving previously from Friedrich Thieberger was in a biblical Hebrew and not the living language of Palestine. In a 1983 interview she recalled these lessons and the fact that Kafka, though always polite and reticent, was very weak: 'From time to time, while we smiled together, he suddenly laid his hand on his chest and leaned back from the acute pain that struck him . . . His mother was very concerned about his illness and sometimes during a lesson she would look in to see how he was.'[12]

There may well be a trace of Milena in the character of Frieda (and of Milena's husband Ernst Polak in the Castle's secretary, Klamm) and K's ruthlessness towards her in pursuit of his admittedly vague and undefined goal might suggest an analogy with Kafka's inability to find a way for relationships to coexist with his literary ambition. At K's first meeting with Frieda he is struck by her 'look of unusual superiority', which recalls Kafka's sense of being overpowered by the force of Milena's personality. 'When that look fell on K, he had the feeling it had already dealt with matters concerning him, matters of whose existence he himself knew nothing as yet, but of whose existence the look convinced him.' K's uncertainty on arrival in the village, his initial pretence that his mission is something else, and his subsequent frustration with the mystifications and obstructiveness of the Castle and its officials, have that universal quality of all Kafka's 'parables', but may equally be read within more precise frames of reference. The fate of the Jew is plainly one of these. But no interpretation is exclusive. From a biographical point of view, Kafka's relationship with his father is another theme which seems in play here, with the Castle seen as an arbitrary symbol of patriarchal power, at once sought and repellent. On his arrival, K discovers that one must ask for permission to stay in the environs of the Castle, as the paranoid victim of arbitrary power feels that he or she must ask for permission to exist. The bell of the Castle sends a tremor through his heart 'as if it was threatened – for the sound was also painful – with the fulfilment of what it vaguely yearned for'. Kafka too may have felt threatened by the fulfilment of his inchoate desires, and K's search, like his own, is not just for a specific goal, but for some sort of reassurance that the goal is correct, or that any goal at all is attainable in this life, and that one will know it when one reaches it. Uncertainty lies within uncertainty like the interlocking paths of a labyrinth. The journey is baffling and there seems little hope of an ultimate deliverance from its false trails and thwarting encounters.

For much of the winter of 1922 and into the spring of 1923, Kafka was ill and confined to bed. He wrote nothing, kept no diary, and sent hardly any letters save for a short note to Oskar Baum in January apologizing for 'shivering'[13] so much that he missed Baum's son's bar-mitzvah (though he sent some books for the boy) and another in March to Minze Eisner, thrilled at the news that she was engaged to be married. In April there was the consolation of a visit from his old schoolfriend Hugo Bergmann, who had gone to Palestine after the war to become librarian at the Hebrew National Library and later professor of philosophy at the Hebrew University. Bergmann stayed in Prague a month and Kafka urged Robert Klopstock to come and meet him. Kafka did what he could to help with Bergmann's Palestine fundraising efforts by writing to friends. He made a brief escape from Prague in early May to the resort of Dobrichowitz (Dobřichovice), which was beautiful but expensive, and was, he told Milena, 'not yet a journey, merely a flapping of the completely useless wings'.[14]

And then in the first week of July Kafka set off for the small Baltic seaside resort of Müritz with his sister Elli and her two children, Felix and Gerti. He was to have an encounter there that would do much to lessen the pain of the last eleven months of his life.

PART IV

Dora

25

On his way to Müritz Kafka stopped off in Berlin to pay a visit to Max Brod's mistress, Emmy Salveter, whom he found charming. He set off with her to visit his Hebrew teacher Puah Menczel-Ben-Tovim, who was running a Jewish children's camp at Eberswalde, but the journey proved longer than he expected and he abandoned it, continuing north to the Baltic.

In Müritz the Berlin Jewish People's Home – the institution for which Felice Bauer, at Kafka's eager prompting, had been a volunteer back in 1916 – had set up a holiday camp for the summer of 1923 in a building called the Villa Magdalene. Kafka had not been in the town long before he became aware of the camp, and he was delighted to watch all its activities through the birch trees from his balcony at the Pension Glückauf, fifty yards away: 'The healthy, cheerful, blue-eyed children give me great pleasure.'[1] The sickly Kafka made repeated mention of these 'healthy, cheerful' children, and their vitality seemed to inspire him. He was still obsessed with learning Hebrew, and continued at Müritz with his lessons. The proximity of all the Hebrew-speaking children at the camp was a marvellous bonus.

The seaside greatly improved Kafka's spirits generally. He had been tired and a little feverish in Berlin, but the first few days of the holiday, as always, set him up. He told Robert Klopstock that 'any effort that lets us escape the ghosts for a moment is sweet; we literally see ourselves vanishing around the corner and them standing there in perplexity'.[2] Shortly before leaving Prague he had referred in his diary to 'The horrible spells lately, innumerable, almost without interruption. Walks, nights, days, incapable of anything but pain . . . More and more fearful as I write . . . Every word twisted in the hands of the spirits . . . becomes a spear turned against the speaker.'[3] Hugo Bergmann, who was now back in Jerusalem (still wanting Kafka to come out and join him), sent Kafka his first letter in Hebrew from Palestine. In his reply Kafka said that the trip to the Baltic had been done 'To test my transportability, after many years of lying abed and of headaches.'[4] Müritz's mostly refugee children, spirited and lively, he characterized as 'East European Jews whom West European Jews are rescuing from the dangers of Berlin. Half the days and nights the house, the woods, and the beach are filled with singing. I am not happy when I'm among them, but on the threshold of happiness.' He 'drew warmth' from the children, and even the sea, which he had not seen for ten years, seemed 'more beautiful . . . more varied, livelier, younger'. The idea of going to Palestine to live with the Bergmanns was tempting, but he did not think he had the strength for it: 'It would have been a voyage to Palestine but in the spiritual sense something like a voyage to America by a cashier who has embezzled a large sum of money . . . the temptation beckons, and again the absolute impossibility answers.'[5] Kafka, however, seems not to have put the idea totally out of mind. He later explained: 'I realized that if I wanted to go on living somehow I would have to do something altogether radical and wanted to go to Palestine.'[6]

It was Kafka's habit, when settled in some new place, to notice the young women in the vicinity, and soon a pretty sixteen-year-old, Tile Rössler (later a leading choreographer in Tel Aviv), hove into view. They seem to have enjoyed each other's company, but soon Tile, who had been volunteering at the camp, had to return home to Steglitz in Berlin. Kafka presented her with a glass bowl she had admired in a shop window and she in turn presented him with a vase.[7] Tile found Kafka 'boyish and lively', a tall, skinny man who played and romped with his nephews, 'although then so near his end'.[8] His last memory of her was when she came to the hotel in the pouring rain to deliver his vase. The pianist in the lobby was playing Grieg 'and you standing there, bowed a little, a little damp from rain, humbling yourself before the music'.[9]

An older Jewish woman, Dora Diamant, a friend of Tile, was also volunteering in the holiday camp, and one day, visiting the camp for supper, Kafka wandered into the kitchen, where he saw her gutting fish. 'Such tender hands and such bloody work for them to do,' he observed.[10] Dora had already noticed Kafka on the beach with Elli and the children and had made the assumption that they were a married couple. Something about the figure of Kafka struck her and she even followed the four of them into town, to see where they were going. Dora was twenty-five and Kafka just forty when they met, although many biographies describe Dora as being nineteen – the persistence of the error due no doubt to the fact that the source was Dora herself in an interview given in 1948. Kafka himself frequently misrepresented his age in correspondence. Both had the faculty of seeming far younger than they were.

Dora recalled Kafka as 'tall and slim and dark-skinned with a loping walk'. He seemed lonely but considerate. 'The essential characteristics of his face were the very open, sometimes even wide-open, eyes, whether he was talking or listening. They were not staring in horror, as has been said of him; it was rather more an expression of astonishment. His eyes were brown [Tile thought them blue; as ever no one could quite settle on an accurate description of their colour] and shy. When he spoke they lit up, there was a humour in them.' And, contrary to reputation, Dora reported, 'Kafka was always cheerful. He liked to play; he was the born playmate, always ready for some mischief.' This shouldn't surprise, for his letters are full of a dry and very subtle irony which Brod confirmed was his natural style in conversations between them. 'His wrists were very slender, and he had long, ethereal fingers which took on shape while he was telling a story,' Dora went on. She and Kafka soon became friends and read Hebrew together on the beach. In a letter to Tile, Kafka described Dora, 'with whom I spend most of my time', as 'a wonderful person'.[11] Kafka was drawn to Dora, she thought, by the fact that she was an Eastern Jew, of the kind that fascinated him: 'I came from the East, a dark creature full of dreams and premonitions.' Though Kafka was intrigued by her origins among the Ostjuden, she herself was drawn to the freedom and enlightenment of the West.

Dora Diamant (she would have used the Yiddish spelling Dymant) was born in 1898 in Pabianice, near Łodž in central Poland. Her father Herschel, a learned man and a factory owner, moved the family soon after the turn of the century to Bedzin in Russian-controlled Silesia following the death of his wife in childbirth. The eldest daughter, Dora became responsible for running the household and looking after her four siblings. Herschel wore the long beard, earlocks, black kaftan and fur hat of the traditional pious Hasidic scholar, a follower of the Rabbi of Ger, and was a pillar of the local Jewish community. Dora's early life was ruled by the pattern of religious observance imposed by her father's religion: she attended Hebrew classes and was strongly influenced by the nascent Zionist movement deriving from Theodor Herzl. In 1917 she was sent to a school in Kraków to train to be a teacher in an Orthodox religious school, but she rebelled and ran away. Her father pursued her, found her at Breslau in Germany and brought her home. When she ran away for a second time he gave up on her. She moved to Berlin in 1920.

Although Dora was steeped in traditional Jewish lore, her literary education was far inferior to that of Milena, and even after Kafka's death she showed little real awareness of his writing. She did not know of the existence of *The Trial* until it was published posthumously in 1925. She treasured Kafka more for his person, his extraordinary character, than as a writer, telling Brod in May 1930: 'As long as I was living with Franz, all I could see was him and me. Anything other than his own self was simply irrelevant and even ridiculous. His work was unimportant at best . . . That is why I objected to the posthumous publication of his writings.'[12] Dora felt that it was impossible to understand Kafka if one had not known him in life. Furthermore, she resented, even in its early stages, the great Kafka scholarly and critical enterprise – what Milan Kundera would call 'Kafkology' – as 'a violent intrusion into my private realm'. Her notebooks, in which she tried valiantly but without conspicuous success to describe this unique, incommunicable personal quality of Kafka, have only recently come to light. After his death she became an active communist and spent some time in the Soviet Union before moving to Britain, where she was imprisoned during the war as an enemy alien and where she eventually died in 1952 (in Plaistow Hospital).[13] She was a passionate, sometimes headstrong, and restless woman, but her vigour was a source of great strength to Kafka in their brief period together.

In early August the shine started to go off Müritz for Kafka. Fatigue, sleeplessness and headaches returned and he wondered whether he were 'not allowed to remain too long in one place; there are people who can acquire a sense of home only when they are travelling'.[14] Some small detail about the management of the holiday camp had rankled with him, though its occupants were still very dear to him, and he stopped going there in the evenings. When Elli said she was cutting short her stay, Kafka said he would return to Prague with her because he didn't want to be alone. On 7 August he travelled to Berlin, where he saw a performance of Schiller's *The Robbers*, and two days later he was back in Prague.

Soon, however, he agreed to make a trip with Ottla and her two daughters to Schelesen. They left Prague in the middle of August and were away for over a month. While he was there Klopstock wrote to tell him that a fellow patient at Matliare, the engineer Glauber, had died. Kafka himself was down to 54.5 kilos, the lightest he had ever been. He told Brod that there were too many 'counterforces' stopping him from recovering. 'I must be a very precious possession of those counterforces; they fight like the devil, or are it.'[15]

At Schelesen a letter arrived from Carl Seelig, a Swiss publisher of luxury editions, who offered Kafka 1000 Swiss francs – a fabulous sum, especially to those who might be starting to worry about the escalating German inflation – for one story. Kafka, however, told Seelig: 'The writings I have on hand from an earlier period are altogether useless; I cannot show them to anybody. Recently, moreover, I have been propelled far away from writing.'[16] But he held the door open to submitting work in the future, which rather contradicts his instructions of 1921 and 1922 that all his work be destroyed.

Kafka was now determined to make one last attempt to escape the clutches of Prague. Palestine was too much for him – his temperature was rising and not enough weight was being put on – but Berlin was a possibility. His pension, payable in Czech kronen, would protect him from the galloping inflation there. On 24 September he set off for the German city, where he would see Dora for the first time since Müritz, seven weeks earlier. The night before he had been filled with anxiety about the step he was taking and was exhausted by the labour of packing trunks. Later, he had come close to sending a telegram to the landlord cancelling the flat. But in the morning he finally left, having 'lovingly quarrelled with . . . Father, [and] looked at sadly by Mother'.[17] To the dismay of Franz's parents and Dora's Orthodox father, the couple set up home in the same house, even though Kafka had said nothing to his parents (confiding as usual only in

Ottla, who was supportive) about Dora and had announced to friends such as Robert Klopstock in advance that he was probably going to stay only for a few days. In fact, he had paid the advance rent for August and September for an apartment in 8 Miquelstrasse in Berlin's Steglitz district, a leafy suburb surrounded by gardens, a short walk from the botanical gardens and even nearer to the Grunewald Forest.[18] In this enclave some of the mounting horrors of the Weimar Republic – hyper-inflation, unemployment and political violence – could be held at bay. The move, he told Oskar Baum, was 'foolhardy',[19] given his state of health, but he may have felt that it was his last chance to escape. 'Within the limits of my condition that is a foolhardiness whose parallel you can only find by leafing back through the pages of history, say to Napoleon's march to Russia.' Kafka was always fascinated by Napoleon, filling his diaries with notes about him, apparently intrigued by the idea of the leader (he sometimes thought of the role of the artist in this way) or perhaps simply mesmerized by the figure of the strong and capable man (like his father) whom he knew that he could never be, even on the page.

In Berlin the first thing Kafka missed about Prague was the excellent butter, and he asked Ottla to send him some by post. (He had hoped it would fatten him up.) He reported to his sister that the centre of the city 'has become a horror to me'.[20] But in Steglitz everything was 'peaceful and lovely. In the evenings, on these warm evenings, when I step out of the house, a fragrance comes to me from the lush old gardens, a perfume of such delicacy and strength as I think I never sensed anywhere, not in Schelesen, not in Merano, not in Marienbad.'

There had, however, been few communications from home in the first weeks of Kafka's stay and he began to be anxious for news. He told Ottla's husband Pepa that he was frightened by the situation in Berlin: 'But is Prague any different? There, how many dangers daily threaten such an anxious soul?'[21] To Ottla herself, he at first seemed to extend an invitation but then pulled back. He confessed: 'This whole Berlin business is such a tender thing, has been snatched with my last strength, and for that reason has probably remained very delicate.'[22] He felt that if his family visited him it would be to extend their influence, to judge him with that 'Prague that I not only love but fear', and thus to disturb his nights. Since he now planned to spend the winter in Berlin, he wondered if he should return to Prague while the weather was tolerable in order to see his parents and tell them to rent out his room, and to retrieve some winter clothes.

Kafka saw Ernst Weiss again (and recommended him to the Swiss publisher), as well as Brod's mistress, Emmy Salveter, but he tended not to go out very much: 'I scarcely go beyond the immediate vicinity of the apartment,'[23] he told Felix Weltsch, describing the charm of the place, whose setting 'for this little emigrant is beautiful'. Money worries, however, soon began to surface. Kafka's pension was being sent to his parents' address in Prague (probably because the terms of his early retirement had stipulated that he remain in the city) and the remittance from home was a little tardy. A large expenditure was looming on a kerosene lamp, since the gaslight was insufficient. If the Institute reduced the pension because he was living in Berlin, an extended stay there might prove impossible.

Kafka, in his fragile state – he watched with wonderment the burly furniture removers who arrived to take away the former tenant's grand piano, and was convulsed with breathing difficulties and coughing if he took a trip across Berlin – was writing little. He told Brod that he had neglected to write to him earlier not because he was trying to conceal anything – 'except to the extent that concealment has been my life's vocation'[24] – but because he was fed up with letters: 'I do not trust words and letters, my words and letters; I want to share my heart with people but not with phantoms that play with the words and read the letters with slavering tongue . . . It sometimes seems to me that the nature of art in general, the existence of art, is explicable solely in terms of . . . "strategic considerations", of making possible the exchange of truthful words from person to person.' At around this time Kafka wrote the stories 'A Little Woman' – which was probably sparked by his landlady and conveys a sense of anxiety about always being judged even when the world generally is validating what one does – and 'The Burrow', which Dora believed was expressive of Kafka's fear of returning to his parents' house. His Prague demons had followed him to Berlin.

Dora Diamant is strangely absent from Kafka's letters in the first weeks and months in Berlin. It is not known when she moved in with him from her room at the orphanage in Charlottenburg, where she was living and working as a seamstress. Kafka was slow to talk about her to his friends and family. A letter to Milena in late November describing Müritz makes a cryptic allusion only to his doubts about moving to Berlin being made possible by 'a solution – surprising in its special way',[25] which of course meant that Dora would be there to remove the impossible threat of living alone.

On 15 November, partly to escape the landlady and her rather patronizing (and possibly anti-Semitic) metropolitan mindset,[26] as well as her demands for ever more rent, Kafka and Dora moved into a new apartment Dora had found near by, at 13 Grunewaldstrasse. This involved keeping mum to the former landlady until the day they left. Kafka managed to miss the move because he had left in the morning to go into the city centre, where he had started to attend events and courses at the Hochschule für die Wissenschaft des Judentums (Institute for Jewish Studies). Just before lunch, as he walked along Friedrichstrasse, he heard his name called and it turned out to be an old acquaintance, a Dr Löwy, who took Kafka off to dine with him at his parents' home. Given the battle to find and pay for food in Berlin at this time of hyper-inflation, it was an offer not to be refused. By the time he returned to Steglitz at six, the move had been completed under Dora's supervision. Shortly afterwards, Kafka told Milena in his penultimate letter to her: 'I live almost in the country, in a small villa and garden, it seems to me I've never yet had such a beautiful apartment, I'm also sure I'll soon lose it – it's too beautiful for me.'[27]

Kafka's mood during this autumnal period in Berlin, while his health was still tolerable, was more gently resigned than it had been in recent years. The continuous and solicitous presence of Dora must have had a great deal to do with this. She later reminisced about the happiness of this period, their loving and playful relationship, the way they would mingle their hands together in a common basin and call it their 'family bath' and share laughter. It is true that he still made occasional references to his ghosts, but he seems not to have been so anxious and unsettled. Max Brod came to visit and claimed: 'I found an idyll; at last I saw my friend in good spirits; his bodily health had got worse, it is true. Yet for the time it was not even dangerous. Franz spoke about the demons, which had at last let go of him. "I have slipped away from them. This moving to Berlin was magnificent, now they are looking for me and can't find me, at least for the moment." He had finally achieved the ideal of an independent life, a home of his own.'[28] According to Brod, Kafka was 'on the right road, and truly happy with his life-companion in the last year of his life, which despite his frightful illness, perfected him'. Kafka had always wanted to find this solid, right basis for living and would not have wished to have been seen by posterity as a prophet of alienation or existential absurdity.

It was during this early period in Berlin that Kafka and Dora, on one of their walks in a local park, encountered a small girl who was weeping because she had lost her doll.[29] Kafka, always touched by the sufferings of small children, told her that the doll was not lost. It had gone on a journey during which it had written Kafka a letter. The sceptical child, during a break in her tears, asked for proof, and Kafka promised to return the next day with one of the letters. After taking great care to compose a letter, he returned with it the next day and read it out to the girl. It explained that the doll had grown tired of living in the same family all the time and had wanted a change of scene. Kafka kept up these daily letters for nearly three weeks, each one making clear that the doll had had to get away and preparing the child for the ultimate realization that she would not be back. In the end the doll met a young man and married him. It was typical of Kafka not only to care but to do so with such painstaking attention to detail.

The new mood of mellowness in Kafka resulted in an unexpected flow of letters to his parents (these remained unpublished until 1990). Although some of these letters expressed anxiety about the non-arrival of his pension payments, he reported positively on his state of health and his diet, and discussed a visit by them which would be 'for me something really to celebrate'.[30] He told them that, in spite of the rampant inflation, he was managing reasonably and was living no more expensively than in Prague. But after the move to Grunewaldstrasse he conceded that there had been 'a colossal rise in prices'[31] which was beginning to affect postal charges. And although the flat was '*so schön*', he still lived 'like a patient in a sanatorium' and did not venture out into the windy city streets very often, although this autumn in Steglitz had been 'more beautiful than any in my whole life'.[32] The deteriorating weather convinced him not to pursue an idea of attending the famous gardening school in nearby Dahlem. Kafka, a man who had written so bitingly about family life, was now making every effort to show interest in the extended family, demanding to know whether Elli's children were yet learning Hebrew and when they were going to write to him in the language.

He was a little more candid to Brod, explaining that he would get up around nine, but then had to lie down a great deal, especially in the afternoons. He was also trying to read a Hebrew novel – *Shekhol ve-Kishalon/Loss and Stumble*, by Josef Chaim Brenner – but he had managed only thirty pages. Generally, he was easily excitable – as when Tile Rössler rang and said she was coming to see him. In the end she did not, but her 'Berlin excitements'[33] agitated him and disturbed his sleep. In the heart of a great capital he was trying to establish his usual protective environment. Although he hardly went out (once to a vegetarian restaurant, where he gorged himself on spinach, vegetable cutlets, noodles and plum compote), he was not cutting himself off. He had visits from Puah Menczel-Ben-Tovim and Emmy Salveter, and was in regular correspondence with Robert Klopstock, who sent him butter from Prague. A letter also reached him from Kurt Wolff enclosing a disappointing royalty statement for 1922–3. A combination of poor sales and the runaway inflation meant that they were closing his account. They were not ditching him, however, and would continue to promote his work because they were 'convinced that at a later time the extraordinary quality of these prose pieces would be recognized'.[34] This was typical of Wolff's courteous treatment of Kafka, even when the latter failed to respond to the publisher's letters because of his illness. Wolff clearly viewed Kafka as a very valuable author, reassuring him of this fact often. As a consolation for the restructuring of their business relationship the publisher offered Kafka some free copies of his own and others' books, which he eagerly accepted.

Rising prices gradually put pressure on Kafka and Dora and they could not afford much else besides food. Theatres were expensive and Kafka sometimes read the newspapers in the windows of the offices at the corner of his street and in the Town Hall Square in Steglitz. Dora was used to improvising and had managed to put together a kerosene lamp by borrowing and buying the component parts when they were still in their first flat. If the weather was good enough, Kafka visited the Hochschule, but spent most of his time indoors – 'all is muted around me, though never too muted. I hear little about the excitements of Berlin.'[35] The Hochschule was, he told Klopstock, 'a refuge of peace in wild and woolly Berlin and in the wild and woolly regions of my mind'.[36] The building contained handsome lecture rooms and a large library. It was also peaceful and well heated. 'Of course I am not a proper student,' he observed, adding that the academy was 'rather odd to the point of grotesquerie and beyond that to the point of intangible delicacy (namely, the liberal-reformist tone and scholarly aspects of the whole thing)'. Dora, who was fluent in Hebrew, delighted Kafka by reading to him every Saturday night the Sabbath prayer 'Got fun Avrum', which she knew by heart.[37] This Hebrew prayer traditionally recited by Jewish women at the closing of the Sabbath asked for the blessing of the 'God of Abraham' over the coming week.

They also shared together the burning of some of Kafka's work. True to his earlier expressed intentions, he now wished to destroy material from the notebooks, and watched while Dora carried out his instructions. Not everything was destroyed, however, and after Kafka's death (unknown to Brod) Dora retained some notebooks and letters from Kafka which were eventually seized by the Nazis. They might one day emerge from the archives.

In a letter to Ottla and Pepa in mid-December Kafka made a rare reference in a family letter to Dora (though, of course, they now knew about her). Thanking them for a parcel of household items, he said that the linen had 'made the greatest impression upon D; she said she really wanted most of all to cry, and actually she nearly did do something of the sort'.[38] Dora then squeezed into the space at the bottom of the letter a word or two of postscript. The autumnal calm, it was now clear, was being followed by a deterioration in Kafka's health. In late December Kafka told Brod that he had had 'disturbances of the most varied kinds and every possible kind of fatigue'.[39] He was reading no newspapers, because of the inflation, 'and so I know less about the world than I did in Prague'. On 23 December he wrote his very last letter to Milena. He apologized for not having written 'for even here the old sufferings have found, attacked, and thrown me somewhat down. At such times everything is an effort, each stroke of the pen, everything I write seems to me too important, out of proportion to my strength . . . I wait for better or even worse times.'[40] He continued, 'I'm well and gently protected here to the limits of earthly possibilities.'

Kafka was well aware of the devotion of Dora, which was total. She was the only woman with whom he had ever lived. His previous relationships, particularly that with Felice Bauer, had foundered on his fear that close proximity would pose an intolerable threat to his writing, which is to say the core of his being. Yet Dora had possessed his life – even to the point of being silently present in the room while he wrote – and this had created no problems for him at all. He read to her everything he wrote during this period (though she remained ignorant of his earlier work) and – with a verve and passion that matched her readings to him (she eventually trained as an actress) – numerous other pieces, especially of the Hebrew works he liked to hear from her. 'Thanks to these readings, I knew more or less by heart the *Schatzkästlein* [*The Treasure-Chest*] of Hebel and *The Marquise of* O by Kleist,' Dora told an interviewer in Paris in 1950.[41] It was Dora who took Kafka first to the Hochschule, where she had studied before his arrival in Berlin, in the earlier part of 1923. Kafka seemed to have found what had eluded him all his life: a natural, sympathetic partner. Underneath Brod's 'idyll' the demons still danced: 'But he spoke of the "ghosts" with the complicit smile of a child who cannot be taken in and which suggested the old bogeymen,' Dora told her interviewer.

'Far from giving the impression of someone morbid or depressed by nature, he had a most joyful temperament, charming, always paying very careful attention to the people he was with.' Dora also disclosed in this interview that, in addition to their pipe-dreams of emigrating to Palestine (they fantasized about running a restaurant, with Kafka playing the part of a waiter), they secretly discussed the idea of going east, to the territory of those Ostjuden whom Kafka so admired. In the flat at Steglitz Dora did the cooking and Kafka ran the errands. He went out in the morning with a basket and a container for milk, and was regularly dismayed to find that while he queued the price of potatoes was marked up by the grocer. This was Germany's hyper-inflation biting hard. The experience, and the suffering of others, mortified him. 'The trip to town was always a kind of Golgotha for him,' Dora later observed. 'In this way he experienced communion with an unhappy people in an unhappy time.'[42] On the rare occasions when they could afford to eat out it was at a vegetarian restaurant after their Hebrew studies at the academy, from whose window he was amused to see a shop-sign reading 'H.Unger'.

Dora was in little doubt that the hardships of Weimar Berlin, however much they tried to shield themselves in their leafy suburb, worsened Kafka's health. As 1923 drew to a close his condition deteriorated and he took to his bed with fever. It must have been clear to Dora, if not to Kafka himself, that the end was coming.

26

In the middle of January 1924 Kafka emerged from the high temperature, chills and fever that had seized him in December, reeling from a doctor's bill of 160 kronen (which Dora managed to negotiate down to half the amount), and with 'a tenfold fear of getting sick'[1] again. Even a second-class bed in the Jewish Hospital cost sixty-four kronen a day, for bed and board only, and with service and the doctor's fees on top of that. The precarious domestic economy of the couple – with no fuel for the stove, they had heated their New Year meal on candle stubs – was based on getting by. Expensive medical fees would surely make their lives impossible. His continuing high temperature inhibited Kafka from going across to the cold room where the telephone was situated in the Grunewaldstrasse building, which indicates his frailty, and which he told Brod was 'a serious obstacle to freedom of movement'. In addition, 'the figures of the doctor's fee float in fiery letters over my bed'. And, as if health problems were not enough, the couple faced eviction on 1 February because of the increase in rent. Brod tried to persuade Kafka to consider a Bohemian sanatorium, but the idea was rejected, probably because it spoke of going backwards: 'I had warmth and good feeding for forty years, and the result does not tempt me to go on trying them.' Kafka felt a 'parasite' on his family, who were supplementing his 1000-kronen-a-month pension, and he could not contemplate any more expenditure on trips to Vienna, for example. Guilty at Brod's generous food parcel, he had Dora bake a cake with its contents and send it to the Jewish orphanage where she had previously worked. The Institute was another source of guilt, for it had acceded to his every request. Kafka wrote thanking the director 'for the kindly understanding which you have shown towards the story of my past year, which may seem outwardly somewhat strange, although inwardly only too true'.[2]

Kafka had just completed 'The Burrow', which he read to Dora. She was convinced that the story had a strong personal element and that it expressed a fear of returning to his parents' home. The narrator of this latest animal story is a creature who describes his carefully constructed subterranean labyrinth, observing: 'I must have the opportunity of immediate flight, for despite all my vigilance may I not be attacked from the most unexpected quarter? I live in peace in the heart of my burrow, and meanwhile from somewhere or other the enemy is boring his way slowly towards me.' Dora saw this as a symbol of Kafka's determination to hold fast to his newly constructed Berlin idyll, to resist the 'enemies' referred to throughout the story, which may have been his personal demons or his parents, waiting to suck him back to Prague. The narrator speaks of his enemies not as external ones only: 'They are creatures of the inner earth, not even legend can describe them, even those who have become their victims have scarcely seen them . . . From such enemies not even that exit of mine can save me, indeed it will destroy me; yet it is a hope, and I cannot live without it.' But Kafka's enemies did not pursue him here. 'Deep stillness; how lovely it is here, nobody outside troubles about my burrow, everybody is engaged in his own affairs which have no connection with me; how have I managed to achieve that?'

How indeed? Not only had Kafka escaped loneliness through loving Dora; he had escaped Prague to find a satisfactory way of living in the full knowledge of the suffering and hardship that lay all around him in contemporary Berlin. Dora later reminisced: 'Time and again he said: "Well, I wonder if I've escaped the ghosts?" This was the name with which he summarised everything that had tormented him before he came to Berlin.'[3] She continued: 'He was as though possessed by this idea; it was a kind of sullen obstinacy. He wanted to burn everything that he had written in order to free his soul from these "ghosts". I respected his wish, and when he lay ill, I burnt things of his before his eyes.' She added that he 'experienced life as a labyrinth . . . For him everything was interwoven with cosmic causality, even the most everyday things.'

There are echoes of 'The Burrow' in a story – 'Investigations of a Dog' – written over twelve months earlier, in the autumn of 1922, when he was also ill and back in Prague from Planá. Another animal narrator finds himself 'withdrawn, isolated, occupied solely with my little investigation . . . we are precisely the ones who live widely separated from one another, engaged in our peculiar avocations that are so often incomprehensible even to our nearest dog neighbour'. His self-analysis is very like Kafka's: 'Recently I have been occupied more and more in reviewing my life, searching for the decisive error that I may perhaps have made and that has been the cause of all the trouble but I cannot find it. And yet I must have made it, for if I had not made it, and had still failed to achieve what I wanted after a long life of honest effort, that would prove that what I wanted was impossible, and complete hopelessness would follow.'

To Robert Klopstock, who was still in Prague at his medical studies, Kafka reported at the beginning of 1924: 'There is little to tell about myself; a somewhat shadowy life, anyone who isn't looking squarely at it cannot notice it . . . If only I could earn something! But nobody is paying wages for lying in bed until twelve.'[4] As a lesson in what earning a living meant in the Berlin of 1924, Kafka told Klopstock about a young friend who was a painter but was forced to peddle books in the street. He stood there in freezing temperatures from ten in the morning until dusk. 'Around Christmas he made ten marks a day, now three or four.' Klopstock, who was not well himself, continued to be very solicitous towards Kafka, sending him chocolates from Prague, even though he had no money to spare. Kafka much admired the young man's sincerity and idealism, and was moved to reassure him that he shouldn't feel bad about writing to him so often.[5] With one of those many letters, Klopstock endorsed a copy of Kraus's *Die Fackel*, which Kafka was always pleased to have in order to indulge 'in those enervating evening orgies [of reading Kraus] of which you know'.[6] Having been given notice at Grunewaldstrasse, 'because I am a poor foreigner incapable of paying the rent',[7] Kafka and Dora moved on 1 February to 25–6 Heidestrasse, an apartment in Zehlendorf owned by a Frau Dr Busse, whose deceased writer husband had been an old-fashioned neo-romantic who would 'certainly have detested' Kafka's modernity. The lingering shade of the landlady's dead husband made Kafka think he might have been tempting fate. 'But I'm moving nonetheless; the world is everywhere full of perils, so let this one emerge if it will from the darkness of all the unknown dangers,'[8] he told Felix Weltsch, who was still sending him regular copies of *Selbstwehr*. On the day they moved Kafka was reporting that he was 'sick and feverish, and haven't been out of the house in the evening through these four months in Berlin'.

An early visitor to the new Zehlendorf flat in late February was Uncle Siegfried Löwy, the doctor. He was shocked by Kafka's condition, and tried to persuade him to leave Berlin for a sanatorium. Kafka was initially reluctant, in spite of his regular temperatures in excess of 100 degrees Fahrenheit, for he did not wish to leave the new apartment, where he could sit out on a veranda in the early spring sun. But he could see that the fever which kept him indoors and rendered any attempt at a walk impossible meant that he had to do something. 'And then again it horrifies me when I consider that I shall be losing freedom even for those few warm months that are predestined for freedom. But then there comes that morning and evening coughing lasting for hours, and the flask almost full every day – that again argues for the sanatorium. But then again there is fear, for example, of the horrible compulsory eating there.'[9]

Kafka's letters were as lively as ever, but there is no doubting his weakness. His letters to his parents – who had sent him warm clothing – continued to be strangely touching in view of his history with them. He concluded one letter with the wistful enquiry: 'In which room are you all sitting tonight?'[10] In another he exclaimed at how good they were to this 'loafing',[11] self-centred person. His request that they not telephone because it was a difficult journey for him to the phone – and what could he do if Dora were not at home? – will have told them how frail he was. On 1 March he told them that if he went to the sanatorium, he would lose 'the quiet, free, sunny, airy flat, the pleasant housewife, the beautiful neighbourhood, the proximity of Berlin, the incipient spring' but he knew that he must go. His last letter to them from Berlin gave thanks for the latest gift of warm clothing: 'That is no waistcoat, it is a marvel, so beautiful and warm!'[12]

On 14 March Max Brod was in Berlin for the first night of Janáček's *Jenůfa* at the State Opera. He had earlier been the one who tipped off Uncle Siegfried to pay a vist to his nephew, and it was now decided that Kafka should travel back with him to Prague. Dora and Robert Klopstock, the latter now in Berlin because of his anxiety about his revered older friend, went to the station to see off Kafka and Brod. Dora did not follow Kafka to Prague until the end of the month. At a crucial time for them both, they were separated. Letters to her from Kafka in this period are among the lost papers of Dora Diamant that were confiscated later by the Gestapo and are possibly still languishing in some obscure archive, along with notebooks and manuscripts. Just when Kafka had been establishing himself for the first time as an independent person in Berlin, happily in love, he was forced to return to Prague. His fears that he would be pursued to the depths of his burrow had been justified. Brod claimed that Kafka saw his return from his life of freedom to his parents' house as 'a defeat'.[13] Almost as if he knew the end was coming, Kafka insisted that Brod come to see him every day.

Uncle Siegfried originally proposed that Kafka go straight from Berlin to a sanatorium in the Swiss town of Davos, but after his Prague interlude he travelled instead to the sanatorium of Wiener Wald at Ortmann, near the town of Pernitz in the Vienna Woods. Shortly after his arrival he wrote to Klopstock, giving full medical details of his treatment. Listing the various drugs which Klopstock, as a medical student, would have understood, Kafka concluded: 'Probably the larynx is the chief problem. Verbally I don't learn anything definite, since in discussing tuberculosis of the larynx everybody drops into a shy, evasive, glassy-eyed manner of speech.'[14] But he had a good room in 'lovely country' and as yet had detected no sign of being patronized. He later called the place 'luxurious, depressing, and yet ineffectual'.[15] When he arrived at the Wiener Wald he weighed only forty-nine kilos in his winter clothes and his voice had declined to a whisper, a process that had begun after the third day in Prague.

During that stay in Prague in March, Kafka had written a story, 'Josephine the Songstress; or the Mouse People'. The narrator, who speaks on behalf of 'us', the mouse people, discusses the beautiful singing of Josephine. Like most of the other stories in Kafka's final collection, *A Fasting Artist*, the concern is with performance. 'Is it her song that enchants us, or is it not rather the solemn stillness which enfolds that small and feeble voice?' the narrator asks, querying the nature and purpose of art and its relationship both with a living community and with silence, just as Kafka would be pondering his own impending silence, his dying voice. The singer feels misunderstood by her audience no matter how much it displays enthusiasm for her art – 'in her view she is singing to deaf ears' – and she 'sings for preference in troubled times' with her 'feeble vocal cords'. The audience feels in some sense that 'this fragile, vulnerable, somehow distinguished creature, in her opinion distinguished by her song, has been entrusted to us and that we must look after her'. Josephine herself believes that 'it is she who protects the people', that the artist has a positive function in society. In fact, 'the thin piping of Josephine in the midst of grave decisions is almost like the pitiful existence of our people amid the tumult of the hostile world'. (Days after this story was completed Adolf Hitler started his jail sentence and the writing of *Mein Kampf*.) The narrator notes both the childishness of his people and the fact that they are 'prematurely old' and 'too old for music'. There are paradoxes in Josephine's art: claiming to save society, it can bring about the opposite result when contemplation of art prevents people from taking the necessary practical measures to help themselves. She herself can be self-deceiving, and asks to be excused from the normal responsibility for earning her living in order to concentrate solely on her art, but the society of the mouse people rejects such a demand out of hand. She is not, however, interested in outward recognition, but is motivated by 'inner logic . . . She reaches for the highest crown not because it happens to have dropped down a little lower, but because it is the highest; if it lay in her power she would hang it higher still.'

When Josephine claims she has sustained an injury her audience is unimpressed by this bid for sympathy – 'if we were to start limping every time we got a scratch the whole people would never stop limping'. She then starts to plead 'exhaustion, dejection, feeling faint. So now we get a theatrical performance in addition to the concert.' And then she finally disappears altogether: 'Of her own accord she withdraws from song, of her own accord she destroys the power she has won over our hearts.' The mouse people will continue on their way and she will be forgotten.

It is impossible not to read this story as anything other than Kafka's literary testament, his last word on the struggle to serve art and truth, and to do so in such a way that meets the needs of a community, that is understood and valued by it, and which puts the artist in a proper relation – a *positive* relation – to that community.

On 9 April Kafka wrote to Brod that it was probably going to be 'frightfully expensive' at the sanatorium and that '"Josephine" must help out a little, there's no other way'.[16] It was published in the *Prager Presse* of 20 April, in the Easter literary supplement of the paper. Brod had already effected an introduction for Kafka to the new publishing house of Die Schmiede (The Forge), which would publish *A Fasting Artist* later in the year, after Kafka's death.

Kafka now knew definitely that his larynx was being destroyed by the tuberculosis. Dora was with him, and was fully aware that his condition was now very grave indeed. On 10 April he was transferred to the University Clinic of Professor Marcus Hajek in Vienna. The car that was sent to collect him, to Dora's consternation, was open on this blustery spring morning. It was a four-hour trip to Vienna from Pernitz and Dora initially wrapped Kafka in blankets, but, feeling the strength of the wind, she soon stood up to act as a human shield. She remained in this position for the rest of the journey.

Just before his departure for Vienna, Kafka had reported to Klopstock: 'It seems my larynx is so swollen that I cannot eat; they must (they say) undertake alcohol injections into the nerve, probably also surgery.'[17] He had a flask by his bedside to collect what he coughed up, and once asked the nurse what it looked like inside. 'Like the witch's kitchen,' she replied. In his next letter to Klopstock he said he was feeling better: the pain when swallowing and the burning in the throat had decreased. There had been no injections, the larynx instead being sprayed with menthol oil. He told his parents that although it was not as pleasant as the sanatorium in the Vienna Woods, he naturally had to stay there while he was unable to eat properly. Dora, who was with him all the time, judged the clinic more harshly, calling his room a 'cell'.[18] She was fearful that this new environment – his bed was between those of two extremely ill tubercular patients – would only hasten Kafka's demise. Nevertheless, on 16 April he told his parents that the weather had become beautiful and the window of his room lay open all day to the spring sunshine, wryly adding that the strict routine was a substitute for the military life he had never experienced. At 5.30 a.m. he was woken, washed and launched into the day by 6.30.

Dora was happier now with his progress after her initial panic and saw him reanimated and full of life. The deaths of other patients, however, understandably distressed him. One morning, when Dora arrived, he pointed to the empty bed of a formerly jovial man who had suddenly died in the night. 'Kafka was not shaken, but positively angry as if he could not grasp that the man who had been so gay had to die,'[19] she said. She never forgot Kafka's 'malicious, ironic smile'. Kafka told Brod on what was his last night in the clinic that he had 'cried without reason several times today'.[20] He added: 'Once the fact of the tuberculosis of the larynx is accepted, my condition is bearable; for the present I can swallow again.'

After a week at the clinic Kafka decided to move yet again, this time to the sanatorium of Dr Hoffmann at Kierling, near Klosterneuburg in Lower Austria, not far from Vienna. The imperious Dr Hajek was not impressed and made every attempt to stop the move, pointing out, reasonably enough, that the sanatorium at Kierling simply did not have the medical resources adequate for someone in Kafka's condition. But Kafka and Dora insisted. Kafka's old faith in natural therapy, fresh air, sunshine and a vegetarian diet had resurfaced in the face of orthodox medicine and its hateful injections (which he would not escape). Nor did he wish to be surrounded by the dying. He was further reassured that he was making the right decision because Klopstock now announced that he was abandoning his medical studies and coming straight to Vienna to help, so there would be some medical knowledge on hand.

Kafka's first days at Kierling involved treatment for a fever which 'consists in lovely compresses and in inhalations. I am fending off arsenic injections.'[21] A week later he again told Brod: 'I am very weak, but well taken care of here.'[22] He described Kierling to his parents as 'this small, friendly sanatorium'.[23] Situated in a building on Kierling's main street, Hauptstrasse, the clinic had been open since 1913 and specialized in lung treatments. It was, however, better known for its hotel-like attributes than for its medical facilities. Kafka's clean, white, south-facing room opened on to a balcony where he could sun himself. He was visited by two very expensive specialists, Drs Neumann and Beck, because the specialist medical care at the sanatorium was minimal. At the end of April Dora promised Kafka's parents that they would be kept informed by her of his progress. Other members of the family regularly telephoned for news.

On 3 May Dr Beck wrote to Felix Weltsch that he had been called to Kierling the previous day by Dora because Kafka was having 'very sharp pains in the larynx, particularly when he coughed. When he tries to take some nourishment the pains increase to such an extent that swallowing becomes almost impossible. I was able to confirm that there is a decaying tubercular action, which includes also a part of the epiglottis. In such a case an operation cannot even be thought of, and I have given the patient alcohol-injections in the *nervus laryngeus superior*.'[24] This procedure gave only temporary relief, and Beck advised Dora to ship Kafka to Prague, since both he and Neumann estimated that the patient had only three months to live. Dora rejected the advice on the grounds that, if it were followed, Kafka would come to realize the seriousness of his illness. (It is hard to credit that he had not already done so.) Beck said he understood Dora's protectiveness and the 'self-sacrificing and touching fashion' in which she was caring from him, but he really was now beyond the help of any specialist, 'and the only thing one can do is to relieve pain by administering morphine or pantopon'.

At some point in the stay at Kierling, possibly at the end of April, when things hadn't looked quite so bleak, Kafka proposed to Dora. He insisted on writing to her Orthodox Jewish father in Poland to ask for her hand. His letter explained that, although he was not a practising Jew in Dora's father's sense, he was nevertheless 'a repentant one, seeking "to return"'[25] and therefore might be accepted. In fact, neither Dora nor Kafka was a practising Jew, in spite of their passionate interest in Judaism. Brod recalled once taking Kafka with him to an admittedly ultra-Orthodox Jewish religious service, a 'Third Meal' at the close of the Sabbath, 'with its whispering and Hasidic chants'.[26] Kafka remained, in Brod's judgement, 'very cool' during this act of worship. He had certainly been moved by the ancient ritual, but on the way home had said to Brod: 'If you look at it properly, it was just as if we had been among a tribe of African savages. Sheerest superstition.'

Dora's father took the letter to the ultimate authority, the miracle-working rabbi 'Gere Rebbe', who read it and pronounced the single syllable: '*Nein.*' Kafka had lost the final battle in his lifelong campaign of marriage-attempts, or *Heiratsversuche*. The recent discovery of Dora's notebooks[27] reveals an entirely new episode in this campaign history. The proprietors of the sanatorium were concerned that the respectability of their establishment was being compromised by the unmarried couple in their care and they began to put pressure on Dora to marry. Their pestering reached its peak when they called her into the office to meet an official from the Vienna Jewish community. He was there to perform the ceremony. Dr Hoffmann and his wife were to be the witnesses. 'It was one of the most horrible moments of my life, to have the most Unimaginable hammered into my head with such cruelty: a life after Franz's death.'[28] Ottla had reluctantly gone along with the idea, but Dora felt it was 'to deprive the dying man of his last happy hours, of his hope'. She refused.

Kafka had been devastated by the rabbi's refusal, and in his last days fell back on the support of Dora and Klopstock. Speaking became very difficult, as did drinking, and he began to write the so-called 'conversation slips', laconic instructions, requests and questions to the friends at his bedside. In mid-May these included Brod, who, fearful that Kafka would be alarmed if he knew Brod had made a special trip to see a dying man, had pretended to have an appointment in Vienna, and saw him in a very poor state. Sometimes the notes were simple, such as: 'A little water; these bits of pills stick in the mucus like splinters of glass'[29] or 'And move the lilacs into the sun.' At other times they reflected the sense that he had been a burden to the other two members of what he called 'the little family', Dora and Klopstock: 'How trying I am to all of you: it's crazy' or 'Of course it causes me more pain because you all are so good to me' or 'How many years will you be able to stand it? How long will I be able to stand your standing it?' At other times a bitterness emerges, as when he recalled the man who died in the night in the Vienna clinic: 'They killed the man beside me; every assistant doctor dropped in and without asking.' And then the galley-proofs of *A Fasting Artist* arrived for him to correct: 'Here, now, with what strength I have am I to write it?' Then there was simple despair: 'Put your hand on my forehead for a moment to give me courage.'

Kafka's last preoccupation was with thirst – 'my craving for water'[30] – which tormented him but which he was unable to slake. 'Franz has become a passionate drinker,'[31] Dora told his parents. 'Hardly a meal without beer or wine. However not in too great quantities. He drinks a bottle of Tokay a week, or other good gourmet wines. We have three kinds of wine available, so that we can have plenty of variety in proper gourmet fashion.' One of the conversation slips reads: 'Given this limited ability to drink, I cannot yet go with my father to the beer garden at the Civilian Swimming School.' At the very end of his life Kafka was groping towards a reconciliation with his father, through this poignant image of sharing a beer with him at last. The changing rooms at the Civilian Swimming School, which had been mentioned in the accusatory *Letter to the Father* as the site of his early humiliations, measuring his puny and inadequate body against the powerful physique of his father, were now being held up as the place where they would once again find each other in harmony over a glass. Surely, in Prague, Hermann's heart would have melted, had he read his son's remarks. Kafka told Dora:

> When I was a little boy, when I couldn't yet swim, I used to go sometimes with my father, who also can't swim, to the place reserved for non-swimmers. Then we used to sit together naked at the buffet, each with a sausage and a pint of beer . . . Just try and imagine the picture properly – this enormous man, holding a little, nervous bag of bones by the hand, how we used to undress, for example, in the little dark cabin; how he would then drag me out, because I was ashamed; how he tried then to teach me the little bit of swimming he pretended he knew, and so on. But the beer afterwards![32]

On 2 June 1924, the day before he died, Kafka wrote his last letter to his parents. He tried to dissuade them from coming to see him – 'I am still not very pretty [*ich bin noch immer nicht so schön*], not at all a sight worth seeing'[33] – but struggled to sound optimistic. He spoke of a possible meeting: 'I mean spending a few days together peacefully in a beautiful locality, alone. I don't remember when the last time was . . . And then "having a good glass of beer together", as you write . . . In the past, as I often remember, during the heat spells, we used to have beer together quite often, in that far-off time when Father would take me along to the public swimming pool.' Kafka's body had always failed him. Dora prised this last letter from his grip and scribbled at the bottom: 'I took the letter from his hand.'

Someone asked him as he lay dying about Felice Bauer, and he scribbled a conversation slip: 'I was to have gone to the Baltic with her once (along with her girlfriend [Grete Bloch]), but was ashamed because of my thinness and other anxieties.' Did he love her, someone seems to have asked him. 'Insofar as it was worth understanding me. She was that way in everything. She was not beautiful, but slender, fine body, which she kept according to reports.'

At four o'clock on the morning of 3 June Dora left Kafka's side, because he was breathing badly, and went to fetch Klopstock. He in turn woke the resident doctor, who administered a camphor injection. Later, shortly after noon, Klopstock gave Kafka another injection which was similarly ineffective and then sent Dora to the post office. This was a previously agreed stratagem between Kafka and Klopstock, to avoid Dora having to witness his death. According to Brod's account, Kafka demanded more morphine and screamed at Klopstock: 'Kill me, or else you are a murderer!'[34] He then made an uncharacteristically brusque gesture to the nurse, Sister Anna, tearing off his ice-pack and throwing it to the floor, saying: 'Don't torture me any more, why prolong the agony?' Klopstock went to move away and Kafka said: 'Don't leave me.' Klopstock said he was not leaving him. Kafka answered in a deep voice: 'But I am leaving you.' A moment later, in his confusion, Kafka thought Klopstock was his sister Elli and told the apparition to leave, fearing he would infect her. Klopstock moved aside and Kafka pronounced what readers of Brod have always taken as his last words: 'Yes, like that, it's all right like that.'

Much later, in the early 1950s, Sister Anna gave her recollections of this June morning: 'About the writer Franz Kafka I can offer no opinion but as a man he is the only patient I cannot forget and whose death took place so simply and was so shattering, that all of us, standing at his bedside, streamed tears.'[35] She said that Dora had rushed back from the post office with a bunch of flowers and urged Kafka to smell them. Raising himself one last time, to the nurse's amazement, he sniffed the flowers. 'It was unbelievable: and even more unbelievable was the fact that he opened his left eye and seemed to come alive. He had such amazingly brilliant eyes and his smile was so full of expression and his hands and eyes communicated when he could no longer speak.'

His last injunction to the doctor had been fulfilled: 'Bring the lilies of the field but no injection.'

Afterword

Kafka's body was returned to Prague and buried on 11 June 1924 in the New Jewish Cemetery at Strašnice. Dora was distraught. Klopstock had written to the family describing her on the day after Kafka's death, lying half awake and murmuring, '*Mein Lieber, mein Lieber, mein guter Du*',[1] and at the funeral she collapsed in grief. Hermann Kafka is reported to have turned his back on the girl from the East as if he repudiated her (or perhaps just her lack of restraint), but in fact she spent some time with the Kafkas after their son's death and was warmly welcomed by them. They even arranged for the modest royalties of his work to be sent to her, as if she really were the wife of Kafka. Hermann himself died in 1931, his wife Julie three years later.

As the body was committed to the grave at four in the afternoon the sky darkened and rain fell. Around a hundred mourners were present as Kafka was buried with the Hebrew prayer for the dead. A week later a memorial service was held at the Kleine Bühne, the Little Theatre, in Prague, where more than 500 gathered to hear speeches, readings and eulogies – giving the lie to the idea that Kafka was obscure and unknown at his death.

Obituaries appeared in the Prague newspapers, the most eloquent and penetrating, as mentioned earlier, written by Milena Jesenská on 6 July in *Národní listy*:

The day before yesterday, Franz Kafka, a German writer living in Prague, died at the Kierling Sanatorium in Klosterneuburg near Vienna. Few people knew him here in Prague, for he was a recluse, a wise man who was afraid of life. He had been suffering for years with lung trouble, and though he was being treated for it, he also deliberately cultivated it and encouraged it psychologically. 'When the heart and soul can no longer bear the burden, the lungs take over half of it, and then the burden is more or less evenly distributed,' he once wrote in a letter, and that was the attitude he took towards his illness. It gave him a sensibility bordering on the miraculous and a terrifyingly uncompromising moral purity; conversely, he was a man who let his illness bear the whole burden of his fear of life. He was shy, timid, gentle, and good, but the books he wrote were cruel and painful. He saw a world full of invisible demons that make war on helpless human beings and destroy them. He was clear-sighted, too wise to live and too weak to fight. But this was the weakness of fine and noble beings who are incapable of fighting against fear, misunderstandings, unkindness, and untruth, who acknowledge their weakness from the start, submit, and so put the victor to shame. He understood his fellow men in a way that is possible only for those who live alone, whose perceptions are so subtly tuned that they can read a whole man in a fleeting play of the features. His knowledge of the world was vast and deep. He himself was a vast and deep world. He wrote the most important books in recent German literature. They embody in untendentious form the battle of the generations in our time. They are genuinely naked and therefore seem naturalistic even when they speak in symbols. They have the dry irony and second sight of a man who saw the

> world so clearly that he could not bear it and had to die, for he was unwilling to make concessions, to take refuge, as others do, in intellectual delusions, however noble. Dr Franz Kafka wrote *The Stoker* (a fragment) . . . which constitutes the first chapter of a beautiful, still unpublished novel; *The Judgement*, dealing with the conflict between the generations; *Metamorphosis*, which is the most powerful book in modern German literature; *In the Penal Colony*; and the sketches *Betrachtung* and *A Country Doctor*. The last novel, *The Trial*, has for years been complete in manuscript, ready for publication; it is one of those books whose impact on the reader is so overwhelming that all comment is superfluous. All his books deal with unwarranted guilt feelings and with the horror of mysterious misunderstandings. As a man and an artist he was so infinitely scrupulous that he remained alert even where others, the deaf, felt secure.[2]

After this powerful and accurate summing-up, how could Max Brod do anything other than arrange the publication of such a writer's works? He began with *The Trial* in 1925, *The Castle* in 1926, and *Amerika* in 1927. English translations by Edwin and Willa Muir started to appear in 1930 with *The Castle*. Introducing that book, Edwin Muir wrote: 'Franz Kafka's name, so far as I can discover, is almost unknown to English readers.'[3] One of those first, and very few, English readers of *The Castle* was Aldous Huxley, who was just clearing his desk at his home in the south of France to write *Brave New World*. 'If you want to read a *good* book, get *The Castle* by Kafka, translated by Edwin Muir,' he wrote in January 1931. 'It makes the other German novelists, even Mann, look pretty thin and insubstantial. For me it's one of the most important books of this time.'[4] Kafka's other works were quickly translated into all the major European languages, but the Czechs were largely indifferent and, after 1938, the new Nazi occupiers banned his 'decadent' work, as the communist authorities would also do after the war. Whatever the criticisms levelled at the editing practices of Brod and the translations of the Muirs (academics of German literature were scandalized to discover that the Muirs were self-taught in German), the reputation of Kafka grew. It could be said that it did so in translation and was re-exported back to Germany, where he is now rightly considered as one of the masters of modern German literature while remaining in a very special sense the property of the readers of the world in so many languages.

The first translation of Kafka into another language seems to have been the Spanish version of *Metamorphosis* in June 1925, barely a year after Kafka's death. The same work appeared in French three years later and other works in other languages soon followed, especially when the three novels began to be issued posthumously. From the 1930s onwards, Kafka's reputation soared, though often his role as a representative of the anxiety of modern man took precedence, especially in the middle years of the twentieth century, over consideration of his artistic achievement. In part this was due to the enthusiasm of Max Brod for Kafka as a religious thinker. Through both his editing of the unpublished texts and his important biography of Kafka, Brod had a powerful impact on the development of Kafka's reputation. Kafka's principal translators into English, Edwin and Willa Muir, were themselves influenced strongly by Brod's assumptions. Many distinguished writers such as Albert Camus and W. H. Auden wrote enthusiastically about Kafka, often in terms that seemed to involve him in their own preoccupations. In France in particular, Kafka enjoyed a high reputation among existentialists and absurdists. In Germany it was not until after the war that he began to be taken seriously by German critics, who often drew him into their contemporary metaphysical and polemical arguments, aesthetic analysis lagging some distance behind. Freudians grew interested in Kafka's apparent sexual symbols, and in due course he was subjected to analysis from most of the dominant schools of criticism of the twentieth century. Yet always he re-emerged as the complex, enigmatic, highly individualized writer known to millions of readers today.

If Kafka's books were said by Milena to have been 'cruel', the decades he did not live to see certainly earned that epithet. All three of his sisters were murdered in Nazi death camps. Ottla, his favourite, refused to hide behind her Aryan husband (indeed, she divorced him in order to save his life) and declared herself to the Nazi authorities as a Jew. She was sent to Theresienstadt, where she volunteered to accompany 1260 children from the camp on 5 October 1943 on a 'special transport'. Their common destination was Auschwitz.

Notes

Abbreviations Used in Notes

Primary Texts in German

B1 *Briefe 1900-1912* edited by Hans-Gerd Koch (1999)

B2 *Briefe 1913–1914* edited by Hans-Gerd Koch (2001) [These are the first two volumes of a projected complete edition of the letters]

D *Drucke zu Lebzeiten* [Published in the author's lifetime] edited by Wolf Kittler, Hans-Gerd Koch and Gerhard Neumann (1994) [Includes *Betrachtung, Das Urteil, Der Heizer, Die Verwandlung, In der Strafkolonie, Ein Landarzt, Ein Hungerkünstler, Ein Damenbrevier, Gespräch mit dem Beter, Gespräch mit dem Betrunken, Die Aeroplane in Brescia, Ein Roman der Jugend, Eine entschlafene Zeitschrift, Ernst Kapitel des Buches, Richard und Samuel, Großer Lärm, Aus Matlárháza, Der Kübelreiter*]

BE *Briefe an die Eltern aus den Jahren 1922–1924* (1990) edited by Josef Cermak and Martin Svatos

BF *Briefe an Felice* [*Letters to Felice*] edited by Erich Heller and Jürgen Born (1967)

BM *Briefe an Milena* [*Letters to Milena*] edited by Jürgen Born and Michael Müller (1983)

BO *Briefe an Ottla und die Familie* [*Letters to Ottla and the Family*] edited by Hartmut Binder and Klaus Wagenbach (1974)

NSF1 *Nachgelassene Schriften und Fragmente I* [Posthumously published writings] edited by Malcom Pasley (1993) [Includes pieces from 1897 to 1917, including earlier *Oktavheften, Hochzeitsvorbereitungen auf dem Lande, Beschreibung eines Kampfes*]

NSF2 *Nachgelassene Schriften und Fragmente II* [Posthumously published writings] edited by Jost Schillemeit (1992) [Includes pieces from 1917 to 1924, including later *Oktavheften, Aphorismen, Brief an den Vater*[

P *Der Prozess* [*The Trial*] edited by Malcolm Pasley (1990)

S *Das Schloss* [*The Castle*] edited by Malcolm Pasley (1982)

T *Tagebücher* [*Diaries*] edited by Hans-Gerd Koch, Michael Müller and Malcolm Pasley (1990)

V *Der Verschollene* [*The Man Who Disappeared*, formerly known as *Amerika*] edited by Jost Schillemeit (1983)

Note: A twelve-volume edition of the fiction, posthumous writings and diaries based on the above Kritische Ausgabe (Critical Edition) but as yet excluding the letters, is available in a popular paperback edition from Fischer in Germany.

Secondary Material in German

Hartmut Binder (ed.) *Kafka Handbuch, Vol. 1* (1979)

EK *'Als Kafka mir entgegenkam . . .' Erinnerungen an Franz Kafka* [*Recollections of Kafka*] edited by Hans-Gerd Koch (1995)

FK Max Brod, *Uber Franz Kafka* (1966)

Kafka-Chronik Chris Bezzel, *Kafka-Chronik: Daten zu Leben und Werk zusammengestellt* (1975)

Wagenbach Klaus Wagenbach, *Franz Kafka: Ein Biographie seiner Jugend 1883–1912* (1958)

TEXTS IN ENGLISH

Brod Max Brod, *Franz Kafka: A Biography* (1960)

C *The Castle* translated by J. A. Underwood (1997)

D1 *The Diaries of Franz Kafka, 1910–1913* (1948) edited by Max Brod; translated by Joseph Kresh

D2 *The Diaries of Franz Kafka, 1914–1923* (1949) edited by Max Brod; translated by Martin Greenberg with Hannah Arendt

GWC *The Great Wall of China and Other Short Works* (1973) Translated by Malcolm Pasley.

LF *Franz Kafka: Letters to Felice* (1974) edited by Erich Heller and Jürgen Born; translated by James Stern and Elizabeth Duckworth

LFFE *Franz Kafka: Letters to Friends, Family and Editors* (1978) translated by Richard and Clara Winston

LM *Franz Kafka: Letters to Milena* (1953) edited by Willy Haas; translated by Tania and James Stern

LO *Franz Kafka: Letters to Ottla and the Family* (1982) edited by N. N. Glatzer; translated by Richard and Clara Winston

M *Metamorphosis and Other Stories* (1992) translated by Malcolm Pasley

MWD *The Man Who Disappeared* (1996) translated by Michael Hofmann

T *The Trial* (1994) translated by Idris Parry

WPC *Wedding Preparations in the Country and Other Posthumous Prose Writings* (1954) translated by Ernst Kaiser and Eithne Wilkins

Notes

Chapter 1

1 Johannes Urzidil, *There Goes Kafka* (1968; trans. Harold A. Basilius of *Da geht Kafka* (1965))

2 D1. 299; T. 466

3 For the date of this much-mentioned incident see Klaus Wagenbach, *Kafka's Prague: A Travel Reader* 1996), p. 65

4 EK.126, '*In diesem kleinen Kreis . . . ist mein ganzes Leben eingeschlossen*'

5 The Altstädter Ring is today known as Staroměstské náměstí; Niklasstrasse goes by the name Pařížska třída, Paris Street

6 The dedicated Kafka *flâneur* should make use of Wagenbach's *Travel Reader* (n. 3 above) and Harold Salfellner's *Franz Kafka and Prague* (2002)

7 Pavel Eisner, *Franz Kafka and Prague* (1950), p. 21, a short but trenchant essay which lays bare the racial and cultural tensions of Kafka's Prague

8 Alena Wagnerová, '*Im Hauptquartier des Lärms*': *Die Familie Kafka aus Prag* (1997), p. 9, '*sehr typischen jüdischen Familie aus Böhmen*'

9 Klaus Wagenbach, '*Wo liegt Kafkas Schloß?*', in *Kafka-Symposium* (1965) ed. Jürgen Born *et al.*, p. 169; Wagenbach reproduces a photograph of the gravestone

10 Julie Kafka, handwritten notes on the family. Ms in Bodleian Library, Oxford, and also in German Literature Archive in Marbach and reprinted in Wagnerová, *op. cit.*, pp. 44–7: '*ein großer starker Mann*'; notes quoted in English in Klaus Wagenbach, *Kafka* (1964; trans. 2002)

11 *Ibid.*, '*Sie war eine zarte und fleißige Frau . . . ihr einziges Glück im Leben*'

12 D1.199–200. 26.12.1911

13 Julius Herz, 'Franz Kafka and Austria: National Background and Ethnic Identity', *Modern Austrian Literature*, XI (3–4), 1978, pp. 301–18

14 See Dietz Bering, *The Stigma of Names: Antisemitism in German Daily Life, 1812–1933* (1987). Only 156 different first names were

permitted in order to achieve the declared aim that the Jews should continue to bear no 'Jewish names or names otherwise unknown in the German language'. See also Hillel J. Kieval, *The Making of Czech Jewry: National Conflict and Jewish Society in Bohemia, 1870–1918* (1988)

15 For a fuller historical account see *ibid.*

16 Joseph Roth, *Juden auf Wanderschaft* (1927) in Michael Hofmann's translation, *The Wandering Jews* (2001), p. 99

17 Brod, p. 6

18 See Anthony Northey, 'Myths and Realities in Kafka Biography', in *The Cambridge Companion to Kafka* (2002), p. 197

19 D1.197. 25.12.1911

20 LFFE.309

21 LF.57; BF.115

22 LF.55

23 LF.287

Chapter 2

1 LF.113

2 Julie Kafka's ms notes in Alena Wagnerová, *'Im Hauptquartier des Lärms': Die Familie Kafka aus Prag* (1997), *'Franz war ein zartes aber gesundes Kind'*

3 *Ibid. 'Es war ein schönes kräftiges Kind'*

4 LF.113

5 Ernst Pawel, *The Nightmare of Reason: A Life of Franz Kafka* (1984), p. 16

6 LM.65

7 *'Ängstlichkeit und totenaugenhafte Ernsthaftigkeit'*

8 Hartmut Binder, *'Kindheit in Prag: Kafkas Volksschuljahre'*, *Humanismen: Som, Salt & Styrka* (1987), p. 83, *'als Muttersöhnchen gehänselt wurde'*

9 This is mentioned in most extant biographies but there is no documentary evidence

10 Pawel, *op. cit.*, p. 42

11 *Ibid.*, p. 44

12 See Johann Bauer, *Kafka and Prague* (1971) for a description of the ghetto at its nadir, pp. 21–2

13 Gary Cohen, 'Jews in German Society: Prague, 1860–1914', *Central European History*, 10 (1), March 1977, p. 30; I am indebted to this research for what follows here

14 http://news.bbc.co.uk/1/hi/world/europe/645506.stm, 16 February 2000

15 Pavel Eisner, *Kafka's Prague* (1950), p. 20

16 WPC.181

17 There is occasionally an unsettling echo of anti-Semitic propaganda in some of the Czech accounts of the lack of rootedness of the Prague German Jews. See, for example, Bauer, *op. cit.*, p. 11. 'The historically progressive, thrusting, biologically healthy Czech element stood in contrast to the German and Jewish enclave . . . an increasingly rootless intelligentsia . . .'
18 Emmanuel Frynta, *Kafka and Prague* (1960), trans. Jean Layton
19 EK.28, '*Immer war er ein Musterschüler, oft Vorzugsschüler; die Lehrer hatten den bescheidenen, stillen, guten Schüler sehr gern*'

Chapter 3

1 Franz Baumer, *Franz Kafka* (1971), trans. Abraham Farbstein, p. 32
2 *Letter to the Father*, WPC.160
3 EK.39
4 EK.38, '*Er war ein stiller, grübelnder und nachdenklicher Typ*'
5 EK.17, '*Wir erlebten zusammen die Erregungen des Nonkonformisten*'
6 Klaus Wagenbach, *Kafka* (1964; trans. 2002), p. 36
7 D1.205
8 EK.29, '*immer sehr rein*'
9 *Loc. cit.*, '*immer etwas entfernt, distanziert von uns*'
10 Wagenbach, p. 268
11 EK.43, '*ruhig, scheu, un ein bißchen rätselhalft*'
12 *Letter to the Father*, WPC.200
13 LM.171
14 *Letter to the Father*, WPC.193
15 LFFE.1
16 D1.14
17 LM.133
18 *Letter to the Father*, WPC.161ff.
19 LM.79; BM.85, '*Und verstehe beim Lesen alle advokatorischen Kniffe, es ist ein Advokatenbrief*'
20 I am indebted, for this insight, to Margaret Jervis of the British False Memory Society
21 See the later discussion of Nadine Gordimer's 'Letter from the Father'

Chapter 4

1 See, for example, Walter Benjamin, *Illuminations* (1955) and Benjamin's correspondence with Gershom Scholem in *Briefwechsel* (1980)
2 For an account of this latter journey of the ms see S (*Apparatband*), pp. 15–16

3 Brod, p. 43
4 Walter Benjamin spoke of his 'immeasurably sad eyes'. Cited in a valuable essay by Gabriel Josipovici, 'An Art for the Wilderness', *European Judaism*, 8 (2), Summer 1974, p. 3
5 EK.157, *'zwei dunkle Augen'*; EK.136, *'sehr großen schwarzen Augen'*; EK.145, *'seinen stahlblauen Augen'*; EK.149, *'große graue Augen'*; EK.92, *'graue Augen'*; EK.168, *'den tiefblauen Augen'*; EK.140, *'den stahlgrauen Augen'*; EK.175, *'Er hatte braune, schüchterne Augen'*
6 Dora Diamant, *Mein Leben mit Franz Kafka*, EK.174ff.; also in English in J.P. Hodin, 'Memories of Franz Kafka', *Horizon*, 97, 1948
7 EK.157
8 EK.87
9 EK.93
10 EK.149
11 LF.283
12 'I don't know old I was at the time, certainly not much over sixteen,' *Letter to the Father*, WPC.206
13 Johann Bauer, *Kafka and Prague* (1971), p. 62, reports documents which indicate that Kafka applied for a passport dated 14 October 1902 valid for a year and asking for permission to spend seventeen days abroad. Since Kafka was under age the documents were signed by his father
14 LFFE.4; B1.14
15 LFFE.5
16 LFFE.5; B1.17
17 B1.24, *'Hier trinkt man Luft statt Bier badet in Luft statt in Wasser und es thut recht wohl'*
18 LFFE.7
19 LFFE.9
20 B1.29
21 EK.58
22 LM.163ff.; letter now dated in BM as 9 August 1920
23 It goes without saying that homosexuality has been adumbrated. See Mark Anderson, 'Kafka, Homosexuality, and the Aesthetics of "Male Culture"', *Austrian Studies*, 7, 1996, pp. 79–99 for a sensitive and judicious exploration of this issue
24 D1.76
25 Quoted by Kathi Diamant in *Kafka's Last Love* (2003), p. 292
26 Brod, p. 37
27 BM.198
28 LFFE.10
29 LFFE.15
30 B1.36

Chapter 5

1 Brod, p. 60
2 See, for example, Ritchie Robertson, 'Fritz Mauthner, the Myth of Prague German, and the Hidden Language of the Jew', in *Brückenschlag zwischen den Disziplinen: Fritz Mauthner als Schriftsteller, Kritiker und Kultur-Kritiker in seiner Zeit*, eds. Jörg Thunecke and Elisabeth Leinfellner (forthcoming)
3 Wagenbach, Chapter 1. Translated as 'Prague at the Turn of the Century' in *Reading Kafka* (1989) edited by Mark Anderson
4 Josef Mühlberger cited by Wagenbach in Anderson, p. 36
5 Cited by Wagenbach in Anderson, p. xx
6 LFFE.233
7 Cited by Wagenbach in Anderson, p. 45. Similar analyses of the linguistic situation are offered by Franz Baumer in *Franz Kafka* (1971); Pavel Eisner, *Franz Kafka and Prague* (1950); Emmanuel Frynta, *Franz Kafka and Prague* (1960); Julius Herz, 'Franz Kafka and Austria: National Background and Ethnic Idenity', *Modern Austrian Literature*, XI (3–4), 1978, pp. 301–18; Leopold Kreitner, 'Kafka as a Young Man', *Connecticut Review*, 3(2), April 1970; Christoph Stölzl, 'Kafka: Jew, Anti-Semite, Zionist' in Anderson, pp. 53–79; Feliz Weltsch, 'The Rise and Fall of the Jewish–German Symbiosis: The Case of Franz Kafka', *Leo Baeck Institute Yearbook* (1956)
8 Erich Heller, *Kafka* (1974), p. 9
9 André Gide cited by Klaus Wagenbach, *Kafka* (1964; trans. 2002), p. 45
10 LFFE.13
11 LFFE.14
12 LFFE.14
13 EK.81–6
14 Johann Bauer, *Kafka and Prague* (1971), p. 106
15 Leopold Kreitner, *op. cit.*, p. 31. See also LF.191 for Kafka's views on the poetry – 'the work of an indiscriminate brain twitching in the head of an overwrought city-dweller'
16 LFFE.21
17 LFFE.22
18 LFFE.24
19 Brod, pp. 107–8
20 LFFE.20
21 Klaus Wagenbach, '*Drei Sanatorien Kafkas: Ihre Bauten und Gebräuche*', *Freiebuter*, 16, 1983, pp. 77–81
22 D2.112
23 D2.159
24 Brod, p. 67
25 Wagenbach, p. 133
26 LFFE.20
27 LFFE.25

28 LFFE.23
29 LFFE.24
30 LFFE.26
31 LFFE.28
32 LFFE.28
33 LFFE.25

Chapter 6

1 Brod, p. 78
2 LFFE.41
3 Franz Baumer, *Franz Kafka* (1971), p. 52
4 LFFE.32
5 LFFE.34
6 LFFE.431n
7 LFFE.35
8 *Ibid.*
9 LFFE.37
10 LFFE.38
11 LFFE.24
12 LFFE.41
13 'The Businessman/A Stray Glance from the Window/The Way Home/The Men Running Past/Clothes/The Passenger/The Rejection/The Trees' in M
14 LFFE.43
15 Reproduced B1.85
16 Brod, p. 82
17 EK.93
18 Brod, p. 82
19 D1.126
20 D1.111
21 Baumer, *op. cit.*, p. 40
22 EK.138
23 Brod, p. 84, '*dem stagnierenden Leben der Akten*'
24 LFFE.58
25 *Amtliche Schriften* (1984), ed. Klaus Hermsdorf
26 LFFE.44
27 LFFE.45
28 EK.88
29 LFFE.45
30 LFFE.47; see also Sander Gilman, *Franz Kafka: The Jewish Patient* (1995), 'Appendix', for medical reports on Kafka at this time
31 For a full account of Kafka and the cinema see Hans Zischler, *Kafka Goes to The Movies/Kafka geht ins Kino* (1996; trans. Susan H. Gillespie, 2002)
32 Brod, p. 104
33 'The Aeroplanes at Brescia,' in M, p. 6

Chapter 7

1 LFFE.63
2 LFFE.64
3 LFFE.65
4 D1.11
5 *Ibid.*
6 *Ibid.*
7 D1.14
8 *Ibid.*
9 D1.24
10 LM.35; BM.21, '*Es hätte so ausgesehn, wie vor dem Jüngsten Gericht*'
11 LFFE.66
12 *Ibid.*
13 See Anthony Northey, 'Dr Kafka Goes to Gablonz', in Angel Flores (ed.) *The Kafka Debate* (1977), pp. 117–19
14 LFFE.67
15 D1.31
16 Ludwig Hardt in EK.189
17 LFFE.70
18 D1.33
19 D1.35
20 D1.39
21 D1.39
22 D1.41
23 Brod, p. 66
24 LFFE.71, '*wie in eine alte Schweinsblase*'; B1.132
25 D1.44
26 D1.45
27 D1.56
28 D1.58
29 LFFE.453n
30 Brod, p. 109
31 Wagenbach, p. 227
32 D1.60
33 D2.244
34 D2.252
35 D2.257
36 D2.259
37 D2.261
38 D2.278
39 D2.281
40 LFFE.74
41 LFFE.75

Chapter 8

1 D1.72
2 Joseph Roth, *The Wandering Jews* (1927; trans. 2001)
3 *Letter to the Father*, in WP, p. 192
4 D1.73
5 D1.75; T1.43, '*die nahe Möglichkeit großer mich aufreißender Zustände, die mich zu allem fähig machen könnten*'
6 D1.75
7 D1.76
8 D1.77
9 For a detailed account of this venture, see Anthony Northey's invaluable *Kafka's Relatives* (1991), pp. 90ff.
10 D1.94; T1.64, '*fetten, schwarzen . . . Juden*'; perhaps the translation in D1 should read 'swarthy' or 'dark-haired'
11 D1.81
12 Ritchie Robertson, *Kafka: Judaism, Politics, and Literature* (1985), p. 16
13 D1.87
14 *Ibid.*; Dora Diamant read this with amusement after his death when the diaries were published, for she too had protruding teeth
15 D1.95
16 D1.96
17 D1.131
18 Cited in Brod, p. 114
19 Isaac Bashevis Singer, 'A Friend of Kafka', in *Collected Stories* (1981), p. 284
20 See Evelyn Beck, *Kafka and the Yiddish Theatre* (1971)
21 D1.191ff.
22 D1.103
23 *Letter to the Father*, in WP, p. 181
24 D1.97
25 D1.100
26 D1.102
27 D1.111
28 *Ibid.*
29 D1.125
30 D1.114
31 D1.128
32 D1.129
33 *Ibid.*
34 D1.133
35 D1.134
36 D1.141
37 D1.184
38 D1.151
39 D1.159

40 D1.160
41 D1.162
42 D1.169
43 D1.173
44 D1.168
45 D1.178
46 D1.181
47 D1.185
48 D1.202

Chapter 9

1 D1.211
2 D1.223
3 D1.215
4 D1.233
5 D1.232
6 D1.235
7 'An Introductory Talk on the Yiddish Language', in WP, pp. 418–22
8 D1.227
9 D1.228
10 D1.231
11 D1.245
12 D1.259
13 D1.261
14 D1.264
15 D1.264
16 EK.95, '*der Impresario präsentiert den von ihm entdeckten Star . . . Schweigsam, linkisch, zart, verwundbar, verschüchtert wie ein Gymnasiast vor den Examinatoren, überzeugt von der Unmöglichkeit, die durch die Anpreisungen des Impresarios geweckten Erwartungen je zu erfüllen*'
17 D2.289
18 *Ibid.*
19 LO.6
20 D2.291
21 D2.293
22 See Klaus Wagenbach, *Franz Kafka: Pictures of a Life* (1984), p. 134
23 D2.298
24 See Klaus Wagenbach, '*Drei Sanatorien Kafkas: Ihre Bauten und Gebräuche*', *Freibuter*, 16, 1983, pp. 77–81
25 D1.247
26 D2.303
27 D2.305
28 Wagenbach (1984), *op. cit.*, p. 138
29 D2.314

30 *Ibid.*
31 LFFE.80
32 LFFE.82; B1.163
33 Edmund Wilson, 'A dissenting opinion on Kafka', in *Classics and Commercials* (1950); also in Ronald Gray (ed.), *Kafka: A Collection of Critical Essays* (1962), pp. 91–7
34 Jorge Luis Borges, *The Total Library: Non-Fiction, 1922–1986* (2000), ed. Eliot Weinberger, p. 501
35 LFFE.83
36 D1.266
37 D1.267
38 D1.265
39 D1.267

Chapter 10

1 LFFE.422 'Conversation Slip'
2 Reiner Stach, *Kafka: Die Jahre der Entscheidungen* (2002), p. 111 – Stach has had access to the Bauer family papers to give the fullest account so far of Felice Bauer and her family
3 Dora Diamant in EK.183
4 Brod, p. 152
5 D1.267
6 LF.5
7 LF.81
8 LF.488
9 D1.268
10 LFFE.85
11 D1.267
12 D1.268
13 D1.270
14 LF.265
15 D1.275; the following journal entry was written in the sixth diary/notebook after a complete text of the story
16 T.355, '*Nur so kann geschrieben werden, nur in einem solchen Zusammenhang, mit solcher vollständigen Öffnung des Leibes und der Seele*'
17 LF.265
18 D1.278
19 D1.277
20 D1.276
21 The point is made by Ritchie Robertson in his 'Introduction' to Sigmund Freud, *The Interpretation of Dreams* (trans. Joyce Crick, 1999), p. xxxiii. See also Gerhard Kurz, 'Nietzsche, Freud and Kafka', in Mark Anderson (ed.), *Reading Kafka* (1989), pp. 128–49
22 LF.297

23 D1.278
24 LF.265
25 LM.191
26 Brod, p. 128
27 LFFE.88
28 Brod, p. 93
29 LF.117
30 LF.10
31 LF.12
32 LF.16
33 LF.15
34 LF.18
35 LF.20
36 LF.27; B1.212
37 Brod, p. 97
38 Franz Kuna, 'Vienna and Prague 1890–1928', in Malcolm Bradbury and James McFarlane (eds.), *Modernism* (1976), p. 131
39 LFFE.93
40 Elias Canetti, *Der Andere Prozess/Kafka's Other Trial* (1969); English translation by Christopher Middleton in *Letters to Felice* (1978), p. 14 (readers should note that this popular Penguin edition of *Letters to Felice* is abridged)
41 LF.30
42 LF.32
43 Found among Kafka's papers after his death; in LF.33
44 LF.34
45 LF.35
46 October 1912; this was first drafted in D1.133
47 LF.37
48 '*Nein, mein und ewig an mich gebunden, das bin ich und damit muß ich auszukommen suchen*'; B1.228
49 These are the words quoted back at her by Kafka in LF.39
50 LFFE.92
51 LF.43
52 LF.40
53 LF.42
54 LF.46
55 LF.54
56 LF.48
57 LF.73
58 LF.55
59 LF.56
60 LF.57

Chapter 11

1 LF.57
2 LF.49
3 LF.58
4 *Ibid.*
5 Brod, p. 128; LF.62
6 Steven Berkoff, *Reflections on Metamorphosis* (1995), p. xv
7 LF.64
8 LF.67
9 LF.74
10 LF.76, '*um zu leben*'; B1.284
11 LF.78
12 LF.80
13 LF.81
14 LF.85
15 LF.97; B1.315
16 Paul Wiegler (1878–1949) in *Bohemia*, 6 December 1912; LF.556n
17 LF.102
18 Brod, p. 78
19 LF.122
20 LF.126
21 LF.132
22 LF.443
23 LF.133
24 LF.134

Chapter 12

1 LF.138
2 B2.15
3 LF.140
4 LF.139
5 LF.141
6 LF.146; B2.26
7 LF.149
8 LF.168
9 LF.177
10 LF.151
11 LF.156
12 LF.157; Buber's speech is in his *On Judaism* (1967), pp. 95–107
13 LF.161
14 LF.164
15 LF.158
16 LF.173
17 LF.174
18 LF.172

19 LF.173
20 LF.187; see Heinrich von Kleist, *The Marquise of O and Other Stories* (1978), trans. David Luke and Nigel Reeves
21 See Anthony Northey, *Kafka's Relatives* (1991), pp. 61–71
22 LF.186
23 LF.187; B2.412n identifies Lise Weltsch as the '*vernünftigen Mädchen*'
24 LF.189
25 LF.191
26 LF.195
27 LF.193
28 LF.196
29 LF.198
30 LF.201
31 LF.206
32 LF.208; B2.422n identifies Kohn as the '*zionistischen Studenten*'
33 LF.208
34 LF.209
35 LF.210
36 B2.117
37 LF.212
38 LF.214
39 LF.215
40 LF.217: Kafka quotes her words back to her; we do not, of course, have the actual letter from Felice
41 *Ibid.*: Ditto
42 LF.221
43 For an exploration of this interest, see Hans Zischler, *Kafka Goes to the Movies* (1996)
44 LF.222
45 LF.223
46 B2.136
47 LF.225
48 LF.226

Chapter 13

1 B2.456n suggests this possibility
2 LF.230
3 LFFE.95
4 LF.233
5 LFFE.95
6 LF.234
7 LF.233
8 LF.238
9 Elias Canetti, *Kafka's Other Trial* (1969), p. 27

10 LF.245
11 LF.247
12 LF.250
13 LF.237
14 LFFE.96
15 For a full and absorbing account of Kafka's relationship with his publishers on this and other occasions, see Joachim Unseld, *Kafka: A Writer's Life* (1982; trans. Paul F. Dvorak, 1994)
16 D1.285
17 D2.21
18 D1.286, '*Die schreckliche Unsicherheit meiner inner Existenz*'
19 D1.287
20 LF.255
21 *Ibid.*
22 B2.186
23 LF.257
24 LF.256
25 LF.259
26 LF.260
27 LF.262
28 LF.263
29 D1.287
30 LF.264
31 LF.268
32 LF.269
33 LF.270
34 B2.211:
35 LF.273
36 LF.274
37 D1.287
38 LF.275
39 LF.277
40 LF.279
41 LF.281
42 LF.293, where it is dated 1 August, but the critical edition of the letters restores the date to 1 July (B2.226)
43 LF.283
44 Reiner Stach, *Kafka: Die Jahre der Entscheidungen* (2002), pp. 350–1
45 B2.226
46 LF.286
47 LF.287
48 LF.289; B2.236
49 LF.289
50 LF.290

Chapter 14

1 D1.292
2 D1.289
3 LF.291
4 LF.304
5 B2.261, '*Ich habe kein literarisches Interesse sondern bestehe aus Literatur, ich bin nichts anderes und kann nichts anderes sein*'
6 D1.296
7 D1.297
8 D1.298
9 LF.306
10 LF.308
11 LF.309; B2.269
12 LF.310
13 LF.313
14 D1.299
15 LF.314
16 LF.315
17 W. G. Sebald, *Vertigo* (trans. Michael Hulse, 1999), p. 142; *Schwindel. Gefühle* (1990)
18 LF.317
19 LF.318
20 LF.317
21 LFFE.100
22 LF.320
23 LF.326
24 Klaus Wagenbach, *Freiebuter* (1983), pp. 87–90; the first visit to Riva was on the occasion of the Brescia airshow in 1909
25 LFFE.100
26 LFFE.101
27 B2.518n
28 D1.301
29 D1.305
30 LFFE.102
31 Mark Anderson, in 'Kafka, Homosexuality and the Aesthetics of "Male Culture"', *Austrian Studies*, 7, 1996, pp. 79–99, offers an important discussion of this theme and presents passages in Kafka's work which could be seen to have homoerotic themes
32 LF.326
33 Cited Anderson, *op. cit.*, p. 86
34 *Ibid.*, p. 89
35 LFFE.167
36 LFFE.102
37 LF.321
38 LF.323
39 LF.327

40 D1.309
41 LF.331
42 D1.309
43 Brod, p. 114
44 D1.310
45 D1.320
46 LF.333
47 LF.334
48 D1.300

Chapter 15

1 LF.336
2 D2.11; the translation should perhaps be: 'What have I in common with Jews?'
3 *Ibid.*
4 D2.12
5 D2.14
6 LF.345
7 LF.349
8 *Ibid.*
9 D2.18
10 LFFE.105
11 D2.20
12 LF.352
13 D2.25
14 LF.352
15 LFFE.115
16 Flesch von Brünningen, quoted in Felicity Lunn, 'City of Angles', *The Royal Society of Arts Magazine*, 79, Summer 2003
17 D2.23
18 Elias Canetti, *Kafka's Other Trial* (1969), p. 29
19 LF.359
20 LF.358
21 D2.26
22 LF.366
23 LF.368
24 LF.372
25 LF.376
26 LF.378
27 LF.383
28 LF.384
29 LF.385
30 LF.387
31 LF.388
32 LF.390

33 LF.398
34 D2.31
35 LF.411
36 LF.415
37 D2.34
38 D2.39
39 D2.42
40 LF.419
41 LF.420
42 LF.426
43 LF.422
44 LF.423
45 LF.425
46 D2.62
47 LF.431
48 LF.430
49 LF.431
50 LF.433
51 LO.8
52 D2.65
53 LF.437
54 D2.65
55 LF.434

Chapter 16

1 LF.435
2 D2.75
3 *Ibid.*
4 D2.76
5 D2.77
6 D2.78
7 *Ibid.*
8 D2.68
9 LFFE.110
10 D2.71
11 LO.9
12 LF.399
13 LF.381
14 LO.9
15 D2.79
16 D2.92
17 D2.93
18 *Ibid.*
19 LF.436
20 *Ibid.*

21 D2.98
22 D2.98
23 Elias Canetti, *Kafka's Other Trial* (1969), p. 61
24 D2.103
25 D2.106
26 Michael Hofmann, 'Introduction' to his translation of *The Man Who Disappeared* (1996), p. vii
27 D2.188
28 See Anthony Northey, 'Kafka's American Cousins' in *Kafka's Relatives* (1991), for a fuller discussion of the connections and echoes in the novel
29 The critical edition of the novel (used in Hofmann's translation), prints this as the second of two '*Fragmente*' at the end of the book, rather than as the final chapter
30 LFFE.113
31 Translation used here by Idris Parry (1994)

Chapter 17

1 D2.107
2 *Ibid.*
3 D2.108
4 D2.109
5 D2.111
6 LF.443
7 LF.445
8 LF.447
9 D2.119
10 LF.449
11 D2.120
12 D2.126
13 D2.127
14 LF.453
15 LF.456
16 LF.457
17 D2.128
18 D2.132
19 D2.129
20 LFFE.114
21 LF.459
22 D2.144
23 LF.460
24 LF.461
25 LF.462
26 Elias Canetti, *Kafka's Other Trial* (1969), p. 63
27 D2.154

28 LF.468
29 D2.154
30 LF.471
31 D2.157
32 LO.13
33 D2.159
34 LF.473
35 LFFE.449n
36 LFFE.117
37 LFFE.124
38 LFFE.126
39 LFFE.127
40 LF.481
41 LF.482
42 LF.500
43 LF.496
44 LF.506
45 LF.502
46 D2.164
47 LF.525; an earlier draft of this letter is in D2.167
48 LF.531
49 LF.528; Kafka quotes this sentence from her letter to him
50 LF.536
51 LF.534
52 Angelo Maria Ripellino, *Praga Magica* (1973); translated as *Magic Prague* (1994) by David Newton Marinelli
53 LF.537
54 LF.538

Chapter 18

1 See Anthony Northey, 'Myths and Realities in Kafka Biography', in *The Cambridge Companion to Kafka* (2002), p. 196
2 LF.542
3 LO.98n
4 LFFE.133
5 *Ibid.*
6 LO.18; but see also LM.146, where Kafka tells Milena that it was in the Civilian Swimming School, not in the apartment, that August that he 'spat out something red'
7 LM.22
8 LO.18
9 LO.20
10 LO.21
11 LFFE.144
12 LO.22

13 D2.182
14 LF.543
15 D2.185
16 Elias Canetti, *Kafka's Other Trial* (1969), p. 91
17 LF.544
18 LFFE.140
19 LF.546
20 LO.24
21 Brod, p. 166
22 LFFE.137
23 See also LM.22
24 LFFE.141
25 D2.188
26 LFFE.140
27 D2.187
28 D2.186
29 D2.190
30 LFFE.147
31 WPC, pp. 42 and 45
32 WPC, p. 72
33 LFFE.166
34 *Ibid.*
35 LO.26

Chapter 19

1 See Klaus Wagenbach, *Franz Kafka: Pictures of a Life* (1984), p. 188
2 LFFE.189
3 LFFE.194
4 LFFE.200
5 WPC.98
6 WPC.103
7 LFFE.199
8 LFFE.201
9 WPC.113–14
10 WPC.119ff.
11 Brod, p. 168
12 LFFE.204
13 LFFE.206
14 LFFE.211
15 LFFE.213
16 LO.107n quoting a letter from Julie Kafka to Ottla, 1 December 1918
17 LO.37
18 EK.121ff.
19 EK.140ff.

20 D2.191
21 D2.191
22 EK.144–45
23 LO.41
24 Nadine Gordimer, 'Letter from His Father', in *Something Out There* (1984)
25 As noted earlier, there is an echo of the modern phenomenon of the 'accuser's letter' recovering hitherto repressed memories of sexual abuse within the family; see Mark Pendergrast, *Victims of Memory: Incest Accusations and Shattered Lives* (1996), a sceptical enquiry into 'the widespread search for repressed memories of sexual abuse' in the 1980s and 1990s
26 Edwin Muir, 'Introduction' to *Amerika* (1949), p. 11
27 Brod, p. 5
28 LFFE.216
29 Ritchie Robertson, *Kafka: Judaism, Politics, and Literature* (1985), pp. 181ff.
30 Brod, p. 140

Chapter 20

1 'Institute Secretary'; Wagenbach, p. 250
2 GWC.104; the sheets on which these were written in the diary were almost all torn out by Kafka and are restored as a complete sequence by Malcolm Pasley (ed.) in GWC, pp. 104–13
3 LFFE.222
4 LFFE.224
5 Brod, p. 75
6 LFFE.227
7 LFFE.229
8 LFFE.224
9 First published in 1968 as *Milena – Kafkas Freundin*; edition used here translated in 1989 by Ralph Manheim; see also Mary Hockaday, *Kafka, Love and Courage: The Life of Milena Jesenská* (1995)
10 LFFE.237
11 LM.19, April 1920; dates are given here for LM in order to allow readers of the English text (which, though in print, is based on out-of-date scholarship) to benefit from the redating in the German critical edition
12 LM.30, May 1920
13 LFFE.233
14 LFFE.236
15 LM.25, April–May 1920
16 LFFE.238
17 LO.49

18 LO.52
19 LM.35, 29 May 1920
20 LM.50, 30 May
21 LM.53, 31 May
22 LM.54
23 LM.56
24 LM.38, 10 June
25 LM.68, 2 June
26 LM.46, 3 June
27 LM.37, 10 June
28 LM.71, 12 June
29 LM.58, 13 June
30 *Národní listy*, 6 July 1924; reproduced in Buber-Neumann, *op. cit.*, pp. 72–3
31 LM.67, 21 June
32 LM.73, 23 June
33 LM.77, 4 July: 'Spoken into your left ear while you're lying there on the wretched bed in a deep slumber for an excellent reason and while you're slowly and unconsciously turning over from right to left towards my mouth'
34 LM.78, 4–5 July
35 LM.84, 5 July
36 LM.104, 19 July

Chapter 21

1 LM.89, 8 July 1920
2 LM.88, 7 July
3 LM.90, 8 July
4 LM.91, 9 July
5 LM.94, 12 July
6 LM.97, 14 July
7 LM.98, 14 July
8 LM.105, 13 July
9 LM.100, 15 July
10 LM.101, 15 July
11 LM.111, 18 July
12 LM.106, 21 July
13 LM.133, 26 July
14 LM.128, 31 July
15 LM.158, 31 July addendum
16 LM.148, 4 August
17 LM.150
18 LM.161, 7 August. For a very original interpretation of this interest in Milena's fashion articles, see Mark Anderson, *Kafka's Clothes: Ornament and Aestheticism in the Habsburg Fin de Siècle* (1992)

19 LM.166, 8 August
20 LM.136, 9 August
21 LO.53
22 LM.179, 17–18 August
23 LM.185, 26 August
24 LM.186, 26–27 August
25 LM.144, 31 August
26 LM.208, 'September'
27 LM.194, 5 September
28 LM.196, 7 September
29 LM.198, 14 September
30 LM.200, 18 September
31 LM.202, 20 September
32 LM.155, 6 October
33 LM.217, 'November'
34 See Gerhard Kurz, 'Nietzsche, Freud and Kafka', in Mark Anderson (ed.), *Reading Kafka* (1989), pp. 128–49
35 LM.219, 'November'
36 LM.220, 'November'
37 LM.222, 'November'
38 LM.223, 'November'
39 LM.213, 'mid-November'

Chapter 22

1 LO.54
2 LFFE.247
3 Ritchie Robertson, 'In Search of the Historical Kafka: A Selective Review of the Research, 1980–92', *Modern Language Review*, 89(1), January 1994, p. 108; see also Eduard Goldstücker, '*Kafkas Eckermann?*' in Claude David (ed.), *Franz Kafka: Themen und Probleme* (1980), pp. 238–55
4 LFFE.247
5 LFFE.248
6 LFFE.249
7 LFFE.252
8 LFFE.249
9 LFFE.254
10 LFFE.257
11 Brod, p. 224
12 *Ibid.*, p. 229
13 LFFE.252
14 Brod, p. 231
15 Brod. p. 233
16 Margarete Buber-Neumann, *Milena–Kafka's Freundin* (1968; trans. Ralph Manheim, 1989), p. 67; see also Maurice Blanchot, *De Kafka à Kafka* (1981), pp. 155–70

17 LO.58
18 Sander Gilman, *Franz Kafka: The Jewish Patient* (1995), appendix, p. 260, gives the final version of the draft printed in LO.57
19 LO.59
20 An alternative version of this meeting is given by Ludwig Hardt in EK.191 where it is claimed Klopstock approached Kafka and asked if he were indeed the author of the book *Ein Landarzt*. Kafka is said to have exclaimed in exasperation: 'On top of everything, this!'
21 LFFE.259
22 '*er lächelt wie ich noch nie einen Menschen habe lächeln gesehen*' in Robert Klopstock, '*Mit Kafka in* Matliare', EK.153–6
23 See Leo A. Lensing, 'Franz Would Be with Us Here: The Posthumous Papers of Robert Klopstock, Including Thirty-eight Kafka Letters', *Times Literary Supplement*, 28 February 2003
24 LFFE.262
25 LO.61
26 Kafka also asked for a copy of *Fear and Trembling*, which seems to contradict Klopstock's account of their first meeting, at which he claimed both were reading this book
27 LO.63
28 LFFE.263
29 LO.72
30 LFFE.271
31 LFFE.273
32 LFFE.279
33 *Ibid.*
34 LFFE.281
35 LFFE.287

Chapter 23

1 LFFE.290
2 Christoph Stölzl, 'Kafka: Jew, Anti-Semite, Zionist', in Mark Anderson, *Reading Kafka* (1989), p. 54
3 LFFE.291
4 LFFE.310
5 D2.193
6 D2.194
7 D2.197
8 D2.198
9 D2.199
10 D2.200
11 D2.202
12 D2.203
13 D2.204
14 D2.209

15 D2.210
16 D2.214
17 D2.213
18 D2.222
19 LFFE.330
20 D2.225
21 LFFE.321
22 D2.224
23 LO.231
24 D2. 228
25 LFFE.324

Chapter 24

1 LFFE.328
2 LFFE.330
3 LFFE.331
4 LFFE.333
5 LFFE.339
6 LFFE.352
7 LFFE.361
8 LFFE.365
9 LFFE.366
10 'Epilogue', to *The Trial* (1925; trans. Willa and Edwin Muir, 1937)
11 See Ritchie Robertson, 'The Last Earthly Frontier', in *Kafka: Judaism, Politics, and Literature* (1985); see also Richard Sheppard, *On Kafka's Castle* (1973)
12 EK.165–7
13 LFFE.368
14 LM.235

Chapter 25

1 LFFE.372
2 *Ibid.*
3 D2.232
4 LFFE.373
5 LFFE.374
6 LO.84
7 A fuller account of this story and of the Müritz stay is provided in Kathi Diamant's *Kafka's Last Love* (2003). Diamant also tells for the first time the story of Dora's subsequent life without Kafka
8 EK.168–73
9 LFFE.377
10 EK.174–85, '*Mein Leben mit Franz Kafka*', Dora Diamant, '*So zarte Hände, und sie müssen, so blutige Arbeit verrichten!*' The translation

here draws on the revised translation by Kathi Diamant, *op. cit.* (pp. 258–61) of Dora's remarks published in an article by J. P. Hodin, 'Memories of Franz Kafka', *Horizon* (1948)

11 LFFE.375

12 Diamant, *op. cit.*, p. 172

13 See Diamant, *op. cit.*, *passim*

14 LFFE.375

15 LFFE.379

16 LFFE.380

17 LO.77

18 Diamant, *op. cit.*, p. 32

19 LFFE.382

20 LO.78

21 *Ibid.*

22 LO.79

23 LFFE.386

24 LFFE.387

25 LM.235, late November 1923

26 BE.34, '*mit . . . ihrem berlinerischen Verstand (sie ist keine Jüdin) unendlich überlegen ist*'

27 *Ibid.*

28 Brod, pp. 197–8

29 The story is told in Diamant, *op. cit.*, pp. 51–2 and by Anthony Rudolf, 'Kafka and the Doll', *Jewish Chronicle Literary Supplement*, 15 June 1984

30 BE.34

31 BE.38

32 BE.43

33 LFFE.389

34 LFFE.489n

35 LFFE.396

36 LFFE.402

37 Diamant, *op. cit.*, p. 77

38 LO.86

39 LFFE.401

40 LM.237

41 Nicolas Baudy, '*Entretiens avec Dora Dymant*', *Evidences*, February 1950, pp. 21–5

42 Diamant, *op. cit.*, p. 258

Chapter 26

1 LFFE.403

2 LO.89

3 EK.179, '*Ich möchte wohl wissen, ob ich den Gespenstern entkommen bin!*'

4 LFFE.406
5 See letter of Kafka to Klopstock, January 1924, in Leo A. Lensing, 'Franz Would Be with Us Here', in *Times Literary Supplement*, 28 February 2003
6 LFFE.409
7 LFFE.407
8 LFFE.408
9 LFFE.410
10 BE.49
11 BE.56
12 BE.65
13 Brod, p. 203
14 LFFE.411
15 LFFE.412
16 LFFE.411
17 LFFE.412
18 See Lensing, *loc. cit.*
19 Kathi Diamant, *Kafka's Last Love* (2003), p. 97
20 LFFE.412
21 LO.90
22 LFFE.413
23 BE.75
24 Brod, p. 205
25 *Ibid.*, p. 208
26 *Ibid.*, p. 153
27 Presented for the first time in Diamant, *op. cit.*
28 Diamant, *op. cit.*, p. 116
29 The conversation slips are appended in LFFE.416–23
30 LO.92
31 LO.121n
32 Brod, p. 206
33 BE.80; previously dated in LO.91 as 'about May 19'
34 Brod, p. 212
35 EK.193

Afterword

1 Bodleian, Kafka MS 4 June 1924, letter from Klopstock to Elli Kafka
2 Quoted in Margarete Buber-Neumann, *Milena – Kafkas Freundin* (1969; trans. Ralph Manheim, 1989), pp. 72–3
3 Edwin Muir, 'Introduction' to *The Castle* (1930), p. 5
4 *Letters of Aldous Huxley* (1969), ed. Grover Smith, p. 345

Chronology

1883 Kafka born, 3 July, Prague
1889 Attends elementary school until 1893
1896 13 June, bar-mitzvah
1901 Attends university at Prague until 1906
1902 23 October, first meeting with Max Brod
1904–5 Writing *Description of a Struggle*
1905 July–August, first affair on holiday at Zuckmantel
1906 April–September, legal clerk in law office of Richard Löwy; 18 June, degree of Doctor of Law; August, second holiday in Zuckmantel; October, start of year's legal training.
1907 Spring, writes *Wedding Preparations in the Country*; August holiday in Triesch, where he meets Hedwig Weiler; October, starts work at Assicurazioni Generali
1908 March, first pieces published in *Hyperion*; July, starts work at Workers' Accident Insurance Institute
1909 Publication in *Hyperion* of parts of *Description of a Struggle*; September, holiday in Riva and Brescia; publication of 'The Aeroplanes at Brescia' in *Bohemia*
1910 Starts diary; March, more pieces published in *Bohemia*; October, trip to Paris with Brod; December, trip to Berlin
1911 Summer vacation to Europe and Sanatorium Erlenbach, Zurich; Autumn, at work jointly with Brod on *Richard and Samuel*; 4 October, first visit to Yiddish Theatre in Prague; winter, at work on first version of *The Man Who Disappeared*
1912 18 February, introduces evening of recitations by Yitzhak Löwy; June–July, with Brod in Leipzig and Weimar and first meeting with Ernst Rowohlt and Kurt Wolff; Sanatorium Just in Harz Mountains; 13 August, meets Felice Bauer; 22 September, writes through the night *The Judgement*; September–October, writes 'The Stoker' and starts second version of *The Man Who*

Disappeared; October, 'A Great Noise' published in *Herder-Blätter*; November–December, writes *Metamorphosis*; December publication of *Betrachtung*

1913 Easter and May, two visits to Felice in Berlin; May, 'The Stoker' published; June, *The Judgement* published; September–October, Trieste, Venice, Riva, meets Gerti Wasner; 8–9 November, visits Felice in Berlin

1914 28 February–1 March, visits Felice in Berlin; Easter, unofficial engagement to Felice; 1 May, Felice visits Prague; 30 May to 2 June, in Berlin for official engagement to Felice; 12 June, engagement broken off; August, starts work on *The Trial*; October, finishes *The Man Who Disappeared* and writes *In the Penal Colony*; December, writes 'The Village Schoolmaster'

1915 17 January, finishes *The Trial*; 23–4 January, at Bodenbach with Felice; January–February, writes 'Blumfeld, an Elderly Bachelor'; 23–4 May, trip to Switzerland with Felice and Grete Bloch; June, at Karlsbad with Felice; July, Sanatorium Frankenstein at Rumburg; November, *Metamorphosis* published

1916 April, to Karlsbad; 3–12 July, with Felice in Marienbad and Franzensbad; 10–12 November, in Munich; 26 November, starts to write in Alchemists' Street stories that were to be included in *A Country Doctor*

1917 March, moves to Schönborn Palace; spring, writes 'An Imperial Message' and 'The Hunter Gracchus'; summer, starts Hebrew lessons and writes 'A Report to an Academy'; July, in Prague for second engagement to Felice; publication of 'An Old Manuscript' and 'A Fratricide' in *Marsyas*; 9 August, overnight haemorrhage; September, moves back to parents' apartment and diagnosis of tuberculosis of the lungs; three months' sick leave; goes to Zürau until April 1918; 20–1 September, Felice visits Zürau; October, 'Jackals and Arabs' published in *Der Jude*; December, second engagement to Felice broken off

1918 April, leaves Zürau for Prague; May, back at work at Institute; 30 November, at Schelesen

1919 Meets Julie Wohryzek at Schelesen; end of March, returns to Prague; summer, engaged to Julie; autumn, publication of *A Country Doctor*; November, wedding with Julie cancelled; 21 November, returns to office

1920 January, starts 'He' aphorisms; April, Merano, corresponding with Milena; July, breaks off engagement with Julie; 8 August, moves back to parents' apartment; 14–15 August, meeting at Gmünd with Milena; December, to Matliare until August 1921

1921 3 February, meets Robert Klopstock; August, returns to work; September, meets Milena in Prague and gives her his diaries; 31 October, special treatment sick leave

1922 27 January, three weeks at Spindlermühle; February, writes 'A

Fasting Artist' and starts work on *The Castle*; June, to Planá; July, pensioned off by the Institute and writes 'Investigations of a Dog'; 20 August, abandons *The Castle*; October, publication of 'A Fasting Artist' in *Die Neue Rundschau*; November–December confined to sickbed

1923 May, to Dobřichovice; June, final meeting with Milena; July–August, at Müritz, where he meets Dora Diamant; mid-August–September, in Schelesen; 24 September, moves to Berlin and lives with Dora; October–December, writes 'A Little Woman' and 'The Burrow'

1924 February, moves house again in Berlin; mid-March, back to Prague and writes 'Josephine the Songstress; or the Mouse People'; March, Wiener Wald sanatorium near Pernitz and diagnosis of tuberculosis of the larynx; mid-April, at clinic in Vienna; May, Klopstock and Dora nurse Kafka; 3 June, Kafka dies in Kierling; 11 June, buried in Prague

Acknowledgements

I should like to acknowledge the assistance of the following institutions and individuals in writing this book: the British Library, the Taylorian Institute, Oxford, the Bodleian Library Department of Western Manuscripts (Kafka Collection), the London Library, the Czech Tourist Authority, Professor Jeremy Adler of King's College, London, Kathi Diamant, Margaret Jervis, Tim Rogers, Anthony Rudolf, Michael Steiner. Eliska Treterová provided both welcome and guidance in Prague.

I owe a special debt of gratitude to Professor Ritchie Robertson of St John's College, Oxford, who was a constant source of advice and encouragement and whose reading of the final manuscript resulted in many valuable suggestions. Any errors which remain, however, are entirely the responsibility of the author.

Index